A DISCOURSE ON HIP

A DISCOURSE ON HIP

Selected Writings
of Milton Klonsky

Edited by Ted Solotaroff

Introduction by Mark Shechner

Wayne State University Press   Detroit

Library of Congress Cataloging-in-Publication Data

Klonsky, Milton.
  [Selections. 1990]
  A discourse on hip :   selected writings of Milton Klonsky / edited
by Ted Solotaroff ;   introduction by Mark Shechner.
    p.   cm.
  Includes bibliographical references.
  ISBN 0-8143-1972-6 (alk. paper)
  I. Solotaroff, Ted, 1928- . II. Title.
PS3561.L628A6   1990
814'.54 — dc20   90-11979
                                                                      CIP

Contents

Preface 7

Introduction 9

One

The End Pocket 39

A Writer's Education 42

Annus Mirabilis: 1932 47

The Importance of Being Milton 70

The Trojans of Brighton Beach 81

Chester, Wystan, Rhoda, and Me:
A Fragment 89

Two

The Old Magi at the Burlesque 105

Greenwich Village: Decline and Fall 106

Maxwell Bodenheim as Culture Hero 117

A Discourse on Hip 131

Three

Jack the Giant Killer 151

Maxim Gorky in Coney Island 154

The Poetry of Samuel Greenberg 169

CONTENTS

Along the Midway of Mass Culture   179
Mc²Luhan's Message, *or:*
Which Way Did the Second Coming Went?   196
Art & Life: A Menippean Paean to the Flea;
or, Did Dostoevsky Kill Trotsky?   208

Four

The Descent of the Muse   261
W. B.⁴: or, The Seer Seen by His Own Vision   263
The Abyss of the Undermind:
Blake's Illustrations of *The Divine Comedy*   297
Speaking Pictures: An Introduction   318
Bibliography   335

Preface

In selecting the writings of Milton Klonsky to be preserved in this collection, I have drawn only upon his published work. Virtually all of the unpublished prose that I came across was from the autobiography of his childhood years. Given the published pieces that bear directly on this period of his life, adding further material seemed to me a much of a muchness.

Otherwise, I have not imposed very rigorous standards of selection and presentation between Klonsky and his readers. A few of the more incongruous, dated, repetitious, or specialized pieces have been left out, but others that may strike readers as bearing these qualities have been included. Klonsky was a writer of relatively few themes and endless variations: to use one of his favorite images, his mind was kaleidoscopic, capable of arranging the bits and pieces of his eclectic learning and erudition into novel and sometimes astonishing patterns. Like the metaphysical poets whose early influence never left him, the incongruous connection and the arcane fact were his meat and drink. To see the murder of Trotsky prefigured in the *Classic Comics* version of *Crime and Punishment* or a Greenwich Village vagrant, focused in the lens of Kierkegaardian irony, turn into Diogenes takes a very special kind of sensibility that needs to be given, as Klonsky himself might say, its head. A number of his essays on Greenwich Village inevitably overlap, occasionally even in phrasing, but the angle and level of observation is a revised and deepening one; roughly, from a point of view to a vision. The details and examples of his essays on mass culture have obviously dated, but the ideas behind them have typically gone from being appropriate to their time to being prophetic of ours. See, for example, the sentences about television, written near the dawn of the medium, in "Along

7

the Midway of Mass Culture." So when in doubt I've stepped aside, giving its benefit to the integrity of Klonsky's small oeuvre and to the different uses his broad range of putative readers—from the scholarly to the iconoclastic—will put it to.

I am grateful to Anatole Broyard, Seymour Krim, and particularly to Mark Shechner for their help in making this book come together, and to Robert Mandel and Lee Ann Schreiner of Wayne State Univeristy Press for giving Klonsky the full hearing he continues to deserve.

Ted Solotaroff

Introduction

1.

One night in 1945 in a bar somewhere in Greenwich Village, Delmore Schwartz announced with excited and gleaming eyes: "1919! 1919! It's 1919 over again." The recollection is William Barrett's and the moment a special one: the Village at the close of the Second World War, when its pinched and angled streets thronged with soldiers and sailors, with young women itching for adventure, with writers and artists drunk on ideas and alcohol — and each other — and a new world seemed on the verge of being born.

The memory is an apt one, for there was a moment in 1945 when New York appeared poised to become the new Paris, with the Village its Montparnasse. That wasn't entirely a delusion. At war's end, the reign of Paris as the international captial of the creative imagination had been destroyed and much of its energy reconstituted in New York. The flight of scientists, psychologists, artists, and intellectuals from Hitler had internationalized the cultural life of New York, and young American writers making a pilgrimage to the Village would find there that intoxicating mix of American rawness, Bohemian libido, and European dialectics that could nourish a proper American renaissance.

Greenwich Village: the name has passed from the geography of America to its dream life. Until it was transformed by high rents and overdevelopment, disheartened by turf wars with local hoodlums, and demoralized by the fallout of the dream itself — all that spiritual impatience in so small a space — it was to most educated Americans a symbol of intellectual freedom, artistic discovery, and sexual opportunity: America's ranking Bohemia and an outpost of the creative spirit against a dreary commercial civilization. When Joseph, the alienated hero of Saul Bellow's first novel, *Dangling Man*, called for "colonies of spirit" to preserve his kind against the life of quiet desperation, he had in mind something like the apartment-cum-salon that his friend Isaac Rosenfeld kept on Barrow Street in the palmy days of the imagination just after the war.

In those days, anything with a roof and running water could be a salon, and for a short while Rosenfeld's apartment was a literary gathering spot, where the regulars included Wallace Markfield, Manny Farber, David Bazelon, and Calder Willingham; and Alfred Kazin, Saul Bellow, Paul Goodman, James Agee, William Phillips, Philip Rahv, Delmore Schwartz, and Clement Greenberg were apt to drop in at any time. And it was just a circle within circles. The New School, just off Fifth Avenue, brought the dialectical imagination downtown. *Partisan Review,* intially on Astor Place, remained a downtown publication even after moving up to 1545 Broadway. The *Chimera*, a journal of contemporary poetry founded down-town in 1942, would later become *Hudson Review*. And artists were every-where: from "the Club" on Eighth Street, where Franz Kline and Willem de Kooning held court and the abstract expressionists, as yet unnamed, were gathering steam for a push into glory, to the Cedar Street Tavern, where action painters sometimes attacked each other as violently as they attacked the canvas, on over to East Tenth Street, just outside the Village, where low rents and low pretensions attracted a gathering of studios and galleries. Even André Breton, the éminence grise of surrealism, lived for a while on West Eleventh Street. Who wouldn't be forgiven for thinking it was 1919 all over, with the avant-garde alive and well just across the street, with *O Altitudo* all around, and the world newly awakened from the nightmare of Hitler and war?

Milton Klonsky was one of the young writers who had been drawn to the Village by visions of a cultural renaissance. Just twenty-three years old in 1945 (born 26 November 1921), he had met both Delmore Schwartz and Isaac Rosenfeld during summer visits to the Cummington (Massachusetts) School of the Arts. Only just beginning to publish — a poem in the *Chimera* in 1942 — Klonsky was an avid reader and an inspired talker who held his own in fast intellectual company. He was, if anything, fast company himself: a protrait of him from those days, by his friend Seymour Krim, describes him as something of a prodigy.

> He had matured much earlier than myself, especially in the minds he had trained with — difficult English poets like Donne, Marvell, Christopher Smart, his much-quoted Blake; the French symbolists, Rimbaud, Baudelaire, Valéry, Laforgue, all the way up to Michaux; plus the most formidable of the contemporary headache-makers like Kafka, Eliot, Pound, Auden, Joyce, Yeats, Stevens and critics like Coleridge, Blackmur, Tate, I. A. Richards.

Allowing for the skewness toward the seventeenth century — the Eliot legacy — this was a full-blown modernist education that a yound intellectual, unfettered by the curricular monotonies of graduate school, was free to absorb on his own. The Rosenfeld cenacle and all the interlocking circles to which it was linked — the *Partisan Review* circle, the *New Republic* circle, the *Commentary* circle — formed the Village's own Institute for Advanced Studies, where education and ecstasy, improbably married by ambition and alcohol, and at times by marijuana, propelled the seminar on into all hours of the morning.

Later, in the fifties, much of this energy would move uptown or out of town entirely, as rents rose; careers, marriage, and children lured some away to the life of quiet desperation; fellowships and professorships summoned a few — credentials or no — to the academy; and other, more aggressive, Bohemias arose. As early as 1948, Greenwich Village was becoming home for decidedly different cultures, a transformation that Klonsky would chronicle with sorrow in his essay, "Greenwich Village: Decline and Fall." But Klonsky himself was not one of the migrants; he never left the Village and never gave up on the spirit of the Village as he first encountered it in his youth. It was the best of all available worlds. "He rarely took a job," his friend Anatole Broyard has written of him, "or entered into a relationship that required him to curb his sensibility — a form of fastidiousness that condemned him to a rather lonely life." He was first and foremost a Village intellectual, meaning that not only did he remain *in* the Village all his life, but that he was quintessentially *of* it as well.

The idea of the Village intellectual, as opposed to the New York or European or university intellectual, conjures up a constellation of images from which we could sketch out a profile of Klonsky without ever reading a line of his writing. What does it suggest? Certainly that he had a restless mind, one that had no truck with received ideas and common wisdom, with "the latest thought-saving ideas," as he called them; that he rejected all temptations to clamber upwards into the middle class, preferring the life of elective poverty; that he scorned any work that did not provide immediate spiritual benefits and even had a casual attitude toward work that did; that he was a wordsmith who preferred the cunning and the elliptical, the pun or the solecism, to the straightforward and the common phrase; that he was a walker in the city and an observer of city life—a boulevardie; that he regarded sex as a calling as well as an indulgence; that he subordinated everything to his ruling principles; orgasm or revolution or satori; that marijuana was a preferred sacrament, as much for its sexual benefits as its visionary ones; that radical politics of some kind was never far from his thoughts, though as often as not he scorned the caucus room and even the voting booth; that music, commonly jazz, was central to his life; that uptown was anathematized as the lair of Moloch; that the bar was his seminar room, the table his podium, the secondhand bookstore his library, the latest young woman his family.

Appropriately shaded and accented—Klonsky preferred Erik Satie to Charlie Parker and was little interested in politics—this composite may serve as an introduction to Klonsky, who was a flaneur, an autodidact, a sexologue, and a spinner of exotic verbal yarns—a Villagiste, in short— who found in this world without as actual what was in his world within as possible, to paraphrase James Joyce's Stephen Dedalus. The Village was his support system, his biosphere, and every tremor in the system became a tremor in his soul, which is perhaps why it was the Village as a subject that concentrated his gifts as a writer, for in writing about the Village he was composing his own moral history. As historian and mythographer of the "decline and fall of the Village," as he called it, invoking Gibbon, he knew his terrain cold, and the three Village essays in this collection show him to be a social observer of rare descriptive powers.

There was, however, an inverse ratio between the quality of his writing and the quantity; for every word there was a dozen silences, and if his name is little known outside a small number of friends and admirers, it is because over a lifetime of writing he produced so little. Until his last decade, the 1970s, when inspired by necessity or by vision or by the need to redem the time—who can say?—he wrote a number of long, elliptical essays and edited five books, including two editions of William Blake, Klonsky was a writer of slender output. Blocked for the better part of two decades, he published sporadically, and were it not for a long character portrait of him by Seymour Krim during that period, his name might have faded from sight altogether.

2.

Klonsky started out in the forties as a poet-critic-man of letters in the manner of Allen Tate or, more to the point, Delmore Schwartz, who, some eight years his senior, was the model of literary-intellectual ambition whom a Jewish boy from New York might aspire to emulate. Krim remembers Schwartz as "the mapmaker, who invented an intellectual world for us all out of Freud, Kafka, Eliot, the New Critics, and the whole modern sensibility that those names implied." The unlikeliest idol of the tribe was Eliot, whose shadow loomed large despite his nasty pronouncements about freethinking Jews. The Eliot modernist portfolio extended back to the seventeenth-century metaphysical poets, whose wit, difficulty, performative excess, and theatrical sense of metaphor had made them allies in the project of "making it new" in poetry as well as ideal testing grounds for the sophisticated exegetical devices that were emerging under the banner of the New Criticism. Typical of its time and symbolic of Klonsky's ambitions was his poem "The End Pocket," published in the *Chimera* in 1942, when Klonsky was all of twenty years old. A smartly tailored little poem in nine stanzas, packing sex, faith, modern astronomy, and Deist cosmology into a single pool-hall metaphor, it was a tour de force of baroque "wit," spectacularly allusive and ferociously clever.

> Haunting these vizored cathedrals
> My lord is rod, my world is green.
> Driven upon its central core
> The ball rebuffed and turned by walls
> Of baize, follows a further plan
> And proves an open corridor.

The billiard balls turn into planets; the cue stick becomes both a penis and God's scepter; the green table becomes a universe and a garden (*homage à* Marvell), etcetera: very cunning, very formal, very labored, and very precocious. Apparently William Arrowsmith, Fearon Brown, and Frederick Morgan, editors of the *Chimera*, thought so too, since they gave it top billing in the second issue of their magazine. It was a major coup for so

13

young a writer, for the *Chimera*, during its brief existence, was a center of downtown poetic activity, publishing poems by John Berryman, Kimon Friar, Karl Shapiro, W. H. Auden, Robert Lowell, Pablo Neruda, and Howard Moss, and essays and reviews by R. P. Blackmur and Kenneth Burke.[1] Klonsky would reappear in the next issue with a brief but bold review of Randall Jarrell's *Blood for a Stranger*, in which he demonstrated a gift for the incisive phrase, the verbal caress, and the drawn sword. Where did these young Jewish boys, many of them from immigrant families, pick up their modernism? Where did they learn to write so?

The answer is, wherever they happened to be: Chicago, Newark, Montreal, Brooklyn, the Lower East Side, much as their fathers, uncles, cousins did a generation earlier in Warsaw, Vilna, Bialystok. It didn't matter; school was wherever you found yourself and wherever you cultivated that keenness of intellect and avidity of learning that you'd brought with you from the street — no, from the crib. Saul Bellow once recalled seeing Isaac Rosenfeld deep in a debate over Schopenhauer at Chicago's Tuley High School while still wearing short pants. In Klonsky's case, the crib was on Staten Island, then called Richmond, and the streets were in Manhattan, the Bronx, and the Brighton Beach section of Brooklyn, a hopscotch of modest locales that were nonetheless as ripe with literary possibility as anything Concord, the Lake Country, or Bloomsbury ever had to offer. Klonsky would write in a summary of his career: "In time, as my appreciation of literature advanced from Bomba the Jungle Boy to Studs Lonigan, and from the poems in the back of the eighth-grade speller to 'The Golden Treasury' to Carl Sandburg, I began, secretly at first . . . , then more and more openly, to write poetry, and with the same passionate dedication with which I used to play street games. These youthful poems, in 'free verse' — meter and rhyme I considered effete and reactionary — were written against: against war and fascism, against poverty, unemployment, slums, discrimination, sexual repression . . . and were modishly communoidal in sentiment and rhetoric."

This training in the poetry of outrage was virtually as common to the Jewish youth of his generation as the Bar Mitzvah, and in some circles even more so. Typically, too, it evolved, toward the end of high school, into a precocious modernism, a championship of Yeats and Joyce, Eliot and Pound, Kafka and Celine, Hart Crane and Marianne Moore and Wallace Stevens, and to the traditions from which they derived.

> My discovery of the English metaphysical poets and the French
> Symbolists . . . was also an act of self-discovery. In the poems

14

of Mallarmé and Marvell especially, with their cinematic shifts
of reference, their amalgamations of imagery drawn from disparate sources, their ironical slant and punning ambiguities cutting both ways, and their intricately plotted structures, which
served to inform and certify words with meaning, I saw a way
of transmuting my own metropolitan experience into poetry.
Marvell and Mallarmé, Mallarmé and Marvell, these two evoked
for me a spiritualized Manhattan.

This spiritualized Manhattan would in time take form as the actual Village, for which the young Klonsky had already prepared himself through
his immersion in the classic texts of modern literature. What one gathers
in Klonsky's frequent evocation of his seedtime is not so much an account
of how a poetic was formed, since there was not enough poetry to declare
a poetic, but how a poetic character came into being, one that could lift
itself up by its cultural bootstraps and transform itself into an advanced
sort of urban being, advanced in thought and feeling and equal to the re-
quirements of the "ghetto of Eden," as he would call it.

By the age of twenty, the young Klonsky was poised at a cusp of the
New York and prepared to hold his own against the contending egos of
the intellectual scene. Yet this auspicious debut was prelude to a slack time;
Klonsky did not publish again until 1947, and the career profile, as seen
from the distant prospect of the bibliography, suddenly goes out of focus:
a reminiscence in *Commentary* on boyhood in Brighton Beach, an essay,
also in *Commentary*, on the ghetto poet Samuel Greenberg, whose poems
are famed for having been raided by Hart Crane, a lament for Greenwich
Village's "age of lead," an essay on the money changers of Paris, and in
1950, a critical exegesis, in the brittle, allusive, and self-confident New
Critical mold, of Andrew Marvell's "The Garden." Taken together, this
is either the profile of an aspiring man of letters, sounding every note on
his pipe as a demonstration of his range, or the sympton of an imagination at loose ends, uncertain of precisely where its gifts lay and lunging
from theme to theme in search of its muse.

Several of Klonsky's *Commentary* contributions in the forties and fifties appeared in "From the American Scene," a regular feature devoted to
vignettes of American Jewish life. Though its contents varied greatly from
month to month, depending on the contributor, the overall vision of "From
the American Scene" was consistent with the cosmopolitan ethos of Elliot
Cohen's *Commentary*: that American Jewish life was American to the core,
and that, allowing for differences of locale, tradition, and history, it was

a variant on familiar American themes. Jewish boys went to the same American schools, played the same urban sports, and were captivated by the same popular entertainment, especially motion pictures. True, they ate matzos and had Bar Mitzvahs and their parents spoke Yiddish and did piecework for a living, but if you pricked them they bled Yankee blue, just like their Irish, Italian, and Polish neighbors. As Klonsky's friend Willie Poster summed up that phase of American Jewish civilization in a contribution of his own to "From the American Scene" in May 1950: "'We are all much more simply human than anything else,' Harry Stack Sullivan wrote some time ago, and since the statement was probably meant to apply to psychiatrists and schizophrenics, it will serve, I hope, to de-emphasize the writer's necessary exaggeration of the uniqueness of what he has seen."

Though Klonsky's contributions, "The Trojans of Brighton Beach" (May 1947) and "The Importance of Being Milton" (October 1952) had their own agendas, the search for auguries of genius, they were finally typical expressions of the general post-immigrant ethos. None of this ransacking of the grammar school years for signs of election is auspicious writing. Young Jewish writers of Klonsky's generation were producing these tenement symphonies by the ream. Most prominently in Alfred Kazin's *A Walker in the City* but also in the novels of Wallace Markfield and the stories of Paul Goodman, Meyer Liben, Michael Seide, Isaac Rosenfeld, and Delmore Schwartz, these arias on the Jewish childhood were to the Jewish literary life what Tin Pan Alley was to music, and what distinguished the best of these was often nothing more than the gift, which so many had in abundance, of acute social observation.

This sort of thing, the man looking back on the boy in search of the man within the boy, has limits, and unless you are Wordsworth remembering intimations of immortality or James Joyce trying on the small wings of Stephen Dedalus, it is best to be modest. Klonsky's Songs of Innocence — and surely the Blakean agenda could not have been far from his mind — have the virtue of their modesty, and along the way achieve minor coups of observation and description.

> The geometrical forms of the city impress themselves upon the consciousness of anyone who grows up with them; they impose a way of seeing and thinking. But the country is natural, that is to say, raw, contingent, unassorted and particular, and must itself be informed by the mind. If a ball is hit on a grass field it can strike a leaf or a stone and shoot off in any direction; but on the street, against hard cement, the angle of return

is determined strictly by the angle of delivery, so that any kid with *chutzpah*, who knows all the angles, can always come out ahead of the game.

There is some tart phrasing here — turning a phrase was Klonsky's stock-in-trade — though no big picture ever emerges. But how could it when one essay is about playing slugball at age eight, another about the pitfalls of the literary life in eighth grade, and a third about Klonsky's diary at age ten?

3.

The Village attracts its own from every state of the mind: some for the faded romance of La Vie Bohème; some to be free of their parents; some out of acedia or wanhope; some to trade in free love; some for art's sake; some because they are zebras on the white plains; some to hide from their failure; some because they'd rather be in Paris; some to do something about *it*; some for a change of mind or heart — but almost all to escape from the stunning heat and light and noise of the cultural mill grinding out the mass values of a commercial civilization.

Klonsky's Brooklyn boyhood essays are likely to seem perishable items now, but their short shelf life was built in; they weren't written for the ages. His Greenwich Village essays are something else again: as fresh as when they were written and of continuing interest, both as writing and history. These compositions of place brought out the best in Klonsky: a painter's instinct for color and line, an anthropologist's eye for the strange amid the familiar; a raconteur's ear for the punch line; a Boschean relish for the topographies of hell; a Jewish intellectual's passion for the jeremiad; a reporter's nose for news. Cartographer and historian of the Village, Klonsky was also the consummate boulevardier, walking the streets of his hometown, chronicling with detachment the vanities that grew like dandelions all around him, and composing tableaux vivants of local delirium and universal folly that were as brisk and pungent as any of the cityscapes composed by his fellow walker in the city, Alfred Kazin.

The three essays on the Village comprise a kind of Bosch triptych, a phantasmagoria of tormented beings that make one wonder if Klonsky was attempting to portray this world or some other. Indeed, an unpublished manuscript, "The Vanishing Characters of Greenwich Village," which is probably a study for the *Esquire* piece on Bodenheim, ends with a conversation in heaven between Joe Gould and Bodenheim, as if Klonsky were contemplating a Village *Divine Comedy.*

Divine or no, Klonsky's Village was certainly a comedy, a lurid and comic vaudeville to which the imagination of America had come to perform its charades of liberation. From its neo-Parisian salad days in the 1920s, when the rest of America "was a No Man's Land, the haunt of the Cyclops," through the wartime and postwar boom, to the 1950s, when the strongholds of Bohemia fell to the developers, the drugsters, and the Bleeker Street Goths, the local hoodlums for whom Bohemia and its inhabitants were provocations to violence, into the 1960s, when the middle-class hippies tried to turn Bohemia into Sunset Boulevard, the Village presented Klonsky with a kaleidoscope of images that stirred his senses even when they repelled his sensibilities, as they often did. The Village may have been the homeland of the heart, but Klonsky kept his heart under wraps, playing by turns Kierkegaard the ironist, Diogenes the dog ("because I fawn upon those who give me anything, bark at those who give me nothing, bite those who annoy me") and Socrates the skeptic, whose "infinite absolute negativity" (Klonsky quoting Kierkegaard on Socrates) appealed to him as the moral posture best suited to confronting the theater of revolt playing outside his door. At its most debased that theater was the agitprop of revolutionism, and some of his sourest comments in "Greenwich Village: Decline and Fall" are directed toward the revolutionists who, in the 1930s, decamped to the Village and conspired to marry "the camaraderie of the WPA" to "bohemian freemasonry."

Thirty years later, agitprop would dissolve into living theater, and as much as he deplored the old Stalinists, Klonsky did not welcome the unregimented new populations of the Village: neither the fashionably hip nor the "etceterogenous muster" of "dropouts, gynanders & androgynes, bike faggots, orgyasmic groupies, stargazers, shamans & warlocks, apocalyptic utopiates, dinamiteros, tricksters & ponces, radical chicsas [sic], bleeders & draculae, and all the rest."

With such jeremiads in mind — and Klonsky could launch an anathema with the best of them — it might be prudent to qualify the statement that Klonsky was quintessentially a creature *of* the Village and say rather that in the tribalized Village he belonged to one of its tribes: the tribe of Fyodor. However he may have tried on the robes of Socrates, Kierkegaard, and Diogenes, or in later years of Blake and Boehme, he was at bottom a Dostoevskian isolato, who kept faith with the "rank and vile of the Village" (Bodenheim's phrase) with whom he had signed up in the forties, before the prospect of being integrated into American society and true to oneself seemed like an honest possibility. "The way of alienation," he would announce in 1948, "is the Jew's badge of Greenwich Village, a way apart that orients itself by negation."

> Life here is the ghetto life, indrawn, with its own tastes and smells, rank and dark and protected as an arm-pit. The native loneliness of Americans is so intensified in the Village that, paradoxically, it becomes a social cement that holds it together. For what is feared even more than alienation from American life is self-alienation, the loss of identity in the melting pot, reduction to the lowest common denominator of dollar and cent values. It is from this fear that Greenwich Village protects its own. Under cover of the most ideal persuasions of self-denial, there is always a private need.

Nineteen forty-eight was a time for such avowals, and everyone was making them. Daniel Bell had spoken for this generation in 1946:

> The intellectual knows too well the ambiguities of motives and interests which dictate individual and institutional action. He cannot surrender himself wholly to any movement. Nor can he make those completely invidious or utopian judgments regarding the nature and needs of man which the cynic and romantic make. He can only live without dogma and without hope. He can only, as an intellectual, realize his destiny — and by consciously accepting it, rework it — through seeing the world, in Friedrich Schiller's phrase, as disenchanted.

Behind such oaths of disenchantment in the second decade of the 1940s — and they were legion — lay the bitter experience of the Marxist fall of the thirties (Spain, the Moscow Trials, the Stalin-Hitler pact) to which was later added knowledge of the Holocaust. Bartleby the Scrivener's "I would prefer not to" seemed no more than common wisdom to a generation that had suffered these shocks and saw no reason henceforth to have faith in anything. In such an age, even Joe Gould and Maxwell Bodenheim in their cups could seem like sages, involuntary sages, perhaps, and Klonsky's light-fingered homage to Bodemheim, "Maxwell Bodenheim as Culture Hero," behind the antic call for a memorial statue "made of broken wine bottles, Sterno cans, rusty bedsprings, old Salvation Army bugles, missing coat buttons," etcetera, was an *ave atque vale* to a hero.

19

4.

For the sake of freedom, but a negative freedom, Kierkegaard adds, the Socratic ironist refuses to cast himself in any other role than that of spectator, preferring even boredom — "this eternity void of content, this bliss without enjoyment, this superficial profundity, this hungry satiety" — to taking an active part in the world's farce.

But alienation comes in many forms, and one man's polemical strategy may be another's moral imperative or another's desperate routine of daily existence. Klonsky's was the last of these, and though he may have adopted it out of moral conviction, it fit him like a second skin and he became the consummate ironist, refusing to take too dangerously active a part in life and exiling himself to the bleachers of spectatorship. He did a disappearing act in the 1950s, going underground in the Dostoevskian sense, as one acquaintance put it, or perhaps after the fashion of Socrates, who, he noted, "*prided* himself upon the simplicity of his life, went about barefoot in a torn, ill-fitting leather coat, and used to say that those who require the fewest things are nearest to the gods." He continued to write, though in the nineteen years from 1949 through 1968 he published, so far as I can determine, only eight essays and three poems.[2] This condition may have been partly imposed on him by a lack of paying markets for his work, due to the esoteric turn of his mind and the baroque turn of his prose. *Commentary*, where he had found early support and approval, underwent a gradual change after the death of Robert Warshow in 1955, which accelerated after the advent of Norman Podhoretz as editor in 1960, and Klonsky's last publication there was "Annus Mirabilis" in 1957. In 1963 he broke into *Esquire* for the first and last time with his Bodenheim memoir, and at the time of his last illness he was writing a memoir of Auden, "First Acquaintance with Poets" (reprinted here as "Chester, Wystan, Rhoda, and Me"), for the *New Yorker*.

Klonsky's resurrection was a slow one, but it significantly coincided with the advent of a publication in which his work was welcome, the *New American Review*, later *Amerian Review*, under the editorship of Ted Solotaroff. Klonsky would publish there four times between 1968 and 1976, one of the pieces being a wild flight of scholarship and fancy, "Art & Life: A Menippean Paean to the Flea; or, Did Dostoevsky Kill Trotsky?" More remarkable than this flurry of long essays was Klonsky's emergence as a scholar and editor. Throughout the decade of the 1970s, he assembled and edited five books, including two on William Blake that must be considered his chefs d'oeuvre.

But in part, too, the man who surfaces in the 1960s is a new Klonsky, Sartor Resartus, with fresh agenda of values and a new spirit of involvement, not with the world, from which he is as estranged as ever, but with his writing, which he now attacks with unparalleled vigor after two decades of lassitude. Like Carlyle's Diogenes Teufelsdrockh, he bursts from his cocoon of despair with a gospel of work. Someone relying essentially on the published record as a key to the man, as I have to, may be forgiven for thinking that something as dramatic as a rebirth has taken place, so different are the axial lines of this work from what Klonsky had been doing before, and so fresh, it seems, is the commitment. Stunningly different too is the ironist's transformation into an enthusiast. Whatever it was that happened in the dark years, it gives the appearance of conversion, possibly even a religious conversion.

Between 1973 and 1980, Klonsky edited five books: *Shake the Kaleidoscope: A New Anthology of Modern Poetry; The Fabulous Ego: Absolute Power in History; Speaking Pictures: A Gallery of Pictorial Poetry from the Sixteenth Century to the Present; William Blake: The Seer and His Visions;* and *Blake's Dante: The Complete Illustrations to the Divine Comedy*, and just prior to these had abridged and edited a nineteenth-century American tract on sex: *Light on Dark Corners: A Complete Sex Science and Guide to Purity.* It is a peculiar assortment of projects, a little of this, a little of that, and some were simply potboilers. What do we make of *The Fabulous Ego*, a selection of essays on history's great despots, from Sardanapalus and Shih Huang Ti to Catherine the Great and Napoleon (but excluding Stalin and Hitler), by a writer whose abiding attitude toward power was wholly in the spirit of Diogenes's demand of Alexander the Great: "Cease to shade me from the sun." The concrete poetry anthology, however, to which Klonsky contributed a few minor pieces of his own, and the anthology of modern poetry were in the main line of his own interests, and the edition of *Light on Dark Corners* would seem to reflect Klonsky's ongoing sexological investigations. If there is a key to this transformation, however, it is in the Blake books, and it is with them that we might want to linger a while.

5.

Diogenes's search for an honest man was conducted on the street; Klonsky took his to the library, and the odyssey that started with a discipleship

21

to Mallarmé and Marvell, the French symbolists, and the English metaphysicals, took a detour through the agora with Socrates and the Greek skeptics, settled in Dublin for a while with James Joyce and *Finnegan's Wake*, came to rest with William Blake and Blake's Gnostic teachers: Plotinus, Emanuel Swedenborg, Jakob Boehme. Klonsky's last projects were the two editions of Blake, and it is clear that these books and Klonsky's sometimes ecstatic introductions are his testaments of where he had come out after twenty years of wandering in the desert. The introduction to *William Blake: The Seer and His Visions*, which was published separately in *American Review* as "W. B.[4]: or, The Seer Seen by His Own Vision," was closer to the experience of conversion and the more personal of the two.

Sometime in the mid-1960s Klonsky had taken LSD for the first, and, he avows, only time, and the resulting experience had been a revelation. He was on Fire Island with friends at the time, and as the spell began to descend, he wandered down from the cabin to the ocean side, where, flayed by the sun's heat, he flung himself into the surf. "The first cold shock of the water went through me tingling with such ecstatic, such baptismal, joy—or was it anguish?—that I felt as if reborn." Suddenly conscious of the unity of all being and feeling the pulse of the sea as indistinguishable from his own, he found himself quoting Blake's "inevitable lines":

> To see a World in a Grain of Sand
> And a Heaven in a Wild Flower
> Hold Infinity in the palm of your hand
> And Eternity in an hour.

As he did so, the world soul within him shuddered and he felt himself dissolve into the universal waveforms of nature.

> The "blue Mundane Shell" (as Blake imagined it) of the sky—a "hard coating of matter that separates us from Eternity"—cracked open for me at that moment, and I perceived the sun with acid clarity as *a* star, one of billions, so many that the grains of sand I then held in my palm would comprise only a handful; and in the same split second the shell of my own time-hardened and encrusted ego, of which the material universe, as Blake thought, was merely the sensual reflection, also cracked, and something within me but not quite me—Ka, or Atman, or Spirit, or Pneuma, or whatever—that had been brooding coiled up in itself, stirred awake.

22

By then, lost in the infinite and crying like a child over the paltriness of his own life, Klonsky still had the presence of mind to come in out of the heat and save himself from a starburn. What Klonsky would later claim to have gathered from that experience was not the existence of a spirit world, "neither visions nor apparitions, no disembottled genii or spirits out of the vasty deep," but a more profound way of seeing, in Blake's terms, *through the eye* rather than simply *with* it, by which Klonsky would mean into the soul of nature and man and into their fundamental unity.

A scholarly edition beginning on so topical a note was not going to enchant the reviewers, and typical of the reviews was Lawrence Alloway's in the *Nation*: "The interspersing of illustrations of Blake with Klonsky's trite grooviness is like a slide lecture by a hip professor. Anybody who needs this as an introduction to Blake does not need Blake." Seldon Rodman in *National Review* was only a tad more generous: "Everything from a self-serving analysis of his own LSD trip to an exegesis of the Prophetic Books delivered in thunderous polysyllabic abstractions is used to beat the poor reader over the head. To no avail. There are sharp perceptions — the recognition that Blake was closest in spirit to contemporaries he never knew, such as Goya and the Marquis de Sade — but a simple biographical text would have been infinitely more useful." Klonsky had picked the wrong moment to wear his Atman on his sleeve; the mid-seventies were years of high indignation in the cultural trenches, and indignation ran highest where anything recalling the sixties and its acid religiosity was concerned. The book also came under fire for haphazard scholarship, which should come as no surprise. Klonsky placed his scholarship, in the service of inspiration, in the service, moreover, of his lifelong project of soul-making, and his researches were bound to be idiosyncratic and personal. (Which is not to say that they were not also thorough and elaborate. I find Klonsky's editions neither trite nor "groovy.") Blake was the metaphor; he himself the ultimate referent. Be that as it may, now that the polemic over the sixties has cooled and the sufficiency of the Blake books as scholarly editions is not at issue, we can go back to them in a less combative spirit and read his introductions as stations in the spiritual odyssey of a Jewish intellectual in search of his own way, which he finds in the most unlikely precincts of charismatic Christianity.

There are many Blakes: Blake the lyric poet and singer of innocence; Blake the radical pastoralist, scourge of the "dark satanic mills" of industry; Blake the agitator for sexual freedom who wrote in his *Marriage of Heaven and Hell* that the millennium "will come to pass by an improvement of sensual enjoyment"; Blake the pioneer engraver and artist of liquid

23

and undulant human forms; Blake the spiritual adept and inventor of his own mythic system; Blake the composer of antinomian homilies; Blake the Gnostic and diviner of Cabbalistic lore; Blake the visionary. Klonsky was devoted to all of these, but the last two in particular, Cabbalist and visionary, seem especially to have caught his fancy.

For Klonsky, Blake was, in Marianne Moore's phrase, a "literalist of the imagination" for whom "What seems to Be, / Is, To those to whom / It seems to Be," and the capacity for belief was the moral underpinning of the imaginative faculty.

> He who Doubts from what he sees
> Will neer Believe do what you Please
> If the Sun & Moon should doubt
> Theyd immediately Go out.

Such faith in vision and so absolute a lack of skepticism could not but put a strain on others, and Blake was widely taken for a madman in his own day. Klonsky himself could be a little murky on the meaning of Blake's visions — are they to be taken literally, morally, allegorically, anagogically? — but like many Blakeans he found it possible to declare for the visionary life without endorsing every cycle and epicycle of the elaborate monomyth, which could be treated as Blake's shorthand for the infinite or an allegory for the transforming power of the imagination itself. "W. B. Yeats, in his essay on the Dante illustrations in *Ideas of Good and Evil*, once character-ized Blake as 'a too literal realist of the imagination as others are of nature.' To which Blake might have responded with one of the proverbs from *The Marriage of Heaven and Hell*: 'What is now proved was once only imagin'd.'"

Still, a Jew might be discomposed to discover his moral center in a vision so profoundly Christian, however heterodox, as Blake's. Blake was brought up in a fundamentalist Baptist household and remained — for all his vision-ary excursions and antinomian rebellions against Old Nobodaddy — a Chris-tian, that is to say, a believer in the divinity of Jesus Christ. Allen Ginsberg, another Jewish ecstatic whose visionary leanings and LSD experiences led him to Blake, seems to have resolved the problem by taking no account whatever of Blake's Christianity and becoming himself a Buddhist, though of a sort that could be mistaken for a Hasidic Jew. Klonsky's solution was to identify in Blake the influence of the Jewish Cabbalists and to situate Blake in a line of succession that runs from the Druids and the Christian Gnostics to the Jewish Cabbalists and the author of the sixteenth-century *Zohar*, the Book of Splendor. Blake's heritage spanned the religions, tap-ping the deepest roots of Judaism, Christianity, and paganism alike for the universal archetypes of which all partake. Blake wrote: "The antiquities of every Nation under Heaven, is no less sacred than that of the Jews. That are all the same thing. . . . All had originally one language and one religion: this was the religion of Jesus, the Everlasting Gospel." Lest this sound too much like common evangelical Christianity, Blake would hold, in Klonsky's words, "that the Druids, who had built the mysterious temple of Stonehenge on the plains of Salisbury, were none other than that chosen and original race descended from the ten lost tribes of Israel." It was with some version of this Hebraic patrimony and Christian gospel in mind that he wrote in the preface to *Milton* the famous lines:

> I will not cease from Mental Fight,
> Nor shall my Sword sleep in my hand
> Till we have built Jerusalem
> In England's green & pleasant Land.

Not "Next Year in Jerusalem," but "Next year this will be Jerusalem." Blake's Christianity, then, is a Judaized Christianity, though Judaized by way of the most difficult and esoteric productions of the Jewish mind, teachings as proscribed by Halakhic Judaism as Gnostic teachings were by the Catholic church. So much the better for imagining a tradition of heresy running from the Druids to the Cabbala to Blake, and ultimately to onself.

Easier to reconcile was Blake's moral posture, which, stripped of the allegorical rigmarole, seems not far removed from the ethos of Greenwich Village. With his gospel of natual law — the moral authority of the senses — his violent anticlericalism, his apocalyptic fervor, the modesty of his material existence, his championship of the creative imagination, his stubborn individualism, and an internal biochemistry that did for him daily what Klonsky and his friends, fortified with marijuana and LSD, could do only spasmodically, Blake was the model revolutionist and archetypal Bohemian. His quarters, indeed, might well have been a rent-controlled Village walk-up.

> During his last years, from 1821 to midsummer of 1827, Blake lived in near poverty and obscurity with his wife Catherine at 3 Fountain Court, Strand, a house kept by her brother-in-law, where they rented two small sparsely furnished rooms on the first floor. The main front room, its walls hung with Blake's own pictures, was described by his biographer Alexander Gilchrist as containing a bed in one corner, a fireplace for cook-

ing and warmth in another, a side table for meals, a second
worktable for engraving that stood at a window overlooking
Fountain Court, and two chairs; while the smaller back room,
apparently little used, provided a view of the Thames shining
beyond, as Blake said, "like a bar of gold."

"Which," Klonsky adds, "was sufficient for the corporeal Blake, but of
course the real Blake, the visionary Blake, lived elsewhere, in what he referred to as the 'Divine Imagination,' and that was expansive enough for
him to contain even Dante's Heaven and Hell." Building his case for the
reciprocity of poverty and vision, Klonsky records that the nineteen-year-
old artist, Samuel Palmer, visiting Blake in 1824, would later write, "Moving apart, in a sphere above the attraction of worldly honours, he did not
accept greatness, but confer it. He ennobled poverty, and, by his conversation and the influence of his genius, made two small rooms in Fountain
Court more attractive than the threshold of princes."

Nor did he cease from mental fight: Blake's edition of Dante's *Divine
Comedy*, the last sustained work of his life, was at one and the same time
a celebration of "the continuous phantasmagoria" (Eliot's phrase) of Dante's
epic and a scalding criticism of its morality, the "algebra of retribution
in the *Inferno* . . . by which the various types and degrees of torment are
meant to be symbolic of the sins themselves, but raised exponentially in
power."

Maybe it was that tension between imaginative powers that rivaled and
challenged Blake's own and a vision of divine justice that Blake found
morally repugnant, or maybe it was the approach of death — Blake worked
on the Dante illustrations on his deathbed — but the subject released all
his powers, and the illustrations of Dante represent his genius in its fullest
flower. It is not hard to see why Klonsky elected this particular sequence
of drawings for his own final labor, though it is doubtful that Klonsky,
who died of lung cancer in 1981, knew himself to be seriously ill as he
undertook the project. But it gave Klonsky the opportunity to celebrate
for one last time the creative powers that Dante ignited in Blake *and* to
second Blake's outrage at the cruel equations of crime and punishment
that "would not permit [Dante] to exempt or pardon even his closest friends,
his benefactors, or his own kinfolk," roasting the father of his fellow poet
in hell for a minor heresy, placing his teacher and counselor, Brunetto Latini,
in a rain of fire among sodomites, and consigning even a member of his
wife's family to hell. Blake's response to such a vision of justice is to depict
Dante's God as a "glum-faced, white-bearded, decrepit old tyrant," Urizen

26

or Old Nobodaddy. The Dante sequence, then, is both an act of homage and a sustained iconographic polemic, a rite of image magic performed as an interpretation of Dante's word magic but also as a kind of antidote, to neutralize and contain it.

Blake's *Dante,* then, is a tug of war between Blake and Dante, a great poet performing what Harold Bloom calls the misreading of a great father poet for the purpose of casting off the father's yoke. If ever the "anxiety of influence" were frozen on the wing so that we could examine it close up, it would be here, and Klonsky, wholly of Blake's party and aware, shows himself a shrewd interpreter of Blake's ambivalence, of the irritable genuflection of one great imagination before another.

Blake's Dante was published in 1980 and Klonsky died in December 1981, leaving this book as his last work and, willy-nilly, his testament. If it can be said that a man writes the meaning of his life into even the most abstract and scholarly of his writings, then the meaning of Klonsky's life, as he understood it, is to be found in these editions, with their praise of the imagination as the supreme moral instrument, their defense of a man's duty to go his own way, and their approbation of the Bohemian life, the life of material self-denial in the name of spiritual and sensual enrichment. They are also impressive feats of scholarship for a man who worked alone without the usual appurtenances of the trade: foundation grants, secretaries, reseasrch assistants, sabbaticals, conferences, subsidized junkets to the world's galleries and archives. These are full scholarly editions with all the conventional apparatus, but they are also the solitary labors of a man who had no professional context and required none, preferring a company of his books and his muse.

6.

Of Klonsky's life we know little. Preferring a secluded and bookish existence, he left behind no stirring memoirs, no exploits to set the world buzzing, and only a few friends and admirers to keep his memory alive. For a while, certainly in the 1940s, he maintained his standing in Village literary circles, and he pops up in Isaac Rosenfeld's journals,[3] in Delmore Schwartz's journals and correspondence,[4] in Chandler Brossard's novel *Who Walk in Darkness,* where he is called Max Glazer, and in biographies of W. H. Auden, in whose life he played a peripheral but curious role. Later he would lose contact with virtually all his old friends, save Anatole Broyard, and were it not for an autobiographical sketch he wrote as part of an application for a MacArthur Fellowship (reprinted here as "A Writer's Education") and Krim's glowing memoir in *Views of a Nearsighted Cannoneer,* we'd know virtually nothing at all. Even Krim's essay, published in 1960, leaves blank the last twenty-one years of Klonsky's life.

Krim describes him when they first met in the courtyard they shared at 224 Sullivan Street, as looking the gangster, the "dark trigger-man" in his youth, "a strange shortish lithe dark-looking cat who would brush by me at the entrance with brusqueness and what seemed like hostility, but also looking me over in a grudging way. There was an under-the-rock air of furtiveness, reptilianism, about the guy; his eyes would never meet mine, never signal hello, but out of their squinting holes they'd flick off my buttons so to speak in one razor-swipe and then stare stonily beyond." Others too have remarked on this air of menace: Broyard remembers him as cranky, mistrustful, and dour, and Krim describes him as occasionally "iceberg-cheerless." He may have yearned for the Blakean empyrean, for the fire of Inferno and the light of Paradiso, but friends remember him as more the Raskolnikov than the Albion.

And yet Klonsky is remembered too as a wit, a raconteur, a formidable autodidact, and a connoisseur of women. I have yet to have a conversation with any of his old friends that did not get down sooner or later to his youthful exploits as a "cocksman," and allowing for the exaggerations of Village talk and the high quotient of sexual envy that lingers even today among that clan, Klonsky's erotic endeavors and sexual vanity are not to be doubted. They were certainly not doubted by his wife, Rhoda Jaffe, whom he married while they were both students at Brooklyn College, and who left him in 1945 over, among other things, his dedicated experiments with new women.

Klonsky was still an undergraduate at Brooklyn College when he met Rhoda (see "Chester, Wystan, Rhoda, and Me" in this volume.) He was just a sophomore, as he recalls, living at home with his parents and contributing to the undergraduate literary magazine, *Observer,* among whose editors was Chester Kallman, whom he would remember thirty years later as a different species entirely from the Marxist literati who otherwise dominated the staff: "a tropical bird in a flock of jackdaws."

> He was then (as he describes himself in a poem looking back
> from middle age) "one of the handsome few," but perhaps
> "gorgeous" would be a mot more juste, with a ripe and finely
> carved mouth, heavy-lidded, dark-rimmed, liquid deep-blue eyes

28

of the kind known as soulful, and wavy blond hair crested by a, suspiciously, blonder forelock trained to appear unruly and break and curl across his brow. While fairly tall and well built, there was nonetheless a Chaplinesque daintiness about him, a certain slight sway and flutter in his gestures and the way he moved that ineluctably spoke its name.

They would become friends in spite of, or perhaps by virtue of, Kallman's announcing that Klonsky was not his type. Kallman, a Jewish boy and son of a Brooklyn periodontist, was also living at home with his father and a Yiddish-speaking grandmother. But he had another, far more dramatic, life that revolved about his relationship with W. H. Auden, whom he had met in April 1939, but which included other men whom Kallman continued to pick up, much to Auden's despair. ("Those dark stripes under his eyes were earned," remarked Klonsky.)

Rhoda at that time was " a revolutionary blond sociology major" who had already had her generation's obligatory fling with the Communist party, from which she had been expelled for some deviation (or "deviationism," as the party liked to call it) and was nominally a Trotskyist when she met Klonsky. But her politics were largely those of atmosphere rather than of conviction, and as their romance flowered Klonsky had no great difficulty in drawing her away from the Trotskyist's table in the cafeteria. She and Kallman, a "co-sexual and subcutaneous sistership," shared an interest in men's sexual capacities and habits and spent flirtatious hours in the Brooklyn College cafeteria with Kallman ransacking his fantasies — or were they recollections? — about the men at each table, "speculating . . . on their inguinal attributes and sexual prowess, sometimes in imagery so graphic as to electrify anyone within earshot. . . ." Normally it was Klonsky within closest earshot, being none too thrilled about a conversation that had precious little to do with his interests. And yet, there seemed no cause for jealousy; Rhoda too was not Kallman's type.

It was at Kallman's home one evening, after blintzes from Kallman's grandmother "*host du gegesen epes?*" and several sides of the 1936 Glyndebourne recording of *Don Giovanni* with Kallman himself, that the doorbell chimed and in walked Auden.

> Though quite tall, about six feet, he was wearing a brown tweed overcoat at least two sizes too big that came down in symmetrical folds to his ankles and gave him the elongated appearance of a carved gothic apostle. His strong-featured, somewhat horsy face was then hardly furrowed; two prominent, cold-reddened

ears poked out askew on either side of his head; and there . . . it was on his right cheek, not so large as I had imagined, about a blueberry-sized, but it held and focused my attention nonetheless.

It was the briefest of hellos, as Klonsky bolted for the door. *"So that was Auden! W. H. Auden! and he knew who I was too!"* Barely nineteen, still nostalgic for the days of stickball with the old gang, Klonsky suddenly found himself on the brink of marriage, faced possibly with a draft (this was 1942), and on the margin of a sexual, political, poetic world far stronger than anything dreamed of in his philosophy. "One thing . . . was sure: whatever decisions I made or were made for me, about both the army and marriage, the chrysalis in which I had lived as a child for so long was soon to be broken."

"Chester, Wystan, Rhoda, and Me" is an uncharacteristically warm and colloquial piece of writing, free of baroque mannerisms and Joycean convolutions that Klonsky habitually indulged. But it was also a commissioned work for the *New Yorker*, through which Klonsky was hoping to gain access to a paying market and a new audience. He was working on it at the time of his final illness and didn't complete it, and it is apparently a prologue to something bigger and bolder that never got written. We know that Klonsky did no military service, that he and Rhoda did marry while still undergraduates at Brooklyn College, and they moved into the Village in 1943. We also know the sequel to the story which may explain why, illness aside, Klonsky did not bring it completion.

The marriage was short-lived, and by the war's end it was on the rocks. During a period of separation, in the spring of 1946, Rhoda went to work for Auden as a secretary and quickly ended up in his bed.[5] Rhoda at the time was in analysis and was notorious for her compulsive psychoanalizing, which set some friends on edge. But as a woman she knew how to put Auden at ease, and for about a year and a half they carried on as lovers. Rhoda was only recently separated from Klonsky, and Auden too was on the loose, his relationship with Kallman being in a state of transition. Kallman had begun denying him sexually perhaps as early as 1942, and their relationship had settled into something like a fretful Platonic marriage: a sexless domesticity punctuated by escapades of cruising by Kallman, who, the more attractive of the two, enjoyed the freedom of his instincts. Rhoda suddenly came into view as a plausible alternative to Kallman — Jewish, blond, from Brooklyn College — and whether Auden entered the affair to sting Kallman or to attempt a sexual conversion to complement his earlier religious conversion or simply because he was attracted to Rhoda, it lasted until sometime in 1947 and dissolved amicably. Indeed, Rhoda would remain his secretary for a few more years. Later Auden would say in a letter, "I tried to have an affair with a woman, but it was a great mistake."

Knowing this, we may find ourselves thinking ahead to the unwritten sequel and wondering how Klonsky was going to handle the difficulties, though the fact that he never handled them may suggest just how difficult they were. Klonsky's only comment after the fact that I'm aware of is a letter he wrote in 1980 to Humphrey Carpenter, Auden's biographer:

> Whenever I met Chester and Rhoda, either together or separately, Auden's spectacular sexual conversion was sure to be discussed and debated and alembicated down to a Freudian vapour, with Chester reciting Shakespeare's "Phoenix and the Turtle" and Rhoda claiming that Wystan had undergone a complete and irrevocable metamorphosis. My own relationship with Wystan deteriorated. . . . He must have felt guilty, I suppose, about having come between Rhoda and me, though our marriage ties were already quite frayed.

The fact that Rhoda remained a part of the Auden-Kallman circle for a few years meant that Klonsky would be excluded from it and from the soirees that Auden and Rhoda hosted on Grove Street. Rhoda's own life would later end tragically, a suicide in the sixties during the breakup of a later marriage, and how Klonsky was affected by it we can't say. There are, it might be added, two literary footnotes to Rhoda's life. She was the model for the woman in Isaac Rosenfeld's story "George" who takes off her clothes at a party and throws the assembled Greenwich Village lechers into confusion. A more tenuous literary transmogrification was into Rosetta in Auden's *The Age of Anxiety,* a figure so poeticized and Audenized that only her recitation of the *Sh'ma'* at the end of a long soliloquy on desolation and heartbreak lets us know, in the most formal and improbable way, that Auden had a Jewish woman in mind.

Klonsky's middle years are not clearly in focus. With his writing at a low ebb, he kept a low public profile. How he managed to live is no small part of the puzzle. For a while, he held a job with a vanity publishing house, Vantage Press, and there was the occasional payday from writing, a pittance by any standard until the seventies, when the editing projects brought in a few modest advances and royalties. Then there were the summer fellowships at artist colonies — Macdowell, Yaddo, Mt. San Angelo — which allowed him to sublet his rent-controlled apartment in the Village for substantially more than he paid, giving him a modest surplus for the fall.

There were brief teaching stints at Hobart College and the Iowa Writers' Workshop and National Endowment for the Arts grant some time in the seventies. For a while, he earned money as a tutor to Hy Sobiloff, a real estate magnate who wrote poetry and employed numerous New York writers to teach him his trade. And there was, it seems, always a woman around to help with the rent, among them Beverly Kenny, a jazz singer who sang with some major sidemen in the 1950s and died in 1960, also a suicide. Still, it was a *luftmensh's* life, and how does a *luftmensh* live?

The rent-controlled apartment figures in the final story, which is touching, painful, and very, very New Yorky. Ignoring signs of failing health, Klonsky entered St. Vincent's hospital in 1981 only after his lung cancer was well advanced, and while undergoing exploratory surgery he suffered a stroke which left him unable to speak when he came out of anaesthetic. Klonsky had been living with Gloria Rabinowitz, an artist whom he had met two years before at the Macdowell Colony, and as his death seemed imminent he and Gloria decided to marry so that she could legally inherit the apartment. With Ted Solotaroff and Anatole Broyard in attendance, Gloria and a speechless Klonsky were married by a rabbi, to the dismay of a medical staff that kicked up a fuss and had to be coaxed into allowing it. Being penniless at the time, Klonsky was assigned to the public ward at St. Vincent's, where the Puerto Rican salsa music could be heard even during a Jewish wedding. Klonsky died two days later. It was a poet's ending: ironic, whimsical, and agonizing.

7.

What can we conclude? Klonsky might be thought of as a failed poet, one in whom the visionary impulse was powerful but the vision weak — nothing at least equal to his ambition. Perhaps it was that he lacked the personal power that poetry demanded, though elsewhere, in his essays, there is power aplenty — intellectual power and emotional power — and the writing is a poet's prose: rhythmic, metaphoric, and allusive. Inspired by Blake and Joyce, Mallarmé and Marvell, he fretted over every figure and every trope, producing at times a prose so compact and vivid that it calls to mind such late Renaissance productions as Brown's *Urn Burial* and Burton's *Anatomy of Melancholy*. Perhaps the failure to transfer this virtuosity to poetry was because, as Krim thinks, too much was asked of him. He was a wunderkind at twenty and under pressure to fulfill his promise. As the years went by and as the need for money became great, even a fabulist like Klonsky began

32

to realize that poetry was a dream that was not going to pay the bills, and he turned to prose and to scholarship, which, making a virtue of necessity, proved to be his métier anyway. He had the poet's transcendental yearnings, the acolyte's fondness for the arcane and the hermetic (which he appreciated as they lent color to the mind rather than as they revealed divine providence), and the poet's devotion to words, but in the end produced scholarship that failed in his eyes to be true Helicon. He once told Krim, in dead earnest, "The poet must think with nothing less than the mind of God." What price such ambition?

But perhaps too it was that he just backed the wrong horse poetically and attached himself to a poetic line, the stifling Eliot/metaphysical line, that gave no scope to his own voice. Klonsky was working against the grain of American poetry, which veered sharply away from Eliot in the postwar decades and took its cues from Walt Whitman, Ezra Pound, William Carlos Williams, and Charles Olson, native poets who sought in their own writing to capture the genius of vernacular American English. The manner of "wit" and conceit came naturally to court poets and other aristocrats of the spirit for whom wit was the extrapolation of a continuing High Church culture, something far different from anything an American Jew from Brighton Beach could ever have experienced. The metaphysical mask was too tight for an urban American face. In effect, Klonsky bound himself to a poetic that made no concessions to his own sensibility or language, and, aspiring to be Donne or Herbert or Marvell, he produced just four poems, not counting his "concrete" poems, in thirty-nine years of writing.

Yet, that failure is hardly the measure of the man or his work. He was, in any event, independent and uncompromising and lived by his own lights, like the Socrates, the Diogenes, the Blake, even, making allowances for irony, the Bodenheim who were his models of conduct, and he left behind a small body of writing that trails clouds of visible glory and demonstrates some hard-earned *sprezzatura*, the deceptive appearance of easy mastery after five years of what Eliot called "raids on the inarticulate." He was a wordsmith of the first rank, a brilliant phrasemaker. Schooled in the routines of high modernism, he was ever in search of the "mot more juste," and often enough he found it. His essays, rooted in a pungent, natural speech, are aglitter with verbal diamonds. Commenting upon Norman O. Brown's quasi-prophetic tracts, he comments on "the ejaculatory style of their marginalia" and observes that "the author of *Love's Body* can jump from ergo to ergo to ergo with as much slippery facility, and has the same prestidigitational expertise with symbols as McLuhan himself." As for Marshall McLuhan, advance man for the new global village and, like Klonsky himself, a sometime Joyce scholar, "As a scholar and critic of Joyce, McLuhan has borrowed much from the Meister in his own glossolalia on the media. . . . The Joycean puns, the palimpsestic style, the cyclical recurrences . . . all are present in McLuhan's own work. . . . As a result, we have . . . a kind of Delphic gibberish, in which metaphors turn into facts and facts are transubstantiated into symbols and symbols blur into myth." Of Chester Kallman he would describe a face like his (Kallman's) father's, but for "just a soupçon, a certain *je ne sais quoi*, of difference around the eyes and mouth." One combs Klonsky's essays for such delights and finds them everywhere. A poet who fell shy of poetry, he pushed hard at the boundaries of expository prose, and other writers sat up and took note.

Yet, brilliant a phrasemaker as he was, he had trouble getting beyond words to a natural flow of emotions. His writing is sometimes word-bound, and, though brilliant in its bindings, it comes up short of the ease and naturalness that ought to be a poet's birthright. Reading Klonsky sometimes calls to mind a phrase of G. S. Fraser in describing Auden's *Age of Anxiety*: "a kind of ruthless and obstinate exercise in pure technical skill." The net effect is a style abstract in the modernist vein, at times more painterly than literary. The excitement of a Klonsky essay at its best is rather like that of a Pollack painting: splashes of color, hints of violence, miracles of form. One is attracted first by the virtuosity; meaning comes in its wake. We might also say that of late Joyce and of the abstract expressionist movement as a whole, which is to say of Klonsky that he was a full-fledged modernist in his writing, albeit in the end of a modernist of scholarhsip. All the same there are stunning moments of clairvoyance when the armory of words seems to dissolve and the writer and his experience are brillantly united. The reader of this collection will find these passages for him or herself: they are stunning and they are everywhere.

This introduction could only have been written with the help of others who were close to Klonsky and were eager to see this collection published. Foremost among them is Ted Solotaroff, Klonsky's friend and literary executor, who assembled these essays and worked closely with me on this introduction. Seymour Krim has been devoted to this project from the start and has been my bibliographer, my critic, and my friend through the writing of it. Others who have been generous with their time and thoughts are Anatole Broyard, Gloria Rabinowitz, David Bazelon, and Saul Touster. They've made this work possible and pleasurable and have saved me from innumerable mistakes. Those that remain are mine alone.

Mark Shechner

Notes

1. The *Chimera* began publication under the editorship of Arrowsmith, Brown, and Morgan in 1942. Its full title for the first two years was the *Chimera: A Rough Beast*, but with volume 3 changed its name to simply *Chimera*, which it kept until its demise in 1947. It underwent several changes in editorship, and in 1947 was edited by Barbara Howes and Ximena de Angulo, but something like a palace coup in 1948 restored Arrowsmith and Morgan, who opened up the format from poetry and reviews to general letters and changed the title from *Chimera* to *Hudson Review*. Klonsky would publish again in *Hudson* in 1952 and 1955.
2. There may in fact be more published writing than I have been able to find, since research into small and transient publications is very difficult to do, and it would not surprise me if some more fortunate scholar should later turn up essays or poems that eluded me.
3. See Mark Shechner, ed., *Preserving the Hunger: An Isaac Rosenfeld Reader* (Detroit: Wayne State University Press, 1988), pp. 443–44.
4. Robert Phillips, ed., *Letters of Delmore Schwartz* (Princeton: Ontario Review Press, 1984); Elizabeth Pollett, ed., *Portrait of Delmore: Journals and Notes of Delmore Schwartz, 1939–1959* (New York: Farrar, Straus & Giroux, 1986); James Atlas, *Delmore Schwartz: The Life of an American Poet* (New York: Farrar, Straus & Giroux, 1977.)
5. For details of the affair between Auden and Rhoda, I am relying on Dorothy J. Farnan (wife of Chester Kallman's father), *Auden in Love* (New York: Simon & Schuster, 1984), and Humphrey Carpenter, *W. H. Auden: A Biography* (Boston: Houghton Mifflin Company, 1981).

35

ONE

The End Pocket

I

Haunting these vizored cathedrals
My lord is rod, my world is green.
Driven upon its central core
The ball rebuffed and turned by walls
Of baize, follows a further plan
And proves an open corridor.

II

The measured poise, the click, the kiss
Of rod and ball, is ritual
That every soul and star repeats
And burns upon its burning space.
Assist! beyond this mass, this hall
Candled by smoking cigarettes

III

That haze the fretted roof with prayer.
I think—the image burns my eyes—
Of those enduring souls I love
Who huddle, clutch and press their fear
In this cold place, yet keep their ways
Fixed by the rod by which they move.

Originally published in the *Chimera* (Autumn 1942).

IV

Waiting, with all their being coiled
And wound upon a shuttling tense
That past and future intricate,
They rage time's come and go, but snarled
Like them I puff my nonchalance,
A school-boy and his cigarette.

V

The body, its key passion can
Open the womb and grave, be poised
Erect within the double wound;
Not soul, soul blunders on a green
And turning world that is amazed,
Its unimaginable goal space-bound.

VI

But rides upon a heaven crossed
By balls of burning black and brown
Planets, and wheeling galaxies,
Where looming stars like rockets burst
Explosions of bright worlds, and burn
New lamps in time, new ways, new laws!

VII

Is it then lost? The hot discharge
That laboured through eternity
This world, before it cooled its wrath,
Does it repeat my bunched emerge
When my torn mother monstered me,
Blind, alive between death and death?

VIII

My spun and billiard words return.
These strategies, these plots, like balls
That cross and cross, how can they meet
And build this world? And stand like stone?
Both ride one law yet parallels
That cannot touch and lunge at fate.

IX

O Master, whose great rod can move
Through ages of immeasurable light
The heavy planets and the stars:
Show us direction of your love,
Restore us, for whose love we wait
Lighting our cigarette from yours.

(1942)

A Writer's Education

I was born on Nov. 26, 1921, on Staten Island, when that borough, then known as Richmond, was sparsely populated and almost countrylike. But before I could put down any roots my family migrated across the river, first to Manhattan, then to the Bronx and then to Brooklyn, going from apartment to apartment and block to block, cubicles within cubes, all over the Mondrian grid of Greater New York (but somehow bypassing Queens), so my early Arcadian memories of Staten Island were gradually paved over by an urban consciousness. The change, the breach in me, was not only psychological but metaphysical, and as wide and deep as that which supposedly separates naturalist and Platonist.

Q. How so, prithee?

A. The abstract geometrical forms of the city impress themselves upon the mind of anyone who grows up with them; they impose a way of seeing and thinking; but the country is natural, i.e., raw, contingent, unassorted and particular, and must itself be informed by the mind. This became manifest to me even in the games, such as stickball and stoopball, punch-ball, boxball and handball, that I played as a kid. If a ball is hit on an open field, it can strike a stone, a twig, a snake, a tuft of grass and shoot off unpredictably in any direction; but on the street, bouncing against brick or asphalt, and on a court enclosed by opposite curbs or the cracks in the sidewalk, the angle of return is determined strictly by the angle of delivery. Any kid, therefore, who knows the angles and how to cut corners, slicing precisely, can always come out ahead of the game. It was, as I say, a metaphysical matrix, Plato in concrete. In time as my appreciation of literature advanced from Bomba the Jungle Boy to Studs Lonigan, and from the poems in the back of the eighth-grade speller to "The Golden Treasury" to Carl Sandburg, I began, secretly at first (for fear of being scorned as a sissy by my friends on the block), then more and more openly, to write poetry, and with the same passionate dedication with which I used to play street games. These youthful poems, in "free verse" — meter and rhyme I considered effete and reactionary — were written against: against war and fascism, against poverty, unemployment, slums, discrimination, sexual repression — come to think of it, not too different from much of the Beat poetry that erupted during the 60's — and were modishly communoidal in sentiment and rhetoric. Several were published in the high school literary magazine, and one, an antiwar poem called "Drums," somehow came to the attention of an isolationist Congressman from Kansas, who inserted it into the Congressional Record.

For in those years known as the Depression (though it had its manic and enthusiastic side) political piety, if expressed fervently enough, was often mistaken for poetry. To see through the one, one had to see through the other. This happened in my case during my last year in high school, at the age of 17 or so, when the politics I had professed seemed to me not only mistaken but a self-betrayal, and the poems inspired by it seemed both flatulent and lumpish, mere windbags of words, "naturalistic" without being natural, and false in tone because falsetto, untrue to my own inner voice.

By then I had begun to read the great modern writers — Yeats and Joyce, Eliot and Pound, Kafka and Céline, Hart Crane and Marianne Moore and Wallace Stevens — and their literary ancestors as well. My discovery of the English metaphysical poets and the French Symbolists — so close to one another in sensibility yet separated by more than two centuries — was also an act of self-discovery. In the poems of Mallarmé and Marvell especially, with their cinematic shifts of reference, their amalgamations of imagery drawn from disparate sources, the ironical slant and punning ambiguities cutting both ways, and their intricately plotted structures, which served to inform and certify words with meaning, I saw a way of transmuting my own metropolitan experience into poetry. Marvell and Mallarmé, Mallarmé and Marvell, these two evoked for me a spiritualized Manhattan. Though I knew little French and had to unriddle Mallarmé's thrice-distilled hermetic poems word by word, over and over, with the aid of Larousse, so that quite often they engraved themselves deeply in memory without ever penetrating my comprehension, that hardly mattered.

For, as T. S. Eliot declared, "Genuine poetry can communicate without being understood."

Eliot's critical ideas, which he had evolved in the course of writing his poetry, dominated modern literature in those days. It was Eliot who had defined the rules of the game, marked off the boundaries of discourse and even, in his most influential essay, "Tradition and the Individual Talent," picked the sides and kept the score. Toward Eliot's "classicism," however, I felt temperamentally opposed. I could agree, for instance, that poetry was not a "turning loose" of emotion, but I could not agree that it was an "escape" from it, for I felt no desire to escape, even if that were possible; and again, though I agreed that poetry was not an "expression of personality," yet Eliot's own unique, even idiosyncratic personality was displayed throughout his work. Finally, if the past, as he said, was altered by the present as much as the present by the past, the literary tradition he had invented for himself could hardly be mine, nor that of any of my contemporaries either. Our sensibilities had been shaped by an American mass culture of which he was unaware. Just as Eliot had declared it necessary to exclude "free-thinking Jews" from his ideal Christian commonwealth, so his literary game was rigged against me and my kind.

During the summers of 1942 and 1943, spent as a fellow at the Cummington School, in Cummington, Mass., a place similar to Yaddo or the Macdowell Colony, I met, among other writers in residence there, the poets Allen Tate and Delmore Schwartz. Both had a formative and lasting influence on me. Through Tate's exacting critical eye I came to discern more clearly the lineaments (and the limitations) of my own work; and by reading with him Andrew Marvell's inwrought and most cryptic poem, "The Garden," with its mazelike ambiguities leading to a concealed but central and radiating metaphor, I saw in it (as mentioned earlier) the prototype of an emerging New York metaphysical style. My first published poem in that mode, "The End Pocket" (which appeared in 1942 in Chimera), was inspired by Marvell's work; and in 1950 I published an essay in the Sewanee Review, "A Guide Through the Garden," which revealed for the first time its Plotinian and Neoplatonist structure.

Delmore Schwartz, whose "individual talent" was too wild and too anomalous ever to be assimilated into Eliot's "tradition," had just completed during the summer I met him a long confessional poem, somewhat in the manner of Wordsworth's "Prelude," on the theme of self-identity. This theme—together with its shadowy counterpart, mutability—had been mine as well, well before I knew Delmore. But afterward it became for me, too, a kind of quest, or inquest, and I pursued it in essay, poem and story through all my old familiar faces, dead phases, masks worn out and seen through. Though I have changed, it has remained the same. Even now I am in the midst of writing a sort of Menippean novel called "White Designs" (the title drawn from a poem by Henry Vaughan and based on the cabalist notion that the white space surrounding the Hebrew letters in the Bible contains its true, that is, mystical, meaning) on the metamorphoses undergone during childhood.

Where am I? Far from where I started, but I mean to get back. I was about to relate how I enrolled in the U.S. Signal Corps, was honorably discharged, took an M.A. at Columbia (writing my thesis on metaphor), got married, divorced, went to teach for a year at the Creative Writing Center of the University of Iowa, returned to New York and began to write for Commentary and Partisan Review, took off for Europe and lived on the margin for almost two years in Paris and London, returned to teach at Columbia for the next two years, then went off to California, where I lived for a year trying to write movie scenarios, quit to return to the Village once more, and so on, as if the past were a rational train of events proceeding down the years from junction to junction, ergo to ergo, to arrive at the I I have become, here and now, writing this. What would be left out en route are all the so-called "coincidences," the missed connections, all those seemingly accidental and arbitrary "constellations" (as Mallarmé came to see them in his last poem, "Un coup de dés jamais n'abolirā le hasard") that have shaped us, as we have shaped them, into what we are. If, as Wallace Stevens once wrote, "Life's nonsense pierces us with strange relation," it is because we ourselves make the connections, for we are the "point."

So then, to get back to where we started, the streets of New York. It is not, as I had so long believed, in a Platonic transcendence of phenomena, rising on tiers of forms to the Good, the True, the Beautiful, that I have found my own truth and my way as a writer, but in the reverse, a descension into the unique and irreducible thisness of things and events, the "haeccities" (as Duns Scotus called them) and what Blake referred to as the "minute particulars." These are so often overlooked because they are beneath our notice and, though all around us, are seen through like air without being seen themselves. Even the games I played as a kid were never that Euclidean, as I now realize, for there was always a thrown-away cigarette butt, a wad of gum, a loose brick or a bump in the sidewalk that could deflect the ball in any direction.

Once, I recall, as the youngest and smallest kid on the stickball team, I was stuck out in the outfield, beyond the second sewer, where in a whole game you might consider yourself lucky if two or three balls came your way; and while I was standing all alone, daydreaming, and not watching home plate, suddenly sensing something, I looked up and there it was, coming right at me like a clenched fist, so that I got set, raising my arms, and yelled, "I've got it! I've got it!" when it swooped and veered off and climbed about the rooftops, not the ball but a bird.

(1982)

Annus Mirabilis: 1932

Like an archeologist in a dream, I opened a dark closet where all the used up and forgotten relics of the past had been slowly accumulated, year after year, and stacked in layers of dust up to the ceiling. The place began to stir. At my first touch, flakes of dust as large as moths rose up and swarmed into the light, almost blinding and choking me as I dug through the pile. Then, near the bottom, I pulled out a box containing a few torn and moldy books; a baseball mask; the rind of an old basketball; a set of yellow report cards bound in a shoelace, recording my Work and Conduct for eight years; a sphinx; a pair of roller skates, the wheels clogged with rust; a bag of marbles and a bag of ball "bearions"—and, buried under all this monumental junk, a little blue book with the word "Diary" stamped in faded gold on the cover.

This was the diary I had kept in 1932 when—as stated on the first page—I was ten years old, four feet five inches tall, and weighed sixty-four pounds. For almost a whole year, until my resolution drained away, I had chronicled the ins and outs of everyday life in a heavy, Palmer-methodized script, the cuneiform of that period, primitive and rough-hewn, as though each page had been laboriously incised in granite. It was hard to decipher my own words; and as I read again the names of my old friends, the record of my trials at school, and those ancient feuds and struggles for survival on the block, it was even harder to believe that the author had once been me.

The dust in the closet had made my hands so black and my clothes so grimy that I looked— *"Look at yourself!"*— as if I had been rolling marbles in the gutter all day long. But who cared? The "I" in the diary was buried in this tomb. Bent over and squinting in the darkness, absorbed in myself, breathing the dust, I lit a match to see by as I turned the pages, and then, slowly, remembered how many times before going to sleep he would make a tent of the blankets and huddle inside, secure and alone, writing down the day's news with the aid of a flashlight. . . .

Suddenly I burst inside and see him in his tent crouched like a gnome over the diary: he turns, he looks up, and with the same start we recognize our self. *Was that me? Is that me?* An enormous waste of time lay between us. And as he, on his side, began to realize that all the breaks, cross turns, and incalculable possibilities of being had led only to me; and I, on mine, saw myself as if in caricature reduced to what he was, essentially the same, we both had to turn away our eyes. I remembered his daydream visions of himself: in the center of the baseball diamond, pitching flawlessly, the bright point of everybody's eyes; or breaking through the forest at dusk clad only in a leopard skin, bringing home the day's kill for his mate; or at the controls of a space ship rocketing out of this world. . . . His eyes seemed to accuse me: *How could I have become what I was?* I felt his contempt and flushed, angry at myself. And I answered: *What did we have in common anyhow?* He was dead twenty years—he had never really been me—he was nothing at all. I exhaled him like a breath. But, in the next breath, as we both knew, I had to take him back, feeling him stretch and expand inside me and his own voice speak through mine.

RESELOUTIONS
1. To gain five pounds more.
2. To be good in school.
3. To be good in hebrew.
4. To get a football.
5. To kiss parents every night.

When I set this down on January 1, 1932, my life had already become entangled in petty snarls of all kinds.

First of all, I was in the midst of a feud at school with a big kid called Harry Adler, who came from a tough neighborhood, and every day during lunch hour I expected the showdown; also, I had been left out of the football team on the block; also, I was quarreling all the time with my older brother, Robert, and mad at my two best friends, Normy and Manny;

also, I was way behind in my club dues at the Hebrew school and threatened with expulsion; and last, and most important, the end of the term at P.S. 6 was approaching, and doubt that I would be promoted made these final days seem long and taut with anxiety.

But I could always escape to the movies.

Jan. 1 – Wanted to go to the Daly teathre, but Frankenstion was playing so I wanted to go tomorrow to the Chester.

Jan. 2 – Went to see Frankenstien but the Chester was too crowded so I couldn't go. The whole block went to see the picture and they all got in except me. I couldn't go to my aunt Becky so I stood home doing nothing.

Jan. 3 – Made a second attempt to see Frankenstein but they charged me 50 cents and I only had 30 cents so again I couldn't see the picture. Papa and Mama went to see Papa's brother in Brooklyn but they told us we couldn't go with them.

Jan. 4 – Today is the first day of school after the Christmas holidays. I got my report card and darn 3 times straight I've got a D in conduct and broke my New Years Resouloutions. I think I'll get a C next month.

Jan. 5 – In school Harry Adler wanted to have a fight with me, but outside he changed his mind. Wanted to go to the library for my brother but when I came there the library was too crowded.

Then, at last, the breaks began to go my way.

Jan. 6 – Had delicatessen for dinner. Enjoyed the meal for it was a salami sandwich, Tangerine and soup. Seen Frankenstein. Think it was the best mystery picture ever seen except, I think, "Dr. Jeckl and Mr. Hyde."

A short disgression on the movies: Inside the Temple of Baal on a Saturday matinee, waiting for the show to begin, there I am in the pit with Manny Mortz on one side and Norman Gebrowitz on the other, a brown paper bag clutched in my hand (containing a chicken sandwich, a pickle, a piece of sponge cake, a tangerine) and hunched forward impatiently in my seat while from all sides I hear the ballyhoo of kids just arriving and searching for friends and friends of friends – "Hey Black-*eey!*" "Hey Yoush-*keey!*" "Hey Ben-*jeey!*" – distant bleats, whistles, Tarzan yells, and shouts of reunion, wrangles over seats here and there and calls for witnesses, the nervous insect cracking of nuts increasing as the moment draws near, and then, abruptly, darkness, a reverent hush, and the projector flashes upon the screen and spreads my eyes with light.

It's the jungle serial! A tremendous yell of exultation bursts from the audience, diminishing gradually to a moderate uproar. When last seen, the good guy had been stabbed in the back, bound with barbed wire, spat upon, and thrown into a den of lions, and some of us doubted that he would get out. Now, just in time, he wrenches himself loose and escapes in a streaky blur while the camera is focused upon the lions. We nudge each other. The scene shifts to the headquarters of the rats. Hearing the news, they begin plotting again, sneering and guffawing in a nasty way. Spies and counterspies shuttle back and forth. Meanwhile, the good guys just horse around their camp and crack jokes as though nothing had happened. Another trap! Beside himself, Manny Mortz stands up in his seat and shouts: "Watch out! Look! They're right behind you!" No use. The good guy — or his best friend or the girl — again is caught in an even more "heart-rendering" predicament, and the chapter ends. There was no catharsis here — who needed it? — only pity and terror unrelieved week after week.

Before the murmurs from the audience had died down, the feature would begin. On Saturdays this was usually a Western starring Tom Mix and his horse Tony; Hoot Gibson, Ken Maynard, Tim McCoy, et al. There was something about these ritual struggles between the Good Guys and the Bad Guys flickering in black and white upon the screen that made their shadows seem even more real to us than the concrete of daily life. We followed them with a zeal that was almost holy. Of course, we liked other movies, such as Our Gang and Laurel & Hardy and Chaplin comedies; murder pictures; war pictures; spooky pictures; pictures with horses, and dogs like Rin-Tin-Tin — just as long as they weren't love pictures or those endless courtroom melodramas that came in with the Talkies and were all talk, talk, talk. But Westerns, naturally, were the best.

Simon De Courcey, the villain (we recognize him by his mustache and his pompadour) *pours himself a shot of whiskey, ruffles a pack of cards, and sneers at Tom Mix.* At the sight of his evil face, many stand up to curse the rat, and with such passion that only the metaphysical bar of the screen kept them from plunging right inside. The plot unreels. *There's De Courcey again with two of his cronies sneaking into the barn, where Tom Mix, his hat off, is politely talking to the girl.* This is too much. Someone always has to leave for the toilet at this point, walking backwards up the aisle so as to follow the action as long as possible. They go in, they do it, they're out in a minute. But even in that brief time, The Chase might already have begun and the whole theater become vaster, darker, more turbulent, with such an abrupt and mixed-up hullabaloo of oohs, ahs, boos, and bahs coming in rapid succession from the audience as first Tom Mix and his pals, then De Courcey and his cronies, flash by across the screen, firing wildly back and forth, that all are indistinguishable.

If no one could hear a word or a gunshot beyond the first couple of rows, it didn't really matter. A large part of the audience would remain for at least two revolutions of the program, learning every word and gesture by heart. Ushers would still be hunting for kids at night sitting quietly and stealthily among the adults.

Months, even years, later, while huddled around bonfires in the street on a winter evening baking "mickies," or just shmoozing in the schoolyard during recess, or hanging around the candy store of an afternoon with nothing to do, the highlights of this movie and other movies would be recalled and relived, having passed into the collective id of the block, mixed with our own dreams and daydreams, the shadowy stuff of our selves.

For this reason (to get back to the Diary) it was a cultural necessity for me to see "Frankenstein" before the year could officially begin.

Jan. 8 — I cleaned the rust from my sled but there is no snow. A new kid moved around the black called Arnold Alper and nobody likes him. Read a book called Modern Art and the Evening Graphic.

Jan. 9 — Got up early and finished the book "Dr. Doolittle's Circus." Didn't want to go out and stayed in the whole day. I comed mama's hair: first I made some like a rose out of the hair and second of all I made curls.

Jan. 10 — Today I quarelled with Normy which was a better fighter, Waker or Smeling. Manny and me were going to an alley but a dog didn't let us go out of the alley. A girl on the block cut herself badly and is getting stitches.

Jan. 11 — Teacher said we are going to have promotion tests tomorrow. She appointed me monitor of the board erasers. Mother bought me shoes and pants. Went to Hebrew and had club. Told joke about what everybody does at the same time. Grow older.

Jan. 12 — When I was going to school I found a penney I looked around and found another penny and a dime. Had geography promotion test. Bought hot-dog with Normy. Normy bought a knish. I wanted to buy a pickel with Normy but his father didn't leave him.

Jan. 13 — Went down for board erasers and cleaned them. First time I never read my composition was today. Went to Hebrew and Mr. Mendelson read us a chapter. Did English and Hebrew homework in schools. "P.S. Am glad I did it."

Jan. 14 — Went to school and put on two different colors on two different stockings. Teacher said there would be a history test tomorrow. Went with Manny at night to P.S. 67. We tried to get in but we didn't. Had bath tonight.

Jan. 15 — Went to school and Harry Adler had to be put back to 4B for a few days. Monday we have construction. Mother and Father looked in Robert's diary and found out that he had a fight with a guy called Fat Leborwitz. Robert is a little cranky today.

The revelation that my own mother had been secretly reading my brother's diary, and mine too — why not? — filled me with a kind of primitive dread. I felt threatened at the *ka*, the innermost moat of my individuality, my self. For if this were allowed, then all the minor victories won grudgingly and painfully over the years — what I would wear, what games I could play, what friends I could have, what I would eat (I won't eat soft-boiled eggs) — all would be sacrificed.

To keep the diary out of her hands, I went over all my private hiding places around the house. I considered stuffing it behind the tubes and coils of the radio, under the mattress, behind the large framed picture of my grandfather in the bedroom, until, finally, I found the perfect plant. It was a deflated basketball, a huge and leathery pumpkin growing casually in the closet, and there I hid the diary and prayed that it would remain undiscovered.

One more good reason for hiding it was this: my last weeks in Class 5B3 were turning nightmarish, and I didn't want my mother to find out.

Jan. 16 — If anyone is reading my diary, YOU MAKE ME SICK!!! I'm not going to write from now on.

Jan. 18 — Today I woke up late and went to school. I got on the late line but sneaked in on time. Went to Hebrew and had club. Didn't pay club money.

Jan. 19 — Went to school and spilled chalk sawdust over the whole closet. Teacher made me clean it up. Played with everybody 3 ft. to germany. Wrote in brother's diary by mistake. He is writing this now while I am dictating.

Jan. 20 — Went to school and had an English test. Teacher

didn't let me be monitor of the board erasers. She picked Harry Adler. Robert was trying to be good to me so I should go to the library and get his card.

Jan. 21 — Went to the library for my brother and got him his card. Had a substitute for teacher today. Played socker and kicked 2 goals on Sam M. Bought the Mirror after a hard quarrel and read it.

Jan. 22 — Got back my Geography test paper and it was 63. Forgot to do some arithmetic examples so the teacher said I might stay in but I didn't. Drizzling all day today.

The weather was out of *Macbeth* — it seemed to be always drizzling. Sometimes, after a long, gray, miserable day at school, I would dream that I was sitting alone in an empty classroom with Miss Moss, my teacher, who pointed her rod at me like an old witch with a hazel wand and said: *"Milton, you've had D in conduct every month and you're going to be left back. . . ."*

My troubles in Class 5B3 had started during the first week of school. Miss Moss, who had a reputation for being very strict, had decided to read aloud a poem in the back of the speller called "How Do I Love Thee?" by Elizabeth Barrett Browning.

"How do I love thee?" she began, looking us all straight in the eye. "I love thee to the height" (she raised her arms high overhead) "and depth" (she lowered them till her fingers touched the floor) "and breadth" (squinching her eyes and mouth like a dog about to howl and flinging her arms violently outward) "my sou-*oool* can reach!" and I couldn't help it, I laughed right out loud.

But nobody laughed with me. Miss Moss began to mutter to herself and agitate back and forth in her chair like an old rabbi, gathering speed, and then she suddenly stood up and quivered, so mad she could hardly speak. When she came to, I was given a note to my mother and sent down to the principal's office, where I had to stay in an hour after school.

From that time on, whenever something suspicious happened in class, I was immediately accused, gaffed, hung with a demerit, flayed with extra homework, so that after a while I just gave up. Besides, I told myself, who wanted to be one of the snitchers and teacher's pets who hung around her desk all day like girls? It was too late to change, anyhow. Once, while Miss Moss was out of the room, I took a quick look at my page in her conduct book and my eyes turned red with all the zeros and X's and questions marked there in indelible ink.

Jan. 25 — West to school and read my composition to the class it was about the Planet Mars. In Hebrew Mr. Mendelson read us a chapter. We had club. But he put me outside so I didn't pay club money.

Jan. 26 — West to school and copied my composition on good paper. Teacher gave me a conduct slip to take home. Went up the school and watched some handball games.

Jan. 27 — I felt a little sick so I stayed home from school. Went with Manny and asked for passes to the movies. We got two. Skated in street for half an hour.

Jan. 28 — Bought the American and read it. But Mama didn't want me to buy the Evening Graphic. Got another conduct slip. Wrote todays diary tomorrow because I forgot to write it today.

Jan. 29 — Went to school and teacher put me outside and told me to call my mother. She chucked me from calling. I mean being monitor of my row. Robby snitched that I didn't pay Hebrew club money and spent it on candy.

Falling through an inner space for five days, I yearned and stretched out for the week end, almost desperately, the way a trapeze artist in mid-air clutches the flying bar.

Feb. 1 — Went to school and Harry Adler told me that he is going to 6A4. Teacher didn't call for mama. But she kept me after class so I came late to Hebrew and had club. I paid 2c. It was rainy the whole day and in the night there was hail.

Feb. 2 — Teacher put me outside class till three o'clock. I missed my drawing. Went with Manny to Washington library because he wanted to join it. I doubt that I'll get promoted.

That was my blackest day. I saw myself coming home with my final report card — *left back* — forced to remain for five more stifling months with kids from a lower class, now my equals, repeating the same lessons day after day and in the same room, most probably, with the same lousy view over the girls' playground, stuck once more with Miss Moss, while all my friends went on to brighter and higher grades.

And my mother — what would I say to her? Could I say: "Mom, I've just been left back?" No. I would say: "Mom, the whole class has been left back." No. I would say: "Mom, they've decided to make public school nine years instead of eight, so 5B is really. . . ." No. It was no use. How

54

could she believe that her own son, her image, her hope, her Phoenix, in short, her me, whom she had extolled and apotheosized up and down the neighborhood, could possibly—the thought was unthinkable—*be left back*?

At that time I would have done anything—study two hours a night, keep neat notebooks, hand in my homework the next morning, never come late again. . . . I was desperate. But, knowing myself, I knew that all this homemade and humble piety would grow stale a week after I had been promoted, and I would have to eat it.

> Feb. 3—Went to school and Priccilla Willonson had the promotion sheet so she told me I will be promted to 6A4. I went to Hebrew and for the first time in a month I did my homework. Went skating at night.
>
> Feb. 4—Went to school and teacher told me that I had 88 in arithmetic. Played basketball with Normen and his cousin. Me and Normy stood Melven and we won him 12-8. When I came up I had very wet socks and shoes.
>
> Feb. 5—Brought Bomba the Jungle Boy at the Giant Cataract to read in class because it was last day of school. I got promoted to 6A4. My marks were as follows: Work—B, B, C, B and Conduct—D, D, D, D, C-. Manny is left back. And Normen is in 6A3.

With what can I compare that day? The joy of Jonah when he was heaved up from the whale's belly was no more than mine as I left Class 5B3 and Miss Moss behind me forever and emerged with hundreds of others into the fresh air of the street, crowing and shouting, tearing up old notes, conduct slips, homework, test papers into confetti and letting the wind blow it around and around the school yard. I felt regenerated, lost and found, my self self-made once more, shining on the world as if the sun itself, that great "I," could look back in amazement at the night it had come through.

The street that afternoon was bulging on both sides with activity, and as compendious in its own way as that huge picture by Breughel in which hundreds of kids are depicted in every game and gambol known throughout the ages, each one given its little place on the canvas. There were games of Ringalevio, Kick the Can, Leap Frog, Johnny on the Pony, Hop-Scotch, Three Feet to Germany; tense. Skelley games were going on within the squares of the sidewalks, and marble contests along the gutters; and boxball, handball, slugball, punchball, and stickball games were in progress, each set of players oblivious to the others. On the curb exchange in the street, "cockemamies" could be traded for checkers, checkers for 'immies," "immies" for bottle caps or political campaign buttons or the lids of Dixie cups, depending upon the season and the fluctuations of supply and demand. And out in the courtyards and alleyways, where their mothers could keep an eye on them, troops of girls were skipping rope and playing potsy (their hopscotch squares drawn bold over the palimpsest of our skelley) while singing their age old matrimonial runes:

Cinderella dressed in yella
Went uptown to meet her fella. . . .

and

If you don't like my apples
Then don't shake my tree;
I'm not after your boy friend—
He's after me. . . .

and

One, Two, Three alarey,
I spy Mrs. Sarey
Sitting on a bumbleary. . . .

and so on.

Meanwhile, roaring in and out of all this chaos, came kids on roller skates. Just as you have to walk barefoot in the country to get the feel of the earth, so to appreciate the pavement you have to put on skates.

Extensions of me like the little wings on the ankles of Mercury, I would clamp them to my shoes so tightly that they bit through the leather and almost into my flesh, then roll off in freedom down the street, clicking over and over the regular grooves in the sidewalk; or grinding, with short, quick strokes, over the rough corrugations of granite pavement that drilled through your bones and made your teeth chatter; or over cobblestones, walking and picking my way painstakingly one leg at a time, like a skier toiling up a slope; or, from the heights, slaloming with a zigzag course around the bumps, fissures, posts, and manholes; or, best of all, gliding downhill with gathering speed over smooth, gray, free and easy blocks and blocks of slate. . . .

No part of the skate was ever wasted. They could be attached to a heavy board nailed to a soapbox and made into scooters; the wheels could serve as pucks for hockey games; or the "ball bearions" taken out of their sockets and used as marbles. But before the wheels were thrown away, they would be ground down further and further to a fine shade, a memory, and even now I can hear them roaring in some deep and narrow tunnel of my mind.

> Feb. 8 — Skated with Normy and Manny to P.S. 67 but we couldn't get in. Lefty told us we might get in on 57, we went there but they told us we've got to join a club. We joined it. We pay 50c a year.
>
> Feb. 10 — Went to school and had Miss Harris. She is a very strict teacher. Me and Sambo wanted to study together but couldn't. Got back my old job as monitor of the board erasers. I had a fight with a boy called Erwin Cohan and bet him up.
>
> Feb. 13 — Went to school and forgot to do the rest of my homework. My teacher got angry and said that she'll show it to Miss Redmond. Played sallugee with Manny and I always took his hat and ran away. But Manny had a cold so I gave him it.
>
> Feb. 16 — I rode to Washington library on the Southern boulevard trolley where I quit. I don't have any time anymore. My uncle from Brooklyn came to visit me. Robert played him the mandelion and it was good.
>
> Feb. 19 — Went to school and teacher asked Herman Fobb if he ever had a "D." He said No. Well said the teacher expect one this month. Played tag with Manny and everybody on the block played also. Saw James Cagney in "Taxi" at Chester.

It was while this picture was being shown that some kid from the Quanee, Jrs., a social club, let loose a boxful of moths he had smuggled inside. They all flew straight up into the projection beam, their enormous shadows flickering on the screen like dragons and throwing the house into a panic. Though caught by an usher and kicked out, his exploit became almost legendary around the block, discussed with awe years afterward.

> Feb. 21 — Today I looked through opera glasses for the first time. The other side makes things small. Went to Hebrew and Mr. Mendelson said he might give me a part in a play.
>
> Feb. 24 — When I gave Miss Harris the homework which my brother did yesterday she said it wasn't my homework and gave ma a conduct mark. I went with Manny, Normy and the new kid Arnold to P.S. 67. But we couldn't get in.

Feb. 26 — Went to school and the teacher chucked Erwin Cohan from being assistant monitor of the board erasers with me. Had race with Jacky and won by two boxes. I should have won by more. Had race with Paul Robbins and lost. Studied part of Topele-tu-taru in play.

Feb. 27 — Went out to the street for 20 minutes, the rest of the time I stood in my house reading Jerry Todd and the Oak Is. Treasure and the Rover Boys at Colledge. Mr. Mendelson gave Morton the part of Berele the thieve.

Feb. 28 — I was reported by Mr. Kressel today and teacher gave me a conduct mark. Wanted to go to atheletic center but I didn't because it was closed and I bought a ticket. Robert is sick.

Feb. 29 — Went to school and got 95 in my geog. test. I met Normy and we skated to Crotona park. I played on a seesaw and I swung on a swing. I read a book called Over the Ocean to Paris.

I went, I saw, I said, I played, I read, I made — I, I, I, I — who were all these braided, pompous, regimental I's identified with me, an endless parade of being, and where were they all marching, anyway? As I look back now, it seems that a certain line of action (perhaps imposed by memory), and a pattern of change, too slow to have been perceived at the time, were emerging from this sensual mishmash like my own fate.

What was most important: my friends and I were beginning to outgrow the street. Long ago, when I was very young and still enclosed by the Family Circle, the street had seemed immense, full of danger, mystery, adventure. But now, somehow, it had become cramped and criblike.

Younger kids — kids wearing their first pairs of knickers — were taking over. Whenever we found them playing on our street we would kick them off or play "sallugee" with the ball, tossing it back and forth over their heads until they began to whimper or, out of nowhere, their mothers appeared. In spite of this, they persisted, even grew bolder, more and more came around, and, in the end, we ourselves were the ones who had to leave.

During our expeditions at night on skates and on foot, we had penetrated other neighborhoods like our own and become aware of the immensity of the Bronx — that mysterious borough built like a Chinese puzzle of blocks enclosed and fitted in other blocks, each one self-contained, with its own circles and inner circles of kids, its social bars, radiations, and cross-connections of status, forming a complex and psychophysical geometry.

Some of these blocks, we discovered, had even organized clubs. The members wore bright two-toned jackets emblazoned on the back with names like The Quanee, Jrs., The Bronx Panthers, Crotona Kings, the Black Dukes. . . . And when we learned that these jackets had been obtained by selling tickets in the neighborhood for raffles — raffles which never had to take place — we decided definitely to form a club of our own.

March 1 — Went to school and teacher made me stay in till half-past four. I sold some tickets for the help of the poor jews in Poland. Played ringelevio with the block and talked about a club.

March 2 — In school teacher gave us a piece of paper explaining hy we should keep our city clean. Wrote the Star Spangled Banner yesterday but I studied it today. Went to a wedding where Aunt Gertie married somebody.

March 3 — Went to a play rehearsel and because there wasn't a lot of kids Mr. Mendelson said it will be tomorrow on 12 o'clock. I had a big fight with Robert up the school. I think I like Manny better than Normy.

March 4 — Went to a rehearsel and didn't bring my part. But I knew how to say it so it didn't matter. I played buttons on the street and came out winning a lot. I won 10c in buttons.

March 6 — Two new stores opened at the same day a dairy and a stationery store. Went to movie and saw Edward G. Robinson in The Hatchet Man. The name of the club is the Blue Falcons.

March 7 — Went to school and gave in 2c for a picture frame which will decorate picture of Georg Washington. Traded Jackie The Rover Boys on Great Lakes and Rover Boys Winning a Fortune for Through Space to Mars and The Iceberg Express.

March 9 — Went to see a movie after school and saw Lena Rivers and a comboy picture. When I came back I played for buttons. I trusted 2 cents from the candy store man and bought buttons. I won 15 buttons and paid candy store man. The first meeting of club is Friday.

March 10 — Walked all the way to Washington library and saw a long line in front of a bank that wasn't moving. While playing association Morty threw a stone on me. The meeting is tomorrow.

March 11 — The Blue Falcons held their first meeting today
and it stinks. Heard Eddie Cantor and Joe Penner on the radio.

The meeting took place at night in a basement storeroom filled with
discarded cribs, kiddie cars, baby carriages, rocking horses — relics of a
past as ancient then as now. The light of a weak bulb dangling from the
ceiling cast huge and despondent shadows on the wall. This room, ever
since we had learned how to break open the lock on the door, had become
our secret hangout. We cleared a space amid all the junk, passed a couple
of cigarettes around, and sat down in council.

Murry Aaronson was there, the hub of our circle, a slick, self-anointed
big shot who had grown up somewhat faster than the rest of us and already wore long pants. There was something sticky and greased-down
about Murry's personality. He was the one who always chose for sides in
a ball game and settled fights, although he really wasn't as good a player
or fighter as he thought. But, so far, no one had challenged him.

Also, *Sheiky Levenhart*, Murry's right-hand man. Sheiky had as many
flares and angles as a diamond and loved the limelight, so some part of
him was always shining in your eyes. As the acknowledged wisecracker,
scop, and gleeman of the gang, he had an every-ready repertory of "dirty"
limericks and "dirty" jokes, whose real meaning even he could hardly
guess, but at which we all laughed anyway. Without warning, Sheiky would
rip "homers" on the flies of our pants, light hotfoots, grab the ball during
a game and play "sallugee" — anything for a gag. You had to watch out
for him.

Also, *Berny Lerner*, our Ajax, quiet, heavyset, a little stupid, maybe,
but the best player on the punchball team since he could hit a ball more
than two sewers. Next to him sat his kid brother *Sidney*, a fat, whining,
useless, and redheaded kid, accepted reluctantly by us only because of Berny.

Also, mean and moody *Morton Malin*, who, only a few months before,
had been laughed at and pushed around, excluded from all our games,
and tagged with nicknames like "Loving Cup" (because his ears stuck out)
and "Water Boy" (because he used to pee in his pants). But so quick and
unpredictable were the ups and downs of status on the block, the seesaw
so unstable, that the Mama's Boy might suddenly rise, while the big shot,
whom everyone had looked up to, come down hard to earth. Morty had
proved himself by a couple of fights on the block; and now, we thought
uneasily, he was waiting to pay back some of the old grudges.

Also, *Seymour Manheimer*, sometimes called "Sambo," a kid with no
special jump or talent, but whom everybody liked. He was a good sport;

he always paid his way; he owned the football. Sambo's father sometimes took us to Yankee Stadium and to the soccer games at Starlight Park, so that we didn't have to sneak in through the fence.

Also, *Norman Gebrowitz* and *Manny Mortz* my best friends. Normy was fat, fair, and soft, while Manny was wiry, kinky, and tense as a spring. I had known and loved them both as far back as I could remember. But Normy, who was a year and a half older than I, seemed to disdain everything that went on on the block. He was always talking about what he wanted to be when he grew up, as if he could hardly wait. Manny, on the other hand, hated to dress up and KEEP OUT, to walk not run, gabble with girls, to behave himself and fetch and carry at the orders of adults. When he was dressed up, he looked miserable; but in his sneakers, with his hands and facy grimy, his knickers torn at the knees, then he was himself. My own feelings were on his side.

Also in the cellar were a few shadowy, half-forgotten figures who sat against the wall in the back (as in the back of my mind) like bas-reliefs, and have never come into the round.

The meeting began with a roll call that lasted for an hour. Then Murry Aaronson took charge. By unanimous vote, the club was officially given the name we had all agreed upon beforehand—the Blue Falcons. Next, we voted that each member of the Blue Falcons had to pay ten cents dues per week; a fine of five cents would be imposed for each week's dues in arrears; and, finally, that anyone over four weeks behind could be kicked out of the club by majority vote. After these preliminaries, Murry was elected chairman and temporary treasurer of the first week's dues; and Sheiky, who wanted the job, was voted recording secretary to take the minutes at each meeting.

Murry made a short, brilliant speech about what we would do with all the dues and the money gained by selling raffles in the neighborhood. There would be parties every month, excursions to the Palisades, a football, soccer ball, and a basketball for the team, a baseball mitt for everyone, and, above all, a jacket for each member in purple and gold with the name the "Blue Falcons" in large red letters on the back. When he finished, everyone was in a glow of enthusiasm.

Then up stood Morty Malin and asked why, if Sidney Lerner could get in the club, shouldn't everyone else's kid brother be allowed to join? What made him such a big exception? And what right did he have to get one of the free mitts, not to mention the purple jacket, since he couldn't play ball anyway?

The mood suddenly turned sour. Then Sheiky stood up and said that Sidney ought to pay double dues for his jacket because he was twice as fat as everybody else. This got a big laugh, the tension relaxed somewhat.

But Morty's wedge had widened the social chasm separating the "big guys" from the "little guys," the older brothers from the younger brothers, and all the lesser chasms in between. Distinctions of rank, protocol, seniority, and precedence were kept as strictly on the block as at the court of Louis XIV.

To settle matters, Murry declared that Sidney would be allowed to attend meetings and pay dues, but be put on probation and not be given a jacket until all the older guys had theirs.

Then Berny Lerner stood up and said, in that case, his brother should pay only five cents dues per week. What's more, he added, Sidney had just as much right to be in the Blue Falcons, and was almost as old — even if he couldn't play ball so good — as Sambo or Manny or Mil. . . .

As soon as I saw the way things were going, I stood up. Speaking for Sambo and Manny as well as myself, I reminded them that I was one of the first to suggest forming the club, meeting in the basement had been partly my idea, and that I played third base on the punchball team. What did age have to do with it? But — I turned around and faced them all — if that's the way they felt about it then we didn't have to belong and they could keep their lousy jackets.

In the silence that followed, with no one trying to stop us, or at least plead with us, we walked out.

> March 12 — Went down and it started raining so I went back and read a book. Went to the Fox Crotona and saw Richard Barthemless and the dawn Patrol and Joe E. Brown in Firemen save my child including 8 vaudeville acts.
>
> March 13 — I stood in the house because no one was in the street. Sambo came up my house and I played him a game of checkers and won. He says I should come back to the blue Falcons.
>
> March 14 — Went to park to trail Robert and his friend Harold but lost them. Manny gave me back my Ballyhoo and Hooey magazine. Almost had a fight with Sheiky. They think I can't beat him up.
>
> March 15 — Went to school and got a conduct mark. We also got a new geography. I missed taking spelling because teacher sent me down to get her ink and when I came up it was over.

Went to Hebrew with Mom and heard a man crack jokes and give a lecture.

March 17—Went to school and found out I had a new substitute. She was Mrs. Hackenburg. Saw Tarzan the ape man in the Lowe's Paradise. This is the first time I ever went to that theater.

March 19—Robert told me today is the first day of spring. A dumb kid called Heshy came around our block. We took him up the school yard and dressed him naked. Played handball and won 21-19.

March 21—Robert is writing this report because papa put medicine and bandages on hand. Climbed school roof and Robert saw. He told parents but they did nothing. Cried when I had medicine put on.

March 22—Robert wants new long pants but he couldn't get them today. He will tomorrow. Papa put glycerin on my hands but it didn't hurt like yesterday. Robert is writing for I have bandages on hand.

March 23—I didn't go to school today because I had 100% fever. Manny came up my house and told me that Sidney Lerner was kicked out of the Blue Falcons.

March 24—Didn't go to school again today because I had a cold. Mamma bought me a Hooey magazine and I read it. Went with mamma and got new shoes and a pair of pants. Robert got a blue pair of longeys.

March 25—Didn't go to school again because I had to rest. Had rehearsal in Hebrew and know it by heart. Gave Morty his part which he lost and I found.

March 26—Tonight was the play and it was very good. Had a big delicatessin dinner and all the relatives were there. Got a watch for a present.

What we had been "rehearsling" and "rehearsling" in the *shul* so long finally came to pass. It was a Miracle Play based on a story from the Bible, and, even more miraculous, the lines themselves were spoken in Hebrew, "the original language of the Holy Ghost," as Coleridge once called it.

After a brief period as a Talmud scholar a year before, during which I sat for an hour each day cheek to cheek with an old rabbi who had a beard like steel wool and kept picking his nose and shaking back and forth as we chanted the words together, I was taken out and sent to this *shule,* a branch of the Arbeiter Ring. Here our parents hoped we would learn Yiddish, a smattering of Hebrew, the meaning of the great traditions, in order to bridge the cultural gulf between us growing steadily wider, wider and deeper, perhaps, than the one between them and their parents. . . .

When I think back, there was something weird and haunted about that night, the place alive with spirits, as if a swarm of ancient kings and prophets shrunken in time to the size of bees and with buzzing names like Homan, Nebuchadnezzar, Jehoahaz, Ahasuerus, had flown there from another world. They were our witnesses. But at the time I could make no connection between the tribal wars of Israel and the struggle for power and status then going on on the block.

> March 28 — Went to school in the afternoon and found out that I missed a Geog. and Arith. test. Teacher sent me a postal card. Went to Hebrew and the new learner in place of Mr. Mendelson is a dope.
>
> March 29 — Went with Sambo and sold raffles from Murry's club. We sold almost $3 worth. I might join the blue Falcons again and pay back dues. Manny doesn't want to. They will get their jackets Friday.
>
> March 30 — I went and played nuts in Hebrew. I won about 25 nuts and I came in with 15 nuts. Mr. Mendelson read us some stories. I practised punchball with the block. Sidney Lerner won't get his dues back from the club.
>
> April 1 — Today is April Fool day and I had a lot of fun playing jokes on the kids. Practised punchball with the block and I hit a home run with a man on 1 and second. The Blue Falcons got their jackets today.
>
> April 2 — The Blue Falcons played a punchball game with the Quanee Jrs. and we lost 15-9. When the game was over Murry Aronson had a big fight with Berny Lerner. The whole block is talking over it.

That day the pavement shook, there were tremors and then more tremors, augmented by the first, and by the time they subsided the whole social landscape was unrecognizable. . . .

The Quanee Jrs., hearing that a club had been formed on our block, challenged the Blue Falcons to a "money game" in punchball. Every player on both teams was to put up ten cents, and the clubs $1.00 each, winner take all. But we expected to win since the game was to be played on our own street, angled like ourselves, where we knew by heart which way the ball bounced.

Early on Saturday morning the Quanees arrived to practice, and we looked them over. They had power. Every man on their team could hit the ball two sewers, while only Berny Lerner, or maybe Murry Aaronson, could hit that hard for us. On the other hand, we knew where to place the ball and how to slice the corners past third and first with sharp grounders. The Blue Falcons were still confident as we got ready to play.

After depositing the money with the candy-store man, we cleared the street of paper and garbage, marked the bases in fresh chalk, and all together pushed the parked cars out of the infield. Then we told them the ground rules. The Quanees had brought along their own umpire, but, rather than accept him, we chose to have none at all. This meant that any doubtful play would be decided by the team with the loudest and most righteous indignation. But both clubs agreed to let Sidney Lerner keep score, and he boxed off the innings in chalk of different color, blue for us and red for them.

The first three innings were scoreless and went by very fast. Then, in the fourth, they scored two runs on a ball that bounced off a parked car in the outfield for a double, and a long fly that Murry Aaronson muffed for a home run. But we came back in our half and got three runs on successive singles and a triple by Sheiky. And so the lead passed back and forth, until, by the end of the ninth, the score was tied, 9–9. For five tense extra innings, Sidney Lerner drew a red goose-egg for the Quanees and a blue goose-egg for us, a red and then a blue. . . .

At the top of the fifteenth, the Quanees, aware that our infield was playing deep, hit three well-placed grounders through first and short and filled the bases. Murry then called time out for a conference. Against all our advice, he made the decision to pull in the outfield for a possible double play. So, when the same kid who had hit the homer before came up, where was Murry laying? He was laying in, right behind second. Naturally, a long, high fly went over his head for another home run, clearing the bases, while all the Quanees whooped and yelled. They scored two more runs before we could get them out; and we went down in our half of the inning 1-2-3.

After it was all over, the Quanee Jrs. collected the money and went back crowing to their own neighborhood. But the box socre—15 to 9—remained on the sidewalk, spread out large in red and blue chalk. Murry Aaronson ordered Sidney to rub it out. And Sidney, as a matter of course, was already scraping with his shoe on the first goose-egg when his brother stepped in.

"Let him rub it out himself," Berny told him.

Everybody turned and watched. There was a ringing silence.

Then Murry said: "What's the matter, Berny? You think you're a wise guy, or something?"

Berny said it to his face. "*Rub the score out yourself.* You yourself, you lost the game."

Murry began to peel off the two-toned jacket of The Blue Falcons, which he had worn all afternoon even though it was very warm. "Here, Sheiky," he said, "hold my jacket."

Sheiky held it for a moment, smelled it for a gag, and then — this was the pay-off — let it fall in the gutter! But Murry was too mad to see what had happened.

"Say that once more, Berny, I'll rub the score out with your face."

Berny said it again.

"Oh, yeah?"

"Yeah."

"*Oh, yeah?*"

"Yeah."

They stood there face to face, vibrating, only an inch apart.

Then Murry touched Berny, Berny pushed Murry, Murry pushed Berny even harder, and the fight was on. We formed a circle around them. Murry landed a wild right on Berny's chest, danced away and got set to throw another, but, before it landed, Berny charged and socked him again and again, got a headlock on him and wrestled him to the ground, where he still kept socking him. When we saw that Murry's nose had started to bleed, we pulled them apart.

It was Berny who had to be held back. Murry just stood there and swallowed his defeat, breathing hard, his eyes watery, one cheek blue and red where it had been rubbed against the chalk scoreboard. When he saw his jacket lying in the gutter, he turned and stared at Sheiky for a long moment, then picked it up without a word and went home.

Murry had lost face. Everyone on the block had seen him beaten up in a fight, humiliated, forced to back down. It was as if a tribal king had fallen, someone from whom we all derived our status on the block; and mixed with our awe and pity for him was concern for ourselves. We sized each other up: *Whose friend is he? Can I beat him in a fight? Will he take my place on the team?* For until someone else could take over and reestablish order in the gang, none of us could feel secure.

April 4 — Went to school and got a "D" in music. I didn't have
no pen so a girl lent me one. Went selling stamps at night to

help the Jews in Poland and came back very late. Papa scolded me.

April 7—Murry's club voted Murry out of it because he thinks he's the whole works. He wants his dues back. I went to the movies and saw The Beast of the City and another picture. I came home 11 o'clock at night.

April 8—Manny says he's moving to Brayton Beach in Brooklyn. Went with Manny and played nuts in Hebrew. I won about 25 nuts and I came in with 15 nuts. Mr. Mendelson read us some stories.

April 9—Wanted to go to a hike with Manny today but he had to go to his aunt so he couldn't but he will go tomorrow. Manny is moving next week. I had a pillow fight with Robert and Pop heard and stopped it.

April 12—Played handball with the whole block up the school yard and won 5–2. Murry had a big fight with Sheiky because he said he threw a stone on him. Sheiky says he'll get even but he's full of it.

April 13—I went to school and the boys had the girls a history match. There were 13 boys left and 5 girls. The boys started talking so the teacher made us sit down and the girls won.

April 14—I went to the movies with Manny, Sambo, Normy and my brother. We saw Wild Women of borneo and the Cohens and Kelleys in holleywood. Took a hike in the Bronx woods with Manny. I played with Manny the whole day today.

April 16—Murry Aronson is back on the Blue Falcons. He had to pay $1.00 to join it. Went to school and the substitute was there. We had a arithmetic, history, spelling and geography test!!!

April 17—Manny gave me a book called Lefty O' the Bush. I gave him my Bomba book. Manny is going to move tomorrow. I mean he is supposed to. I took a long walk with Manny at night and talked.

Manny, my best friend, Manny and his whole family were leaving for good, moving out of the Bronx, across Manhattan, a thousand miles away into the depths of Brooklyn. I couldn't believe it. I might never see him again. And I felt, hard in my throat, the unswallowable lump and catch of mortality. . . .

That night Manny and I cut our thumbs and sucked each other's blood.

No matter what happened, we swore, we would see each other again. We exchanged books. We made plans for a hike to the Palisades. And yet we both knew — and knew the other knew — that time and ten thousand blocks of New York would surely come between us.

April 18 — Manny moved today. I helped him with the moving van and his mother gave me a nickle.

WHY I LIKED MANNY

1. Because he was a good fellow.
2. Because he was no traiter.
3. He laughed at every funny thing.

MANNY WAS MY BEST FRIEND

April 19 — Went to school and we still had the substitute for a teacher. I had an arithmetic and history test. Saw Will Rogers in Business and pleasure and Douglas Fairbank Jr. in Union Depot. Very warm today.

April 20 — I went to a sader at Uncles Hilly's house and gave my cousin Bella a book called Wonderful tales. I wrote Manny a letter and sent it. Sheiky came up my house today. Very warm.

April 22 — I took a hike with a new kid called Arnold. We went to the Bitanical gardens and came back by way of the Bronx Park. I got lost there but finally got out. When I came to the lion house I couldn't find Arnold so I went home alone.

April 23 — Manny sent me a letter today from Brooklin. The Blue Falcons broke up and all the guys want back their dues. Murry wants to make a new club. There are a lot of moths today. I never saw so many.

April 24 — The moths are still here and I killed them.

It was a living snowstorm, something unheard of, a blizzard of moths that turned the sky suddenly gray, drove people indoors, stopped traffic on the streets, steadily coming on and on in gusts and flurries of wings all day until by nightfall, as if they had been waiting for a signal, they swarmed over all the street lamps in the neighborhood and put them out, crawling and flopping on top of one another in layers of white pulp an inch thick. Even with all the shades pulled down that night I could still feel them out there, peering and probing, and occasionally a soft thump, thump, thump on the window would wake me up. And the next morning strange birds of all kinds would casually take off from their perches in easy dives and snap one, two, three on the wing without breaking the arc of their flight. The laziest cats would strike them down with their eyes half-shut. And we ourselves, we beat them with rolled up newspapers, squashed them underfoot, packed them like snowballs, tore off their wings and stuffed them in milk bottles. And still the moths kept coming on.

They stayed for two days and nights, and then as abruptly as they had come, they left. Some of us thought they had been blown in and then blown out by winds from the south; and others said no, the moths had been ripened too soon by the warm weather, and birds had driven them from the park; but within a week everybody on the block had forgotten about it. Had there been any prophets and augurs around, as in the great days, such a freak of nature would have been enough to start wars, foment revolutions, and make or break kings.

(1957)

The Importance of Being Milton

It's no use trying to blame or to justify the mortal taste, so long ago, that passed over Morton and Mortimer, Marvin and Melvin, and fixed, irrevocably, on Milton as just right, a name which would become me. It was a bond, not a brand — for what became of me can be traced back to that one fatal choice. Whenever I hear it swelling under and rising above the choir of other names, I feel again identified with "the organ voice of England" (as Tennyson called him) — "Milton! a name to resound for ages!" Descend, Urania!

My mother must have heard the echoes in the boroughs of New York, without knowing their source. She had never read *Paradise Lost, Samson Agonistes, Comus,* or any other works of the poet; Milton seemed to her not only a nice name, but the closest to my deceased grandmother's, Malke. No garland was intended for John Milton. Even among my friends on the block the great name was slanged around in a casual way, nicked and diminished to Milty or, more often Milt. Who cared? In those days, when the fruit of good and evil was still green, I would plunge frequently into a forest daydream "with native honor clad in naked majesty," where I was known as Bomba the Jungle Boy. And what — the question is laughable — would Bomba have to do with poetry, a puling girl's game no better than potsy or rope-jumping? If I had been told then that I belonged to the same totem as John Milton, a poet in

Originally published as "The Importance of Being Milton: That Talent Which Is Death to Hide," in *Commentary* (October 1952). All rights are reserved by *Commentary*.

the 17th century who wore his hair in long curly locks, I would have laughed and plunged back into the forest.

This primitive attitude was bound to change, and did, as my own voice lost its shrillness and took on some of the deep undernotes of the organ. During my last year at P.S. 100 in Brooklyn, I became the editor of the 8B3 *Gossip*. I was not only the editor but the production chief, editorial writer, and circulation manager of the *Gossip*, since it was my idea in the first place. In a sense, I *was* the *Gossip*. Of course, most of the creative writing was done by the rest of the class and there was an editorial board consisting mainly of girls but I set the style and policy of the *Gossip* from the start. Only the name was not my own. I would rather have called it the 8B3 *Bugle*, or something with more force, but the board decided otherwise.

With the special privileges granted the editor of the *Gossip*, I could escape the feeling of crib, the ennui, the routine of bells, the mill in the halls, and the endless perspectives of desks which I had endured for eight years. In the morning, while attendance was being taken, I'd sometimes saunter out past the monitors at the doors into the schoolyard, and watch the blackboard squad, trying to make their job last as long as possible, beating the chalk dust out of felt erasers until the air around them was white. Then, if in the mood, I would walk into the street — always somewhat unreal and romantic between 9 and 3 — where, my lungs enlarged by the spirit of freedom, I would light up my cigarette and inhale the divine afflatus. What a lift it gave me! At such times, as though I had taken the food of the gods, I would look down from an enormous height while the blackboard squard picked up their erasers and reluctantly went inside, the monitors shut the doors, and, occasionally, someone late for class would come charging down the street in an open panic, unlaced and unbuttoned. I was above all that. Only the sound of bells ringing vaguely inside could bring me down a little, and I'd go back to my place with class 8B3 and dawdle through the day, still abstracted.

My real work began when school was over. For the sake of the *Gossip*, I might stay in the empty halls as late as 5 P.M. to accept and reject manuscripts, assign reporters, revise copy, set deadlines, and award by-lines. Whatever I said, went. When students from the 8B's, as well as from the lower classes of P.S. 100, came to me with their ideas and compositions for the *Gossip*, I would attend patiently to them all and offer my criticisms. Even if a stickball or punchball game was taking place on the block, I chose to remain at my desk day after day. And yet, behind my back, there were some grudgers, bitches, and malcontents — especially Gloria

71

Lockoff—who said that I, who started the *Gossip* in the first place, was getting to be bossy and conceited! I never bothered to answer them, though I knew who they were, letting my work speak for itself.

Gradually, the shape of the *Gossip* began to emerge from the hodge-podge of contributions, and I saw it was going to be good. On the front page, of course, would be important items such as the Principal's speech in the assembly on citizenship, the results of the intramural sports contests, a report on the P.T.A., and my editorial on "World Events." Then there was an anonymous column called "School Bromides" which listed the boring refrains of the faculty under the subtitle "History Repeats Itself, So Do Teachers." For this I contributed Mr. Stackenfeld's "I remember when I was a boy . . . ," Miss Dinkel's "Now this test doesn't count," Miss O'Leary's "You're dealing with Miss O'Leary," and one or two others. Also we had reports on the Cooking Club called "Cook-Coos," the Campers' Club, which had recently hiked to Bear Mountain, the Stamp Club, and the Debating Society. A short story called "Triumph," by David Goldstein, though obviously derived from Grayson in *Garry Grayson His Speed*, had a quality of its own and was accepted.

Most of my trouble came from the book-review section, called "The Bookworm Turns," by Gloria Lockoff. In my opinion, it didn't satisfy the editorial standards of the *Gossip*. But since this Gloria Lockoff was the pet of the library teacher, Mrs. Kohn, and Mrs. Kohn was supposed to be the *Gossip's* faculty adviser, I thought it more politic, in the end, to accept her contributions. Everybody agreed that the *Gossip* should do something for literature; but who, I felt, would be interested in a review of *Il Pagliacci* such as this:

> Do actors while amusing a public forget that they are merely dramatizing what someone else's pen has written? Why does Canio, the clown of a troupe of actors, tell Tonio, the head of the troupe, that his wife, Nedda, has made a secret tryst with Silvio, a peasant, when he knows that he is very hot-tempered? Tonio at first does not believe him for he knows that Canio has a lying tongue, but his doubts are soon confirmed for he sees Silvio in the front row of seats with eyes for Nedda alone who looks at him and blushes. Will anyone be able to disentangle this web of hearts? Why not read *Il Pagliacci*, this heart rendering *opera* and find out for yourself the outcome of this tragedy? The *Tales of the Opera* are to be found in the music shelf of our library.

72

We even had to take a second review by Gloria Lockoff on Richard Harding Davis's "In the Fog," which wasn't much better.

> What had happened to Lord Chetney? Nobody knew. Suddenly a report was received: "Lord Chetney found dead with Princess Zicky, in a house with furnishings of Russian origin, location unknown." Reported by Lieut. Sears, an American, who was found in the vicinity of the police station wandering about apparently lost in the London fog. Who had committed this atrocious murder and then vanished, swallowed up in the fog, leaving only a trail of blood behind him? Was the princess Zicky only an imposter who, preying upon rich men's purses, suddenly met her fate, killed by one of her recent admirers, whom she had stripped of every vestige of honor, and now, seeing her entertaining someone else, had returned to commit this ghastly deed? Nobody knew. Who was the Queen's messenger? Was it not queer that nobody had ever seen or heard of him before? I cannot answer these questions as skillfully as the author, so why not read "In the Fog" by Richard Harding Davis which you will find in the book called *Fourteen Great Detective Stories*.

I insisted, however, that we publish a report by our sports editor, Edwin Kanner, on the final game in the P.S. 100 baseball tournament between 8B2 and 8B3, even though we lost. It was a game in which I played right field.

> Spectators went wild with excitement, and dazzled by the form of the players, waited anxiously for the beginning of the 8B3–8B2 championship game. Mr. Stackenfeld, athletic director, called the captains of the two teams together. 8B2 luckily won the toss and chose to be last up at bat. In the first inning, 8B3 with bases loaded and one man out, realized that they had a chance to score. 8B2's pitcher turned nervously around to see if his team was ready. With the shouts of encouragement ringing in his ears, in two successive pitches retired to the side. 8B2 was cheered lustily as they came to bat. By superb playing of 8B3, they were retired scoreless. The second and third innings were scoreless and the crowd murmured to the effect that it was a pitchers' battle. After exceptionally good fielding, 8B2 retired 8B3 in the beginning of the 4th inning. 8B2 with determined thoughts now came to bat. Ben Krakowsky, one of 8B2's

star hitters, singled. Heavy hitters then sent Ben around to
score 8B2's lone tally. Filled with desperate determination, 8B3
came to bat. Their efforts were futile as 8B2 retired them scoreless and disheartened. The game was over and losers and vic-
tors joined lustily in a loud cheer.

When all the copy was in and approved, the Art Squad prepared an
emblem for the masthead showing the silhouette of P.S. 100 with "8B3
GOSSIP" in a banner waving across the page. I then took the *Gossip*
down to Mrs. Schwartz, the Principal's secretary, who prepared it for
mimeographing. Mrs. Schwartz worked all afternoon, typing page after
page, while I turned the handle of the mimeograph machine. A poem in
tribute to Mrs. Schwartz, written by Vivian Kuskin of 8B3, was printed
in a box on the front sheet.

> A TRIBUTE
> Mrs. Schwartz is the queen
> Of the mimi-machine.
> When our inspiration was ripe
> She worked on the type.
> As class 8B3
> So thankful are we,
> We don't have to be taught
> Mrs. Schwartz is a sport!

For me that was a great day, bugled and spangled above all others, when
the *Gossip* made its debut in P.S. 100. It was sold in stacks, it was read
all over the neighborhood, I was named and acclaimed by everybody. At
the school assembly that week, right after the pledge of allegiance to the
flag, the Principal himself asked me to stand up again and be introduced.
With all the classes in 8B there to witness, I rose — *O Altitudo!* — and walked
down the aisle toward the platform, my legs a little stiff and shaky as
though I were on stilts, my head in an aureole, looking straight ahead and
not turning while friends on all sides whispered "Hey Milty! Hey Milty!"
as I passed, until, after a long stretch, I reached the platform and shook
hands with the Principal. It was the peak of my eminence.

But within a week, only a few days, it began to crumble, the *Gossip*
seemed nearly forgotten, and I found myself on level with the rest, back
at the mill. During lunch hour, I would sometimes see scattered pages of
the *Gossip* blowing around the schoolyard, along with old exam papers,
pieces of comic sections, and torn sandwich wrappings. I could no longer

get outside the building in the morning, to smoke my cigarette, and no one came to me for advice in the afternoon. Yet what hurt almost as much was the indifferent response to my editorial, "World Events," from those who should have known better. In my high days as editor, I had thought of "World Events" as a visionary down-look (so to speak) from the top of the masthead. But now, so far had I fallen, I was even told by my history teacher that it showed the bad influence of the editorial page of the *Daily News!*

Without the *Gossip* to sustain me, I would arrive late in the morning and leave as soon as the bell rang. The chafes, contumelies, and all the kid-stuff of school grew more intolerable. Each period the door that shut on the class stifled an open yawn of boredom, and the halls narrowed and narrowed so that I could hardly squeeze my way through to the end of the day. While I sat inside the classroom, my spirit flew out of the window. The teacher had to call my name two or three times before I could return in time to recollect myself. And then, in a daydream, the idea came to me.

"O for that warning voice!" — but no voice was heard. The toad came and squatted, hissing in my ear. From a mere speculative vagary, a speck, the idea bouldered in concreteness and importance until, in the end, it took up all the space in my mind. And one night, at the instigation of Auld Scratch himself, who "set himself in glory above his peers" and "thought to have equalled the most high," I did it. I wrote the following letter to the Principal:

> Dear Sir:
> I've read the paper put out by the students of P.S. 100, and I've never read a paper as good as the *Gossip*. As a member of the P.T.A., I want to congratulate you. I especially liked the editorial "World Events," which had a real understanding of history.
>
> Yours sincerely,
> Mrs. S. Falk

As soon as I had deposited this in the mail box, I felt in my bones the awful knowledge of Will and Fate. I wished I could have undone it, and yet I knew I would have done it again. It was knowledge bought dear, as it always is, by knowing ill. Of course, I considered it very unlikely that the letter would be traced to me — *who's Mrs. Falk?* — but I was irritable with suspense. The next day in class, every time my name was called I heard it at once and winced, expecting to be summoned before the teacher, accused, judged, and sentenced. Only a small abyss separated my desk from the teacher's. And though this day passed like any other, my anxiety remained. By the end of the week, just as I was beginning to feel secure again, an incident occurred during the gym period which was an omen of things to come.

Gym was one class I really disliked. That afternoon it was 8B3's turn to play basketball on the small basement court painted in a flat, peeling, municipal gray, a dim and stuffy place where echoes resounded from side to side like the ghosts of old balls, a place larded as it were with an ancient smell of sneakers and stale underwear. We used to keep the same uniforms in our lockers throughout the term; and the joke, as old as the school, stated that socks were to be changed twice a year—in summer, if they stuck when you threw them against the wall, and in winter, if they stood up by themselves and you had to pull them on like boots. The basketball court itself was hardly large enough for a regulation-sized game, yet thirty or more players would be crowded on the floor. You might sometimes rush around for a whole hour without ever touching the ball. Anyone who managed to get it in his grasp would defend it against anyone else, teammates as well as opponents, since they were all out to take it away.

As it happened, fate tipped the ball into my hands. I bounced it once, looking around for a possible shot at the basket, feinted, and then dribbled sideways down the court, jumped and placed a perfect lay-up right through the hoop. Then the whistle blew. Mr. Stackenfeld, the gym teacher, claimed that I was hacking, holding, and running with the ball! The decision was so unjust, and fell at such a triumphant moment when I had almost recovered my sense of glory, that I threw the ball away, cursed, and burst into tears. I was dismissed from the class.

It did not seem possible that Mr. Stackenfeld's decision against me could have been influenced by the column "School Bromides" printed in the *Gossip*. Yet what other explanation was there? Furthermore, I had never had anything to do with those obscene glyphs and caricatures on the walls of the Boys' Room showing Mr. Stackenfeld with Miss Dinkel, the science teacher, though it was a broad joke throughout P.S. 100. The thought of his ingratitude, and my own humiliation, made the Adam's apple swell in my throat. My eyes blurred again, and I plunged into myself conjuring images of revenge and redemption.

By the time I reached the next class, Mrs. Kohn's library period, I was already in such a deep mood that I could hardly emerge to hear her calling my name. But somebody nudged me, pointed, and I crossed the Bar and small abyss that separated us. Mrs. Kohn made me stand and wait while she looked at me steadily without saying a word. Then, turning, she put it on the table.

I took the letter and pretended to read my own unmistakable, Palmer-methodized handwriting, searching for a way out.

"That's a fine letter," I told her.

Mrs. Kohn kept looking at me.

"*Who's Mrs. Falk?*" I said. And felt the jab of a pitchfork in my conscience.

Finally, the teacher spoke. "All right, Milton, that's enough." And then, a little sadly: "You know, I once thought of promoting you to the '1' class."

She was referring to an occasion, the year before, when I had almost been elevated to 8B1, the select class in P.S. 100 for those with the highest grades and the best conduct, instead of being stuck in the catch-all 8B3. But that was a light-year ago. Standing there, with my head down, I wished to be neither in the "1" nor the "3" but in a null class by myself, and nameless if possible, a nonentity conceived by a sin of omission, X and nowhere. It was all over.

After a conference of the Dean, Mrs. Kohn, and Mr. Stackenfeld — who had already reported the incident in the gym — a note was sent to my mother. She arrived solidly in school with me the next morning, prepared to fight it out as usual. My mother had been to such sessions before, over minor issues of unsigned report cards, ink fights, etc., and had always managed to prove me right. But all the testimony against me this time, capped by the fatal letter of Mrs. Falk, was too much even for her, and she subsided in silence.

The Dean proposed that my mother take me to see a certain professor of child psychology at Hunter College who specialized in "hard" cases. Since that seemed the easiest way out for me, and, besides, would offer a day's surcease from school, I agreed. Accordingly, an appointment was made with the professor, and that same week Mr. Stackenfeld himself drove us to Hunter College in his car. My mother sat beside me in the back seat looking as resigned and mournful as possible. To distract myself on the long ride to Manhattan from Brooklyn, I took along a book which had never failed before, *Through Space to Mars*, but somehow the weight and gravity of the situation held me down. I was even more depressed by the time we arrived.

Hunter College was the largest school I had ever seen, and it swarmed with women. Mr. Stackenfeld guided us through a wide corridor where women smiled and gurgled with pleasure when they saw me, as though they knew who I was, until, around a bend, we found the professor's office. Here Mr. Stackenfeld and my mother both left me, and I sat down waiting for the ordeal.

77

In a little while, someone called me by name and led me across the hall into a room where the professor held his classes. It was a seminar or laboratory in advanced child psychology, and I was the advanced case. The room was a sort of pit-like, sloping auditorium and at the bottom, behind a desk, was an old man with a tuft of gray beard who smiled and glowed and pointed with a pencil to a high chair for me to sit down. The light reflecting upon his glasses hid his eyes, and was triangulated by a gold disk that hung upon a chain around his waist like a little sun. The scene was weird. On the high chair, "by merit raised to this bad eminence," I looked around and saw that the class was filled with women all beaming at me and taking notes.

The first question the professor asked turned me deeply into myself: "Which do you like better, Milton, your father or your mother?"

As a man playing basketball suddenly receives the center tap, and swerves, looking for an opening to pass or shoot or dribble down the court, while, on all sides, he sees nothing but milling and confusing arms, the shouts of his own teammates wrangling with those of his opponents, some crying here and some crying there, until the ball swells in his hands and the hoop contracts to a little far-off ring, and, at last, the umpire blows his whistle to end the play — so I sat baffled and uncertain of what to do. Who could answer a question like that? When he saw that I was confused and holding, the professor quickly changed the subject.

He poked his long finger into my past and put words in my mouth I never knew were there. In the presence of the girls in the class he asked me a highly personal question. I felt reduced and exposed. And all the while, I kept trying to penetrate the glare on his glasses, to see what he was seeing. But it was as though the light came from behind.

When I turned my head away, I succeeded in recovering my poise. After a few stammers, I began to anticipate and then parry his questions, asked him one in return, made a few asides to the audience, even cracked a joke and was beatified when all the smilers burst into a loud laugh. The oppressive atmosphere of the class lifted. Since the professor wanted to hear about the *Gossip*, I outlined its history from the start — my work as editor, its contents, the trouble with Gloria Lockoff, described the policy of the paper, and expanded some of the ideas in my editorial "World Events" — omitting nothing but the letter from Mrs. Falk, which he knew about anyway. By the time the class bell rang, with the same angry finality as at P.S. 100, I was in a high state of self-esteem.

What a fool I was! A minute later, I realized how he had deliberately duped and tempted me to expose myself, exalted me only to make my fall

78

more abject, and I felt, in the pit of my stomach, the vertigo of descending in an elevator very rapidly. As the class emptied, I saw him saying something to my mother at the door; and from the way his beard jerked in my direction from time to time, I was sure the news was evil. We left together in a lingering mood, with the world all before us. "What's going to become of you, Milton?" she told me. My mother had often said that, even in small things like liver or soft-boiled eggs, I didn't know what good was. And as we sat in the back of the car going home, she repeated again and again that the professor thought I was too wild, spoiled, conceited, and unaware of the difference between right and wrong. That was his opinion.

The professor's solicitude did not end with my ordeal at Hunter College. For weeks afterwards students from his class would drop in to see me at home and chat with my mother, still smiling at us and taking notes. From a special case I had become a project. But, in time, these visitations became less frequent, and even the memory of the *Gossip* faded to a distant blue. I fitted myself into the cramp of school again.

Then the warm weather of spring and the approaching day of graduation brought a carnival excitement to class 8B3. As though we were all celebrities, everybody was signing everybody else's autograph album. David Goldstein wrote in mine: "In the golden chain of friendship, regard me as a link"; Helen Lavoy: "Roses are red, violets are blue, a face like yours belongs in a zoo"—but she really liked me; Rubin Bayliss: "Take the local, take the express, but don't get off till you reach success"; that jerk, Albert Moscowitz: "Consideration, tolerance, and a fatalist's perspective, and you cannot help but make your work"; and Gloria Lockoff, without rhyme: "I wish you all the success in the world and if you ever become a newspaper editor let me know or rather Mrs. Kohn. She'd love to see what you turned out to be. If anything." This was typical of her.

I had always imagined the end of school as a day of absolute freedom and revelation when I would see the other side of the moon. For years I had longed for it. Yet as the time came closer, I began to feel sentimental about good old P.S. 100. I visited my earliest teachers from the lower grades, carved my initials deeply and finally on my desk, and sang the school anthem in a loud voice at assemblies. One morning in the auditorium, during a dress rehearsal for the great day, while I was marching up and down the aisle in my "graduation suit"—with long trousers instead of knickers—a note came that the Principal wanted to see me.

When I entered his office, the Principal was sitting ensphered behind a wide round desk, in a white office, with an American flag on the wall over his head. What a difference from the gloomy pit where I had been tormented by the professor! I had seen the Principal at assemblies and heard his name whispered in awe ever since I was first enrolled at P.S. 100, but we had never exchanged more than a few solemn and stilted words. Now he beckoned me to sit down. He began by asking me the serious question that has bored generation after generation—what did I want to be when I grew up? And I answered, as I always did, that I didn't know for sure. While he talked, my attention wandered over the school plaques and trophies in his office, to the walls smiling with photographs, through the window looking out over the schoolyard—arrested occasionally by the sound of the words "Gossip" and "World Events"—and returned to find him standing enormously above me. At this cue, I too stood up and we shook hands as we had once before on the stage of the auditorium.

"Milton," he said, "Milton, you know you're named after John Milton." No I wasn't. "He was a Puritan and a great poet." And there it was.

A large picture hung in the assembly hall showing a group of Puritans on their way to church on the first Thanksgiving Day. And though I had heard vaguely of John Milton by then, it was difficult to think of a poet as one of those grim characters dressed in black knickers, stiff collars, and what looked like firemen's hats. Nevertheless, I was impressed.

I went to the library that day, and for the first time opened *Paradise Lost.* The "organ voice" thundered at me: *Of man's first disobedience and the fruit Of that forbidden tree, whose mortal taste Brought death. . . .*— and all the words seemed to be sounding at once. What was he talking about? I read the lines again, and again they gibbered in my mind like words without meaning. Was this poetry? It was nothing like those easy poems printed in the back of the *Eighth-Grade Speller* which we had been forced to memorize and recite in class. But even without understanding why, I couldn't forget that great blind voice with its oceanic range, broad and powerful enough to be heard across three centuries of time.

Ah well, Urania—"the meaning, not the name, I call"—you know what I'm going to say. Whether we make our choices or our choices are made for us, like our names, it all comes to the same thing in the end. What thing? There is a ring where name and image join. As I was deaf to my own name and its meaning, so at last I was identified with Milton, blind to his own image by a kind of visual amnesia. But I don't have to justify myself before you. Only by accident can we ever find an Eternal Providence in our lives, although, to come down to earth, for our ways to have crossed that way in Brooklyn was a revelation of poetic justice—as if there were any other kind.

(1952)

80

The Trojans of Brighton Beach

When my grandfather was alive he could walk up and down six thousand years as though it were a little narrow room; for him, all history could be contracted to the span of memory; and, since the Jews were the People of History, the memory of each one was a monad which represented the history of all. The time was always now. When anything happened in the house or the neighborhood, he could fish up a correspondence from the Bible at the drop of a line. If you asked him a simple question he would answer by a parable; and all his questions were usually rhetorical, like God's own. The Greek philosophers thought of God as an Engineer or an Architect, and the Christian theologians as a Judge, but the Jews made him One of the Family—and I think the God of the old days must have been like him, a brooder in dark corners, minding everybody's business and keeping himself aloof, jealous, stroking his ego like a beard. *Olav hasholem.*

Anyway, my grandfather's insight was true in at least one respect: fifty centuries after Moses my family still had traces of the old desert restlessness in their blood. Of the true breed of *luftmensh!* After living up in the air for a whole year, they would pack up the apartment like a tent and move off to a greener oasis, quieter, where the people are more refined, from Staten Island to the Bronx to Manhattan to Brooklyn (somehow bypassing Queens) so that with each shift I had to pull up my stakes in the gang and the neighborhood and start all over again.

Originally published as "The Trojans of Brighton Beach: Life on the Old Block," in *Commentary* (May 1947). All rights are reserved by *Commentary.*

By the time we finally settled in Brooklyn in the late summer of 1930, I had absorbed so much street savvy up and down town that I was already something of a Culture Hero, with new accents, new games, new angles. But with or without Culture—to be a new kid in a strange neighborhood is an all-day lonely drag. We lived in a lower-middle class section of Brighton Beach dominated by one gang of kids, the Trojans, who would have nothing to do with me.

At first I didn't mind eating cold chicken by myself, since there was so much to see and do. From where we lived I could smell Coney Island in the daytime frying in its deep fat; and at night, of course, there were Wonder Wheels, Freak Shows, Arcades, Coasters, Whips and Reels in a blaze of neon down to the slums. On the other side was Manhattan Beach, "a community of prosperous homes and gardens," fronting on Sheepshead Bay, which was filled with fishing boats and yachts. Brighton itself was the middle-class axis of this seesaw, sometimes tipping its families up and sometimes down. And in those early days of the depression, when capitalism was afraid of its own shadow and there was nothing to fear but fear itself, I could sense the anxiety of everyone to keep his place on the balance.

Until the cold weather came, I spent the days hunting and exploring.

But nothing can be more barren than a summer resort in winter, especially when you're without friends. Loneliness drives you out of the house and back up again— *"Et faim [fait] saillir le loup des bois,"* as Villon said, who knew what it meant. You can read the old books over once more, Bomba the Jungle Boy, Poppy Ott, Tom Swift, Baseball Joe, etc., but there's no one around with whom you can trade and discuss the fine points. You daydream. At night the "heys" and whistles of kids aren't for you. When you see them in school, or after school in the candy store wearing their blue flannel jackets with red blazon: TROJANS, there's no familiar greeting, only a scraping of curious foils—but their eyes glance you through and through.

Any move you may make toward rapprochement in this stage must be lightfoot, delicate, since at the least blunder in protocol you can lose Face, or be tied with a nickname for years like a tin can to a dog's tail. They ignore you, they cut you out. And then the contumely of *nebichs*, mama's boys, and small fry! Your pride rebounds like a billiard ball wincing from buff to buff in angles of refraction.

But at last from hanging around so much, the day does come when one of the Trojans is missing from a punchball game and they need an extra man. If you're any good, you're in. And now that the breach is opened you learn their names, the same set as on any other block: of course a

Peewee, a Fatso, a Lefty; and a Herb, Willie, Sy, Izzy, Delmore, Manny, Dave, etc. There's always a sissy and a tough guy, a wisecracker, a bully, a nice guy, a blowhard. All of them size you up more closely, watching the way you throw a ball and your style at the plate with questions in their eyes: Can they beat you up in a fight? Will you take their place on the team? These issues can be settled only after months of playing ball together and one or two fistfights. If you can beat up Willie, and Willie can beat up Sy, then you can beat up Sy and your rank is proven by syllogism—but still, the social equilibrium is so unstable that the sissy, whom everyone despised, might suddenly shoot up to a hero or the wisecracker lose his verve. Because I had acquired so much outside experience, I already had an edge sharp enough to penetrate the Trojan enclaves. Ulysses was needed no less than Hector. And when, for example, I introduced the game of slug-ball from the Bronx, my position became really solid, since any new game is a victory in the constant battle against big-city cramp.

The streets of New York must have been virgin once, artless and unenhanced. But, by our time, the vacant lots and fields where the kids used to play baseball and football had already been supplanted by five- and six-story apartment houses until there wasn't a gap for miles. Where and how to play what was a problem. Parks were crowded with mothers wheeling baby carriages, and the schoolyards were taken up by girls playing potsy and skipping rope:

> One, two, three alarey
> I spy Mrs. Sary, etc.

It was no use trying to drive them out of the yards by terror, they would run to the custodian on any provocation. There was only one thing to do: take over the street. The brickwork and moldings of buildings, stoops, abutments, cornices, rungs on fire-escape ladders, the squares of sidewalks, even sewer covers were adapted to some sport which was then given a set of rules and a name.

Slug-ball was so conceived. The day I first introduced it was a hot afternoon in August, and a few of us were sitting around on the curb with nothing to do, wondering whether we should hitch a ride on the back of a trolley to Prospect Park or gyp some candy from Epstein's store on the corner when, suddenly, I remembered slug-ball. A smash! Unless the war has broken the great tradition, the ball is still being slugged in Brooklyn.

Slug-ball is played off the sides of apartment houses on a court that is four sidewalk boxes in area, with the cracks serving as boundary lines. As one of a large family of games such as stoopball, boxball, hit-the-crack, etc., which are enclosed and restricted by the sidewalk, it demands an ability to manoeuver freely in tight Mondrian forms. Weight and strength are no advantage: only celerity, jump, a shrewd eye, and a quick hand. The kid who knows how to slice the ball and to cut corners with precision can trim anyone bigger and stronger than himself.

In the country, positions would have been reversed. But that is the difference between the City Character and the Country Character, which is, really, a difference in state of mind and disposition of soul. Between the two there is a breach as wide as that which divides Plato and Aristotle. The geometrical forms of the city impress themselves upon the consciousness of anyone who grows up with them; they impose a way of seeing and thinking. But the country is natural, that is to say, raw, contingent, unassorted and particular, and must itself be informed by the mind. If a ball is hit on a grass field it can strike a leaf or a stone and shoot off in any direction; but on the street, against hard cement, the angle of return is determined strictly by the angle of delivery, so that any kid with *chutzpah*, who knows all the angles, can always come out ahead of the game.

We played hard with a will to win so strong it willed itself. Sometimes we became so engrossed by a punchball or a stickball game that night would fall without anyone's being aware of it, and only our fathers coming home from work cranky, on the El, or the cross yells of mothers from both sides of the street, frantic over dinner growing cold, could ever break it up. If any one of us tried to leave in the middle of a tight score, he had to fight his way out.

When the immie (marble) season rolled around in the spring, a fever of acquisitiveness would erupt over the whole neighborhood, and we would play for them by day and by night under the street lamps. We pitched them along the curb, letting nothing stand in our way, sometimes scooping through puddles of mud and even under parked cars. My hands would be grimy and warted from the gutter; I smelled of the gutter — but O the sweet stink of property! To fondle in my pocket the cool, round smug glass immies like cats' eyes, purple, green, orange, lemon; heavy reelies made of steel; transparent glassies; milkies as pure as the white of egg; to feel them there was a capitalistic joy that transcended and eclipsed the vulgar interest of Rothschild or J. P. Morgan.

Sudden passions for checkers, bottle-caps, political-campaign buttons, the tops of Dixie cups, would rise and fall like jags on the stock market. The currency didn't matter much since everything was redeemable at the street exchange, six bottle caps for one immie, two buttons for a checker, etc., depending upon the season and the fluctuations of supply and demand. Sometimes the bottom would drop out of the Dixie cup market,

84

leaving those who had speculated in them with a stock of worthless card-board. But immies and checkers were always secure. You couldn't go wrong with immies and checkers.

No matter what went on at the curb—immies, hop-scotch, ringelevio, or slug-ball—they were all attacked by mothers who complained because they had to complain, and, even more, by the old ones, those *zedas* with embroidered *yamelkas* and their white beards worn like orders upon their chests. They wondered whether we were Jews or a new kind of *shagitz*. On a sunny day they would take down their chairs and sit out on the street, massive and still as Druids, rarely exchanging a word with one another, but watching us with their slow eyes. At such times we would always take care to go to the other end of the street, as far as possible from their Klieg-light scrutiny like the stare of conscience. But sometimes we couldn't help meeting one coming from the synagogue, and then we would all have to stand by sheepishly while he asked us questions in Yiddish about our mothers and fathers, how much Talmud we knew, etc., until he left us, shaking his head from side to side.

They cramped our style, these old ones. If we wanted to play a game which involved some roughhouse, like Johnny-on-the-pony—in which one side would line up against the wall with their heads under each other's legs and their backs up, while the other team across the street would take running leaps and pile down hard on top of them, trying to break the buck-ing pony—for such games we had to go out of the neighborhood. And even then we could never feel secure. If anyone were hurt the news would surely be blown like a cloud over every family on the block and a gray continual nagging would rain indoors for weeks.

Nevertheless, we couldn't give up these games. Our text was not from Isaiah, but the Book of Kings. To the North were the Falcons: a gang of kids with names like Pat, Mike, Danny, Frankie. And to the South were the Wolverines: kids called Tony, Angelo, Pete, Rocky. When they burst out of their own neighborhoods and descended on ours, as they frequently did in rough gangs, we had to stand up to them.

Halloween was the traditional time for street fights. And the night be-fore, we filled all the silk stockings we could find with flour, broke up crates and boxes and rubbed colored chalk on the slats of wood. In the morning when we met one anther we compared our weapons, whacking them on the sidewalk and on fireplugs in anticipation. We were never disappointed, they always came.

"Here they come!" The street contracts like a heart. There on the corner, two or three Philistines, standing close together to pool their courage, survey the street. Behind them is the rest of the gang, the bigger and tougher kids whose faces we know from the past. Soon these too come from around the corner with a swaggering nonchalance. We exchange insults.

> They: (personal) Hey Moe, ya fader sleeps wid ya muder.
> We: (political-satirical) Hey Angelo, watsamada ya no lika da Mussoleen?
> They: (religious) Hey Ike, we got what da Rabbi cut off.
> We: (the last word) Send it back to da Pope; he needs it.

Suddenly we are caught unprepared by a fusillade of prune pits which they had concealed in their pockets. We rush them, and they fall back. They rush us and we fall back. A free-for-all begins. And the hullabaloo arouses the whole neighborhood. Somebody's mother opens a window and heaves out a pail of water—*pishach!* A butcher, leaving his store and his customers, charges out in his bloody apron to separate us. Suddenly someone spies the blue coat of a policeman racing toward us, and the alarm is CHICKeeeee! We scatter.

It was all over in fifteen minutes. Later when we emerged from basements and lobbies, still pumping for breath, we sat down on the curb and crowed. We didn't give a hoot for the interdictions and naggings and curfews which would follow. In that first release of tension and sweet lift of gravity after battle, none of these things weighed a feather.

When the Old Guard heard about it, as they always did somehow, they were triumphant—we were growing up hooligans, bums, outcasts, Cossacks! They painted a picture of our decline and fall stage by stage down to the steaming fosse of Perdition, until someday we would be eating pig and pulling beards on the streets of New York.

The issue between them and us was drawn. And any kid who put on more than an outward show of religion was regarded as queer, on their own side. Our fathers mediated, improvisionary patchers, trying to play both ends against the middle. The dazzle of America was still so bright in their eyes, it blinded them to what was happening on our side of the street. Although it was their generation which had inverted the Messianic hope of the Jews into socialism, they could still not let go of the old ways. And who could have blamed them if sometimes they mistook the vision of Elijah for the figure of Uncle Sam with his glad hand, high hat, and star-spangled vest? Confused, troubled, they were pulled by the old and the new, but, as time was on our side, they let us have our way which was more and more becoming theirs as well. And when *zeda* died, the old life he represented passed with him.

(His picture in a gilt frame was first hung in the parlor; but after a few years we found it didn't look "nice" with the new furniture, and so *zeda* was relegated to the bedroom. A Van Gogh print was put in his place.)

American holidays began to displace the Hebrew, just as American newspapers displaced the *Day* and the *Forward*. The Friday night candles disappeared, and the two distinct sets of ware, one for meat dishes, one milk, were washed in the same sink. I remember — I am ashamed — I would shush my parents whenever they spoke Yiddish on the subway or the street. Everybody knew that the more Americanized families had the jump on success, and who didn't want to be a success? Don't be a sucker. $ was the sign of the Good Life.

Of course, certain of the more important Hebrew holidays were still celebrated: Rosh Hashonah, Yom Kippur, Passover. When *zeda* was still alive and could fire the four great questions at us over the matzoh and the wine, the Passover had a holy zeal.

Then it was: *l'shana habaa b'ara d'Yisrael.*

But now: This year in Flatbush; next in Forest Hills.

For two or three days of the festival there would be nothing but matzoh on the table — matzoh meal, matzoh balls, fried matzoh, egg matzoh, whole wheat matzoh, matzoh plain, until the whole family was thoroughly fed up with matzoh in any form. We longed for our daily bread. And once, this was the turning point, I think it was my eleventh or twelfth year, I was secretly given money in the middle of Passover and sent to an Italian grocery a few blocks away to buy a loaf. To avoid meeting anyone I knew I plotted a long route to the store, and I even carried an old knapsack to hide it from the neighbors. Everyone on the block must have been doing the same.

It was the neighbors who had to be placated by a show of religion, the neighbors who minded everybody else's business; and as for God — he was a very distant relative who never visited us any more, in business for himself.

My friends and I were at that time attending the Talmud Torah in preparation for Bar Mitzvah. Three afternoons a week after school, we would sit cheek to cheek with an old Rabbi who had a beard like steel wool, swaying and chanting with a copy of the Talmud open before us, he in his cracking bass, we in our rising treble. When things were going well, he would sit in his velvet chair, his eyes half shut, picking his great bearded nose with his little finger while he mumbled after us. But whenever the noises of the street pulled us away from the lesson, we were pulled back again by a rough rap on the knuckles or a cuff on the side of the head. We were glad to get up and get out.

The year of the Bar Mitzvahs—then we were alive! We were climbing the last hump of childhood. From an inner distance, we could hear the reverberations of sex growing closer and louder. Some of my friends were actually dressing up (no more knickers), and even—this was prodigious—giving up a punchball game to hang around with the girls. The girls themselves had known the exhilaration of heels and silk stockings long before, the little harpies, waiting to pay back the old grudges.

In that twilight period when the values of the adult world came into collision with our own, some of us surrendered to them entirely, others tried to compromise, and there were some who resisted until as late as sixteen joining groups of small fry. For the first time, the family position and fortune made a difference in our own status. Even a touch of anti-Semitism came in—it did not pay to look too Jewish, especially for the girls. There was, also, a breakup of caste—the athletes felt the mace of power growing soft in their hands, while the rich, the smart, and the merely good-looking felt it stiffening in theirs.

I remember the whole time as a continual bazaar of parties and celebrations. Every other week, one after the other, I saw my friends rise up and declare their manhood while the rest of us sat in the back rows, apart from the relatives, giggling and throwing spitballs, with our *yamelkas* slanted on the side of our heads at a sharp angle.

So then, we were admitted.

But where? For what had we been prepared? Certainly not for the ritual despair of our forefathers, the Wailing Wall, the lost Temple and the rest, although we knew we could never resign from the old contract with the past, our long history bonded by memory and always annealed in the present. But what was our point of view?

What, in short, was the angle?

A New York question, rhetorical, rebounding from its own answer! It was New York we were prepared for, and New York, half-Jewish, which took us in.

New York! Ghetto of Eden! We go back always where we come from, in memory, to and from ourselves. The things that made us what we are made you. With your five bright boroughs of a superlative quincunx and your streets laid out in gyres, diamonds, squares, and rhombs like those perfect forms which Plato thought lay in the burrows of the Mind and which Nature could only roughly approximate, to see you is an intellectual joy, to think of you is to be re-identified with oneself!

(1947)

88

Chester, Wystan, Rhoda, and Me:
A Fragment

When W. H. Auden fell out of the sky I was just walking dully along West 4th St. in Greenwich Village late on Saturday night, returning home after picking up a copy of the Sunday *Times* at Sheridan Square, and as I got to Charles St., passing by the lamp post on the corner, I flipped the paper over to scan the headlines on the bottom half. There was his face — or rather what the years had made of it — as wrinkled and cracked and reticulated with deeply grooved crisscrossing lines as a dried creek bed, staring quizzically up at mine, as if curious to see my reaction, for above the photograph in large type was the news that he had died in Austria the day before. In a flash, of heart failure. The shock made me fumble and almost drop the paper, clutch for it and momentarily lose my balance, lurching sideways, so that I had to reach out and embrace the lamp post to steady myself. Right then, it so happened, as if meant to happen, by design to complete the scene, two Saturday-night suburban-looking couples doing the Village came sailing by arm in arm and pointed me out to one another, gleefully, no doubt elated by what must have seemed to them something amazing yet also ludicrous and typically Villageois: a local drunk, or maybe a junkie, corkscrewed around a lamp post while reading the Sunday *Times*. Only who cared? Without budging, rapt and transfixed ("Now, now," I can hear him say in the nannyish tone he occasionally affected, "that's a bit over-*donne*, Milton, it won't do") beneath the lamp post, ob-

Originally published as "First Acquaintance with Poets" in *From Mt. San Angelo: Stories, Poems, & Essays,* edited by William Smart (Sweet Briar: Virginia Center for the Creative Arts and Associated University Presses, 1984).

livious to the stares and double-takes of people hurrying by, I remained there for some time peering through the dim light at the small print of his obituary until my eyes started to blur, the words hazed over, when I broke off, looking about at the by now nearly deserted street, and reminded myself that while Auden's quest, his lifelong Icarian flight ("Now, now . . .") had ended, and with scarcely a splash in the world-at-large, I still had somewhere to get to. . . .

That was on September 29, 1973, approximately thirty, though it seems more like XXX, years after I first met him. But even before then I had already encountered his poems and read and reread them, to puzzle out their meaning, so closely that I got to know many by heart, making them my own with the sort of proprietary enthusiasm and exultation that can only be felt by an adolescent bardling of sixteen or so, such as I was at the time, for whom the discovery of a new poet speaking, in a manner of speaking, his own language is also an act of self-discovery. Of all the poets both English and American who had emerged during the thirties, Auden, I thought, had the most original and prophetic voice. No matter that his early poems were so riddled with secret passwords, personal references, double-entendres and innuendoes intended exclusively for those already in the know, that crucial lines and even whole passages despite all my efforts to understand them seemed nothing but gibberish; for me it was a delphic gibberish; and besides, as Coleridge tells us, "Poetry gives most pleasure when only generally and not perfectly understood." What most pleased, and overawed me too, was the voice itself, unlike any I had ever encountered before in English poetry, the voice it seemed of an ancient Scandinavian skald or tribal scop, terse and abrupt, elliptic, grunty with Anglo-Saxon vocables, that might have issued from some autochthonous source in the fjords of his own psyche. Despite that it was no less modern, even à la mode, and fashionably Freudian and communoidal as well, its grim prognostications of doom, doom and death, "death of the grain, our death, / Death of the old gang" in the coming of Marxist apocalypse set off by tom-tom alliterative meters, slating atonal dissonances, half-rhymes as surprising as puns. And at the time of which I was writing, with Hitler dominant over Europe, it was just what I wanted to hear.

In those days I was a sophomore at Brooklyn College, living at home with my parents, and a timid contributor (an essay on e.e. cummings, rejected derisively, and a Shelleyan love poem, grudgingly accepted) to the undergraduate literary magazine, the *Observer*, one of whose editors was the poet Chester Kallman. It was through Chester that I later came to know Auden, but when and where I first met Chester escapes me now.

He seems to have popped up present in my life without antecedence. One clue: he was the cousin of a close friend of mine, Jack ("Yecky") Freilicher, a precociously hip and talented jazz pianist with whom in my earliest pubescent years, when I had just grown hair and self-conscious, I used to share a magical joint or two and discuss Sex, Art and Politics during midnight rambles on Brighton Beach, and chances are that "Yecky," who often mentioned his cousin the poet as someone I definitely ought to dig, would at least have tried to bring us together. But if he ever did somehow, I wonder, could I have forgotten?

Among the glumly solemn young Marxist literati who roosted on the staff of the *Observer*, Chester stood out like a tropical bird in a flock of jackdaws. He was then (as he describes himself in a poem looking back from middle age) "one of the handsome few," but perhaps "gorgeous" would be a mot more juste, with a ripe and finely carved mouth, heavy-lidded, dark-rimmed, liquid deep-blue eyes of the kind known as soulful, and wavy blond hair crested by a, suspiciously, blonder forelock trained to appear unruly and break and curl across his brow. While fairly tall and well built, there was nonetheless a Chaplinesque daintiness about him, a certain slight sway and flutter in his gestures and the way he moved that ineluctably spoke its name. Homosexual of course he was, and he flaunted it, but not *a* homosexual, for that wasn't the most substantive of all the things that made Chester Chester. It took some time, but once we broke through the psycho-socio barrier between us—he had told me from the start, *sotto voce* and gently, so as not to hurt my feelings, but to my immense relief, feigned to spare his, that I wasn't his "type," which made it easier—I came to see what a tough-minded bird he was under the fancy plumage, strong-willed and independent in his opinions, and with a range of experience, though in age we were scarcely a year apart, far wider than mine. My social and intellectual life was then almost entirely centered around the college; his, it seemed, began only when classes were over.

Those dark stripes under his eyes were earned. On several occasions, coming across each other by chance in the hallway or cafeteria, he'd greet me with the hassled, breathless air of someone late for an urgent appointment, pause and assume the sidewise stance of a relay runner waiting anxiously for the baton, his rear pivotal leg extended for a fast getaway and one arm stretched out to touch my fingertips, meanwhile straining himself apart inch by inch as he apologized for not being able to stay but promised to see me soon, asked how I was and what I was up to and if I was writing, all in one blurt. On his way to the exit, should he meet any of his many old friends, he might go through the same routine two or three

91

times before taking off. Not to have known him, as they say in Latin, argued oneself unknown. But of his private affairs, except that they kept him on the run, I knew hardly anything for months after we first became acquainted.

Then one afternoon, at an informal conference of *Observer* staff members and contributors held in the cafteria, at which he wasn't present, I heard the astonishing news, astonishing to me but an already well-gnawed and desiccated bone of gossip to everyone else, that "Wystan—which I translated mentally into W. H. Auden, the way I invariably thought of him, an awesome surname preceded by those two Shakespearian initials stamped on the cover of a book—and Chester were intimate friends, more than just friends, lovers in fact, like Oscar & Bosie or Verlaine & Rimbaud, and had been inseparable ever since Auden arrived and settled in this country in 1939. Not willing to expose my own naivete, I remained silent while their relationship was knowingly discussed and bantered about at the table. Afterward, by asking around here and there, I heard the tale of how Chester and a friend of his, Harold Norse, similarly blond, homosexual and a poet, had attended a reading one night by Auden and Christopher Isherwood sponsored by the League of American Writers with the hope of later arranging an Anglo-American liaison. It was Norse who received an invitation from Isherwood to call at the hotel where they were staying but Chester, either through calculation or miscalculation, who took the card upon which Isherwood had written their address. When he arrived and knocked at the hotel door the next day, Auden is said to have opened it, stared at Chester, and exclaimed, "but it's the wrong blond!" But it was the right. Some three years later the affair thus started was still continuing and as fervent as ever.

Of homosexual love, in its physical aspects, nearly all I knew at that time was based on traditional street lore passed down from generation to generation and on what I could glean, furtively and guiltily, in the public library from the tomes of Kraft-Ebbing and Havelock Ellis, where the most interesting parts were curtained off in Latin. It baffled (*How can people do things like that?*) and somewhat embarrassed but did not morally offend me. As a private vice deserving public censure it fell somewhere, in my estimation, between stamp collecting and reading other people's mail. Nor did I feel either tempted or threatened by it. My own commitment to love between the sexes was exclusive and firm, never firmer than then, though I had little opportunity to prove it.

But that soon changed, and the course of my life as well, when I began my first "serious" affair, with a revolutionary blond sociology major named Rhoda Jaffe, whom I met one fall day sitting apart from the others at the Trotskyites' table in the cafeteria. It was she who approached me, getting up smiling from her place to ask me to sign a food-smudged and ink-bespattered petition (but it had the effect of a love philtre) against, I believe, war and fascism, which I did in a daze without reading it through (strains of the "Liebestod" sounding from afar), and one thing led to another. On my part it was both love and self-love, equally and reciprocally. I was then about nineteen. At the age of thirteen or so I would sometimes filch a couple of cigarettes from my father's open pack of Camels and go off on solitary walks at night along the tree-shrouded mall on Ocean Parkway in Brooklyn, smoking one going and one coming; and on an evening I've never forgotten a car pulled over to the curb and a man, seeing only the glow of my cigarette in the darkness, stuck his head through the window and shouted, "Hey, Mister! How do I get to the bridge?" That was the first time anyone had every called me "Mister." And with Rhoda, at the commencement of our affair, I felt the same rush of instantaneous maturity and self-esteem. Greater even, for she had seen and selected me for herself in broad daylight, me, though she was obviously desirable, sexy, charming, beautiful enough to have had anyone else she pleased instead of me, a sophomore still living at home with his parents and dependent on them for pocket money.

A month before we had moved from Brighton Beach, where I grew up, to an apartment on Ocean Ave. and Ave. H. in Flatbush, only a couple of blocks from the college but a long train-ride from my whilom stickball-and punchball-playing friends in the old neighborhood, so that I felt exiled and lonely. My romance with Rhoda changed all that; and surprisingly, though I couldn't imagine him ever playing stickball, it coincided with a growing friendship with Chester. Between them, each in his/her own way, they took charge of my wordly and sentimental education.

Chester was then living as Auden's guest in Brooklyn Heights at the now near legendary 7 Middagh Street—a dilapidated three-story building transformed into a sort of sixties-style commune of Olympian bohemians, and run as a boadinghouse, whose members at different times included Carson McCullers, Louis MacNeice, Gypsy Rose Lee, Golo Mann, Paul and Jane Bowles, Salvador Dali, Benjamin Britten; but whenever Auden left town to read his poems or lecture somewhere, which happened frequently, Chester would come down from the Heights and stay with his father and grandmother at their house on Ave. J, within close walking distance from where I lived on Ave. H. As a result we saw each other more and more often, both on and off campus, passing by slow gradations from acquaintances to confidants.

Or rather I became Chester's. He had already, as said before, typed me as not his and thereby banished me in his mind to a sexual Limbo somewhat like Dante's, "where those without hope yet languish in desire." Knowing our circles would never intersect, and that whatever he told me would remain secret, he enjoyed setting me up as his heterosexual "straight" man and startling me with tall tales and inside stories of the Homintern (as he dubbed it), illuminating the darker recesses of the closet with flashbulb glimpses that left me momentarily wide-eyed. Over the years he had acquired a raunchy homoerotic nomenclature as extensive and subtly precise in its way as the working vocabulary of Eskimoes to distinguish among the manifold appearances of snow; no doubt for his reasons similarly practical; but new to me, it served to heighten his sometimes stercoraceous revelations à la Jean Genet into a kind of poetry.

From the tales of his own romantic adventures, and there were plenty, I gathered the obvious inference that despite his ongoing affair with Auden, he had not forsaken all others. In the course of conversation he might remark, "Wystan thinks such-and-such" or "Wystan and I met so-and-so," at which I would at once clear my mind expectantly, hoping to hear more, but it hardly ever went further than that. Nor did I wish to embarrass myself and possibly disgust him with country bumpkin questions of the "Hast thou seen Auden plain?" variety. Chester, however, often asked me about Rhoda; but under the mistaken assumption that as a homosexual he would be antipathetic toward women, I was apprehensive about introducing them. Needlessly. By their second encounter, no later, they entered into a cosexual and sisterly intimacy, so much so that at times in their company it was I who felt like the third party.

The place where we all invariably met was—had to be—the cafeteria. During that early wartime, the students and teachers abruptly dropping out from week to week to join the service, and classes subject to cancellation in midterm, the cafeteria was not merely a place to eat, the stomach, as 'twere, of the student body, but its social heart and intellectual brain center as well, a crowded, bustling, feud-ridden, volatile, and at times cacophonous place that had a continuous life of its own apart from that of the college itself. Dispersed among the undifferentiated mass of students, who sat anywhere and left soon after having lunch, there was: a jocks' table adjacent, by a mutually appreciated *discordia concors,* to a chess-players' table; a self-segregated Wasps' table, blacks' table, and Orthodox Jews' table; a Newman Club Catholics' table where all the prettiest girls, it seemed, wore tiny *noli me tangere* gold crosses trembling in the cashmere valleys of their bosoms; a Stalinists' table separated by the length of the room and the breadth of an ideological abyss from a Trotskyites' table; a plague-on-both-your-houses heretics' table of anarchists, socialists, Lovestoneites, Luddites, Shachtmanites, syndicalists, "Crullers" (Committee for Revolutionary Labor Action), and other such disgruntled utopians; a nonsectarian but perpetually squabbling and faction-ridden psychoanaloids' table; a jazz-oriented hipsters' and (conspiratorially secret but reekingly obvious) pot-smokers' table; and many others I suppose, concealed here and there in the throng, but whose *point d'appui* was unknown to me.

After I succeeded in wooing Rhoda away from the Trotskyites' table — which proved fairly easy, for, as she liked to say, she had always been a "democratic narcissist" at heart — we tried the heretics' then the psycho-analoids' and then went off to sit by ourselves at one of the anonymous free-for-all tables. There we'd remain through the afternoon, talking and smoking and talking and chain-drinking Cokes and coffee, as the hourly classroom bells rang out several shifts of scene and personae in the cafeteria, but break off at some point to find a secluded spot under the athletic field grandstand, if it wasn't too cold, or in an empty lab if it was, and return to the same table afterward. Occasionally we'd join or be joined by friends, chief among them Chester, for whom I kept an expectant eye cocked, as did Rhoda as well.

Whenever Chester made one of his entrances he'd pose, as if preoccupied, at the doorway for a moment, ruminating, while his eyes rapidly cruised up and down the cafeteria in search of an appealing or, failing that, familiar face, and then, having assessed all the possibilites, slowly insinuate himself through the crowded aisles, "the observed of all observers," bestowing as he went a nod here or a snub there, until he reached the table of his choice. As often as not, but most often if he had just written a poem he wanted to try out on me, or had had a romance he wished to confide to Rhoda, he'd join us. The welcome would always be warm.

As I envision them now, converging in memory as they lean across the table to embrace and greet each other with little yelps of affection, they seem as closely akin as Hansel and Gretel. If opposites, as they say, attract, it's astonishing that two people so much alike could have liked each other so much. Each, to begin with, through some genealogical fluke, was a natural blond, with the blond's distinctive chlorophyll, yet behind their eyes, and in a certain unerasable millennial palimpsest that came through beneath and shaded their features, both had to be Chosen. Their way of laughing and what, with almost equal frequency and decibels, they laughed at were also similar, Rhoda's laugh being rather low and throaty and Chester's a half-note higher than the norm, so that they met on approximately the same register. These physical traits aside, there was something else, even more important, that they shared only with each other and that drew them still closer: they had each at an early age lost their mothers, Rhoda and her two sisters as a consequence having been raised in foster homes and orphanages, and Chester, an only child, at home by his grandmother. It left them with a need to belong and be loved solely for being that could never quite be satisfied, as I see now; but steeped, and nearly smothered, in maternal schmaltz as I was then, I envied them instead their independence and freedom from family ties.

At the table Chester, if in an antic or a roguish mood, might continue aloud his assessment of the student body in the cafeteria, but this time tête-à-tête with Rhoda, offering critical comments on any of the male gender he found worthy, admiring some limbs and disparaging others, speculating as well on their inguinal attributes and sexual prowess, sometimes in imagery so graphic as to electrify anyone within earshot, his voice rising to an ecstatic coloratura trill of syllables poured forth in one breath and run pell-mell together (*"Parlor-sizedbarelythat bututterly–utterlydiv* I-I-I-*ne"* — and perch for a long high moment on that sustained dieresis before slowly fluttering down — *"my dears!"* all the while slyly encouraging Rhoda to express her own opinions. I'd sit there grinning stolidly. Rhoda, with reassuring knee-nudges under the table and side-glances in my direction, would always demur, or else modestly murmur something noncommittal, yet somehow I always had the feeling that if I weren't there her response would have been more wholehearted. Both of us well knew that what inspired Chester's performance was mischief not malice and, primarily, a desire to reaffirm with Rhoda their co-sexual and subcutaneous sistership. But to be jealous of Chester? It was absurd.

The aria over, and his hilarity having subsided, Chester would become aware of my glum silence and realize that he had ignored and possibly offended me as well; whereupon to make up for it, for unless carried away he was always gentle and tender towards others, he'd turn to me contritely and ask in a serious voice, "Have you been writing?" Which I took as a sure sign that he had, and I'd politely ask him the same. He'd hedge, I'd hedge, *à la manière* d'Alphonse et Gaston or of Abbott and Costello, until finally, after a few self-deprecating shrugs and signs and disclaimers that it wasn't much and wasn't finished, "with sweet reluctant amorous delay" he'd yield, extracting from his inside coat pocket a much folded and re-folded tattered sheet of paper scrawled all over with lines that had been scratched out several times, then rewritten and reassigned to distant cor-ners of the page, with arrows pointing helter-skelter this way and that way to their new locations, out of which mess would emerge, like a nymph from a sewer, spruce and clean-limbed, a sonnet perhaps or a villanelle or even a sestina.

Since it was of course illegible, he'd consent to read, make that croon, the poem to us in a low, solemn Gregorian plain chant which he'd lower still more where required for dramatic emphasis, so that to hear him at all amid the babble of voices and clatter of dishes in the cafeteria we had to lean forward and listen intently. Throughout the recital I'd be ransack-ing my mind for something cogent or at least unstupid to say when it was over.

Chester was then under the spell of Thomas Campion's lyrics; but the violin-like phrasing and complex harmonies of that most musical of Eng-lish poets were beyond his range. What his own youthful efforts evoked instead was the fin de siècle tinkling preciosity of Lionel Johnson's or Ernest Dowson's music box. Auden's influence was evident only in the avoidance and, possibly, in his predilection for traditional verse forms and elaborate stanzaic patterns. As a self-styled "courtly maker," Chester ab-horred the lumpish "proletarian" free verse—precursor of the tub-thump-ing Beatnik type that erupted a generation later—in which left-wing politi-cal virtue tried to pass as poetry in those days, and I was with him there; yet for all their technical skill his own poems, most of them inspired by homosexual love, were evasively ambiguous, squeamish almost, and primly conventional in diction, with none of the pungency of his own natural speech. But how tell him that? I was so painfully aware of the pains taken in their composition that I was reluctant to seem ungrateful.

My comments at the table, offered apologetically and larded by admira-tion for the poem as a whole, would be confined to what I considered a tepid epithet here or a bumpy meter there. Even so one ran a risk. Chester felt each critical pinprick like a wound in his own psyche, and would re-spond with scorn, implying that I was too obtuse, with a sensibility too obfuse, to appreciate what he was up to. As he went on to defend and explicate his work, pointing out shades of meaning thrice distilled and metaphorical nuances dimly pinnacled, I'd nod as if in agreement, while convinced more and more that he was describing some ideal Platonic poem existing only in his imagination rather than the one that lay bleeding before us.

At this point Rhoda, who loved a political but loathed a poetical wrangle, would remember a protest rally she had promised to attend, give each of us a neutral kiss and depart. Chester and I would then continue the discussion sometimes until deep into the afternoon — and on many such afternoons, conflated in my mind, so that they now, with a single exception, seem like one long afternoon and one long discussion — and remain there until the cafeteria employees started clearing the table of dirty dishes and sweeping rubbish around, and over, our feet, muttering to themselves meanwhile, when we too would have to leave.

On the afternoon that stands out from the rest, rather than break off the conversation then and there I decided to walk Chester home. It was a cold, windy day in November, and when we got to his place — a "private house" (as it used to be called), with a screened-in front porch, a kitchen large enough to serve as a dining room, a basement and even a back yard, of the sort that once lined the side streets of Flatbush but have since been torn down to make way for high-rise apartment buildings — he invited me inside to warm up. While we were sitting in the parlor Chester's grandmother, then well past eighty, shuffled into the room wearing a faded housecoat and floppy bedroom slippers and asked him, in Yiddish, "*Host du gegesen epes?*" ("Have you eaten anything?"), in a small, frail, quavering voice, pure as a mew, then shuffled out again and returned a minute later bearing within two trembly hands a plate with a smoking pair of blintzes covered with sour cream. As she set it down she offered me one too, which I refused because it was getting dark out and supper would be waiting for me at home, but either because she was hard of hearing or preferred not to hear, perhaps both, she brought me a plate anyway. Those blintzes were delicious. It must surely have been from here, come to think of it, that Chester acquired the culinary skills that made him in later years such a superb cook.

She enjoyed watching us while we ate, seating herself meekly in a corner of the room, and though Chester implored her, "Please, Bubba, go lie down, rest," she paid no attention but kept following us with her eyes unto the last forkful, then got up to collect the plates. As she bent over the table she stroked Chester's hair, as she must have done a thousand times before, but by that one instinctive gesture, like the touch of a magic wand, he was suddenly transformed in front of me into a little boy again.

For most of his life she had raised Chester, as before him she had raised her own son, Chester's father, Dr. Edward Kallman, an orthodontist of some importance with a large practice in Manhattan, besides being an amateur landscape painter and, in those days, a reverential member of The Party. I had met him briefly on a couple of previous visits to the house, each time hurrying in and out with a different distaff comrade in tow, on his way most likely to a meeting at the local catacomb, when he would pause only long enough to say hello to me and exchange a few words with Chester. I had the impression, which deepened, that politics to him was merely periodontics on a world scale, and, having looked into the maw of capitalist society and found all its institutions too far gone in decay for any patchwork therapy, had concluded that the whole mouthful must be pulled, the sooner the better, and replaced it with a set of Marxist dentures. Perched on a buffet against the wall opposite me stood a framed picture of him, taken as a young man, looking earnest, normal, reliable, respectable and substantial, in sum a very *mensch*, and all the things that Chester was not, yet featured remarkably like him, with just a soupçon, a certain *je ne sais quoi*, of difference around the eyes and mouth. So go figure it. There must have been, I imagine, a clash in the beginning between father and son, between the rival claims of Homintern and Comintern, but during the years I knew them and observed them together they treated each other always with respect and affection.

It was getting dark out. I stood up to leave, but Chester, who had recently received a present of the 1936 Glyndebourne recording of *Don Giovanni*, with the superb baritone John Brownlee in the role of the codpieced "Dissoluto," insisted that I remain a while to hear one side — "Just one," he said — but one side and one aria led to another — "The last!" he'd promise — until finally I had to outshout his protestations and put on my coat. As we were standing in the foyer saying goodbye, the bell chimed outside and Chester opened the door.

In he, unmistakably and corporeally, like an idea personified, came, blowing his fingers and stamping his feet with cold, yet I couldn't have been more astonished if his mythological near namesake Odin had just entered the room. Embracing Chester, he was as yet unaware of my presence, so I had a chance to look him over unobserved. Though quite tall, about six feet, he was wearing a brown tweed overcoat at least two sizes too big that came down in symmetrical folds to his ankles and gave him the elongated appearance of a carved gothic apostle. His strong-featured, somewhat horsey face was then hardly furrowed; two prominent, cold-reddened ears poked out askew on either side of his head; and there (I looked for it, remembering the lines from his "Letter to Lord Byron," "Conspicuous . . . a large brown mole; / I think I don't dislike it as a whole.")

it was on his right cheek, not so large as I had imagined, about blueberry-sized, but it held and focused my attention nonetheless.

Pretty soon he noticed me gazing at him, and Chester introduced us. As we shook hands he held mine a touch longer than usual, a flicker of recognition passing across his pale grey eyes while he tried to equate my image with what Chester must already have told him about me, then burst into a high-pitched neigh of Oxfordian vocables from which I could make out nothing but my own name repeated a couple of times. Flushed, I suppose, and mumbling how glad I was to meet him, I backed out the door into the street.

So that was Auden! I told myself. *W. H. Auden! and he knew who I was too!* Exultant at having met him at last, I started running home through the streets, but halfway there I stopped, deliberately, and slowed down to a walk, for what impelled me to run almost as much, as I realized in self-disgust, was the primordial childhood fear of being scolded for coming late to supper. Here I was nineteen already, going on twenty, and had just met the most famous modern poet in England, yet I was still living at home cribbed and confined and spied on by my parents. So far my mother knew nothing of my affair with Rhoda; but I had been staying out later and later with her at the small apartment she shared with another girl at East 84th St. in Yorkville, sometimes not getting home till 2 or 3 A.M., and even staying overnight a couple of times. Sooner or later, I knew, she'd begin asking questions.

And then there was the war. Several of my friends, anticipating America's entrance into the war, had already volunteered for some branch of the service—"Yecky," for instance, had learned to play the tuba in order to join the military band at West Point, where he was now blowing Sousa marches for the duration—and my own number in the draft might be called at any time. Rhoda's political weather vane, recently shifted toward pacifism, urged me to declare myself a conscientious objector, but to that, as a craven cop-out, since I fully supported the war against Hitler, I could, and did, conscientiously object. Within the past few weeks, however, suggesting it at first casually and, she insisted, solely as a means for me to get a deferment in order to finish school, then more and more zealously, she proposed that we get married. *Me?* I thought. *Barely nineteen? And married? No.* In a vision I saw parallel rails stretching ahead year by year through deserts of conjugal eternity. Appealing to her own political conscience, I reminded her of her oft expressed belief, which I shared, that love was free and needed neither state sanction nor religious sanctification; but our case was different, she replied, for we were using the state, not being used by it; and with the issue thus joined between us, there was hardly a time we were together, especially just before or after making love, sometimes during, when she did not raise it.

One thing, though, was sure: whatever decisions I made or were made for me, about both the army and marriage, the chrysalis in which I had lived as a child for so long was soon to be broken. . . .

(1981?)

TWO

The Old Magi at the Burlesque

Pulsing from phase to phase, far-off, a bright
American star that sheds itself in flares
Of jazz, she hides behind the light she bares
Revealed and veiled by spangles, white in white,
As if her solid flesh were made of light,
Light of their eyes, the flesh of dreams and prayers,
Substance of nothingness, O wheel of stares,
Ishtar, Mama, first wish come true tonight!

So she, at last, unspangles all but one
Unknown triangular zone of swaddling bands.
Hearing their cries, the endless jazz begun
Again she comes and hides, with her bare hands
Upon the patch, death like a dazzling sun
And the invisible for which it stands.

(1955)

Originally published in the *Hudson Review* (Winter 1955).

Greenwich Village:
Decline and Fall

Rabbi Joseph ben Shalom of Barcelona maintains that in every change of form, in every transformation of reality, or every time the status of a thing is altered the abyss of Nothingness is crossed. . . . Nothing can change without coming into contact with this region of pure absolute Being which the mystics call Nothing. . . . It is the abyss which becomes visible in the gaps of existence.

—Gershom Scholem

Once last summer I was crossing north on Sheridan Square, thinking of nothing; suddenly the green light turned red, and there, dodging in the middle of traffic with me, I caught sight of a man whose face was so blotched, pitted, and scabbed by disease that, modestly (having been ravished before by so many obscene stares), he cast his eyes down with the refined coquetry of a beautiful woman. Where did he come from? And what was he doing out there in the broil of midday?—this phantom escaped from the undermind! When I reached the curb, I looked for him up and down the seven streets that radiate from the hub of the Square. But he had already disappeared, leaving behind him only a sulphurous after-image which, even now, still burns and holds its shape. What a scream, I mean what a laugh if this image of mind were his only claim to being—yet I choose to regard him with a straight face.

Now in the rational light uptown, above 14th Street, which is cut off from the Village like the Ego from the Id, I would have seen him for what he was. "There is the world dimensional," as Hart Crane called it, "for those untwisted by the love of things irreconcilable." But downtown, everything obvious is immediately suspect; and obviously, the most hidden secrets are dressed in the loudest fashion, if you know what I mean. Even the streets of Greenwich Village have so many twists, dead stops, gaps, trailing ends, and sudden inspirations out of blank walls that it sometimes takes years of free association to find your way around.

There is no straight way. Nobody wants to be tagged — you're *it*! Intellectuals without glasses, poets in business suits, gynanders and androgynes, the shapes of figures blur and metamorphose like the images of a dream. *Come out from behind that beard! Ovid, old Roman spy, you haven't changed, who do you think I think you are — Sigmund Freud?*

Where was I? I was standing on Sheridan Square one night waiting for the electric horse on Jack Delaney's marquee to jump over the neon stile. But just as the light turned, I saw, out of the corner of my eye, a drunk walk on his hind legs like a dog, stagger, fall on all fours, and heave up on the street. One of the Bleecker Street Goths who hang around this neighborhood pushed him from behind with his foot so that he slumped face down in his own stew. When he tried to jack himself up on his elbows, he was shoved down again, even harder than before. Standing there, I identified myself so closely with the poor croak that it was almost as though I had been kicked, and I who was sprawled out on the street with my head in vomit. But I knew it would be dangerous to interfere, so I swallowed my disgust and walked diagonally away across the Square.

Wherever you go you run into these young toughs, the "internal proletariat" of the Village, each one of them with a little fuse of violence smoldering under his shirt. They issue every night from the ranges of ulcerous tenements along Bleecker, Christopher, Macdougal, Sullivan, etc., in order to escape from the squalor of immigrant family life in crowded cold-water flats. Since the "nice" girls of the neighborhood are called in by their parents before the long Village night is even half over, they are forced to gather on the corners by themselves in male packs. Then to see Othello walking hand in hand with Desdemona, or the lay sodalities of fairies (a caricature of themselves), makes them ache with jealousy. They even grudge the sexual freedom of the Village artists and intellectuals who, like themselves, are barred from the commercial mills uptown. But here at least the artist and the conscientious objector to American culture have some sort of status. The Goths have none. Therefore, the drunk must eat his vomit.

Sometimes I'd come across them pitching coins against the wall of the Christopher Street poolroom and then, while the next pitch was held up until I passed, they'd look me over. *Was I a Jew? How did I do? Did I show any fear? What was I doing here?* Their philosophy is as hard as the cement under their feet. Everything is a racket; the game of life is to beat the racket; and anyone who says no is a liar or a sucker. Their true heroes are the bookies, the prize-fighters, and the racketeers who once rose out of their own ranks and now operate the Nite Clubs and park their Cadillacs in front of the poolroom. One question they can never figure out, and so what never fails to impress them, is this: why anyone with a chance to play for the blue chips uptown, or why any girl born with a privileged face, should choose to live in these slums? And every year they see new recruits coming down.

The Village attracts its own from every state of the mind: some for the faded romance of La Vie Bohème; some to be free of their parents; some out of acedia or wan-hope; some to trade in free love; some for art's sake; some because they are zebras on the white plains; some to hide from their failure; some because they'd rather be in Paris; some to do something about *it*; some for a change of mind or heart — but almost all to escape from the stunning heat and light and noise of the cultural mill grinding out of the mass values of a commercial civilization.

But not all who live in the Village are at home there. There are also writers, private secretaries, dancers, copy writers, actors, illustrators, and musicians on the make, who come down from the provinces to be close to the Big Time and leave as soon as they can. Graduates of the toney Eastern colleges for women such as Vassar, Bennington, Bryn Mawr, and the rest comprise one of the steadiest sources of recruits. But after a brief flurry of excitement and uplift, these also dry up fast like summer rain. And then there are the fellow-travelers of Bohemia, whose home base may be anywhere at all, but who keep up the Village line through the auspices of friends. Not to mention an etceterongeneous muster of characters for whom any classification would be inherently contradictory.

The places where all these people live range from the plush and marble apartment hotels on the Gold Coast of lower Fifth Avenue to the cold-water tenements with communal toilets and no baths that once housed the masses of immigrant workers at the beginning of the century. Here and there a few of the old type of one-family brick houses still stand, relics of the Henry James and Lillian Russell era when Washington Square and its environs was the hub of New York society. Most of these have been split into two- or three-room flats, each one inhabited by its own colony of extra-ordinarily sensitive roaches with long, delicate, trembling wands and Hamlet-like refinements of indecision, a breed peculiar of the Village. The interiors are furnished in a style which, through the years, has become almost as standardized as Bronx Department Store Gothic or Terre Haute monde moderne: chairs and tables and couches wavering between junk and the antique like the houses themselves; framed reproductions of Rouault's "The Old King" or Picasso's "Woman in White" or that picture by Henri Rousseau of a lion in the moonlight sniffing the feet of a sleeping gypsy; floors painted red, yellow, green, brown; collapsible shelves loaded with books on psychiatry, books of modern poetry, books of prints by the Paris school, some second-hand or inherited, but most of them borrowed and never returned; and so on. With only minor changes, it is recognizable as the period style formed at the end of the First World War — the time Greenwich Village first became self-conscious — and reflects all the nostalgia for those good old days.

As seen from the fox-hole perspective of the Village during the 20's, America was a No Man's Land, the haunt of the Cyclops. Only in Europe could the good life be found:

> Là, tout n'est qu'ordre et beauté,
> Luxe, Calme, et Volupté.

The boulevards of Paris were as crowded with Villagers as Washington Square in the Spring.

By the 30's, the spiritual homeland had shifted a thousand miles to the East amid the gilded domes and cupolas of the first Worker's State. (It was at this time, incidentally, that young Jewish intellectuals from the outlying boroughs of New York entered the Village as a group.) The depression fell like an incessant damp, cold and miserable and everywhere. What remained of the enthusiasms of the 20's was sublimated into political passion: Dionysius was reborn as Nicolai Lenin. And, conversely, the café and speakeasy society of those days was transformed into cafeteria society — Life Cafeteria, Stewart's, the Waldorf — where, until far in the night, the history and destiny of mankind was measured out with coffee spoons. To the Bleecker Street Klans on the other side, who sat in the steam of tobacco smoke and watched these tables seethe and boil with Marxist pronunciamentos, appeals, denunciations, charges, and countercharges, all this talk and all this fervor were just so much sucker bait.

Still, in those first years the marriage of bohemian freemasonry and the camaraderie of the WPA was almost perfect. The open collar and the grimy pants served both as well. But afterwards the foundations of this union split so wide (corresponding to the political divorce in the Worker's State itself) that, when the bastard Stalinist type appeared with his slogans, his cast-iron frame of mind, his dog faith, and his carefully cultivated mediocrity, it was a shock to recall his parentage. And the radical splinter groups that followed with their perpetual cries of "Rape!" and their tedious apocalypses — what could be expected from them?

109

By the end of the 30's Lenin's mummy had begun to stink.

Not the Revolution, but the Great War itself—that was the apocalypse so much dreaded and so long anticipated it was almost a relief when it came. Greetings! "Bababadalgharaghtakamminarronnkonnbronntonnerronntuonnthunntrovarrhounawnskawntoohoohoordenenthurnuk," as James Joyce said. But ah, those days of innocence! O lost Arcadia! I never saw so many drooping fawns and dying swans. The war put a stop to all that. And nothing could ever be the same any more.

While the war was going on, every night in the Village was Saturday night. Soldiers and sailors of all the Allied armies jammed the bars and the main streets of Greenwich Village hunting for a wild time. But that time was gone. With the moral dikes broken everywhere, and the whole country engulfed by the flood, the Village, strangely enough, was left high and dry. All the tabooed "dirty" words had been rubbed clean by everyday use. Of course there was as much freedom, in the Village as before; but since this was equalled and even surpassed by Main Street, where was the defiance and the revolt against convention which, previously, had been the spur? The celebrated Village campaign for sexual independence had ended in a strange victory: free love was driving the professionals off the streets. And the baby-faced V-girls walking arm in arm with sailors down Broadway were wearing their mothers' high heels. In this situation, only the operators of the honky-tonks on Sheridan Square and in the side alleys made sure, somehow, that the sinister reputation of Greenwich Village was preserved.

The good old days when nobody had a job and nobody cared were over. Even the panhandlers who wander down to the Village from the "smoke" joints on the Bowery would touch artists and intellectuals on the street who were never good for a nickel before. And now that there was so much money around, apocryphal stories of the Depression were revived with nostalgia: how this musician split his personality and collected four pay checks from the WPA music project as a string quartet; how someone else had lived off the Waldorf Cafeteria for a year by demanding a free cup of hot water for a second cup of tea without buying the first, and then, by pouring in enough ketchup, had brewed a thick bowl of tomato soup on his table, etc, etc. But for the majority of Villagers, rejected by the Army on psychoneurotic grounds, the slush money to be had uptown was irresistible; and, without too much loss of face, some erstwhile bohemians were even able to join the great herd shoving at the trough. This was not altogether a betrayal of principle. It was, I think a means for absolving the secret guilt of not being in uniform. For them the despair within had

110

at last been equalled by the hysteria without, thus providing common ground for a *modus vivendi*. But a return later on to the past life was almost impossible, as most had, in the meantime, contracted a new apartment, an analyst, a wife, or other expensive habits.

Perfect circles of friends drifted apart and disappeared like smoke rings. And one by one the old hangouts were lost. George's Bar (the ancestor of the San Remo today) was taken over completely by sailors and their quail; and even the last remaining forum of cafeteria society, the Waldorf, fell to the Bleecker Street Goths, who now had it almost completely terrorized. Boredom followed everywhere you went: boredom, barroom hysteria, confessions regretted by morning, cracked marriages, affairs over in a week, violence for reasons forgotten during the violence . . . Then the war suddenly ended.

After the block parties and the parades under the Arch, it was wry to see the new recruits to the Village come down expecting to find the Golden Age of the 20's or the Silver Age of the 30's, but hardly prepared for this, the Age of Lead. Morale was worse than in the army. It was impossible to rent an apartment without "pull" or a great deal of cash. Through their GI loans, some managed to open new book shops with a room in the back; and there you could see them sitting all day and part of the night surrounded by second-hand books and piles of old literary magazines — *Partisan Review, Kenyon, Sewanee, View,* etc. — chatting with friends and customers most of whom came to sell rather than to buy. A dull business, once the edge had worn off.

What they had dreamed while regimented in the army was a vision of the palmy days of Paris Bohemia with a slight admixture of the American Frontier — but by now, alas! the Left Bank had been eroded by sentiment, and the frontier had contracted to the five senses of the individual. The underground names and passwords of a generation ago were already shopworn, with the new ones kept under the counter. It was also harder to break into certain Village cliques by mere brilliant talk and the flash of personality alone. Somehow the cross slogan of American business — "How much does he make?" — had been taken over by the Village: "Where does he show?" — "What has he published?" — the bark of an official dog. Artists and poets did their "work" like everybody else.

During the war, Greenwich Village had been exposed as never before to the total glare of American mass culture, a light that had long blinded everyone with excess of light. Then, with the liberation of Paris, came the first influx in five years of the new paintings by Picasso (with their cartoon shapes) as well as work by Braque, Bonard, and young French painters such as Dubuffet; the poetry of Eluard and the cryptograms of Queneau; and, most astonishing, the Existentialist philoshopy of Sartre and Camus, which drew heavily for its examples on the tough-guy heroes of American fiction and gangster movies. The anticipation was nothing compared to the let-down. And when European artists and writers again came to America, guided by their customary arrogance toward the natives, they were given a close look. They were like us—only smaller, fussier, dingier, and even (O Ghost of Henry James!) more innocent of the facts of life. Despite all their bitter experience, they had not yet been through the mill of a total commercial civilization—and that was the Real Distinguished and Distinguishing Thing. Their day and night were not ours.

Europe had already probed the nerve ends of modern art to the points of their most exquisite attenuations, from Mallarmé to Proust, from Redon to Mondrian. By seeking to re-barbarize their own culture through American jazz, movies, comic strips, etc., European artists and intellectuals had in the end redirected America up its own alley. (A final irony is that, even in this, America is still following the lead of Europe.) But now there was no turning back.

In the past, these debased forms of popular culture had been something to be poked with a long stick. Now that they had acquired such foreign respectability, their very coarseness was subtly admired. O Polyhymnia, sacred slut, sing for us (if you don't mind) of the furious drives of Dick Tracy, L'il Abner, and Moon Mullins struggling in their boxed and aimless worlds; and of the shadowy Olympus of Hollywood where the old forms of Greece are overthrown by a mechanical Prometheus; and of the soap dramas on the radio where the drabness and stupidity of life is celebrated, and the movements of the bowels are announced with trumpets. . . . Maybe the old alienation of artists and intellectuals in America could be adjusted by a common bondage. Maybe this was the way out at last. But even if this were true, the sad fact remains that a way out is not necessarily a way in, nor is "culture" a revolving door.

The way of alienation is the Jew's badge of Greenwich Village, a way apart that orients itself by negation. Life here is the ghetto life, indrawn, with its own tastes and smells, rank and dark and protected as an arm-pit. The native loneliness of Americans is so intensified in the Village that, paradoxically, it becomes a social cement that holds it together. For what is feared even more than alienation from American life is self-alienation, the loss of identity in the melting pot, reduction to the lowest common denominator of dollar and cent values. It is from this fear that Greenwich

Village protects its own. Under cover of the most ideal persuasions of self-denial, there is always a private need.

The radical movement of the 30's was engaged not only with politics but with more personal considerations: political parties were places where you met and made your friends. And the same function was served by the arty societies of the 20's. But times change — now's now and then was then.

Free and easy love in the Village is a thing of the past. The night wanderer from bar to bar searching for the rare encounter finds only wanderers like himself, always on the prowl, always restless, never satisfied. The more intellectual can spend hours sitting in the gas chambers of the New School, bored to extinction, but hoping to meet a true friend in such cultured atmosphere. The fairies are the most driven — their nervous cruises down 8th Street, 4th Street, the Park, and back again are like a man pacing up and down a room. And even when all these find what they want and still want it, the gossip spreads so fast and the Who's Had Who in the Village is so faithfully compiled — although nobody cared enough to snoop before — that a lasting relationship is rare.

If the most important single event in the erotic life of Man during the past century has been the gradual disappearance of animals from the cities and farms, then the next — although probably there is no connection — has been the emergence of Woman to the rank of full and equal partner. Women in the Village are often as aggressive as the men, who are inclined to be somewhat backward as a result. The illusion of emancipation, however, satisfies most. On the corner of Greenwich and 6th Avenues stands the House of Detention, or jug, for women, which hides its grim interiors behind the facade of an apartment house — even numbered, 10 Greenwich Avenue: a demure symbol and monument of the suffrage movement. Like the men of Greenwich Village, women here suffer from the fact that love is not an immolation of the self, but the proof of it: *Copulo ergo sum.* And those causes and movements which once supplied additional proof are no longer viable.

Without any unifying political or artistic center, the Village has fragmented into small groups who go to the same parties, hold the same views, and know each other too well. The Society of Neurotics Undergoing Psychoanalysis is the only one at present with something of the old catholicity, yet with this important difference: it is a secret society, and the membership is hidden even from those who belong. Still, it's a connection. And it takes only a minute for those who are, or who have been, or will be analyzed to smell one another out. First, the shy query: Have you been analyzed? Then: How many years? And next: Who is he? How much does he charge? And then: what party? — Freudian, Reichian, Adlerian, Horneyan, Jungian? This last question is charged and the wrong answer can explode any further conversation.

For when the political cliques of the 30's lost their passion and died, they never really died but rose to the bosom of the Father and were strangely transmogrified. Psychoanalysis is the new look, Sartor Resartus, but the body underneath is the same.

A competent analyst can read their minds like a book by Freud, which is what some of them become after two or three years on the couch. The desperation, however, is real. Looking into themselves, they've seen the Gorgon. It does no good to pat its ugly snout, or to feed it lump sugar. The monster sits deep inside covered by the muck of the undermind and with its eyes always open. In order to charm it to sleep, or to pierce its heart by a sharper insight, they lie on the psychoanalytic couch in the dark room with Perseus on his rocker behind them, his pen in hand, taking notes. *O why was I born with a different face? What can't I find a lover? or a job? or a friend? Why don't people admire me? Why do I hate the sound of clocks? Why can't I dream? Why can't I get up in the morning? Why do I bite my toenails? Why don't you ever say anything? O tell me it's true and it's not true! Show me the open way! Make me feel that everything will be all right.* So it goes on. Job, covered with boils and sitting on a stone in the field, asked the same questions.

There is a circle apart, however, even from the Village which is itself apart, where all the answers kiss the questions and all those who are afflicted with wanhope or acedia can make peace with themselves. I mean the jazz-narcotics coteries, the "hipsters," so-called. These are drawn from the spiritually dispossessed who form the underground of Village life. Since they are unalterably aginst The Law, they have their own rites and passwords and worship their own forbidden God — The One Who Puts Out The Light. The Hipster societies — if they are such, since nobody in them thinks they belong — may be considered the draft-dodgers of commercial civilization, just as Villagers, in general, are the loyal opposition or "conscientious objectors." They take no stand, for any stand would have to be inside the group and therefore against themselves, against their negative principle. The mood which infect them all is, perhaps, a tender American version of that underground nihilism which erupted in the forms of Dada and fascism in Europe — anti-art and anti-morality. What they believe in is benzedrine, "tea," and jazz.

Jazz and "tea" (marijuana) form a bridge to Harlem, the other ghetto uptown, and many on both sides use it to cross over. The midpoint is 52nd Street where all the cats, black and white, can get together in the cellar clubs to dig the latest jive and to hear Dizzie or the Bird or the Hawk blow their valves. Black jazz is the only art whose moods and ecstasies reflect their own, whose pace is equal to the terrible inner speed of the drug. When marijuana loses its drive there are some who learn how to saddle and ride the "horse" of heroin. But once on that nightmare, as everybody knows, there is no dismounting until the other side of the Bar has been crossed. For such release, life itself is a handicap.

Around the track of all these gyres and circles in Greenwich Village, no matter where we start from we arrive at the same place in the end — beside the point. Without a common focus, images are fractured on everybody's point of view; and meanings shift without pivotal reference. The boundary between inner and outer reality is blurred. What is real or good or beautiful is a matter of taste. Since for our time, and in the Village especially, truth itself has become a sentiment, the search for an Absolute is maudlin. All the beards of authority have been cut off, and anything goes: Ovid is Freud is Karl Marx is Joe Gould is I AM. Which brings us by a commodius vicus of recirculation back to Sheridan Square and environs, like a barber's pole forever disappearing into itself.

I cut diagonally away across the Square, leaving the drunk on the sidewalk, and headed for the cover of darkness in the movies. The theater was packed, people were standing five deep behind ropes, yet, somehow, probably because I was alone, the usher signaled for me to follow as soon as I arrived. While we were walking down the aisle, a sudden blow of laughter from the audience struck me so hard that, even without knowing why, I laughed along with the rest.

My seat was in the middle row, the best in the house, and, what was even more uncanny, two others right next to it were vacant! I smelled them, I looked under them, I felt them — nothing was wrong. But why wasn't anyone coming down the aisle? There was another blow of laughter, and then another even harder, the effect augmented by itself. I looked up at the screen. *A man was being hit over the head by a lead pipe.* Although he seemed in agony, every time he screwed his eyes and made mouths the laughter from the audience became louder. A woman was whispering behind my back! I turned around, but quickly she looked the other way. ME? Now the whole house was screaming. *A blindfolded man was about to walk into an open sewer.* I shut my eyes, but his after-image remained. The beam of the inner eye cast his figure on my mind with as much power as the projector upon the movie screen. As I wavered, two women in gray

115

and black came down the aisle. There was no other way out. I ran up the stage, and, while my shadow wavered on the screen for a moment as though undecided whether to follow, plunged into the abyss of nothing. The man tore the bandage from his eyes and clutched at me as I passed. But the film of reality which separated us was as wide as the abyss itself.

Down Fifth Avenue and under the Arch I ran to the cement circle in Washington Square. It was a bitter night without stars or a moon and the park was deserted. But from nowhere someone called "Klonsky!" — my name. I saw him then as he came loping towards me, his face so flat and black I could hardly separate the features. "Give me some skin, man," he said, "I want you to dig some of this new charge."

Ah well, ah well, it was my friend Saggy, an old viper out of Harlem, always frantic, always high, the kind of tea-pusher who'd pull a hype on his own mother if he knew who she was. Under his sleeve his wrist was pocked with a thousand bites of the needle. He took out a long white fuse of tea from his pocket and bit open one end. Then he lit up with a deep sigh of smoke and, as the image of the burning match reflared upon his eyes, I saw in that sudden flash of insight that they were pitch-black! they had no whites! — like the sooty fire-place with the orange flame burning inside it before which I am writing.

(1948)

Maxwell Bodenheim as Culture Hero

Just as I remember him, the character, he makes his entrance. "MOSCOWITZ! MOSCOWITZ! Well, well, well, well, wel-come in, come in, Mr. Moscow-, it's Mr. Moscow-, it's Mr. Mos-cow-*iiiitz!* MOSCOWITZ!" I was sitting with some friends in the San Remo in Greenwich Village at the time, long ago — it must have been the Winter of 1952 — when we heard the shouts and the laughter all around us. What happened? We all turned to look. As usual, a dense grey smoke screen of tobacco in the place made everything seem hazy, so that now, peering backward through the years, I have the strange sense of being present once more. At the espresso urn was the *padrone*, Joe Santini, bowing toward the door with a glow of ecstatic malice on his face, and still shouting *Moscowitz! Moscowitz!* at a tall, glum, scraggly, hawk-nosed, long-haired, itchy-looking, no doubt pickled, fuming and oozing, Bowery-type specimen; and yet, for a' that, something austere and even classic about his ruins — Old Roman, not just any ordinary human junk heap — made me look again. It was Maxwell, the Bard himself, Bodenheim, at bay.

So why "Moscowitz"? I've often wondered about that. Maybe it was a political rib thrust at Bodenheim, with an added *itz*-twist of anti-Semitism, for being a fellow traveler; or, since there was a men's clothing store called Max Moscowitz' around the corner, an attempt to ridicule the poet by association; maybe both; but anyway, at each tremendous MOSCOWITZ! a kind

Originally published as "Squash & Stretch: Maxwell Bodenheim in the Village," in *Esquire* (December 1963). Reprinted with permission of *Esquire*. Copyright © 1963 by Esquire Associates.

of seismic rumbling and trembling went through him. He seemed to heave and swell up; heave and swell up. At the bursting point, when one more MOSCOWITZ! might have done it, Santini stopped. The scene was set.

By now, too, most of the customers, packed three-deep at the bar, were watching, and a couple of prompters near the jukebox called out: "Hey, Max, let's have a powm! Recite us a powm!" Abruptly, wheeling about, he glared them into silence. Though Bodenheim had come to the San Remo for that purpose, to read his poems in exchange for a few beers, his name was at stake, his quid, the nub of his being, that irreducible *yerde* without which he would have been Moscowitz, and he made a move as if to leave. But other hecklers, each one igniting the next and too many to suppress, took over: "Come on, Max, don't just stand there, make up a powm! A powm! A powm! Let's have a powm!" His head, as if twitched by invisible strings, kept jerking this way and that as he tried to spot them in the crowd. Once his eyes crossed mine and held them, in full blaze for a moment, and I felt a flush of guilt for being there at all. Why didn't he leave?, I wondered. Why didn't *I* leave?

Then someone, from way in the back, yelled "MOSCOWIIIITZ!"

That did it. He drew in his breath, about to say something, and paused. Everybody waited. Magnificently, he stretched out his arm; the one remaining button on his coat popped off. Ignoring this, despite all the guffaws, with a sweeping gesture he wrapped that old dung-colored horse blanket of a patched overcoat, like a purple toga, more closely about him, as heroic — all right, mock heroic, even ludicrous, cornball, but still, in his own way, heroic — as Marc Antony when he faced the mob around Caesar's bier. (*The will, the will! we will have Caesar's will.*"), and then, from the depths of God-knows-what source of inspiration, he dredged up, shaped each word and just before he left spewed out his farewell to us all:

"Pimps! Patriots! Racetrack touts!"

What an exit! The door still slams in my mind. Up until then, I suppose, I hadn't really appreciated the nobility of the creep; afterward I never forgot it. They kicked him and he bit their feet; they spat in his face and he held up a mirror; they mocked him and he took the words out of their mouths. In a lifetime of playing himself, that was without doubt one of his greatest performances.

But it was also, for me at least, his last, for during the years that followed, leading up to the double murder of Bodenheim and his common-law wife, Ruth Fagan, by a demented seaman (whose confessed motive was to get his name in the papers), I caught only rare and disconnnected glimpses of the poet. And always in motion, *agitato*, darting in and out of bars and restaurants on Eighth Street, with a decrepit manila envelope of poems, held together by a shoelace, tucked under his arm; or crisscrossing through Washington Square during summer, gesticulating and talking to himself; and once, as a crowd collected, I saw him on Waverly Place passionately denouncing a traffic light for being a symbol of The Whole System; and another time, toward the end, I ran into him and his wife, after they must have made the rounds of the "smoke" joints along the Bowery, staggering hand in hand down Bleecker Street; but most often I'd see him hurrying alone through the Village night, going somewhere, *fato profugus*, as if he were late for some urgent appointment.

When I splice and connect all these separate occasions in my mind, then reel them off, like the rushes of an old-time silent movie that jump and sputter, flash and grow dim, the film unwinds itself faster and faster, skipping months, years, until it suddenly breaks off, frozen, at the last still: *a furnished room on the lower East Side, with all the shades drawn; a naked bulb suspended from the ceiling by a cord, swinging violently back and forth; a smashed wine bottle on the floor in a spreading puddle of wine; a couple of chairs overturned; a few panic-stricken roaches rushing for cover; against the wall an unmade bed on which a woman lies sprawled in an odd twist, motionless, ripped and flung aside, with the stuffing coming out, like a kewpie; and in the foreground, closeup, surprised in his bare feet, Bodenheim, himself, Bodenheim with the bullet already in his heart, tottering, not even looking at his murderer, but with his face turned for the last time to the audience, to me, openmouthed, stretching out his arm, about to say something, and then. . . .*

And then, nothing. The End. Words failed him, and without words, what was he? Anonymous, neither Bodenheim nor Moscowitz, sunk in the age-old silences.

. . . or so it seemed. And yet, somehow, who knows how, but knowing him, the character, with his genius for comeback, I had a hunch he wouldn't take this lying down forever.

Since his death a strange thing has happened. Though the old Village to which he belonged has receded in memory, and grown and flatter and dimmer year by year, at the same time, standing out against the present like a bas-relief, the essential Bodenheim of Bodenheim can be seen even clearer and bolder than when he was alive. I don't mean to preach a risen and exalted Bodenheim, which would be ridiculous; nor do I mean to "revive" him as a poet. Actually, he was a lousy poet. What I mean is that for us, now, Bodenheim has come into his own as a kind of bohemian

119

culture hero, an Urbeatnik, so to speak, though his beatification has been long overdue.

Only Joe Gould, Bodenheim's contemporary, and the author of that lost, mysterious opus, *An Oral History of the World*, can be compared with him as a Village character. But what a pair! Judged by their appearance alone, each could have been the image in a Coney Island mirror of the other; while Gould was squat and bald, Bodenheim was lank and shaggy; and while Bodenheim sometimes needed a shave, Gould was magisterially endowed with an heraldic blazon of white beard. Yet the difference between them went even deeper than that, into their life styles, the roles given them by fate. Bodenheim's old-time bohemian evangelism inspired almost everything he did: even in bed, at the moment of truth, he must have thought of himself as striking a blow for sexual freedom. For more than forty years he tilted his crazy lance at all the grundies, killjoys and vaticides of American life who protect us from being ourselves. But Gould, if he stood for anything at all, was an anti-hero; a pinpricker; a pain in the ass of pomposity; and no matter what the scene he always played it down and cool at an angle. He neither joined The System nor fought it, on principle, but kept himself apart, hip and aloof, to follow his own unique cross-purposes. . . . And so forth. In fact, like Shem & Shawn, or Cain & Abel, or Yin & Yang, or Don Quixote & Sancho Panza, Gould & Bodenheim could appear together as a team in the great tradition of literary vaudeville, costarring nowadays as *The Hipster & the Beatnik*.

Since this is Bodenheim's story, however, not Gould's, there's no need to give them equal billing here. But for our purposes Gould deserves at least to make an appearance, perhaps as devil's advocate—the same role he played so well in life—putting the hero on and setting him off by contrast.

Almost all modern authorities on the origin and meaning of myth, such as Otto Rank, Carl Jung, Lord Raglan and others, agree that there are certain unmistakable signs by which a true culture hero can be identified; and these have been summed up by Joseph Campbell, in his book *The Hero With A Thousand Faces*, as follows: "A hero ventures forth from the world of common day into a region of supernatural wonder: fabulous forces are there encountered and a decisive victory is won; the hero comes back from this mysterious adventure with the power to bestow boons on his fellow man." This universal pattern of withdrawal-initiation-return applies to the mythic heroes of every people of mankind, and also (as any unbiased survey of his life will prove to Bodenheim. If only as a spear carrier he belongs in the same exalted company.

According to the Village legend, Bodenheim was born in 1892 or '93 in a small town in Mississippi, though some say Missouri, the only son of respectable middle-class German-Jewish parents ("Eat! Eat!") who earned their living by dry goods. Up to the age of fourteen he grew up like any normal American schoolboy of that time, miching and swapping, stealing apples, sneaking into the nickelodeon, reading the Yellow Kid and Horatio Alger. But Character (as Freud himself said) is Destiny. And when the change came, as it had to, it must have come as a shock. He let his hair grow out, avoided his old friends, took long lovely walks by himself at night, and secretly at first, then more and more openly, began to write poetry. Alarmed, his parents begged him to spare them the disgrace, insisting that they had sacrificed enough already, and urged him instead to join the family business and write his poems, if he still felt like it, "as a sideline." When this failed, they threatened to burn his books. The young Bodenheim thereupon left home and took to the open road.

For more than a year he wandered about the American wilderness as a boy bum, a gadling, à la Rimbaud, drinking canned heat and sharing a pot of stew or a fleeced chicken in hobo jungles all over the South and Midwest. What "fabulous wonders" or "supernatural forces" he encountered there, who can say; but from then on Bodenheim always found kinship among the drifters and irreconcilables, the misfits and outcasts of society, whether on Poker Flat or the Bowery. And he must also have acquired, during this formative period, a tolerance for venomous liquors which enabled him to survive the years of Prohibition in the Village. But that test was still far off. . . .

Now, about 1910, when he was only seventeen or eighteen, Bodenheim boosted his age to enlist and served a four-year hitch in the Army, plus a year's stretch, after going A.W.O.L., in the Federal penitentiary at Leavenworth. Without doubt his lifelong and irrepressible unpatriotism can be traced back to this ordeal. And yet, in a larger sense, being swallowed up and buried alive in prison was for Bodenheim a symbolic, and necessary, descent into the labyrinth, the whale's belly, the infernal regions beneath society. He won a "decisive victory," the end of his initiation. For all this while he was rehearsing his fate and shaping his lines, coming more and more to resemble himself, so that when he finally emerged, scowling, into the light of common day, baleful and shaggy-haired, with a decrepit manila envelope of powms stuck under his arm, he was already unmistakably in character.

To Chicago then he came, burning. . . . This was during the First World War, and Chicago was then the chief revivalist center for the arts in America—the Chicago of Frank Lloyd Wright and Thorstein Veblen,

Dreiser, Jelly Roll Morton, Vachel Lindsay, Edgar Lee Masters and Carl Sandburg and Sherwood Anderson. The avant-garde *Little Review* and *Poetry* magazines (though both were being masterminded from London by Ezra Pound) had just set up publication in Chicago. But most important for Bodenheim, a large bohemian colony, vintage 1914, of Wobblies, pacifists, Eugene V. Debs socialists, vers-librists, naturalists, Objectivists, short-haired and flat-heeled feminists, muckraking novelists, Ash Can and Cubist artists, and so on, with all their etceterageneous camp followers and kibitzers, was sprawning on Chicago's North Side.

Those who knew Bodenheim at the time recall especially his dark, brooding, almost Dantesque countenance and his pale, remarkably pale, eyes which seemed illuminated from within and to flare out of this darkness. Though he carried himself with an hidalgo pride and swagger, making his exits and entrances in the grand manner, he also smoked an intellectual pipe. Bodenheim was noted as well for his dry, cachinnating laugh, of the sort described as "bitter," and with it went an explosive talent for mockery, plus a ready command of billingsgate and the blackjack epithet, which made him a dangerous opponent in any literary argument. Men thought of him as weird but talented, or talented but weird; and women, wherever he went, regarded him highly as a threat to their virtue.

With so much going for him, Bodenheim — or "Bogie," as he was called by his friends — was able to move freely between Chicago's literary parlors and the more roughhouse and bohemian hangouts in the Tenderloin. Soon he began to publish his early poems in free verse in most of the important literary magazines around such as *The Dial, Poetry, The Little Review*, the *Smart Set*, the *Century*, the *Yale Review*. Though these poems seem nowadays surprisingly pastel and conventional in tone, with their florid and hoity-toity, almost prissy, diction (in which the eyes of a "factory girl" are "dry brown flower pods / Still gripped by the memory of lost petals," and a chorus girl's voice is "a rose fragrance waltzing in the wind"), at the time they appeared he was acknowledged as one of the most phosphorescent of the new Imagist poets. In 1917, for instance, he appeared side by side with the leaders of the "Others" movement in their annual anthology — the Others being T. S. Eliot, W. C. Williams, E. E. Cummings, Marianne Moore and Wallace Stevens. From London Ezra Pound, already established as a one-man brass band for modern poetry, requested a contribution from Bodenheim for a collection he was putting together — then changed his mind, afraid that his German-sounding name might be found objectionable while England was at war with the Huns. (A frankfurter with sauerkraut in those days was known as a sausage with Liberty cabbage.) Pound eventually decided to accept the poems, but played it safe, publishing them under the initials "M.B."

War or no war, Bodenheim was still Bodenheim, nevertheless, and refused to trim himself down. Even after the U.S.A. joined the Allied armies "over there" in 1917, he remained as staunchly subversive as before. A wider public now began to hear of him, not so much as a poet but as a torchbearer for "Flaming Youth." For as soon as the Kaiser was beaten, and the postwar mood of radical and fashionable disillusionment set in, Bodenheim and his cohorts on the North Side suddenly found themselves oddly enough, in the vanguard of the national bandwagon.

Together with his closet friend, Ben Hecht, then a young newspaperman and aspiring novelist, Bodenheim devised a number of surrealist pranks and hoaxes in Chicago, somewhat similar to the ones being perpetrated at the same time by Tristan Tzara, André Breton, Marcel Duchamp, and the rest of the capital cities of Europe. For instance, the two hired a hall for a literary debate, and the word got out that it was to be on the theme: "Resolved, that people who attend literary debates are imbeciles." (When the debate took place Hecht merely stood up, looked around the audience and said, "The affirmative rests"; then Bodenheim got up, also looked around, said, "You win," and everybody went home.) Another time, using the nom de plume of René d'Or, he launched a fake poetic movement called the "Monotheme School," complete with the usual manifestos and denunciations, and ran a nationwide contest on the subject of "Bottles." And there were other capers, too, of the same sort, all of which were reported in the Chicago press along with the more practical assaults on society by Al Capone and Big Jim Colosimo.

A spirit of youthful and fundamentally American innocence still lingers about them, and has survived intact into the present. Above all, they meant well. Compared with the Dadaist and Surrealist demonstrations in Europe, which sometimes ended in riots and cracked heads, their aim was not to confound, but to convert the "bourgeoisie." To what? Free love or free verse or the repeal of Prohibition in those days, Zen Buddhism or Bop or the free sale of marijuana in ours, it doesnt' matter. The slogans might change, but the banner of uplift remains the same.

Anyhow, it was this missionary style, this booster bohemianism, that Bodenheim brought with him, sometime in 1920 or '21, as a "boon" from Chicago to New York.

The rumor of his exploits in the Midwest had already reached the inner circles of the Village; and as soon as he arrived and was taken in, he took charge. Chronicles of Village life in the Twenties, such as Albert Parry's

Garrets and Pretenders and Allen Churchill's *The Improper Bohemians*, relate his progress in a tone of awe and astonishment: how he presided over a series of all-night poetry readings in various speakeasies on Macdougal Street, using a sledgehammer as his gavel; how, with the millionaire playboy-poet Robert Clairmont and other cronies, he founded the "Greta Garbo Social Club," dedicated mainly to the seduction of schoolteachers; how his reputation got so notorious that newspapers from Paris to Hong Kong reported his escapades — and even The New York *Times* took notice after two teen-age flappers committed suicide in the same year, blaming it all in their farewell letters on unrequited love for Bodenheim; and how, despite all this activity, he found time to write a half-dozen volumes of poetry and at least fifteen novels in the years from 1920 to 1930. One of these novels, a mildly cantharidian work called *Replenishing Jessica*, had the good luck to be condemned by the Society for the Prevention of Vice, and so became a national best seller.

Whatever money he made on it — as well as on *Georgie May* and *Naked on Roller Skates*, his two other successful novels — he spent as fast as it came. Being a freeloader or a free-spender didn't matter too much during the boom years of the Twenties. Besides, Bodenheim's early initiation into hobo life had made him as indifferent as Elijah to the next meal or the need to keep up a front.

Then, with the coming of the Depression, the mood of the Village soured. After the Jazz Era, the Depression was like a long hangover, symbolized by the switch from bathtub gin to coffee, from saloon to cafeteria society.

About this time, Bodenheim and the other charter members of the Greta Garbo Social Club used to make a regular habit of finishing up the long Village night at a cafeteria called Hubert's on Sheridan Square, across the street from the IRT subway. Here they would hold court and pass their hip flasks around until the sweet birds sang, and then linger in the blue light to watch the earliest office workers and clock punchers scurrying down the hole on their way to their jobs. The fame of Hubert's as a bohemian hangout soon spread, attracting crowds of tourists as well as new arrivals in the Village. And at the center of it all, of course, was Bodenheim, as the following bit of vintage doggerel reveals:

In Hubert's famous cafeteria
The girls all suffer from sex hysteria;
They drink a glass of gin or wine
And make a dash for Bodenheim.

From Hubert's the scene shifted over the years to the Life cafeteria, then to Stewart's, then to the Waldorf . . . and with each shift the cast of characters kept growing larger and more varied.

Those vast and tumultuous parliaments of the Marxist Thirties, apocalyptic bull sessions, dumas in which every faction and subfaction of political and sexual malcontent was represented, within them an entire generation sat waiting for Godot and meanwhile passed the time in talk, talk, talk, talk, as if trapped, they were all tyring to talk their way out of life. Here Joe Gould must have filled up at least a half-ton of nickel notebooks for his endless *Oral History*. Sometimes the smog of kitchen fumes, stale breath and tobacco grew so thick that it would drive the customers into the street, still talking, but they always returned to finish the conversation, night after night.

When Godot finally arrived, in the guise of World War II, there was hardly antyhing left to be said; and by the end of the war the doors of the last remaining old-style cafeteria, the Waldorf, stopped revolving forever. Their ghosts still haunt the Village. Just as in the Middle Ages, when a fountain or a flowering tree would miraculously spring up to mark some hallowed spot, two large new banks now occupy the sites where Hubert's and the Waldorf used to stand. . . .

But to get back to Bodenheim. As the Depression deepened, the arc of his career also slumped, and kept on slumping. To the puritanical and self-righteous Marxists who largely took over, his type of bohemianism was considered nothing less than a "petty-bourgeois" deviation. The Greta Garbo Social Club broke up, its members, and the members of their successors. The nymphs too went back where they came from; and their successors in the the local cafeterias, those whey-faced maidens who wore no makeup and boycotted silk stockings ("Down with Japanese imperialism!"), must have thought of Bodenheim as a stimulating conversationalist in bed, but useless on the barricades. Of course he could, and did, Leninize & Stalinize with the best of them; and he even wrote poems in the accepted "proletarian" style, with such glumly descriptive titles as "Home Relief Bureau," "Southern Labor Organizer," "Answering a Trade Union Man," and so on; but it did no good: they knew their man. A more likely commissar there never was.

When his novels fell out of fashion, and publishers stopped handing out advances, Bodenheim joined the W.P.A. Artists' Project. This didn't last too long, for some reason, and he learned how to get by from day to day on petty grift, handouts disguised as loans, heisting books and records from Village stores (that oversized overcoat of his!) and, especially, selling manuscripts of his poems or making them up on the spot in bars and cafeterias.

Through the Thirties and into the war years, he could be found every night at Stewart's or the Waldorf, usually sitting alone, his manila envelope at his side, his pipe fuming, his eyes fixed on the revolving door, waiting for a mark. Already he had the characteristic vulpine expression of his last phase. Whenever he felt hungry he might make a glass of tomato soup out of ketchup and water, or a sandwich out of mustard and relish, then disappear into the Men's Room to wash the stuff down with swigs of raw alcohol tintured with codeine. The management, though disgruntled, tried to look the other way — after all, he was still an attraction for tourists, some of whom could remember a sheiklike Bodenheim. Late at night, after he had collected enough small change to pay for a flop and a bottle of wine, and only then, would he take off and head for the Bowery.

The Bowery, in fact, soon became his haunt as much as the Village. Sometimes he wouldn't be seen for days, and then show up looking rheumy-eyed and bug-ridden, his clothes stained with vomit, talking to himself. Every variety of good-natured and denatured alcohol — the canned heat, the speedballs, the Sneaky Pete, the red-eye, the white-eye, the dead-eye — which he had swilled in such huge quantities over the years, now fermented and heaved up inside of him; and periodically, after blowing his top, he'd be committed for longer and longer spells to the Bellevue Alcoholics Ward.

His old friend Ben Hecht (who was later to write a play based on his life, called *Winkelberg*) used to send him some money once in a while to help out. The money enabled him to live in simple squalor, for a month or so at some fleabag hotel, until he felt well enough to go back on the bum again. Each time he reappeared scrawnier, shabbier, more haunted.

It was this hallucinated Bodenheim, drifting in and out of his mind like the moon through the clouds, muttering at shadows, sniping cigarettes out of the gutter for pipe tobacco, flopping in basements and alleys in the winter and wherever he fell in the summer, the Bodenheim of the late Forties and early Fifties, the poor guy, whose image replaced that of the once flamboyant poet and Village philanderer. Job or Jonah had nothing on Bodenheim. His pride still sustained him, of course, as always, but it also left him open to ridicule and made the stones he ate stonier.

This is where we came in. . . .

About three years before his death, when he was already past Sixty, he met Ruth Fagan, an ex-schoolteacher, ex-reporter, who was destined to share his last great moment with him. She was about thirty years younger, vaguely pretty until you looked close, bright, even literary, but with a long record as a patient in mental institutions. Here if ever was a chance for the heroine of American soap opera to nurse her man back to Health with the balm of her Love and inspire him to reach Success. Instead she gladly went down to his level. And even to keep themselves there, she wasn't too shy to turn a trick now and then, for $5, $2, a bottle of wine, whatever the John would offer; nor was Bodenheim against drumming up trade. It wasn't the first time for him.

During World War II, for instance, when hundreds of lonely sailors used to roam the Village at night looking for action, he is supposed to have supported himself by the following ingenious racket: Spotting a sailor at a crowded bar, Bodenheim would sidle up confidentially, wink, point to any well-stacked wench who happened to be in the place without an escort, and claim to be her agent; then, after collecting her fee and his commission in advance, he'd disappear. (Sometimes, so they say, neither the girl nor the sailor would ever find out how they had both been had.) Bodenheim always maintained a lofty disrespect for private property, sexual or material, his own or other people's.

Procuring for his wife, therefore, was no indication that he didn't love her. On the contrary. And though they had their brawls and quarrels (once they were seen standing on opposite sides of Eighth Street, taking advantage of the moments when the heavy intervening traffic would allow them to catch a glimpse of each other, to hurl quick insults back and forth: "Bitch!" "Wordbotcher!" "Lousy schoolteacher!" "Conniving clodslucker!" and so on), but these quarrels would always be patched up, and then they'd be seen walking arm and arm together as if nothing had happened. In many ways they might have been considered an ideally married couple. They drank out of the same bottle, slept in each other's arms whenever and wherever they could, divided their orts and scraps equally and tenderly.

After their double murder — she ripped open by a kitchen knife, he killed by a bullet in his heart — the newspapers ran their picures and featured articles about them for days, gloating over every detail of the tragedy. The headline in one paper read: HE DIED DEFENDING HER HONOR.

The story goes that they had agreed, reluctantly, to spend the night with the killer in his sleazy furnished room off the Bowery, knowing all the while he was a dangerous psychopath, because it was midwinter and they had no other place to stay; after they arrived Bodenheim sat in a chair near the steam pipe drinking wine and reading Rachel Carson's *The Sea Around Us*, until he dozed off; but was awakened suddenly by screams to find their host trying to rape his wife. Bodenheim jumped up to help her, but the man turned, pulled a gun out of his pocket and shot him at point-blank range, then dropped the gun, picked up a kitchen knife from the table and stabbed her brutally and rhythmically more than twenty times. . . .

Just once more, this time positively, for his final appearance, we'll bring him back. And on the principle that every Yin must have a Yang, matter its anti-matter, and anything that can be stretched can also be squashed, let it be in company with his opposite numero, Joe Gould. "Either," as Shakespeare once said of a similar pair of co-stars, "was the other's mine": they co-substantiate and belong to each other.

One place where Gould & Bodenheim must have met during their careers in the Village was at the Raven, a beat but pre-Beat literary and social club that used to hold poetry readings in various lofts and basements from time to time. Each poet/member-of-the-audience (it was hard to tell which was which) had an equal chance to declaim his poetry to the rest, by mutual sufferance, give and take, something like those old-time Russian steam baths on the East Side where the patrons take turns beating each other with soapy palm fronds. Bodenheim, of course, was always one of the main attractions; but since free wine was usually passed around for inspiration, Gould, too, seldom missed a session.

Most of the time Gould sat silently, with a deceptively absent expression on his face, peering out behind his glasses, behind his eyes, twice-removed, a long cigarette holder tilted between his store-bought teeth at a jaunty angle (so as not to singe his beard) and helped pass the bottle around. But Gould was also a fearsome heckler, with a sharp, Yankee, detergent wit that could cut the crap, quickly and cleanly, whenever the poetic effluvia grew too ripe to bear. After being given the bum's rush one night, for jumping up on a chair, flapping his arms and screeching like a sea gull about to take off, he retaliated by picketing the Raven's outdoor poetry exhibit in Washington Square with a placard which read: "Poets of the World, Ignite! You have nothing to lose but your brains."

Gould's "hipsterism" (for that's what it was, in contrast to Bodenheim's "beatnikism"), combined with his Yankee cracker-barrel shrewdness, gave him a distincitve flavor. He traveled lighter than most people, unburdened by the gravity of self-importance that weighs them down. But how "hip"? And in what way? Of the various kinds and degrees, ranging from the zomboid catalepsy of the junkie to the aesthetic dandyism of a Baudelaire, and from the social poise of Joseph in Egypt to the catstep of a Harlem Negro at a Debutantes' Ball in Georgia, Gould's style was marked by a kind of puckish audacity, somewhere between chutzpah and hubris; his political attitude, noncommittal; his point of view, wry.

But Bodenheim, no doubt, would have considered him a traitor to The Cause.

Anyhow, it is in such a tableau, at the rave, that I like to imagine them: Bodenheim standing within a circle of candlelight on the stage declaiming one of his Beat-style poems against bourgeois fornication, denouncing The System, and Gould sitting in the shadows apart, like an attentive spy or agent-provocateur, taking down his words; or sometimes the picture changes, and there's Bodenheim mounted on a broken-down caballo, sticking his neck, his lance, his inside, out, ready to charge, crying *"Poetry for the Masses! Down with the W.C.T.U. Dieu Defend le Droit! Up yours! . . ."* and with Gould on a burro headed the other way.

Already a new and hungry generation (the "rank and vile" of the Village, as Gould once called them) has appeared on the scene. Yet the cast, as always, contains the same types but with different faces as the generation before: daubers and wordlings, utopiates, psychoanaloids, Raskolnikovs, argonauts up the creek, genies out of a bottle, nymphs in their prisons, hustlers and ponces, misfits and sterlings, breeders and draculae, wreckers and Trotskyites, gynanders and androgynes, Goths and Romans, Pagliaccis, pascudniks, slum-faced grubniks, Calligulae-Calligularum . . . and to many of these newcomers, Gould & Bodenheim may be no more than a pair of names.

So, for their sake, now, and for the sake of newer and even hungrier generations to come, something ought to be done. What I have in mind is nothing grandiose — perhaps a pair of memorial statues in the "constructivist" or junk school of modern sculpture, to be erected in some out-of-the-way corner of Washington Square Park. And they must be abstract, too: for as symbolic Hipster & Beatnik it's hard to tell whether the contours of their personalities are self-defined or belong to the social space that rounds and presses in on them from all sides.

Gould is easy. He can be represented by a working model of one of those old-fashioned barber poles (the kind that swallows up itself), and with a housewrecker's basketball-sized steel ball set on top bristling all over with spiky penpoints. As for Bodenheim, his statue should be at least ten feet high and set in the foreground, as befits a hero in the same class at Theseus and Finn Maccool. Let it be made of broken wine bottles, Sterno cans, rusty bedsprings, old Salvation Army bugles, missing coat buttons, and such, all wired and soldered together in eccentric cubist planes and angles; with the whole mass tilted precariously forward, as if about to topple, but checked and balanced by a long pole, perhaps a fireman's pole, protruding boldly and defiantly. And to crown the figure, a battered and punctured aluminum soup pot, upside down, like a knight's casque, should be slanted obliquely so as to focus the rays of the setting sun through two holes in the bottom, and allow them to blaze down into the eyes of his admirers.

(1963)

A Discourse on Hip

Our age demands something more: it demands, if not lofty then
at least loud-voiced pathos, if not speculation then surely results,
if not truth then conviction, if not honesty then at least affidavits
to that effect, if not emotion then incessant talk about it. It
therefore mints quite a different species of privileged faces.

— S. Kierkegaard, *The Concept of Irony*

He must have seen me coming a half a block away at the same time I
spotted him, a ? stooped over an I, in the alcove of a combination Health
Food & Head shop on 8th St. where he had set himself up for the night.
No doubt a panhandler, I figured, but even for the Village *what a panhandler.* His tall and wiry frame was bent over what seemed, at first, a
kind of pilgrim's staff but was really, I saw as I came closer, an old mopstick, with a VOTE FOR BELLA ABZUG shopping bag crammed with his orts
and scraps and other personal garbage at his feet, which of course were
bare, scabbed, and encrusted with funk, and though it was mid-August
he had draped himself in a thick brown army blanket, folded double, with
a hole cut in the center, through which his bald and knobby peanut-shaped
head, festooned beneath with a beard like Father Time's, poked out balefully and periscopically as he watched me coming toward him, step by step,
staring down as I went at the scuffed-out graffiti on the sidewalk (ZOOS
φυχs AFFERDITE), then over my shoulder (not out of fear, but hoping
that someone might come by and pass ahead of me), then off into an inner distance, anything to break the social contract we had sealed with that
first exchange of looks, but every time I risked a glance in his direction
I felt the needles of his eyes fixed and flashing in mine, it was too late,
he knew I knew he knew he had me, glommed, so that I found myself
unconsciously slanting toward the edge of the curb, half teetering there,
in a hurry now to get past and go free, and almost had it made, I thought,

Originally published as "Down in the Village: A Discourse on Hip. Or, Watch Out
for the Cynosure," in the *New American Review* 13 (1971).

when he abruptly raised and jabbed his stick like a long extended middle finger straight at me, at the same time thrusting out his neck and his jaw as far as the sinews could stretch, and barked: παρακαραττειν το νομισμα — or something like that — but with such rabid and convulsive fury that I jumped, astonished, back off the sidewalk, as if I had just heard a talking dog.

His cachinnations woke up the whole street. From a hallway nearby a junkie, nodding, roused himself from his catatonia for a moment to hold out a cupped hand and burble, "Man . . ." as I went past, shaking my head, but right into a midnight-blue black in a flowered dashiki, with a topiary afro to match, who spread-eagled his arms to stop me, "Brother . . ." so that to dodge him I had to cross over to the other side of the street, where a girl with that blue gaze (*which lies!*) and a privileged face, no doubt no more than sweet sixteen, but already turned rancid, brushed up to me, smiling her mouth, "Sir . . ." and as I shook her off, finished in one blurt, "Spare 'nychange?" and . . .

Where do they all come from? Suddenly one day, one month, one year — I'm not sure which — there they all were as if spontaneously generated by the times. And that first character, the Cerberean dog who had snarled and barked at me from the alcove, he seemed almost uncanny, an apparition out of the ancient world, and yet in a way the leader of the whole park. Of all the changes on the Village scene, their appearance nowadays is without doubt the most protentous.

You can run into them at any time along the curbs, an entirely new breed of local *bhikku*, more like bill collectors from society at large than mere beggars. They outnumber the winos from the Bowery and even outhustle the familiar Village clochards who once had the streets to themselves. And with few exceptions they are mainly young, making out from day to day by making do on small change and petty grift because why not. Except for a stash of pot, maybe some acid now and then, and a sufficiency of pills, their needs are minuscule. Accordingly, they travel light, without the usual baggage of the superego (having seen through the foutrescence of it all), refusing not only to provide a good or a service to the community but also to pay their dues, like decent panhandlers, by feigning gratitude or shame. Like Mao's guerrilla fish, they survive in the bottom sea of Village life by mingling with the hoi polloi of heads, dropouts, gynanders & androgynes, bike faggots, orgyasmic groupies, stargazers, shamans & warlocks, apocalyptic utopiates, dinamiteros, tricksters & ponces, radical chicsas, bleeders & draculae, and all the rest. Very few of them can get up the steep rents required to live here; yet they still consider the Village turf their own, as the rightful heirs of bohemia, and cling to it, though the grass may actually be greener and cheaper somewhere else. At the end of the long

> — *Man, is this the same shit you laid on me the last time?*
> — *No, this is some new shit. This is better shit.*
> — *Man, this had better be better shit than the last shit.*
> — *You know I wouldn't just shit you, man, this is the best shit around. This is good clean shit.*

Village night they go back (if not to their parental homes) via F train to the dense cloacal slums of Harlem or via crosstown bus to crash pads in the lower intestinal depths of the East Side, where they come from.

Yet as part of a still inchoate international and quasi-religious movement, they might just as well have come from communes on the shores of the Red Sea, by way of Katmandu or Marrakesh or Angkor Wat, after starting out, perhaps, by smoking the eucharist among cells of true believers in Dubuque, say, or in the catacombs of Chattanooga, or . . . from anywhere at all, in fact, where the gospel of the Hip has penetrated — to rearrive by the usual underground commodius vicus back to Washington Square and environs, where it's still supposed to be at. *It* being the Scene, *at* what you make of it. And to swell it, also coming from all over, like the mendicant hippies, to do their own numbers, the spear carriers of various Hip-related causes have made their entrance in recent years.

At the corner of 8th and Sixth outside of Nathan's *Famous* — as if the Village had become a freaked-out Coney Island — there are sometimes a half-dozen different factions competing for space and decibels: Black Panther teen-age militants in tennis shoes and leather jackets selling the party newspaper (*Check it out, brother! Hip yourself to the truth. Check it out!*) mainly to honkie sympathizers; also, "Legalize Marijuana" martyrs smoking pot in the open and grabbing passersby off the streets to sign petitions; also, Women's Lib and Gay Lib activists picketing the sexists and straight-and-narrows; also, part-time student anarchists, "Free Palestine" graffiti commandos, Maoists, and the like, scattering leaflets and shouting their slogans sometimes a yard apart. And once in a while, to blow everybody's mind, there arrives a troupe of Hare Krishna addicts in saffron robes banging cymbals and hopping about while chanting their mantic chant, "Hare Krishna Krishna Krishna Hare Hare . . ." endlessly, with their own surrealistically pink and earnest mid-American faces, plain as pie despite the shaved heads and the Indian getup, contrasting oddly with the crushed, harried municipal-gray types that hurry on past.

Once again, it goes without saying, hardly any of the aforementioned

133

weirdos and agitators actually live here. In fact, even homegrown Village weirdos and agitators have gradually been forced out and compelled to move somewhere else. Likewise very few starving artists can afford to starve here any more.

For what with rent controls and the passage of laws designating the Village a "national historic area," or whatever, to keep it from being bulldozed by speculators, the Village has slowly become fossilized instead. Those decrepit old brownstones and sagging townhouses on the side streets, whole rows of them, where the young just starting out or people just making out could live, almost all have now been taken over as private residences by those who have made it or already had it made for them. And even those raunchy walk-up-six-flight tenements and loft buildings, with their communal johns in the hallways and warped and tilted Dr. Caligari walls and floors, but which provided large artists' studios and cheap apartments, have been eviscerated and the hulks chopped up into high-rent cubicles. The facades are the same, but the people behind them are different. Someone once remarked—maybe I did, but it doesn't matter—that the Village, with its unpredictably digressive streets and twisting free-associational byways, was divided from the straight and squared-away world uptown like the ego from the id; but the universal solvent of money on one side, and the adoption of a fashionable Hip style on the other, coming together, have blurred that distinction. Nevertheless, since the facades of the Village have remained the same, like a stage set, anyone who has lived here long enough to have passed through various personal metamorphoses and transfigurations can encounter on almost every street the ghosts of former selves, lost personae, forgotten identities. It is, not to be too analytical, the widespread Village affliction of anamnesis, or *déjà vu*, the feeling that one's past may be lurking about somewhere, psychologically equivalent to the head-swiveling backward-looking tie of people afraid of being mugged by someone coming up behind them. . . . But I digress.

Like the buildings themselves, all those avant-garde and bohemian causes first proclaimed in the Village have also, though keeping their facades, become somewhat fossilized. For instance, now that prudery in the U.S. has been wiped out almost as thoroughly as polio, the erstwhile "sublimation" of sex into vaporous spiritual inanities has been turned about, arsyversy, by an equally false "inspissation" of the spirit into mucky sexual inanities. Again, the feminist demands for equality and freedom, put into practice long ago in the Village, have now become the ideological dildoes of Women's Lib. In politics, too, the passionate yet sectarian radicalism that once inspired (and also consumed) a generation of Villagers has come

134

to provide parlor patter for well-to-do ne'er-do-wells and, as staled in the mouths of the somewhat less than New Left, with their mindless and self-righteous sloganizing and

ceduceduceduceduceducedu
ce*duceduceducedu*cedu
ceduceduceduceduceducedu

Know Nothing violence, it has inadvertently pointed the way for any future American fascism. *Also sprach Zarathustra.* In sum, the nonconformist and dissenting spirit of the Village, in art, literature, manners & morals, has by its very success (Marx would have called it a "negation of the nega-tion") resulted in the establishment of a new kind of disestablishmentarian Establishment. (Of which the *Village Voice*, with a circulation of over 150,000, may be said to be the echo.) Yet the facades, naturally, are still the same.

The life-style of the Village since World War II, the Hip, has undergone the same sort of transmogrification. *"Mais où, dîtes-moi, où . . ." sont* the snows and the tourists of yesteryear, who used to come down to the Village with their maps and guidebooks, cameras dangling from their necks, and nudge each other whenever they spotted a typical beatnik or maybe a boheme. They've all gone Hip. ("Yet utter the word Democratic, the word En-Masse.") For with the advent of the Hip as a mass evangelical move-ment, heralded by all the media, what has emerged is not, as sometimes claimed, a sub- or a counter-, but part of the boss, culture, right now the most booming and successful new stand on the American midway.

Having heard the call at last, thousands of weekend communicants from the square 9-to-5 world out there — people born with corners, but recently turned on and converted — take over the Village scene. They are the same so-called "middle" Americans, members of that "Lonely Crowd" described by sociologists, who, fifty years ago might have attended chruch festivities. During the week they are involved in getting and spending, making it in one fashion or another, but the competitive "scrimmage of appetite" and status-seeking that was the mode of life for generations before theirs has lost meaning for them.

Comes the Sabbath, therefore, and as night begins to fall, tourists of all ages, colors, classes, and genders throng through the streets of the Vil-lage in long slow peristaltic waves, spilling over the sidewalks into the honk-ing, even slower-moving traffic, going nowhere but anywhere in search of the Way Out, which is the Hip *tao*, the Far Out, past psychedelicatessens offering vibrators, electric dildoes, pot papers, water beds, hubblebubble pipes, Kama-Sutra Oil, black lights, Day-glo decals, phallic candles, stained-glass granny specs (*"Spare 'nychange?"*), and on past gay leather shops, mod schlock shops, rock record shops, past reeking incense carts and reekier pizza parlors, carts selling tacos. souvlaki, organic heroes, Tibetan prayer beads, ankhs, past newsstands stacked with the latest *Stud, Screw, Box, Eat, Flesh, Orgy,* with a pervasive sexual fever, as the night grows late, rising among them, the fairies cruising up and down for trade, girls of all ages alone or in pairs looking for action ("The Female equally with the Male I sing") just as aggressively as the men, pickups and putdowns, swaps and cross-connections being made and unmade all around, here and there a black-white or white-black couple, arm in arm, passing through, yet no one casting a stony glance, and with many in the crowd, obviously, spaced on acid or zomboid on junk, some even lighting up and passing joints around right

> *—Man, where do you get this shit? You call this good shit?*
> *—Just give the shit a chance, man, don't rush this shit.*

in the open, the smell mingling with all the other reeks and stinks so that no one, not even the cops, knew where it came from, or cared. The scene, after all, belonged to them. So Rome in its time must have been taken over by romanized Goths, Greece by hellenized Romans.

Sometimes the temptation arises to shope me in the latest Hip shrouds, like Piers the Plowman, with a beard and a fright wig to match, and join that "faire felde ful of folke" . . . but the impulse as quickly fades. It's their scene. And should any long-time Villager—Hip, too, like, but of an older dispensation—happen to be caught abroad in that crowd, maneuvering his way through along the curb with a copy of the *Times* under his arm, he would no doubt appear to them the way tourists in the past had once seemed to him: displaced, cornered, and uptight.

History, as it turns, has a reverse left-handed and ironical spin of its own.

Which leads us back to our first question: *Where do they all come from?* And then another: *How did they all get here?* and finally: *Whence cometh the Hip?* Here follows then, with constant reference to the Village scene, a brief speculative discourse on the history, phenomenology, sociology, and soteriology of the Hip.

To start with, take the circle in Washington Square, that inverted mandala around which generations of Villagers have met and turned each other on. As the consecrated navel of bohemia, it was for them no less allowed a spot than, say, the omphalos at Delphi for the Greeks or the double ring of menhirs at Stonehenge for the Druids. But this can also be interpreted as a kind of cryptogram of the Village ethos. Enclosed within its own Hip circle of values, the Village was able to keep its distance from, yet still orient itself ironically toward, the square world outside. But now that the Hip has become a life-style for millions, with an ever more expanding circumference, an almost miraculous presto-chango transvaluation of values has occurred: the Village has been squared within its own circle, or, as they say, blown its cover. . . . Never to be recovered.

The irony in this turnabout, with the Hip being outhipped, is irony conceived out of and against itself: *for the Hip, as manifested in the Village, is merely the local habitation and the name assumed by irony in our times.*

Kierkegaard, himself an Ur-Hip prophet, saw it coming long ago: "Should a new manifestation of irony appear, it must be insofar as subjectivity asserts itself in a still higher form. It must be subjectivity raised to the second power, a subjectivity of subjectivity, corresponding to reflection on reflection."

The "I^2" autistic and anarchist Dadaists around World War One would have been viewed by Kierkegaard as fulfillment of this prophecy. When the French Dadaist Marcel Duchamp, for instance, painted a moustache on the face of the Mona Lisa (who must have been smiling expectantly through the centuries waiting for him to do just that), it was graffiti applied to the face of the entire traditional, i.e. "square," esthetic and moral order she represented, to "*épater les bourgeois,*" as they used to say. Yet even — I mean especially — for the bourgeois themselves, that order has now disappeared. No case of a bourgeois being épatéd by art (except perhaps in the Soviet Union) has been reported in the last fifty years. What has taken the place of the established art of the past is, of course, the avant-garde, featuring Dada itself. How then can another moustache, "corresponding to reflection on reflection," be painted on that moustache? Come to think of it, the dadaization of Dada into official culture, enshrined in all the museums, may actually be that Higher Moustache — what Kierkegaard, in another context, must have meant by "the secret trap door through which one is suddenly hurled downward . . . into the infinite nothingness of irony."

Back now to the Village. Shortly after World War II, when the social conditions out of which the Hip emerged were still without form, and void, the prevailing mood was one of disenchantment with the jejune radical politics of the thirties. Of course there were still many faithful Stalinoid and Trotskyite utopiates around in those days, waiting patiently for the first Workers' State

That enormous self-consuming rat
That piecemeal nibbles itself fat

to wither away, but most of the Village intelligentsia had finally come to recognize that concentration camps, police terror, bureaucratic censorship, and even murder, of artists, the racial extinction and uprooting of whole peoples, etc., no matter how rationalized by ideologizers, were not what they had meant by "socialism" at all. The "party line" was for what it always had been, a "line." During the same period, the new venerable "modernism" that had kept American artists swaddled by Europe began to seem more and more constrictive. The unswaddling occurred with the so-called "Action" or "Abstract Expressionist" painters (centered around the old Cedar Tavern and the San Remo in the Village), through whom Kierkegaard's "subjectivity of subjectivity" was at last realized and the act itself of painting the painting itself became its own content.

But the chief, if not "onlie," begetter of the Hip in those years, from which it derived both its name and intrinsic features, was jazz. I mean the "cool," oblique, and involuted jazz of the late forties and early fifties, as often cacophonous as lyrical, sometimes called "bop," conceived by Charlie Parker, Dizzy, Monk, Mingus, Miles, Coltrane, and many others not so well known. In the uptown as well as Village dives where they appeared, they came on more like a conspiracy of soliloquists than a band of "mere" musicians. The subtle and complex interiors and angles of refraction of this new jazz gave the emergent Hip its mirror image. And along with it, in the roles of performers, hangers-on, or dealers, there entered the Village scene a much larger and distinctive caste of uptown blacks (known as Negroes in those days or, if the personal coefficients worked out, spades), but all nephews of Uncle X, who brought with them — new at the time — heroin, as well as an easy supply of grass. Their cultivated "cool" — similar to the classic Greek *ataraxia* — was a practical virture, enabling them to maintain grace under pressure of a hostile white society. For they had to remove, by whatever solvent, a stain on the psyche deep-dyed by generations of slavery and near-slavery: the black original sin of being black. Going for them, too, was an elaborately ritualized Aesopian jive, irony employed as a verbal screen, by which they could manage to remain within and yet apart from the ofay culture.

That jive, of course, has now become the *lingua franca* of the young, black and white, throughout the U.S., and so no longer Hip but square. But the intent of those original bop hipsters was no different from what the late Joe Gould, years ago, discerned as the real motive behind the boost in the subway fare from a nickel to a dime; "To keep out the hoi polloi"; and was certainly no worse, either, than what snobs and pedants intend when they create their own apartheid by quoting Greek and Latin tags.

So then, to condense this chronicle (brief enough to be printed small on one side of a strip of ZigZag): by the mid-fifties in the Village the Hip style had already been formed — *adoxia*, contempt for public opinion, whether in politics or art; *anaideia*, a profound "jemenfoutiste," or Fuck You, attitude in matters of sex, drugs, living habits, morality in general; and *adiaphoron*, a cultivated indifference to the social hangups of race, religion, status, money, etc. By the mid-fifties, too, the first psychedelic drugs, peyote and, somewhat later, LSD, appeared behind drawn shades; and to provide atmospheric cover for the sunbursts of illumination and/or hallucination imploded by these drugs, such native as well as Far Eastern esoterica as Zen, yoga, vedanta, tantric Buddhism, ESP, astrology, shamanism, and the like, found many converts. The Village scene, too, was transplanted onto college campuses, among faculty as well as students, with large colonies of the Hip in Chicago and San Francisco. Grass, tea, shit, boo, fu, hemp, birdseed . . . name your metonymy, was by now become foison o' the glebe — and, incidentally, as an absurd cultural byproduct of the immigration of Puerto Ricans into New York, the tag for the stuff became affixed as "pot," after the Spanish *potiguaya*, meaning the crude, unstrained weed with its twigs and seeds. It had been Herbert Hoover, after all, who had warned as far back as 1932 that grass

> — *Man, do you really get high on this shit? This shit's got no wings, man.*
> — *Man, even if you can't get high on this shit, it'll at least turn you sideways. I mean, get lost.*

would grow in the city streets if Roosevelt were elected; and he was right; but he couldn't have foreseen that it would also spread to the previously lush suburbs . . . and so throughout middle America. And wherever there's grass, the Hip way of life is sure to follow.

Notwithstanding, there was a low-barometric dead calm of boredom during those late Eisenhower years of the sort that precedes social hurricanes and private hysteria.

When it hit the fan, finally, the newborn yawp of the Beat movement was heard across the land, then further amplified by a responsive bleat in all the media. Not too long after, Timothy Leary's Transcendental Medicine Show arrived on the scene, which by now was the American big-time, promoting Instant Hallelujah Cubes for the suffering masses under the slogan: "Tune in! Turn on! Drop out!" To millions of the young and not so young, yoked to treadmill jobs or stuck in the adolescent detention camps of high schools and schools of higher learning, it was

139

a call to freedom and self-fulfillment. There followed, as we know, a mass conversion.

Since jazz had become both too far-out and too hermetic, as if grudging the intrusion of an audience, the gospel that suited these new converts best was rock, with its free-for-all revivalist enthusiasm. Much more was involved, however, than merely a generational shift in taste. The "cool" and ironic suspension of disbelief by the old Hip, tolerating your truth, his truth, my truth, everybody's true truth, was replaced by the clairvoyant certainties of acid and the instantaneous soap-bubble absolutes of pot. This also permitted the neo-Hip to take up a variety of social causes (including the cause of Hip itself) with the fanatic self-righteousness and eagerness for martyrdom of a church militant.

The entire movement that originated in the Village has thus been split into what might be called a hinayana and a mahayana Hippism, with the Lesser Vehicle as doctrinally pure as ever because free from all doctrine, though now somewhat creaky and running down, and the Greater still gathering converts and momentum along the moebius curve of the seventies . . .

. . . Which is a curve that twists backward on itself. For having taken Kierkegaard's concept of irony, in its latest avatar as the Hip, right up to the present, we now have to turn back, along the same curve, to the very source of irony among the Greeks of the fourth century B.C. And when we do so, peering at them reflectively as through the wrong end of a telescope until they dwindle in the mind, dwindle and diminish into minikins, diminkins . . . we also must do a double-take, for there *we* are, as large as life!

What I mean is that the ironic style had social consequence for the Greeks similar to our own, resulting in a "proto-Hip" movement throughout the ancient world.

As the chief exemplar and master there stands the baffling figure of Socrates. Since his very existence was grounded in irony, he is as difficult to perceive in himself (Kierkegaard well knew) as "to depict an elf wearing a hat that renders him invisible." Of course this is not the noble drag-queen Socrates ventriloquized by Plato in his dialogues, too Good to be True (or Beautiful), but the cranky, bibulous, henpecked and argumentative old layabout of Athens, the ironical Socrates, who confessed his ignorance so as to confound the wise, and under the pretense of being taught, taught others. He deliberately went about Athens seeking philosophical arguments with the Sophists and other pretenders to the truth, making himself a pain in the ass of hypocrisy and pomposity; and very often, as one of his biographers relates, "he was treated with great violence and beaten, and pulled about, and laughed at and ridiculed by the multitude. But he bore all this with great equanimity." The "dialectical method" (so called) employed by Socrates in these street debates with Sophists, proceeding through paradox and antithesis back to the *a priori* grounds of their beliefs, which then gave way, to leave them dangling on the reversed hook of his ¿, was meant as much to conceal as to reveal his own thoughts. His irony was thus conceived by him as a stratagem by which to bypass the mind's printed circuits of rehearsed responses and acceptable ideas. It was, in the old Hip word, "down."

Kierkegaard described it as "infinite absolute negativity," and explains: "It is negativity because it only negates; it is infinite because it negates not this or that phenomenon but the totality of the present age; and it is absolute because it negates by virtue of a higher [i.e., future] actuality which is not." For the sake of freedom, but a negative freedom, Kierkegaard adds, the Socratic ironist refuses to cast himself in any other role than that of spectator, preferring even boredom — "this eternity void of content, this bliss without enjoyment, this superficial profundity, this hungry satiety" — to taking an active part in the world's farce.

When he was brought to trial for his life, as an enemy of the Athenian democracy, he explained his apolitical attitude (as set down by Plato in *The Defence*):

> I go round privately thrusting my advice on everybody and you may well wonder why I do not take my place on the speakers' platform and offer it to the *polis*. I have often told you why. It is due to the divine voice that has attended on me since I was a boy. This is a voice that never prompts me to do anything, but only forbids. It orders me not to engage in politics and I have nothing but gratitude for its advice. Well you know, Men of Athens, that if I had meddled in politics before now, I should have been dead and of no use to you or to myself.

And yet he was executed for his nonparticipation as well as if he had engaged in plotting against the state. When his wife said to him, "You die undeservedly," he is supposed to have answered, "Would you then have me deserve death?" Socrates, who was a stone-cutter by trade (some say a slave), *prided* himself upon the simplicity of his life, went about barefoot in a torn, ill-fitting leather coat, and used to say that those who require the fewest things are nearest to the gods.

Upon the death of Socrates in 399 B.C., one of his closest disciples, an Athenian rhetorician named Antisthenes, determined to put into practice the preachments of the master by living as a mendicant philosopher, indifferent to external circumstances and public opinion. He used to lecture, it is said, near a gymnasium called Cynosargus, as a result of which his adherents became known as Cynics (literally, "dogs" or "snarlers"), meant to be pejorative, as "beatniks" and "hippies" in our own day. He himself was tagged with the opprobrious nickname of Haplocyon ("downright dog"). Antisthenes chose to go about Athens dirty and barefoot, let his hair and beard grow long, and dressed winter and summer in a ragged double-folded cloak, under which he wore nothing at all, as if to show his contempt for appearances. (Once, while Socrates was still alive, Antisthenes turned a rent in his cloak outside, and Socrates is said to have remarked: "I see your vanity through the hole in your cloak.") With the addition of a walking staff and a sack to contain food and other necessities, Antisthenes' costume became the standard garb for all the Cynics. Again following the lead of their master, they went out of their way to offend and outrage convention by the use of scatological language and by defecating, masturbating, and copulating in public.

The immediate predecessors of the Cynics were itinerant and mendicant Orphic preachers, who taught that there was a blessed life after death in which all the world's wrongs would be righted; but Antisthenes inverted their doctrine, claiming that only in this world, because it was the only world, were justice and happiness possible. He advocated a return to a state of nature, without shams and hypocrisies, and the reduction of desire, ambition, pleasure, love of others as well as of possessions to a point of extinciton. Antisthenes also taught the inherent equality of men and women — as, for that matter, of all classes and races of human beings — and called for the creation of a world state, or rather, non-state (coining the word *Kosmopolis*), where there would be neither ruler nor ruled. As the greatest of all blessings, he named freedom; for which reason he also chose Hercules as patron saint of the Cynics, for Hercules was a mortal who had lived without constraints and had risen to be a god by his own efforts.

It was not the founder, however, but a later disciple, the celebrated Diogenes, who became in the world's eyes the cynosure (there it is) of the Cynic movement.

Diogenes was whelped in the Milesian colony of Sinope on the Euxine Sea, and important trading center at the time between Greece and the Near and Far East. He must therefore have early become acquainted by means of travelers passing through Sinope with the religious teachings of the Magi of Babylonia and the Hindu gymnosophists of India. His father was a money-changer; and there is a disputed story that Diogenes during his youth became involved in a conspiracy to adulterate the currency of Greece. After consulting the Delphic oracle for advice on whether to continue in this fraud, he was seemingly encouraged to do so; but Diogenes did not comprehend that the oracle was really advising him to alter the *customs* of Greece, since the word νομισμα is ambiguous, meaning both "coinage" and "customs." This Delphic utterance was later adopted as the slogan of the Cynics: παρχαραττειν ("Change the Currency," or, "Revaluate Values).

For his crime as a forger, Diogenes was banished and sold into slavery, becoming the property of an Athenian named Xeniades. His pride was such that when he was put on the block, and the auctioneer asked him what he could do, Diogenes answered, "Govern men — give notice that if anyone wants to purchase a master, there is a master here for him." Transported to Athens, he served as a tutor in Xeniades' household for a number of years, after which he was given his freedom. He soon attached himself to the Cynics surrounding Antisthenes, becoming the most noted of all upon the death of the leader in 371 B.C.

Two tales concerning Diogenes have become legendary: first, that he made his home in a barrel (like John Q. Taxpayer in American cartoons) and took it with him wherever he went; and second, that he walked through the streets of Athens in broad daylight with a lit candle looking for an honest man. But it doesn't seem likely that the Cynic who tried to reduce his needs to nullity would have wasted a candle on such a (to him) hopeless quest; and as for the barrel, it was really a large wine jar, an idea that came to him, so he said, when he observed a snail carrying its shell around. Diogenes even gave up eating off a plate in favor of a hollowed-out loaf of bread, also threw away his bowl when he realized he could drink water out of his cupped hands. In order to inure himself against hardship, during the summer he would roll naked in the hot sands, during the winter embrace marble pillars covered with ice and snow. Once he was seen begging alms from a statue, and when asked why, replied, "To get into practice in being refused." He visited whorehouses to wrangle with the whores, hoping in this way both to sharpen his tongue and learn how to bear insults without losing his *ataraxia*. Once when he was mocked by the people for having been sold into slavery as a forger by his native city, he said, "The people of Sinope condemned me to banishment, but I condemned them to be themselves and to remain where they were." Another time, when he was seen going into a theater while everyone was coming out, and was asked why, replied, "It is what I have been doing all my life." One day as he was squatting down in the marketplace to eat his mess of leftovers, and several bystanders reviled him by calling out "Dog!" he retorted, "It is you who are the dogs for standing around and drooling while I am at dinner."

Diogenes felt no shame or impropriety in stealing from temples dedicated to the gods (just as hippies nowadays rip off department stores and credit card agencies), arguing as follows: "Everything belongs to the gods; wise men are the friends of the gods; and all things are shared among friends. Therefore, everything belongs to wise men." He repeatedly declared that an easy life had been given to men by the gods, but that they had spoiled it by seeking for luxuries and pleasures. By indolence and apathy the Cynic could display his indifference toward society, for he felt that to engage in trade or manual labor would be to lose caste; on the contrary, as a philosopher he considered himself at least the equal of emperors and kings. When in need of money for food, so that he had to go out and panhandle along the curbs of Athens, he said that he was merely reclaiming what belonged to him, not begging. He took immediate advantage of whatever place was convenient, whether public gardens or the porticoes of temples or the colonnades of state buildings, to sleep in or to answer a call of nature, asserting that "the Athenians had built him a place in which to live."

Diogenes apparently had no sexual needs, and would lecture anyone who cared to listen that copulation was the business of those who had nothing better to do, citing with approval the opinion of the philosopher Democritus that "Orgasm is merely a slight attack of apoplexy." Yet he also held that marriage as an institution should be nullified and all women be possessed in common, with the children of such unions becoming the responsibility of society at large. And . . . so forth.

Finally, Diogenes made this boast: "I have vanquished poverty, exile, disrepute; yea, and anger, pain, desire, fear, and the most redoubtable beast of all, treacherous and cowardly, I mean pleasure. All alike have succumbed to her . . . all, that is, save myself."

Most of the Cynics, however, were not opposed to pleasure, sexual or otherwise, merely the excessive pursuit of it; and no doubt would have approved of the present drug culture for the immediacy of the satisfactions it offers. Diogenes' bone-dry asceticism was a function of his own personality.

When Plato, who lived in Athens at the same time, was asked to characterize Diogenes, he replied, "That man is Socrates — gone mad." A statement of which Kierkegaard (though for some reason, the Great Dane never gave the Cynics their due as the heirs of Socrates) would have approved, for he perceived that the ultimate effect of the Socratic irony would be to "reinforce vanity in its vanity and render madness more mad." Diogenes himself used to say that most men were within a finger's breadth of being mad; for, he argued, if anyone were to walk through the streets of Athens while stretching out his middle finger he would be considered mad, yet if it were his forefinger, no one would pay any mind. On one occasion, when he was asked, "What sort of man, O Diogenes, do you think Socrates?" he replied, "A madman," thereby turning the tables on Plato through his own master. What he meant was a higher madness, a condign madness, so to speak, suited to a mad world. All metaphysical speculation on the ultimate nature of reality he ridiculed as a symptom of this madness, akin to the endless cupidity of misers and the insatiable ambition of kings. Once, while Plato was discoursing at a banquet on his Ideas, and using the terms "tableness" and "cupness," Diogenes interrupted, "I, O Plato, see a table and a cup, but I see no 'tableness' or 'cupness'"; and another time, to refute Plato's definition, "Man is a featherless biped," he plucked a chicken and brought it into the Academy, saying, "This is Plato's man," then added to the definition, " . . . with broad flat nails." He loved to play the yippie clown.

The life of Diogenes (412–323) and that of Alexander the Great (356–323) were regarded by their contemporaries as mirror opposites: the anti-hero and the hero, slave and emperor, the old man who had reduced desires to nothingness and the youthful conqueror of the world who wept that there were no new worlds to conquer. It was Diogenes' claim that he enjoyed life in his wine jar as much as any king in his palace. And Alexander seemed to agree, for when he asked at one time who he would rather be, other than himself, he answered, "Diogenes." According to tradition (or to the myth engendered by their contrast), Diogenes and Alexander died on the same day of the same year.

A meeting between them actually took place in Corinth, in 336 B.C., when Diogenes lay sprawled out in the marketplace, basking in the sun. Alexander, who had just taken the city, saw him there and left his entourage to stand beside him, saying:

"I am Alexander, the great king."

"And I am Diogenes the dog."

"Why are you called a dog?"

"Because I fawn upon those who give me anything, bark at those who give me nothing, bite those who annoy me."

"Then ask any favor you wish."

"Cease to shade me from the sun."

This incident occurred during the first year of Alexander's reign, when he was only 22 years old; but ten years later, after the battle of the Hydaspes had opened up the whole northern India and the Punjab to his armies, the astonished emperor encountered what must have seemed like hundreds of carbon-copy Diogeneses baked black in the sun, "a people" (Alexander wrote in dispatch) "professing a rigid and austere philosophy, yet even more frugal than Diogenes, since they go altogether naked." These were the gymnosophists (literally, "naked philosophers") whose religious ideas Diogenes had encountered as a youth in Sinope. Quite possibly, too, Alexander and his armies might also have met with monks worshipping the Buddha, whose "Fire Sermon," preached 150 years or so earlier, was the ultimate expression of salvation through renunciation:

> Everything, Bhikkus, is on fire. . . . The eye is on fire, the visible is on fire, the knowledge of the visible is on fire, the contact with the visible is on fire, be it pleasure, be it pain, be it neither pleasure nor pain. By what fire is it kindled? By the fire of lust, by the fire of hate, by the fire of delusion it is kindled, by birth age death pain lamentation sorrow grief despair it is kindled. . . .

> Knowing this, Bhikkus, the wise man . . . becomes weary of the eye, he becomes weary of the visible, he becomes weary of the knowledge of the visible, he becomes weary of the contact of the visible, he becomes weary of the feeling which arises from the contact of the visible, be it pleasure, be it pain, be it neither pleasure nor pain. He becomes weary of the ear: pain. He become weary of the nose: pain. He becomes weary of the tongue: pain. He becomes weary of the body: pain. He becomes weary of the mind: pain.

> When he is weary of these things, he becomes empty of desire. When he is empty of desire, he becomes free. When he is free he knows that he is free, that rebirth is at an end, that virtue is accomplished, that duty is done, and that there is no more returning to this world.

Upon the homecoming of Alexander's soldiers to Greece, the ascetic religious values they had absorbed and brought back gained currency — or rather, as the Cynics kept insisting, changed it — throughout the empire. The great majority of the Cynics and their supporters were drawn from the lowest classes, the slaves, outcasts, beggars, and also from among the women. From out of the same social matrix, centuries later, emerged the congregations of the primitive Christian churches. The monks and anchorites who fled from the declining Roman civilzation into the wilderness were actually late heirs of the Cynics. The Cynic movement itself endured far into classical times, a familiar part of the Roman scene as it had been of the Greek . . . and is now under another incarnation, part of our own. The Emperor Julian (the Apostate), as late—or as early—as the fourth century A.D. said of it: "Cynicism seems to be in some ways a universal philosophy, and the most natural," For it also seems to erupt most dramatically when the currency of values with which people spend their lives has been altered, and devalued, not by themselves but by historical forces beyond their control. Kierkegaard again: "For the ironic subject the given actuality has completely lost its validity; it has become for him an imperfect form which everywhere constrains. He does not possess the new, however, he only knows the present does not correspond to the idea of this future."

The death of Diogenes, when he was close to 90, befitted a man who had preached self-denial and renunciation: he simply held his breath until he was suffocated. The Corinthians are said to have erected over his grave a pillar, surmounted by a dog carved in Parian marble. Shortly before his end, he had asked to be buried on his face; and when asked why, replied, "Because in a while, everything will be turned upside down." And so it was, and many times thereafter. While he lived, however, Diogenes placed his own ! under the Socratic ?, depending his very being on it . . .

. . . Which is where I came in. *Where was I?* I was standing on the corner, about to step off the curb, when I suddenly remembered—*of course!*— and turned back, half running, as if late for some urgent appointment. It was one of those Village nights, after 4 A.M., when all the bars are closed, and only junkies, footpads, prowlers, muggers, and other hobgoblins seem to be abroad. Even the shadows throw their own shadowier shadows. I kept close to the curb, head down, in a hurry to get there.

At the combination Health Food & Head shop where I had first seen him—how long ago was that?—I peered, even sniffed, around the alcove for his spoor, but he had vanished. Maybe the cops had grabbed him, I thought, maybe . . . *the park!* Where else? If he were anywhere, that's where.

Up to the corner and then down Fifth, at a lope, I passed under the Arch and then went straight to the stone circle. Except for a low moon, skulking behind clouds, there was hardly enough light to see by; but I went carefully around the rim clockwise, then counterclockwise, then clockwise again, looking into every possible nook. Nothing. Reluctantly, still unsatisfied, I walked away, turning to glance back a couple of times.

At the base of the herm erected to Alexander P. Holley, three compacted

147

shadows lay sprawled, an empty wine bottle poking out of a brown paper bag on the ground beside them. One of them, seeing me, roused himself and called, "Hey! Brother, c'mere . . ." and when I didn't, got up and took after me, touching my elbow. "C'mon, man, you c'n spare me some change. I'm your brother."

This time I dug into my pocket, but all I could come up with was a nickel, covered with lint, and a penny, which I then placed in his palm. Cupped there, pinched between thumb and forefinger, I could see a lit "roach" glowing like a small red third eye.

"That's it," I said, "Sorry, but all I've got else is just bills."

"Gimme a dollar, man," he told me, then pulled out a handful of coins, "and I'll change it."

Some vaguely amorphous recollection, like the contents of a bowl of oatmeal flung out and caught in midair by a circumference, momentarily passed through my mind.

"No, man," I said, dodging around him, and away.

He looked at the nickel and the penny I had given him once more, as if he couldn't believe it, then took a deep drag on his "roach," blowing out sound through the smoke, "Sh . . . sh . . . sh . . . sh . . . sh . . . sh . . . sh . . . sh . . . sh . . ." his stercoral ejaculations finally suspired in one long dieresis, "Shhhhhhhheeeeeeeeeeeeeeeeeeeeit, man! What kinda shit is 'at?"

I heard a thunk, then a clink, as he threw the coins after me.

Down 4th St., on my way home, I went by the Maoist Peace Church— once a real honest-to-god church—in the middle of the block, then stopped, went back, and took a good look. There he was, all right, in the rear portico, laid out flat on his back in the shadows, with only his horny feet protruding into the open. The mopstick was stuck straight up into the shopping bag beside him. He seemed dead to the world . . . but was surely just asleep, like Dionysus, for the time being. Once his big left toe twitched, barely, either in blessing or derision, maybe both.

(1971)

THREE

Jack the Giant Killer

As I lay alone and bone-cold stiff in bed
  My dream was olive oil and fur,
But he stalk like an eel slipped through my head
  So fee-fie-foed and foamed with blood
    That I fell with a shudder
Of moons, waning in black and white
Spasms of darkness, spasms of light,
Waning and waking while the slow
Pulse of neon shone on my window.

O Mother light, light years away, the Bar
  And midnight sun for all your crowd —
Eccentric planets gathered to a star —
  I spied, behind the glass, their loud
    Hands like the deaf and dumb:
Junkies with jaundice; drunken jews;
A Djinn, two Gorgons, and a Muse;
Fey women and fairies in a mock-
Fight or cock-fight without a cock.

My dream, like theirs, dissovled into a stain,
  What could I do but join that swarm
Of eyes like darting little wasps of pain?
  Stung, I looked up, there stood the form

Originally published in the *Hudson Review* (Autumn 1952).

Of malice cool and calm—
One of the mob from Bleeker St.
With cement under his two feet.
Odds and angles were all he knew.
F—— you was his How do you do.

I smelled the gas that holds the spheres apart.
    And smiled, gagging, smiled though I feared,
Knowing for him, and all like him at heart,
    Masses like him, that time had sheared
        The Golden Fleece of power—
Greece of her jewels, Egypt of bones,
And Memphis of colossal stones—
The sheared Lamb turning on a spit.
And yet their teeth shall break on it.

Ah well, for all my blague, my one long shot
    On fame, niched in the dark—the juke
Box plays for him immortal jazz. And what
    If what he swills all night, turns puke
        At dawn? Now, here and now,
He winds all with his winning hand:
Cadillacs, greenbacks, cognacs, and
Girls skinny as Memlings, and girls
With breasts as round and smug as pearls!

Now, while he scowled and screwed his brows to size
    Me up and down, turning my stare,
A match he struck reflared upon his eyes
    And caught my image burning there
        (Lensed in an orange fire)
That blurred and puffed to disappear
Into the phantom eye and ear
Of echoes reechoing echoes,
Mirrors admiring mirrored rows.

Match-fire, beer-foam, and fear, fire, foam and foe
    Seemed like a dream's mirages mired
Deep undermind—but wisps and drifts as slow
    As smoke-rings, broken, arched and gyred
        Their hoops around the whole!
Then all my moons came out and shone

152

In rings of light cold and alone!
And white, white, burning in one white
Flash and open stare of insight,

I saw the blocks and symbols of New York
   Rising in tiers, higher and higher,
A stalk, a flower, and then another stalk
   Of smoke, blooming in orange fire,
     Twin bulbs and pods of fire,
And from these pods the seed of time
Drained downwards to a little slime,
The light blew out, and my full moons
Shrivelled and hung like spent balloons.

All gone, all gone, O Mother now who'll buy
   A fur coat of the beards of kings?
Who'll kill the Giant? Who'll clean the world's sty?
   Stunned when she heard the news, the Sphinx
     Burst into tears and died.
Who'll suck my narrow bones? Or sup
My soft eyes, boiled, in an egg-cup?
Who'll match my teeth upon a string?
I don't know, I don't know a thing.

(1952)

153

Maxim Gorky
in Coney Island

What may have been the first encounter between the American Puritan conscience and Russian Communist evangelism occurred nearly fifty years ago, in the Age of Innocence, when both were still tender and unworldly.

In the early spring of 1906, the eminent Russian novelist and revolutionary, Maxim Gorky, arrived in New York harbor on a mission to raise money in America for the Bolshevik cause. A large and enthusiastic crowd came to meet him at the pier. William Randolph Hearst's *American*, for which Gorky had written an article in 1905 on conditions in Russia, estimated the size of the crowd as "more than several thousand," while Gordon Bennet's *World*, engaged at the time in a circulation war with Hearst, figured it as "no more than a thousand." Accompanying Gorky as he disembarked, and sharing his bows, was a young and pretty actress from the Moscow Art Theatre, Maria Andreyeva, who was understood to be his wife.

Gorky could not have chosen a more favorable time to visit the country. The brutality with which the Czar had suppressed all opposition, the officially inspired pogroms, and the poverty and misery in Russia after the war with Japan had aroused the sympathies of the American public. A Committee to Help the Russian Revolutionists, consisting of William Dean Howells, Mark Twain, Arthur Brisbane, Robert Collier, Edwin Markham, Peter Finlay Dunne and Jane Addams, had arranged for Gorky's admission to America. Gorky assured the immigraiton authorities he was a Bol-

"Maxim Gorky in Coney Island" was first published in *From Mt. San Angelo: Stories, Poems, & Essays,* edited by William Smart (Sweet Briar: Virginia Center for the Creative Arts and Associated University Presses, 1984).

154

shevik, not an anarchist, and his purpose was to deliver lectures rather than throw bombs.

Once in New York, the literary lion of the Revolution was fed the raw meat of flattery and feted and petted until he purred. At a banquet held on the evening of his arrival, Arthur Brisbane dictated an editorial appeal for the Bolsheviks to be run in all Hearst papers across the country. Symposia in honor of Gorky were sponsored by Charles Scribner of *Scribners*, Richard Watson Gilder of *The Century*, and W. C. Allen of *Harper's*. The most influential literary figures of the day came to his support. It was even rumored that an invitation had been sent him by President Theodore Roosevelt to dine at the White House.

H. G. Wells, who was present at one of these dinners, describes Gorky as "a big quiet figure with a curious power of appeal in his face and a large simplicity in his voice and gesture. He was dressed in peasant clothing, in a belted blue shirt, trousers in some shiny black material and boots. Save for a few common greetings, he had no language but Russian." A contemporary photograph reveals a face modelled in flat planes and angles like a cubist sculpture, with small, dark, indignant eyes set behind the high cheekbones; a wide, thin, mouth; and a pair of plump and luxuriant mustaches drooping down below the chin. The contrast with the pretty and fashionably dressed Maria Andreyeva, who was always at his side, must have been impressive.

From his suite in the Hotel Belleclaire, Gorky granted exclusive interviews to reporters from the *American* in which he attacked the Czar and appealed for aid for the exiled revolutionaries. A nationwide lecture tour, arranged by Professor John Dewey of Columbia, was expected to raise more than a million dollars. Faneuil Hall in Boston put in a bid for his first appearance outside New York, after which other cities as far west as San Francisco were to have their chance. And as Gorky's popularity rose higher and higher, the success of his mission seemed certain.

Then, all at once, the air was let out of the balloon. The Imperial Russian Embassy, dismayed by his reception in New York, informed the editors of the *World* that Gorky was not only living in sin with Maria Andreyeva, but already had a wife and child somewhere in Russia. The *World* pounced on this opportunity to embarrass Hearst by exposing his pet Bolshevik. Gordon Bennet, who was then, coincidentally, living in Paris with a young Russian countess, wired his paper to publish this exposure of Gorky. The next day the *World* came out with a grisly, heart breaking description of Gorky's wife and child out there in the frozen tundra, cold, hungry, and abandoned, while Gorky himself, grown fat on capitalist royalties, sported all over the world with his mistress. On the front page was a recent photograph of Gorky and Maria Andreyeva next to one of his wife and child.

Reverberations of moral indignation in the American press, pulpit and parlor were instantaneous. For his part in the Gorky affair, the expulsion of Professor John Dewey from Columbia was demanded. The banquets were cancelled, the committees disbanded, the lecture tours postponed indefinitely. The manager of the Hotel Belleclaire requested that Gorky and his mistress leave the premises. They departed for Hotel Lafayette-Brevoort in Greenwich Village and again they were forced to pack up and move, this time to the old and decrepit Hotel Rhinelander across the street. The pair then left to attend a socialist meeting and, on returning after midnight, found all their luggage piled up on the sidewalk in the rain. If not for the intervention of Mr. and Mrs. John Wilson, who invited them to their house in Staten Island, they would have been forced to spend the night in Washington Square Park.

Hearst's *American*, in a belated attempt to answer the *World*, asserted that Gorky was really married to Maria Andreyeva all the time, but could not reveal the details of his divorce from his first wife "without endangering the lives of scores and perhaps thousands of his countrymen." The newspaper took that chance, anyway. "It is here made known for the first time that there exist in Russia today a provisional government with a set of laws. . . . Gorky received his divorce under these laws." But no one, not even Gorky, was convinced by this explanation. And though his first wife, hearing the news, cabled the *World* that she and Gorky had parted by mutual consent and she was now happily remarried, it had little effect. Only five days after his arrival, Gorky learned that the Puritan conscience might tolerate political revolution in Russia but not sexual immorality in America.

Aleksei Maximovitch Pyeshkov — Gorky, meaning "The Bitter One," was his pen name — was especially bitter over the failure of Mark Twain to come to his aid. He had literacy affinities with Twain, since the boy from Nishni-Novgorod and the boy from Hannibal, Missouri, both made use of folk material drawn from their childhood and wrote in a vernacular style; and they even resembled one another, superficially, in appearance, since they wore the same flourishing handlebar mustachios — though Twain's had already turned white while Gorky's was a rich brown. Now the "Russian Twain," as he was called, felt that the "American Gorky" had betrayed him. When Twain was informed of these feelings of former friend, he replied, "Gorky has made an awful mistake. He might just as well have come over in his shirttails." And, he added, "Certainly there can be but one wise thing for a visiting stranger to do—find out what the country's customs are and refrain from offending them. Custom is custom—it is built of brass, boiler iron, granite." But Gorky, on his side, felt that Twian had joined an international capitalist conspiracy against him.

The writer and his mistress spent the next few weeks in Staten Island and then moved out to the Wilsons' cabin in the Adirondacks. There he began his most famous novel, *Mother*, and, except for occasional visits from the faithful John Dewey and H. G. Wells, remained in seclusion. The furor caused by the exposure of his private life in the *World* had almost subsided when, in August, an article by Gorky appeared in *Appleton's Magazine* called "The City of Mammon." In the doom-heavy tones of a biblical prophet come down from the Urals to judge New York, he delivered himself of the following fulmination:

> It is the first time I have seen such a monstrous city and never before have people seemed so insignificant, so enslaved. Yet at the same time I have never seen them so tragi-comically self-satisfied. There are many energetic faces among them, but in each face you notice before anything else its teeth. No inner freedom, freedom of the spirit, shines in their eyes. . . . Theirs is the freedom of blind tools in the hands of the Yellow devil—Gold. . . .

As if to prevent any misunderstanding, he also sent a telegram to the I.W.W. leaders, Charles Moyer and "Big Bill" Heywood, who were in jail awaiting trial for the assassination of the governor of Idaho.

"Greetings to you my brother Socialists. Courage! The day of justice and deliverance for the oppressed of the world is at hand. Gorky." The newspapers published this telegram and excerpts from his article, "The City of Mammon," renewing their demands that the Russian Bolshevik, novelist, and adulterer be deported. Whatever support Gorky still had in high and literary places now left him. Ambrose Bierce, whose stories on the Civil War Gorky had admired and recommended to Tolstoy, wrote of the incident to his friend George Sterling:

> Having been but a few weeks in the land, whose language he knows not a word of, he knows all about us and tells it in generalities of vituperation. . . . He is a dandy bomb thrower but he handles the stink pot indifferently well.

Even Hearst's *American* felt that Gorky had stayed too long in the United States. Without waiting to be asked by the immigration authorities, Gorky made plans to leave for Europe with Maria Andreyeva on an early steamer.

It was about this time that Gorky's remaining friends, in an effort to show him the American Dream from the inside, took him to "that happy island of illusion," (as the Guide Book called it) "where the sweltering masses of the monster city may forget the dry realities of work-a-day life and steep themselves in harmless frivolities amid the cooling breezes of the eternal sea."

Coney Island—then pronounced "Cooney"—had undergone a great transformation by 1906. Right after the Civil War it had been the head-quarters for gangs of smugglers and rum-runners operating off Norton's Point, a center of gambling, skullduggery, and prostitution, and a kind of Casbah for criminals on the lam. (Boss Tweed was able to hide there for two weeks after his conviction before taking a boat for Spain.) The lowest and toughest dives in Texas and Colorado were sometimes called The Coney Island; and, so infamous had the name become in the 1870s, that a reform movement in Brooklyn seriously proposed to change it to Surf Island "without the peculiar and somewhat embarrassing associations of the old." But all of this was over when Gorky made his visit in the late summer of 1906. "The long bare unfrequented shore," recalled nostalgically by Walt Whitman, "that I had all to myself and where I loved to race up and down after bathing," was then the playground for more than 300,000 people who came every day by steamboat, horse and buggy, and trolley car.

> A trip up the Hudson or down the Bay,
> A trolley to Coney or Far Rockaway,
> On a Sunday afternoon—

was a favorite song, the strains of which Gorky might have heard as he travelled to Coney on the Culver Line.

The trippers had already begun to come in increasing numbers in the 1880s when Coney's reputation improved and ocean bathing became popular. "A Day at Coney Island," written in heroic blank verse by Tad (J. P. Sweet), in 1880, celebrates the resort of those days:

> We hail with joy that geologic morn
> When Coney Island from the sea was born.
> As time sped on, with each succeeding year,
> The Oceanic's widening sand appear;
> This near the day when Caesar entered Rome—
> Then thy beach, Brighton! rose above the foam.

The poet goes on to describe the crowd on the beach — "The maiden whose sweet frizzes hang / In tufts inverted fashionable Bang," "the athlete ponderous with the brawny limb," "the spruce Apollo with his parted hair," "the ancient hay-bag," "the country rustic and the city swell / The western beauty and the city belle," "the Jersey farmer with his honest face." "It was" (as another writer described it) "the ordinary American crowd, the best natured, best dressed, and best smelling crowd in the world." Gorky, of course, saw a much larger and more heterogenous throng pushing through the Midway and lying on the beach in their rented bathing costumes. Tens of thousands of recent immigrants out of Germany, Russia, Poland, Austria, Sweden, Italy, many still speaking their native languages and wearing Old World clothing, mingled with this "ordinary American crowd," even aborbed it, and shared the communal sun and the great mechanical toys of Coney Island.

Steeplechase, Luna Park, and Dreamland, the three amusement parks on the island, were then almost brand-new and in their hey-day. The use of quantities of electric lights for display had recently been developed. From the Chicago Columbian Exposition of 1893, in which impermanent structures of steel and plaster were shown molded into various shapes, Coney Island adopted its own timeless style of architecture. Entrances to all the rides and exhibits were built to resemble Egyptian pylons, Malmein pagodas, Arabian minarets, Babylonian ziggurats, all white-washed, with their weird forms outlined and festooned at night with thousands of electric bulbs. Luna Park, constructed in 1902 at a cost of 2 million dollars, had 250,000 electric lights; while Dreamland — the park Gorky visited — built in 1904 at a cost of 3.5 million dollars and intended to be two times bigger and better than Luna, employed over 500,000 bulbs as well as many beacons and towers of light. The 1906 Guide Book states:

> Dreamland at night glows and sparkles with an electric radiance. . . . For thirty miles at sea, the tall beacon tower may be seen like a gleaming finger. It is a marvelous fact that with all the profuse use of fire in electrical form, the element has never escaped from the control of the corps of experts in charge.

As for the rides, they were among the most Rube Goldbergish and ingenious contrivances of nineteenth-century mechanical science. There were "feeler" rides like The Old Mill, in which long narrow boats filled with couples floated through mysterious tunnels of love; "tickler" rides like the Virginia Reel, invented by H. E. Riehl in 1890, in which round cars revolved and twisted downwards in a circular descent like pinballs; "round" rides like the carrousel, or the Airship Swing in which a series of steel arms lifted gondolas faster and faster and higher and higher in ever widening circles; and "gravity" rides, such as the switchback railway invented by Lamarchus A. Thompson in 1884, in which cars rolled down on their own momentum from peak to lesser peak and around curves unbanked to swing the couples together, until, the momentum exhausted, all the passengers got out while the motorman switched the car to another peak.

One of the many variations of the "gravity" ride was the famous Loop-the-Loop, a roller coaster which made a 360 degree turn inside a bow in the center, passengers being held in place by centripetal force; and, another, The Dragon's Gorge in Luna Park, with forty-eight hundred feet of track, where — says the Guide Book — "the passengers start from the North Pole and visit in rapid succession Havana, Port Arthur in winter, the Rocky Mountains, the bottom of the sea, and caverns of the lower regions besides experiencing a dash under a great cataract." A topsy-turvy take off on the "round" ride was the Ferris Wheel, a wheel of light turning sixty feet in the air, which dominated the Coney Island skyline. And, in a class by itself, was the colossus of all sliding ponds — Captain Roynton's Shoot the Chutes. Of all the rides on the island this was, truly, a Russian invention, having been first devised as an artificial incline for tobogganing during the winter fairs of Moscow. In 1823, it was brought to Sadler's Wells in London as "The Celebrated and Extensive Russian Mountains," and then, seventy-five years later, to Luna Park. There the ride was Americanized by sending, each night, a live elephant "sliding down the steep incline with frightful rapidity toward the lagoon in the center of the Plaza." Dreamland built two Shoot the Chutes, each one more jumbo than Luna's, with two elephants crashing down "with frightful rapidity" two times a night.

Others shows, rides, exhibitions, and spectacles offered by Luna and Dreamland were: Lilliputian Buildings, a fifteenth-century German town in miniature inhabited by dwarves; The Great Deep Rift, a section of a coal mine in operation; The Creation, a cycloramic presentation in which "the waters part, the earth arises, inanimate and human life appear," and its sequel, The End of the World, "according to a dream of Dante"; a Snake Dance by a tribe of Moki Indians; Le Voyage on l'Air, in which "the passenger, with the aid of ingenious mechanical and electrical devices, gains the impression of an air flight over the skyscrapers of New York . . . made possible by photographs taken originally by two daring aeronauts"; The Great Train Robbery, a cycloramic spectacle later made into one of the earliest movies; Twenty Thousand Leagues Under the Sea, a submarine excusion à la Jules Verne; A Trip to the Moon, a sort of scenic railway from which Luna Park derived its name; The Streets of Delhi, an oriental pageant with elephants, maharajahs and dancing girls; and that wasn't all for the hundreds of thousands of Ladies and Gentlemen who came each day to Coney Island.

On the Bowery, a midway barred to wheeled traffic, were all the fire-eaters, sword swallowers, rope dancers, jugglers and freaks — with huge "valentines," portraits of the Monster-osities, framed in electric light. A section of the Bowery between West First and West Third Street, called The Gut, was the orignial Tin Pan Alley of New York. Occasionally, important boxing matches, such as the Fitzsimmon-Jeffries fight for the Heavyweight Championship, were held on the commons. There were cabarets, dance halls, vaudeville, and kinetoscope shows on the side streets. Except for the smells of hot dogs, hot corn, hot fries, the swarming crowds, and the untuned and interfering clamor of barkers, hawkers, and pitchmen, a walk down the radiant alleyways of Coney Island was like walking up and down and in and out of the channels of a TV set.

The author of an article on Coney Island for *Munsey's Magazine* in 1907, Lionel Denison, commented on "the disposition of people to make their amusements so like their daily life." He continues:

> Like the circus horse driven around the ring from left to right, every day, on Sunday to rest himself went around from right to left. . . . So these city people, tired by the jar and noise and glare and crowds of the street, go for recreation where all these are intensified. The switch-backs, scenic railways, and toy trains are merely trolley cars a little more uneven in roadbed, jerky in motion and cramped in the seat than ordinary trains, but not much. . . . The Ferris Wheel and gigantic see-saw are but exaggerations of the ordinary elevator, and the towers are not unlike office buildings.

Nelson's *Views of Coney Island*, one of the many guide books of the time, takes an opposite position:

> It is no use to criticize the Island; it exists and will continue to exist because it offers to all, gentle and simple, poor and rich, a rare feast of fantastic illusions and wonders, complete enough to quench the mysterious thirst for active excitement as an alternative to monotonous work. . . .

But the essence of the Midway, perhaps, lies between. The normal, the upright, the average — made freakish in the crazy mirrors of Coney Island

and upset and unbalanced by all sorts of mechanical contraptions — was, after all, straightened out and reaffirmed for the great American middle class.

> Look into the pewter pot
> To see the world as the world's not,

as an old English rhyme of the sixteenth-century expressed it.

A few weeks before Gorky's own pilgrimage, Mr. Albert Bigelow Paine, a magazine writer in the genteel tradition and a close rhyming friend and biographer of Gorky's enemy, Mark Twain, came to inspect the playground of the masses. His article, entitled "The New Coney Island," was published in *The Century* magazine that summer.

Paine was pleased to find that the old, disreputable Coney Island, with its leagues of gamblers, thugs and prostitutes, was no more. He recognized the difference even on the trolley car going over. "There was a crowd of people; and the fact that in numerous cases the ladies were given seats while the men held on to straps, was evidence that Coney had changed." And as the trolley approached Surf Avenue, Paine heard the "undercurrent of excitement."

> A number of passengers were making their first trip, though these were inclined to speak in whispers as the wonder of the spectacle gradually lifted before them. . . . First came the chariots where the tickets were sold; then a row of entrance gates; and beyond them an enchanted story book land of trellises, columns, domes, minarets, lagoons and lofty aerial flights. And everywhere was life — a pageant of happy people; and everywhere was color — a wide harmony of orange and white and gold under a cloudless blue. It was a world removed — shut away from the sordid clatter and turmoil of the streets.
>
> Of course, it was still a whirl of noise and exhibition and refreshment — but the noise was within the limits of law and order and the exhibition and refreshment were more wholesome. Kinetoscope shows of a gay but harmless variety seemed to prevail where once painted and bedizened creatures attracted half-sotted audiences with vulgarity and display.

Among the lawful noises he heard on the Midway was the barker's "*Hu*-rry! *Hu*-rry! *Hu*-rry! Step-right-up-Ladies-and-Gentlemen!" and the pitchman's "Ve tell your name! Ve tell your age! Ve do not know you! Ve nevare saw you!"; and the hullaballoo of booths where "the passerby was incited to hit the colored man whose face decorated the center of the curtains to get thereby a good cigar"; and the clanking machinery and diminishing screams of passengers on "innumberable gravity railroads and chutes and whirling air-ship swings . . . [which] the appetite of the American people for rapid motion has produced." Paine himself was tempted to take a ride on the dangerous Loop-the-Loop, but thought better of it in time. He left well-satisfied with the afternoon and glad to recommend Coney Island to all the readers of *The Century.*

To Carthage then came Gorky, burning, burning, burning and brooding over the failure of his mission, exposure of his private life in the newspapers, betrayal by friends—and prepared to see what he wanted to see. He saw it; and then sailed two weeks later with his mistress for Capri. There, in a small, seaside villa on the ancient pleasure island of the Emperor Tiberius, he wrote his impressions of the American playground of the masses and the way of life it represented. The article, entitled "Boredom," appeared in the *Independent* magazine in the summer of 1907.

Gorky took the trolley to Coney at night when the great electrical display could be seen. Like those jewelled birds on the golden tree and the two gold lions in the throne room of Byzantium, which would warble and roar on the approach of an ambassador, the myriads of brilliant electric lights at Coney were intended to overwhelm and dazzle the eyes of any observer. The ambassador from Russia to Dreamland was suitably impressed.

> With the advent of night a fantastic city all of fire suddenly rises from the ocean into the sky. Thousands of ruddy sparks glimmer in the darkness, limning in fine sensitive outline on the black background of the sky, shapely towers of miraculous castles, palaces and temples. . . . Fabulous beyond conceiving, ineffably beautiful, is this fiery scintillation. It burns but does not consume.

But after this propitiatory hymn to electricity is over, Gorky invokes that "Yellow Devil—Gold" once more, and says what he really thinks of Coney Island and New York.

> The City hums with the insatiate, hungry roar—the ceaseless bellow of iron, the melancholy wail of Life driven by the power of gold, the cold, cynical whistle of the Yellow Devil scare the people away from the turmoil of the earth burdened and besmirched by the ill-smelling body of the city. And the people

go forth to the shore of the sea, where the beautiful white buildings stand and promise respite and tranquillity.

And Gorky tells what they find when they get there.

> The amusements are without number. Boats fly in the air around
> the top of a tower, another keeps turning about and impels
> some sort of iron balloon. Everything rocks and roars and bel-
> lows and turns the heads of the people. They are filled with
> contented ennui, their nerves are racked by an intricate maze
> of motion and dazzling fire. . . . The ennui which issues from
> under the pressures of self-disgust seems to turn and turn in
> a slow circle of agony. It drags tens of thousands of uniformly
> dark people into a sombre dance and sweeps them into a heap
> as the wind sweeps the rubbish of the street. Then it scatters
> them apart and sweeps them together again. . . .
> They swarm into the cages like black flies. Children walk
> about, silent with gaping mouths and dazzled eyes. They look
> around with such intensity, such seriousness, that the sight of
> them feeding their little souls upon this hideousness, which
> they mistake for beauty, inspires a pained sense of pity. The
> men's faces, shaved even to the mustache, are grave and immo-
> bile. They enjoy the tinsel, but too serious to betray their plea-
> sure, they keep their thin lips pressed together and look from
> the corners of their eyes, like people whom nothing can astonish.
> The men with serious faces seat themselves on the backs of the
> wooden horses and elephants of the merry-go-round. With a
> whoop they dart to the top, with a whistle they descend again.
> After this stirring journey, they draw their skin tight on their
> faces again and go to taste of new pleasures.

Then Gorky, drifting along with the crowd in his own search for pleasure, found himself inside an exhibition called "Hell." This was an old-style
morality play, stern, solemn, and ceremonial, which attempted to show
the consequences of sin. As an attraction, it was just as popular as any
other in Dreamland. P. T. Barnum had discovered in the nineteenth-century
that the American public liked their circuses with a touch of revivalism,
and their revival meetings with a touch of the circus; and so, even in his
advertisements, the old master huckster never failed to mollify the Puritan
conscience and to adopt biblical words and references wherever possible.

While Gorky watched the performance of "Hell," he seemed to see the hand of that Puritanism which had pinned the scarlet letter on him and Maria Andreyeva only a few months before. This was his chance to even the score.

> Hell is constructed of papier mâché and painted dark red. Everything in it is on fire — paper fire — and it is filled with the thick, dirty odor of grease. On one of the stones sits Satan. He rubs his hands contentedly like a man who is doing a good business. He must be very uncomfortable on this porch, a paper stone, which cracks and rocks. But he pretends not to notice his discomfort, and looks down at the evil demons busying themselves with the sinners. The atmosphere in Hell is stifling. The demons are insignificant looking and feeble. Apparently, they are exhausted by their work and irritated by its sameness and evident futility.
>
> A girl is there who has bought a new hat. She is trying it on before a mirror, happy and contented. But a pair of little fiends seize her under the armpits and put her into a long smooth trough which descends tightly into a pit in the middle of the cave.

The same treatment is given a man who has drunk a glass of whiskey and a girl who has stolen money from a companion's purse.

> The audience looks on these horrors in silence with serious faces. The hall is dark. Some sturdy fellow with curly hair holds forth to the audience in a lugubrious voice while he draws the moral. He says that if the people do not want to be the victims of Satan with the red garments and crooked legs, they should not kiss girls to whom they are not married because the girls might become bad women. Women outcasts ought not to steal money from the pockets of their companions and people should not drink whiskey or beer or other liquors that arouse the passions, they should not visit saloons, but the churches, for churches are not only better but cheaper.
>
> At the conclusion, a nauseatingly beautiful angel appears on a wire holding a wooden trumpet pasted over with gilt paper between his lips. On catching sight of him, Satan dives into the pit after the sinners.

Gorky then proceeds to draw his own Bolshevik moral from this Puritan morality play.

Everywhere the one commandment is repeated: "Don't!" For it helps to crush the spirit of the majority of the working people. . . . On the right, they are intimidated by the terrors of eternal torture. "Do not sin," they are warned, "Sin is dangerous." On the left, in the spacious dancing hall, women waltz about, and here everything cries out to them: "Sin! For sin is pleasant."

Not far from the orchestra is a cage with bears. One of them, a stout brown bear with the little shrewd eyes stands in the middle of the cage and shakes his head deliberately. All this is sensible only if it's contrived to blind, deafen and mutilate the people. Then, of course, the end justifies the means. But if people come here to be amused, I have no faith in their sanity.

To conclude, Gorky himself, like that "nauseatingly beautiful angel" in Hell, places the "wooden trumpet pasted over with gilt paper" between his own lips and blows a call for revolution — an event as near and far for him then as the Day of Judgment.

One thing alone is good in this garish city. You can drink in hatred to your soul's content — hatred of the power of stupidity. . . . Mean panderers to debased tastes unfold the disgusting nakedness of their falsehood, the naivete of their shrewdness, the hypocricy and insatiable force of their greed. The cold glare of the dead fire bares the stupidity of it all. Its pompous glitter rests upon everything round about the people. The soul is seized with a desire for a living, beautiful fire, a sublime fire, which should free the people from the slavery of a varied boredom.

Gorky's essay against our own Coney Island followed a long tradition of similar jeremiads against other and older Coneys, throughout history, by poets, preachers, and prophets. William Langland's "Vision of Piers Plowman," with it's "feeld ful of fok," was a take-off on the great Winchester Fair in Fourteenth-century England; the fair at Sturbridge in the Eighteenth-century was the model for "Vanity Fair" in Bunyan's allegory "Pilgrim's Progress" and William Wordsworth's description in "The Prelude" of Bartholomew Fair — the spiritual progenitor of our Coney Island — seems almost to have taken the words out of Gorky's mouth:

All out-o'-the-way, far-fetched, perverted things,
All freaks of nature, all Promothean thoughts

Of man, his dullness, madness, and their feats
All jumbled up together, to compose
A Parliament of Monsters. Tents and booths
Meanwhile as if the whole were one vast mill,
All vomiting, receiving on all sides . . .
O blank confusion! true epitome
Of what the mighty City is herself
To thousands upon thousands of her sons,
Living amid the same perpetual whirl
Of trivial objects, melted and reduced
To one identity, by differences
That have no law, no meaning, and no end . . .

But all these were inspired by a desire for moral and spiritual uplift and a religious regeneration of the masses; while Gorky's indignation was directed at the American people for wasting their time at such low and trivial pleasures when they should be attending meetings and demonstrating against the government.

The editor of the *Independent* inserted the following comment on his article:

> To most people Coney Island, the playground of the metropolis, seems a place of gayety and comparatively innocent though somewhat vulgar amusements. But to the man who has assumed the name of "Gorky," The Bitter One, it only affords further evidence of the stupidity and depravity of the human race and of the tyranny of capital. When Maxim Gorky was in this country last summer he seemed to find life and its conditions everywhere as bad as in darkest Russia. Finally, to cheer him up, his friends took him to Coney Island and this is the impression it made on his sensitive mind. After reading it one knows better how to interpret his pictures of Russian life.

When Gorky and Maria Andreyeva left America for Italy, he was interviewed on shipboard by reporters from the newspapers. In answer to a question on the kind of activity he regarded as necessary for social advancement, he replied:

> Circulate cheap editions of classics, the great histories, novels, poems, dramas, provide picture exhibitions for the wage earners and lectures on natural science. Already your workmen

have a plethora of material goods; their souls are stuffed with fatness; they, like the rest of America, have no souls.

But more than twenty years later, with the USSR already a reality and the first Five Year Plan for the industrialization of Russia about to begin, he changed his mind about the American "plethora of material goods." Confronted with his own criticisms of America while he was here, he said, simply: "I was a Russian rustic then." In 1928, Gorky was persuaded to return to Stalin's Dreamland as the chief literary figure of the Revolution. He lived luxuriously in a mansion overlooking Moscow, once inhabited by Napoleon during his Russian campaign.

Dreamland in Coney Island was destroyed in 1911, when that "element" which the proprietors boasted had "never escaped from the control of the corps of experts in charge" broke out one night due to a short circuit in a ride called "Hell Gate" and burned the playground of the masses to the ground. Gorky himself died in 1936, also as a result of fire, and under weird circumstances.

As the best-known Soviet writer of his time, he had held on stubbornly to his faith in the Revolution and continued to believe in the "sublime lie" of communism (as he called it) rather than the "petty truths" of Western democracy. Except for various official speeches and articles, his literary output was nil. Then, in 1936, rumors began to reach friends in Europe that Gorky was trying to escape from the Workers' Paradise and, that same year, his death by bronchial pneumonia was announced dolefully over the Moscow radio. Two years later, his decease was called murder by the Soviet government and became the pretext for the famous Moscow Trials, with their sinister overtones of medieval trials for witchcraft. Under cross-examination by the chief prosecutor, Andrei Vishinsky, a certain Dr. Levine made this "confession":

> Gorky's great passion was fire. He loved the flames and we exploited this passion. . . . We lit a fire for him in the open air, at a time when he was fatigued and weak. Gorky stood next to the hot fire and this was very bad for his lungs, resulting in his death.

Almost all of Gorky's old pre-Revolutionary friends — called "assassins, spies, deviationists and wreckers" by Vishinsky — were made to confess in torture chambers and sent to the firing squad. In a wax museum in Coney Island today, there is a replica of one of those Russian torture chambers.

(Undated)

The Poetry of
Samuel Greenberg

For the tragic life of this poet, clipped at the age of twenty-three, an apology is required — but from whom? Who is to blame? "God's only excuse," said Nietzsche, "is that he doesn't exist" — but since when is that an excuse? Job, who knew all His historical sleights of hand and philosophical disappearing acts, would never have accepted such an apology. And anyhow, since the court of Highest Appeal is forever adjourned, Sing O Muse and adjust the fate of Samuel, Jacob and Hannah Slimovitch's son, driven by the flood of history from Vienna to imperial New York, where, as a child of nine, he burrowed with his family in the slums of the East Side, played hopscotch and stickball in the streets, read Horatio Alger, the pulps and the comics, went to PS 160 on Suffolk Street, but had to leave in the seventh grade to work in a luggage factory, contracted tuberculosis, wrote his poetry in the dead calm between fits of madness, and died in a Staten Island charity ward in 1917 at the age of twenty-three.

Greenberg left more than six hundred poems, scribbled on the backs of calendar sheets, envelopes, postcards, in nickel notebooks, etc., which were regarded by his family and even by the author himself, in his words, as "nonsense to real literature of careful judgment" (Greenberg's *Autobiography*).

After his death, the whole mass was given to a friend, William Murrell Fisher, who preserved them curiously for years. But then, by chance, the young Hart Crane saw some of those poems at Fisher's house in Wood-

Originally published as "The Poetry of Samuel Greenberg: 'Neither the Time nor the Poet was Ripe,'" in *Commentary* (October 1948). All rights are reserved by *Commentary*.

stock, N.Y., and was so struck by the power of their rhetoric—much like his own, as though Greenberg had taken the words out of his mouth—that, fortunately, the greater poet took them back and condescended to plagiarize, without which service who would have heard of Samuel Greenberg? The sudden evaporation of promising talent, leaving only the waste in the melting pot, is one of the sad characteristics of American culture.

Greenberg's life as an "apartment Jew" was spent at the height of the exodus from Eastern Europe, a turbulent period, when shipload after shipload of immigrants were landed on Manahattan like an invasion army, and the downtown bridgehead teemed with our own foreign faces and foreign languages, strange food smells, beards, *yarmulkas,* gabardines. Yet this experience, which formed his sensibility, left no impression upon the actual stuff of his work. At the time Greenberg wrote, the attempt of the Imagists to appropriate small tough lumps of the daily life for poetry was unknown to him, and even if known would not have been understood. His sense of the contemporary life was weak. As a result, Greenberg's diction is often pseudo-literary, filled with the outworn poeticisms of another age and irradiated only by his own fever.

But even if Greenberg, with his undeveloped technique, could never propound the City, the City itself (metaphorically speaking) spoke through him, in tongues, a kind of Delphic gibberish of imagery.

He was a New York poet—the pastoral scenery of his poems has the depth of vaudeville flats. It is not only his high metaphysical voice, however, or the cinematic flow of images, the speed of his imagination to catch swift ideas and feelings on the fly, that make Greenberg, I think, the ancestor of an as yet unrealized Big Town style. There is also a curious Chinese-box effect of "in-wit" in some of his poems (which we shall examine later on), interiors of the mind enclosed in themselves. The intellectual toughness of the City and its irony—billiard "english"—are lacking; yet no one would expect a poetical *naif* like Greenberg to think out of the side of his mouth.

In applying such an interpretation to the poems, it is true that we look for what we want to find; as James Joyce remarked, we wipe our glosses with what we know. According to the predisposition of his critics, Greenberg has been claimed as a surrealist, a primitive, a neo-Romantic, etc. But, in the end, the poet himself is responsible for that. The almost sibylline unconsciousness in which he wrote his poems tempts us to impose our own catergories upon them.

Greenberg's most ambitious work is "Sonnets of Apology," a group of poems written during his last months in a tubercular ward when the visions of fever became confused with the appearance of things as they are.

> . . . the beam
> Of fire from the sun cast mine own
> To slumber in imagination of spheres.
> Under the heavens of moon-like shapes
> Mine eyelids shut; I fell into unfelt realms.
>
> (from "Enigmas")

In his charge, the rational outline of the sonnet form based on the medieval syllogism, with its statement, counter-statement, and resolution, now bulges with disfigured images packed to fit the required fourteen lines. Even the original shock of these poems absorbed for us by Hart Crane, still we are not prepared for this. The main influences, Shelley, perhaps Blake, certainly Emerson, and those poets of the Romantic movement included in Palgrave's *Golden Treasury* and the back of Greenberg's grade-school reader, these are undigested. As a result Greenberg's poems are loaded with Romantic apparatus: clouds, blood, death, stars; sudden apostrophes to Platonic abstractions; and the characteristic amputations and contractions of "'pon," "'pelling," "'frain," "o'er," "e'er," etc.—even without the excuse of metrical exigency.

Despite the great rise of some lines and passages and even whole poems, the nose sniffs—gas or pneuma, the true afflatus or flatulence merely? Greenberg's language strains under a weight of meaning it can hardly bear, both because his technical control was slight and the gravity of his experience too heavy; so that, frequently, his words drop their burden of significance altogether and float off like runaway balloons, in a Shelleyan *extase*, pinnacled dim in the intense inane. The opening lines of "Man" are typical.

> O perfect lay of deity's crested herb
> Thou art as the winsome seed afloat.
> Whose power e'en fear doth warmly note
> Upon the slave of mortal earth to curb. . . .

Paradoxically, it was the cramp of Greenberg's limited vocabulary on his ideas—"rather poor in careful selection of grammatic assistance unguided"—which forced him to invent new words and constructions, and, sometimes, to charge verbs and epithets with an intense focal brilliance: "Mythology helped the modern life *upbraid*"; "Thou hast in plea Mankind's thirsty juggle, to *upheave* its concept"; "Doubting conscience's concentration and *behave*"; "The orator follows the universe / And *refrains* the laws of the people," etc. Artistic limitations, when they are understood, not only prevent but inform.

A close reading of Emerson gave him his bias, his cue, and even a degree of control. Emerson's gnomic style is pounded by Greenberg into flat declaratives, and used to anchor his own Transcendentalism, but a naive version, sometimes almost ludicrous, as in these lines from "To Darwin": "And within the oversouled hush / I breathed the prayers, reliance." Greenberg's use of universal titles — "Peace," "Life," "Force," etc. — which serve as neo-Platonic essences or forms for the poems and so predicate their contents, was also derived from Emerson.

What attracted him to the Transcendental philosophy with its sharp Kantian disjunction of existence and essence, image and reality, good and evil, was precisely this cleavage. Greenberg was in love with the dualities, the master symbol of Yin and Yang.

> The great color and sacred Mary
> Were whirled in the eyes of Venus and Mars,
> But the large sun-circle kept on
> With the moon-disk and stars
> (from "Thus Slave Through Nature)

His own consumptive fever, which cast him intermittently from the apparently real world to the truly unreal, must have seemed like a symptom of this basic metaphysical duality.

But whether he understood its implications or not, Greenberg left Emersonianism at a crucial point. The passage from "Enigmas" already quoted ("the beam / Of fire from the sun cast mine own / To slumber in imagination of spheres. . . .") contains a notion of insight, the mind's internal beam, as the moon of reality *reflecting* the true light of day — in distinction from the Emerson-Kant view of the mind as imposing its own categories on nature. It may be reckless to try to piece out a consistent philosophy with quotations from a poet often confused and contradictory (or from any other poet), but I think this does show Greenberg's adherence to a Biblical naturalism, which presupposes a gap between the intelligences, but not the universe, of God and man. Without the acceptance of this gap — and the possibility of a prophetic leap across — mysticism is disqualified.

Throughout his poems, Greenberg refers to the senses as "bubbles" that can pop at any moment: "the bubble of senses bright," "eye bubbles dissolving water shade," and in one of his best poems, "The Glass Bubbles,"

the frailty of sight is metaphorically identified with the frailty of what is
seen.

> The motion of gathering loops of water
> Must either burst or remian in a moment.
> The violet colors through the glass
> Throw up little swellings that appear
> And spatter as soon as another strikes
> And is born; so pure are they of colored
> Hues, that we fell the absent strength
> Of its power. When they begin they gather
> Like sand on the beach: each bubble
> Contains a complete eye of water.

The modulations of metaphor here are extraordinary in a poet who never
read Donne or Marvell. First, the bubble-images are thrown up by a spout
of vision-water, and "spatter" as others strike and are born; as they break
they dissolve into hues of color without substance (like an after-image)
so pure "we feel the absent strength of its power"; until, finally, the terms
of the metaphor are identified and the eye-spout and its image-bubbles
contain one another. The gritty hardness of the image of sand — "When
they begin they gather / Like sand on the beach" — is thrown into our eyes
just as the transformation takes place. Figuratively speaking, the whole
poem is a metaphysical wink of the inner eye that transcends appearance.

But even the possibility of such a transcendence in poetry — "the weaving fictions of chromatic truth" — serves only to confirm the gulf between
sensory perception and the reality. This theme is further rehearsed in "The
Master's Triumph," with its powerful cadence reminiscent of the later Blake.

> Behold all this jagged beauty; I bare the test alone of perfec-
>   tion too imperfect.
> The choir spirit in order weaves it own gauge in the song of life.
> O detail! must thou trail endless, as fables of yore forever create
> Harmonies, while we breathe broad and simple? We pray to this
> Abandoned universe; that critic looms high in chaos, whether
>   it contains
> Sensual or divine restriction. . . . Or perhaps the infinite charm
>   is cursed.

No matter how God-like in this "abandoned universe" the act of creation
may be, the poet's task is not redemption but to deliver himself from the
necessity of having to be redeemed.

He sat as an extricable prisoner, bound
To essence that he sought to emancipate.
                              (from "Poets)

Or, as he says elsewhere, following Emerson: "The essence of life remains
a screen"—an essence which is not screened by anything else, but *is* a
screen, a screen that screens itself. The "within the within" noumenal
character of reality is mirrored by Greenberg's image (or the other way
around), thereby exemplifying in itself what it asserts. One of the lines
Hart Crane appropriated from Greenberg for his own poem, "Emblems
of Conduct," was of this sort: "For joy *hides* its stupendous coverings."
But Crane, exercising his *droit de seigneur,* misread or deliberately transformed the line to "For joy *rides* in tremendous coverings," and so spilled
its meaning.

"Emblems of Conduct" was composed by Crane out of a congeries of
lines taken from five unrelated poems of Greenberg: "Daylight," "The Lau-
reate," "Perusal," "Immortality," and, of course, "Conduct," from which
it originated. The result was only a crude amalgam, lacking the spontaneity
and dramatic tensions of the original. Here is Greenberg's "Conduct,"
another of the "inwitted" poems where his images have a Realist auton-
omy and follow their own leads:

By a peninsula the painter sat and
Sketched the uneven valley groves.
The apostle gave alms to the
Meek. The volcano burst
In fusive sulphur and hurled
Rocks and ore into the air—
Heaven's sudden change at
The drawing tempestuous,
Darkening shade of dense clouded hues.
The wanderer soon chose
His spot of rest; they bore the
Chosen hero upon their shoulders,
Whom they strangely admired, as
The beach-tide summer of people desired.

The vast landscape of volcanoes, valleys, and beaches is crowded into
small context of the poem, and even further diminished by the figure of
the Titanic painter who sits "by a peninsula" to sketch the "valley groves."
(Freudian criticism can make a fuss over the peninsula and the groves—

as indeed the whole poem is symbolical of the act of creation.) A strange apostle gives alms to the meek, just as the painter gives form to what he sees. All nature is in a geological confusion like the first week in the book of Genesis or the painter's own mind. Abruptly, this identification of the creator and the object of creation is made explicit as the volcano bursts — "Heaven's sudden change at / The drawing tempestuous / Darkening shade of dense clouded hues." Then, just as suddenly, the painter resolves his confusion and finds a "spot of rest." His mental landscape becomes a summer beach, and here the artist-hero is acclaimed and borne upon the shoulders of the crowd.

Crane sometimes incorporated Greenberg's imagery with a greater degree of flexibility than in "Emblems of Conduct." Philip Horton's biography of Crane contains an account of the change suffered by a line from Greenberg's "Shadowings" before it was finally annealed in the second part of "Voyages." "Silhouettes set the scepters roving" became, by stages: (1) "Shadowed sceptres roving"; (2) "Circled by sceptres roving"; (3) "Enlisted by what sceptres roving / Wide from isle to isle have churned"; (4) and then, the form in which it was used: "The sceptred terror of whose sessions rends. . . ." (At this point Crane interpolated a line from Greenberg's "Man" — "All else than Deities green crested herb" — which he later removed.) The final version reads:

> The sceptred terror of whose sessions rends
> All but the pieties of lovers' hands.

Contrasted with the molten issue of these lines, "Emblems of Conduct" is a slag-heap.

Crane's conscious attempt in "Emblems of Conduct" to impose a rational order on Greenberg's associational flow of imagery without first estimating its depth or current was a violation of his own theory of extralogical poetry. In an article published by Crane in 1925, two years after he had made copies of the Greenberg manuscripts, he wrote: "Via . . . their metaphorical inter-relationships the entire construction of the poem raised on the organic principle of a 'logic of metaphor' which antedates so-called pure logic and which is the genetic base of all speech, consciousness, and thought extension." But despite his prescriptive criticism, Crane was always ready to supply a rational gloss for his own poems, perhaps trying to join the two terms "logic of metaphor" and "so-called pure logic" not metaphorically but literally. Certainly as the subject of his own poetic analysis he associated the figures of logic and metaphor too freely; even his use of the term "logic" — in this connection deprived of any usual denotation — is purely metaphysical.

The method advocated by Crane, evidence of which he found in Greenberg's "Sonnets of Apology," was originally developed by Rimbaud and especially by Mallarmé in his later poems. The structural rigor of Mallarmé's work was, perhaps, an attempt to make his poems self-sufficient and autotelic in a time of chaotic cultural values — "Monads have no windows." By omitting the social connections of syntax, the symbols and metaphors of poetry (like the symbols of a dream) attain their relevance to one another and to the world only within the formal context of the poem itself. The vision of the poet can be made manifest by being filtered through a significant form — for without this objective technical correlative for his vision his symbols are merely spots before our eyes. As William Blake pointed out: "The artist's conception is as his execution and no better."

An architecture of metaphor was never achieved by Crane, and never attempted by Greenberg. Greenberg's ultimate failure — and Crane's to a lesser extent, as his ambitions were greater — was due to the lack of such a controlling technique.

The affinity of both poets is clear — New York. Crane's talent was magnetized by New York, and in the "Proem" and "The Tunnel" sections of *The Bridge*, as well as in "For the Marriage of Helen and Faustus," he found his pole. Although these poems absorb without self-consciousness the artifacts of the machine age, they avoid the lumpish naturalism of early free verse — Whitehead's "fallacy of misplaced concreteness" in poetical guise — and the style Crane wrought instead with its slang, thick *impasto* of diction, high tonal pitch curved on the inside, elliptic shifts of reference, etc., was considerably more flexible. Greenberg, on the other hand, had none of this literary sophistication. He had only a sensibility formed in the streets, but, in expressing himself, he unconsciously anticipated and sometimes even surpassed the art of Crane. With his technical handicap he could never sustain a unified vision, and, in the end, fragments are his whole achievement.

Greenberg's life and his work were cut too soon, with all the dangerous (for us) pathos and sentimentality of ruins, shards of poetry that "crumble within view and palm." Neither the time nor the poet was ripe. The immigrant culture of the East Side was then still more European than American, and the effort of adjustment from the crawling villages of Eastern Europe to the pace of a 20th-century megalopolis, the cockpit of mankind, engrossed every other concern. This Greenberg saw clearly.

I live in an age where the age lives alone
And lonesome doth it rage
Where the bard dare not come.
              (from "The Tempest")

His freak genius was the product of his struggle to achieve personal
authenticity, a "self gathering of natural prevention in the ways of life's
action," while still assimilating to the new American life. His problem in
poetry, like that of assimilation in general, was enormous, Hamlet's problem: To be or not to be — what? For it is much more painful to live without
one's self than to live as a pariah, without society; just as it is better to
be in exile than to be dead. The symptoms of the afflictions which led
to Greenberg's death — his schizophrenic madness and the tubercular shred-
ding of his lungs, the source of inspiration — were true symbols of a greater
social disorder. We wheeze in spirit. And the elastic of self-alienation has
already been stretched so far that all are in danger of being struck down
by it, as by a sudden snap of the mind.

What is supposed to be the last poem Greenberg wrote, found on the
back of a postcard addressed to his brother and dated March 14, 1917, is
composed in tight and regular stanzas, unlike "Sonnets of Apology."

The advantages of such a strict order, where the slightest shift of meaning or value can be made emphatic, is obvious for a disoriented poet like
Greenberg. And yet pattern is not form, as conformity is not style. Despite
the superb finish and pure tone of this poem, it is Greenberg's sprawling
"Sonnets," with their rank tropical overgrowth, gorgeous and grotesque,
which are much closer to his own nature.

Here is "To Dear Daniel," which comes almost as a summation of Greenberg's life.

There is a loud noise of Death
Where I lay;
There is a loud noise of life
Far away.

From low and weary stride
Have I flown;
From low and weary pride
I have grown.

What does it matter now
To you or me?

What does it matter now
To whom it be?

Again the stain has come
To me;
Again the stain has come
For thee.

(1948)

Along the Midway
of Mass Culture

1.

A tourist snapshot of Hell, or the entrance of Hell: Coney Island on a hot Sunday during the summer with millions of people stretched naked on the sand, or wallowing, stumbling and falling over one another in the surf. The beaches are so jammed they can occupy only as much space as their bodies. Against the walls of the apartment houses or in the courtyards of the huge Baths facing the ocean, the echoes of all their millions of little voices are reflected back and compounded into a stunning roar — the "strange tongues. . . . words of pain, voices deep and hoarse and sounds of hands" which Dante heard in the outer ring of the Inferno, where the outcasts of Hell turn "in the air forever dyed, as sand when it eddies in a whirlwind." These are the great swarm of humanity who lived their lives "without blame and without praise, but were for themselves," and so were spewed out by both God and the devil.

The masses were put in their place — outside — and socially restricted by Dante even from his Infernal freakshow. In the plays of Shakespeare as well, though he himself was a plebeian, the appearance off-stage of the mob, that "beast with many heads," could evoke imagery of profound nausea. When the mass man was given an individual role, it was either as a clown or the butt of ridicule. And yet the revulsion of both poets, deep as it was, merely reflected the universal prejudice of their own ages. The culture of the Renaissance could allow the dignity of

"Along the Midway of Mass Culture" first appeared in *Partisan Review* 16:4 (April 1949).

Man only in the abstract, or in great individuals, but never in the whole lump.

It is, then, more an historical than a literary problem to account for the gradual leavening and rise of this lump in time — from the domestic tragedy of the seventeenth and eighteenth century, to the pastoral sentimentalism of Grey and Crabbe; from the poor-but-proud "a man's a man for a' that" defiance of Burns and Wordsworth, to the celebration of the "divine average" by Whitman; and from the depiction of low-life in the novels of Dickens up to the psychological casing of debased urban and rural types in Dreiser and Faulkner. By the nineteenth century, this social leavening process had gone so far that Tolstoy, in an attack on the new French symbolist poetry, could even question the sanctity of Art itself and prefer "Uncle Tom's Cabin" to Shakespeare and Russian folksongs to Beethoven (although he himself knew better), solely because they appealed to a greater mass of people.

The Coney Island culture is, of course, a phenomenon of the twentieth century.

> The age demanded an image
> Of its accelerated grimace,

as Ezra Pound said, which it was quick to find. Comic strips, pulp fiction, movies, radio serials, commercial jazz and the rest are a direct result of modern technology and public education. Whether we choose to dignify these products by the name of Art is a semantic problem — what is central is that they usurp the functions of traditional art in setting the styles, the manners, the images, the standards and the goals of life for millions, almost as though they were the organs of an un-official state religion. And in its scope, this sub-culture is wide enough to include the millionaire and the dime-store clerk, the president of the United States and the Negro sharecropper, the old and the young, in a truly classless and democratic consonance of spirit.

Whitman imagined that the new forms to be developed by a democratic art would be a further revelation of the old, and could be exposed merely by stripping off the outer layers of decayed sensibility. But even the form of the novel, which had been the chief literary vehicle of the middle-class since its inception, now, in the hands of such writers as Proust or Joyce or Kafka has become as highbrow and aloof as any other genre.

The hope persists that, somehow, in the fullness of time, either through the Grace of a revolutionary state or, gradually, through the dissemination of Great Books, the values of advanced art can be sifted down to the mass. But this is a pathetic consolation, Whitman's booster optimism turned rancid. It may have some validity in the case of *kitsch* art exemplified in best-selling novels, jukebox adaptations of Tchaikovsky, choral works like "Ballad for Americans" or "Freedom Train," modern dancing in Broadway musicals, etc., that petty-bourgeois "uplift" by which Americans punish themselves for really preferring Moon Mullins. (And, incidentally, the type of culture fostered in the Soviet Union today by fiat of its most authoritative critics.) The base forms of mass art have autonomous values and a parallel momentum of their own. Moreover, their pervasive power is such, like the political slogans of authoritarian states, that any influence is most likely in the reverse direction. Neither the bohemian ghetto nor the university provide a hiding place.

When comic strips, jazz, pulp fiction and the rest are not intellectually snubbed, they are regarded as the bastard products of modern civilization, mere artifacts like juke boxes and slot machines, without any cultural ancestry or tradition. Their lineaments of descent, however, are unmistakable. Just as the leading forms of bourgeois art were derived from medieval sources — the novel from feudal *gestes* and romances, the drama from miracle and morality plays performed in the market place, etc. — so these new upstart genres are grounded in middle-class culture of the past. To trace even one of them back to its origins, the comic strip for example, reveals certain early characteristics that apply to all.

2.

During the first half of the eighteenth-century in England, a period which saw the consolidation of British mercantile power and the establishment of the Protestant ascendancy, there was a new security of person and a freedom of opinion that was shared by all but the lowest classes. That vertical chain or ladder of Being on which feudalism had based its cosmology and its hierarchical social relations was about to be tipped over on its horizontal axis by a levelling of class values. The *canaille* were now citizens with a stake in Parliament and even an interest in the arts. Common Sense — that great virtue of the average — was elevated to a rank as high as all the others. God himself, turning the screws of an erector set universe constructed according to the rational blueprint of Newton and Leibnitz, could have no patience with any monkish hyperdulia or aesthetic faradiddle.

181

The five great comic novelists of England, Smollett, Fielding, Stern, Richardson and Defoe, as well as the cockney artist Hogarth, appeared at this time almost in a group. All of them had an intimate connection with early journalism, sharing its time-sense as a series of discrete moments, each without self-possession, as well as its notion of the "concrete" as residing in the particular entity or even sensorily observed. The scenes and actions of Smollett's novels, especially, frequently resemble detached anecdotes taken from a newspaper or magazine of the period. With their tortuous plots unwinding upon the spool of a foregone conclusion; their crude characterizations drawn almost to the point of caricature; and their uncertain structure wavering between the narrative and informal essay (just as the journals of the time wavered between reporting and editorializing); yet with everything drawn in bright color, full of slapstick vigor and spiked with climaxes — these early novels could hardly hope to compete for literary esteem with poetry or drama. On the other hand, by their rootedness in the common daily life they had immense appeal, and achieved an audience for literature greater than any before.

During the same period, this new mass audience was shared by the cartoon art of William Hogarth and his successors. And in the fusion of the two — the early English novel of Smollett and Fielding and Hogarth's drawings — the style of the comic stirp was conceived.

Hogarth's declared purpose in his little-known book, *The Analysis of Beauty*, was "to treat (his) subjects as a dramatic writer." What he did achieve for the first time in "The Rake's Progress," "Marriage a la Mode," "The Harlot's Progress," and his other cartoon series, was, in effect, a translation of novelistic situations and character types into pictures. (Of course the medieval paintings and stained-glass windows illustrating Bible stories and the lives of the Saints for the laity preceded Hogarth; but these had a religious rather than a social perspective, as, also, miracle and morality plays compared with Elizabethan drama.) Hogarth's ambition was not to methodize nature, but to see her in all her literalness and materiality — to strip the Quattrocento ideal of any mysticism and reduce it to a physical average. In his work, the knobs, twists and bulges of flesh of ordinary mankind superceded the perfect forms of Venus and Apollo. Yet as he came to understand later on, the concept of the Average was an ideal as abstract as the concept of the Beautiful.

Hogarth served to widen the split between "high" and "low" art, reflected during the eighteenth century by the more academic dispute between the Ancients and the Moderns. For those artists surrounding the official court painter Joshua Reynolds, and for the "connoiseurs," so called, who admired the Italian schools exclusively, he could never restrain his contempt. There was, unmistakably, the bray of the true philistine horse-laugh in the way Hogarth ridiculed the claims to "divine inspiration" and the "*Je ne sais quoi*" or Grace, of these artists. His own compositions were often cramped with detail and unbalanced; and his line was coarse, enclosing rather then revealing form, so that his pictures actually improve when they are reduced in size for publication. All his immense inventive genius was restricted by default to the depiction of a literary subject matter: — caricatures of London daily life, both high and low, as seen from the inside.

But since satire and caricature were the dominant modes of art in the eighteenth century, Hogarth was eminently fitted for his age. The social order of England at that time had such stable foundations, (or thought it had), that the distortions of view in Hogarth's pictures, like the crazy-mirror expansions and contractions in Swift's *Gulliver's Travels* or Pope's *Rape of the Lock* could easily be refocused and adjusted to the norm. The artist's "slant" was his point of view. Hogarth even posited a standard "line of beauty," the serpentine line or spiral, which was for him the secret grace of the Greek and Italian styles; but, when this spiral twist was flattened or bulged or distorted in any way, it emerged in the shape of caricature. The deviant, the non-average, was also the freakish that could provoke either laughter or disgust, according to the intent of the artist. And, as his pictures show, the wit of connecting "improper" forms in caricature was equal to the wit of connecting "improper" ideas and images in satire.

With this, the general theory underlying the comics was about complete. Hogarth's successors and imitators gradually abandoned hs moralistic tone as well as his hopeless battle with the "connoisseurs." His cartoon art was endowed to the daily newspaper rather than to the museum. The development of illustration and caricature by Rowlandson, Cruikshank, Gilray, Seymour and the rest coincided with the growth of modern journalism in Europe and America. By the time Outcalt's "Yellow Kid" appeared in the New York *World* in 1896—generally considered the first of its kind—an embryo comic strip art was already gestating which, upon the consolidation of mass newspapers and syndicates by Pulitzer and Hearst, emerged at last full-grown in the way we know.

3.

Those visionary figments—Mutt and Jeff, Smilin' Jack, Blondie, Dick Tracy, Daisy Mae, The Gumps, Popeye, Moon Mullins—every day, exposed in their boxes of light and jails of purposeless energy, they glow in the minds of millions. The services they perform and the needs they fulfill are real. Like the newspapers themselves, the comic strips re-enact a vast solemn American ritual—The Strip Tease of Time. With each issue, suspense is aroused and discharged in a little climax without relief, anticipating only another climax tomorrow and tomorrow, until, just before the final black-out, time's overwhelming secret is almost but never revealed and always hidden again. As the goal or reward of a culture founded on materialism is the very activity taken to reach it, so the comic strip leads to no final revelation and exhausts itself in immediacy. Its rigid daily pattern is repeated in an overall timeless and shapeless continuum.

And not only the comic strip, but also jazz, soap opera, the movies, pulp fiction have this one great structural principle (or lack of principle) in common. As a consequence, any criticism of the mass arts based on the authority of traditional art, is baffled from the start. From the standpoint of organic form, the various genres of mass culture seem closer to artifacts than to art.

To attempt a formal definition of the comic strip, therefore, would be a contradicton in terms, since the very concept of form in art entails unity of time and space and action. Its form—as for the movies, pulp fiction, jazz and the rest—is really formula, whose prescription never varies. Jazz, whether hip or commerical, from blues to be-bop, must serve out its time constricted behind the thirty-two bars of the average record; although, during a performance, it can be extended indefinitely by the addition of new choruses or longer rides. As for the movies, the convention of plot and character are always so rigid that the circular continuum of feature to newsreel to double feature can be breached at any point without loss. No wrench is suffered during this transition by the audience, which arrives and departs in the same darkness. And in soap opera and serialized pulp fiction, the comic strip device of the strip tease in time is used to provide suspense and direction in a plot going nowhere. But since the strip tease can never be pared down to its essence, these are never formally completed but, rather, discontinued or exhausted.

Moving always on the surface of appearance, it is impossible for any of the mass arts to plunge beneath this surface and into a depth of meaning, symbolic or anagogic, which form alone provides.[1] For this reason, the casts of characters in comic strips, like the stock types in pulp fiction and the stars of Hollywood, who always play themselves in whatever roles they are cast, are mere concretions of characteristics, animated types or "humours" rather than persons. All these characters are self-contained,

184

hermetically sealed by the formula from any growth or change. Once set in motion, they can go on and on for years in a kind of somnambule inviolability.

The most successful and famous comics often survive their authors, and, in rare cases, even the newspapers where they first appeared. It takes a major change in the American *ethos* to effect even a slight alteration in their formulae. But when, after many years, one of these strips recasts its characters and plot, or expires, that is an event as significant as a style of dress or slang going out of fashion. The cocky, sadistic, tough-talking "Yellow Kid" of the 1890s — from whose name, incidentally, the term "yellow journalism" is derived — has been superceded by the still more violent, sophisticated and sensational comics of our own time, just as the old-fashioned demagogy of Pulitzer and Hearst has been streamlined by their successors. In modern comic books and newspaper strips, read by all classes and age-groups with equal fervor, there is such great emphasis on mayhem, arson, murder and pathological sex as to necessitate laws for the protection of public morality. "Krazy Kat," "Happy Hooligan," "Mutt and Jeff" and "The Katzenjammer Kids" were products of a more genteel era that has passed away. Sometimes, however, a comic strip remains embalmed in the juices of another time, unable to renew itself, yet too valuable a property to be abandoned. "Maggie and Jiggs," for example, a strip burlesquing the social *gaffes* and foibles of the immigrant *nouveau riche*, has lost much of its point now that the upper and middle classes have learned to forget their manners. In any event, none of the really important old-timers are ever forgotten. Their names and typical wisecracks color the daily speech, and their faded pictures merge gradually into the family album of American life where they are preserved.

For it is the great indistinction of both the mass arts and contemporary life that they reflect one another so closely, feature by feature, it is almost impossible to tell the image from its source. Both collaborate to form a common myth, that vague gray area of the "collective unconscious," where psychoanalysis and sociology overlap one another. The fictive heroes of this myth are the archetypes to which the masses try to conform, and the dies from which they stamp their own behavior. Consider the style of the city gangster, in all his synthetic moods, from the brash hood to the smooth operator; the style of the strong and silent Western cowboy; the style of the country Gable and the hick siren; the style of the Cynical reporter on a metropolitan newspaper; the style of the Woman-with-a-past and her fallen sister, the Whore-with-a-heart-of-gold; and the characters that kids throughout the U.S. assume when they play at War or Cops and Robbers or Cowboys and Indians—all are derived to a greater or lesser degree, from the classic types of the movies, pulp fiction and comic strips. But with this demurrer—the spell cast by the these mythical images would be broken, their charm unwound, without the simple faith of the masses.[2]

As the power of the religious and artistic value has shrunken, the mass arts have taken over. The collapse of Puritanism, for example, has opened a vacuum in the interior lives of millions—the secret world of the daydream and the forbidden wish—which is now filled almost entirely by the sexual codes, styles of courtship, and erotic images derived from the mass arts. Even the comic strips exhibit women as lush as those of the beer and cigarette ads; while some like "The Gumps" and "Winnie Winkle," where sex was once a minor display, have had to be revamped to satisfy their public. (The formulas of new strips concerned with aviation, such as "Terry and the Pirates" or "Smilin' Jack," place equal emphasis on sex—new evidence, perhaps, for Freud's theory of the dream symbolism of flying.) In Hollywood, an elaborate and knowing technique has been developed, known in the trade as the "continental touch," in order to keep within the bounds of propriety, and for an audience quick to take a hint. As a result, the provinces today are as cultivated as the large cities.

Romantic and confessional pulp fiction, the most lurid as well as the tender adolescent varieties, employ the same conventions as Hollywood but affect a kind of mincing virtue which is all their own. Under all romantic persiflage, however, there is a bond of understanding between author and reader not to take it all too seriously. Love is a bedtime story, but sex is real and earnest. Nevertheless, the readers of *A Girl Can Dream* by Phyllis Pool, *Appointment with Love* by Clinton Dangerfield, *Banished to Paradise* by Blake Reed, etc., shop girls, school girls, stenographers, housewives in their millions demand to see themselves as heroines of romance along with the queens and grand-dames of the past. Romantic love has been democratized in these magazines and sold on every newsstand. The ads on the back pages, however, are a pathetic commentary and as real as a dirty joke—ads for Loans, Cures for Stammering, Foot Powder for tired feet, Reduce! Pictures of your favorite Hollywood stars, Stop B.O., and so on.

The moonshine of these romances derives from the movies, from Hollywood, where the stars like gods and goddesses of a new Olympus merely play at being human. Their love affairs among themselves and, sometimes, with favored mortals outside the movies, recounted years later around every American fireside, bar and soda fountain are already part of our national folklore. The stock characters of romantic pulp—and of Western, Detective, Sport and Horror stories as well—are only copies of these larger-than-life originals in Hollywood. There the daydream is given a local habitation and a name.

Accordingly, what was at first joined only as a metaphor—the Hollywood constellation and the Pantheon of ancient Greece—now present certain real points of contact. The stars of Hollywood can be conceived as archetypes existing apart from us, in a preternatural dimension of their own, for the images on the screen are ikons rather than photographic representations of real persons. In this sense, Clark Gable and Lana Turner are merely actors who represent CLARK GABLE and LANA TURNER. These great shadow-gods, entering our lives in all the guises of Zeus—the Swan, the Bull, and the Shower of Gold—and their goddesses, with their smooth, lovely faces unlined by any trace of anxiety or intelligence, together living, loving and dying but always rising again on other screens in other films, immortal and grand, what have they in common with our petty cares and interests or even, for that matter, with the lives of the actors who portray them? The archetypes persist under many transmogrifications even when the actors who originally portrayed them are dead. Their cosmetic masks are forever renewed. Yet the gossip columns and picture magazines where the stars are worshipped, and the press agents who are their priests, all conspire to identify these ideal images with the physical beings of actors and actresses. And for the millions who surrender themselves and surrogate their passion to these images in daydreams or (with their eyes closed), even in the very act of love, they are more real than the bodies they are possessed by or they themselves possess.

The star system undoubtedly is the most original invention of the movies— in a synecdochal sense, it contains and *is* the movies. European film studios, which have been unable to develop a comparable system of their own, seem to lack the glamor and enchantment of Hollywood. American movies are preferred by the masses even in foreign countries; and this despite the handicap of a strange language and the fact that, from the standpoint of theater art, French and English films are often superior. An actor in foreign films, whether from the Comedie Française or from the Abbey Theater, is merely an actor, but Betty Grable in America is a star. Hollywood can ingest directors, writers, technicians and actors into its thearchy, "the finest that money can buy," with the same divine and imperious appetite with which the Olympians must have devoured the local deities of Greece. It is only after elaborate rites of beatification by press agents, gossip columnists and movies magazines, however, and the further proof of their box-office magic, that the taint of Europe and mortality can be washed away. In this manner, after changes of name, personality, and appearance, some of the highest stars have ascended in Hollywood. American actors, however, whose features might stamp them as minority racial types, are condemned to roles of a sinister and/or sophisticated kind.

The Italians suffer mainly from this prejudice. Jewish film stars are frequently able to "pass" without special observance; but, in the parts of Jews, they are restricted to standardized *schmaltz* characterizations, unctuous, self-sonscious, and embarrassed by a fulsome desire to please. On the other hand, it is almost impossible for a Negro to play a romantic or heroic part in the movies. Even the best Negro players are invariably shown as domestic servants or musical clowns or the butts of ridicule—the same roles, incidentally, which were bestowed on the lower classes in Elizabethan drama. What motivates these restrictions is as much political as it is financial. For the collective daydream of Hollywood is as jealous and exclusive as the individual's; and the rise of a new romantic star from a minority race or nationality signifies a rise in social rank for the whole group.

As it has developed, the mythopoeic power of the movies, inherent in its very method, has given it a quasi-religious status and a structure that differs radically from any other literary or theatrical genre. As the anecdote is the concrete substance of the short story and novel; gossip of the drama; soliloquy of the modern poem; so the daydream, with its moving images beamed inside the mind, is the concrete substance and focal point of the movies. The movie theater itself is like a working model, or templet, of a huge mind. While the brilliant hypnotic screen converges all light and movement in the darkness, a simple faith on the part of the audience ("the camera never lies"), suspends any disbelief in the projected reality of what it sees—for both the private darkness within and the public darkness of the theater are illuminated at once by the same image. What a machine for the cretinization of masses! The deadpan with which the camera records its pictures is like the reassuring legal prose of Kafka's dream narratives, whereby, keeping a straight face, the most incredible characters and events are detailed with such a consistently monotonous gravity of emphasis that the fantastic can be taken at its face value. Conversely, the matter-of-fact events shown in the newsreels of Senators speaking, flood waters rising in Iowa, famines in China, etc., are somehow transformed to the same illusory plane as the feature production itself. The shadows of the movies flicker between the black and white world of positive fact and the chrome world of fantasy, unreeling both on a single beam of light. But this spooky lighting effect is a device of ritual much older than the movies:—

188

Darkness in churches congregates the sight;
Devotion strays in open daring light,

as a poet observed in the seventeenth century. The silver screen, the hush, the darkness—it *is* a kind of secret Mass where all who attend partake of the Host in common; and, to project along this line into the near future, the movies may yet find in television a comparable Reformation, in which the individual will be left to face his own screen alone.

Whatever style television may ultimately compose for itself is now hidden in a primal chaos of all styles, a super-Vaudeville large enough to include the movies, sports events, grand opera and news events all on the same bill. The earliest films, in turn, were little more than photographic imitations of stage plays or cirucs tricks, agitated dumb-shows, until the camera learned to move and to participate in the action. But from this discovery emerged the great motif of The Chase, a motif which is dominant in Chaplin's early comedies, Westerns, cops and robbers melodramas, cartoons, etc., and, in one way or another, figures in almost every kind of film. The Chase was not only a fulfillment of style, but, even more, created a ritual form out of a mass psychological need. In the spellbound attention with which a newsreel audience watches a football player running and twisting down a broken field away from hands that clutch at him from all sides, there is, under all the excitement and tension, a release from the common nightmare of being pursued by someone or something with the pursuer gaining closer and closer. It is almost as though time itself were the pursuer, that "cinematic" time (to use Bergson's appropriate metaphor), conceived as an absolute, free and mathematical essence with an existence of its own. What better place for the apotheosis of our "cinematic" time than in the movies?

The name of Benjamin Franklin glows on the marquee, appearing as The First American. For his many indigenous qualities, but, especially for having made a fetish of time, which is money, everyman's commodity, the stuff of life, Franklin was recognized by Europe as the representative type of a different *ethos*. During his lifetime, of course, main outlines of this ethos were still obscure. But by now the American fetishism of time has exposed itself through many nerves of anxiety—e.g., the obsessive dread of losing one's youth or virility, the dread of growing older without "having lived" (Rip Van Winkle), the dread of missing one's chance or "golden opportunity," etc. It is no contradiction, however, that Progress is conceived to be as steady, irresistible and cumulative a process as the ticking of a clock. The new *must* be better, for the same reason that the go-getter

189

must come out ahead — or else something is radically wrong. The comic strip "Moon Mullins" provides a negative sort of testimony for this credo — Moon, a character in the old picaresque tradition, never does any work, sleeps too much, chases after women, wastes his money and never thinks of tomorrow. But to balance Moon, at the other end of the evolutionary scale there is "Buck Rogers," "Flash Gordon," and, of course, "Superman," Tarzan's city bred and more neurotic cousin, who can hear a dripping faucet miles away.

Now the most remarkable fulfillment of these notions of time and progress in the mass arts is, certainly, science-fiction (so-called), whose lineage goes back to Lucian, Kepler, Donne and Swift; yet, paradoxically, this literary tradition has been crossed with the still more ancient ghost story, to produce something essentially different from either and pecuiar to our own times, a scientific demonology. The faith of the masses in scientific progress, which has largely superceded faith in Biblical revelation, can call up its own superstitions of the possible as terrifying as those of the occult. In *Astounding Stories, Wonder Stories, Amazing Stories* and the like, the demons and devils that once haunted mankind have been driven thousands of light years away into the interstellar regions where anything goes. But this is where the paradox unfolds itself — for, to the superstitious mind, the farthest movements of the stars and the innermost movements of the soul (exemplified by the pseudo-science of astrology), are the two poles of one axis.

One of the most original writers of Gothic science-fiction, H. P. Lovecraft (whose paranoid tales of the pre-creation race of Chthulu are in many ways reminiscent of the old Kabbalistic legend of the Breaking of the Vessels), was so possessed by sub-conscious demons that, like W. B. Yeats in *A Vision,* he even invented an elaborate list of Chthulu tracts and incunabula to buttress his stories. Their names could be recited at a black Mass: — 1) The Micronomicon of the Mad Arab, Abdul Alhazred; 2) Pnakotic manuscripts; 3) R'lyeh text; 4) Book of Dzyan; 5) Seven Cryptical Books of Hsan; 6) Dhol Chants. In his public life, Lovecraft was a respected citizen of Providence, R.I. and, like many of his profession, declared himself to be an orthodox "mechanical materialist."

The bulk of the science-fiction stories published in pulp magazines — in distinction from the more sophisticated varieties — have, by now, evolved a set of conventions so widely accepted that their fantastic plots can be told straight, without any literary sleight-of-hand, like the tales of ghosts in the Middle Ages. The casts of characters in these stories are cut from the same pattern as Western or Romantic pulp: there is the hero himself (who is the usual daydream hero), an evil scientist (who could be a cattle rustler or suave nightclub operator as well), and, inevitably, a good scientist and his beautiful daughter. Formula proscribes form. And neither space ships, ray blasters, time machines or all the rest of their Gothic furniture can raise them above the level of pulp fiction.

For any of the mass arts, questions of aesthetic value are supererogatory. But the uncertain cultural status of science-fiction, ranging as it does from high to low, presents a problem in criticism that applies to all: namely, whether a transvaluation of the mass arts can be effected, while still maintaining their democratic base, so as to make them serve as vehicles of advanced art. What this really entails is that both halves of our schizoid culture be joined and made whole by an act of the artistic will. In the past, of course, folk songs and country dances were formally developed in the symphonies of Beethoven and Schubert, and the old popular ballads recast in the poems of Wordsworth and Coleridge. Yet the poetry and music of the Romantic era was no more available to the broad mass of people then, than it is now; and, in any case, the natural forms of ballads, folk songs and country dances were derived from the same organic principles as traditional art, which are essentially opposed to the technological art products of our own time. To attempt to anneal the two, therefore, even if it were socially possible, would result in an aesthetic hippogriff, a prodigy as strange as any Shakespearean marriage of the Phoenix and the Turtle.

Those experiments of Stravinsky and Gershwin, while appearing to offer a structual synthesis, are really a hangover of late Romantic "program music" — (the equivalent of *collage* in painting) — in which bird calls, cannon shots, cow bells, train whistles, etc., were sounded off to counterfeit reality. These works may be musically successful notwithstanding, but jazz has its own ways and its own means. By a reciprocal process, when jazz bands strain to achieve a larger statement by imitating symphonic forms, as in Duke Ellington's suite *Ebony Concerto,* the result is foredoomed to be a humorless parody of both. The movies, infected by the same notions, tend to produce elephantine spectacles or mere photographed versions of stage plays; and comic strips, likewise, when they abandon their cartoon style for devices of chiaroscuro and realistic drawing, resemble the *kitsch* illustrations in *Good Housekeeping* or *The Saturday Evening Post.* Limits and rules, even for the mass arts, define themselves by an excess of their own ends.

So then, to recapitulate what has been assumed all along: the base forms of popular culture have an autonomous system of values indifferent to the standards of artistic criticism, and a career separate from that of traditional Western art. As a corollary to the "cinematic" time sense which they embody, all are committed by formula to the appearance of things presented by immediate sensation. And since, by definition, it is impossible for them to evaluate experience by means of form, the glass they hold up to modern life is a mirror that focuses certain aspects sharply but reflects nothing in depth. It is this two-dimensionality that makes them seem closer to artifacts than to art.

4.

Along the midway of our Coney Island culture is jazz or ragtime or blues or swing or be-bop, of many names but one homoousian substance. The nature of jazz music has not been treated in any detail so far, and yet, in a sense, it may be considered a prototype of all the mass arts. For in no other are ideas and feelings presented for their immediate effect at the very moment of conception, nor are the restrictions of formula so exacting and necessary. Only the 2-4-2-4 structure and the 32 set bars of jazz can control the vagaries of improvisation. Consequently, these crude arrangements of popular tunes, stamped out as though by a machine to fit the time of a dance or the length of a record, are in contrast to a highly complex rhythms and elaborately figured variations of theme. Many jazzmen, who may be virtuosos on their own instruments, are yet unable to read even the simplest musical score.

Jazz arrangements are usually devised beforehand by the band leader-entrepreneur, but the performance itself is a corporate activity in which the inspiration of each musician is pooled. The American system of checks and balances in a free enterprise system has no better working model. Those jam sessions where musicians get together after hours to play for their own satisfaction constitute an open market for the mutual exchange of ideas. Any new "riff" or "break" of value becomes the property of anyone present and is quickly passed on—one reason why the most original innovations in jazz are often anonymous. As ideas catch and connect, an altogether new style of playing, such as be-bop, can suddenly emerge as though it were "in the air" all the time, the air the trumpet or saxaphone man blows through his mouthpiece.

European mimicry of American jazz, especially the French with their quaint Hot Clubs, can never quite approximate its tone. Their very aesthetic seriousness is un-American and gives them away. The brass toughness and disreputable history of jazz, whose origins among the Negroes in the South can be traced to slave plantations, gambling boats on the Mississippi, the dives and cathouses of old New Orleans and Memphis, up to the seamier clip-joints along Fifty-Second Street and in the Harlem ghetto, where it is now enshrined (not to mention its sinister association with drugs and late hours), all this has flattered even the most prosaic Local 802 hipster with a kind of Villon-esque underworld glamour. Among the coteries that surroung jazz, a distinctive jabberwocky composed of carnival slang, thieves' argot and Harlem jive has been cultivated, in order to separate the hipsters from the squares.

But at this point certain further distinctions ought to be made. Black jazz, the only chaste and true variety, is but a narrow band at the extreme end of the Tin Pan Alley spectrum, the rest of which ranges from the mixed pied-piper outfits of Benny Goodman or Woody Herman, all the way around to the huge all-white orchestras of Tommy Dorsey, Glen Gray and Harry James, For these last, the commercial bands that blare on the radio and in the movies, jazz improvisation is ruled out altogether, and every number is rehearsed and mechanically regulated to the smallest crotchet. Yet it is mainly the loudest and most vulgar which are most popular throughout the U.S., perhaps for that reason; while the best colored jazzmen, from whose work all the others are derived, are kept waiting in the kitchen of American success. In Hollywood's recurrent jazz operas, Negro musicians are rushed in and out as discreetly as waiters. By some absurd double irony, however, the great majority of the Negro population penned in the Northern and Midwestern ghettos actually prefer bleached imitations of commercial jazz or even the white varieties themselves — driven by the same levelling pressure of the Boss culture that makes them straighten their hair or value lighter colored women as more sexually desirable; as, for whites of second-class nationalities, it compels many to change their names, their manners, their religions, or even their faces.

But the absorption of Negro jazz by the Leviathan is only one sign of its power. For the American mass culture is also an imperial culture, whose authority is as great abroad as it is at home. It is no exaggeration to state that it occupies a comparable relation to its ethos as Protestantism once held for the British Empire, or the classic Pantheon for ancient Greece and Rome. The base forms of mass culture are capable of undercutting the most rooted traditions of art and religion in Europe, not by any competition of values — they are aesthetically neutral — but because, on the broadest social level, these traditions are already exhausted. The Soviet

Union, which would like to fill the vacuum with its own imperial prescriptions, carries on a steady, virulent offensive against American movies, comics and jazz.

In its present setup, however, mass culture is not necessarily confined within the matrix of contemporary society, for it can operate with equal or even greater efficiency under a totalitarian as under a democratic system. Its nature is so closely bound to technology that no one can predict what new shapes and genres it may yet evolve. The real artist behind American culture is Vulcan himself, the great artificer surpassing all his old devices year after year. The invention of television, for example, has at once confined movies, comics, spectator sports and even newspapers within the scope of a single screen and enlarged their view enormously. And there is always a new ride or a new sideshow down the midway.

In contrast, the traditional arts of Europe are gradually freezing into a museum culture, with the trophies of the past hung side by side with those of the present. It has even been suggested seriously, by Malraux and others, that reproductions of the greatest art works in Paris and other capital cities be circulated around remote areas—a sort of French "Freedom Train" for artistic documents—as though this funeral exhibition could substitute for the creative energies of a living art. After the first World War, such piety toward past values would have seemed a ridiculous excess; but Dadaism and Surrealism could afford to paint the moustache on Mona Lisa only because these values were still viable.

Of course, works of art of a high order, equal to the best of the past, can still be produced, though increasingly rarified, professional and aloof. For the tradition begun with the Renaissance is ending. As the advanced arts have surpassed themselves in the refinement of sensibility even to the point of nullity—the blank page of Mallarmé and the empty canvas of Mondrian—so the mass arts have become more violently sensational and garish. Following parallel directions, both lead to an equal exhaustion. The humanistic and scientific tradition of the Renaissance, of which American mass culture is the ultimate product, has strained itself over the centuries to lay those eggs slowly hatching under the deserts of New Mexico.

(1949)

Notes

1. The symbolic devices of certain movies, such as the white gulls in *Potemkin* intended to express freedom, or the Freudian emblems in other "art" films (described by Arnold Hauser in his article "Can 'Movies' Be Profound?" in *Partisan Review* (January 1948), are of a different order from those in painting and literature. They should be regarded instead as cues calculated to arouse a definite response from the audience, as, e.g., a dog howling to evoke foreboding, or a baby gurgling to evoke maternal sympathy.
2. During World War II, the type of Rover Boy beach charger and fire fighter celebrated by Hollywood was an open scandal in every camp, but too shocking and too ludicrous to be taken seriously, almost like the war itself. And, for another example, those great lovers of the silent screen, Valentino, Theda Bara, John Gilbert, et al., seem to be playing in a farce when they are shown today.

Mc²Luhan's Message, *or:* Which Way Did the Second Coming Went?

That snake seems to have bitten its tail again, another age come full cycle, *in saecula saecularum,* and lo, from the bogs of the undermind, certain primordial fears and superstitions have emerged, oozing, into our own enlightened times, resurrected by the same science that was supposed to have buried them forever. *For instance, what are those spectral presences (or UFO's) that appear and disappear at will, being and not-being both here and there and now and then? Where do they come from? What do they want? And those strange signals recently detected by radiotelescopes, the so-called "mysterium phenomenon," emanating from somewhere within the Milky Way, do they contain a message for us? And for how many billions of years has the phone been ringing unanswered? Also, what about the discovery by subatomic physicists of antimatter, which has led to the conception of an antiuniverse that mirrors our own, Ahriman to our Ormuzd (or the other way around), with both mutually annihilatory? Or the equally mind-spinning theory of Russian scientists that the two small moons of Mars, Demos and Phoibos, are really artificial satellites, relics of a vanished Martian race? What happened to them? Can it happen to us? Once more, does the sin of having plucked the nuclear apple mean that Cosmic Man, like the old Adam, has been cursed with mortality? And how will we be saved this time? . . . And so forth.* God or no God, if figures, the universe must be haunted.

A generation, born since World War II, for whom science fiction has become science, can hold no truths to be self-evident, no speculations too

Originally published in the *New American Review* (January 1968).

far out. So where, *dictes-moy où,* are the old-time peepers and mutterers, seers and aurists, apocalypsos and doomsdaters who used to be around? All snowed under. Instead, as the millennial countdown approaches 2000, an entirely different breed of prophets, "new hatcht to th' woeful time," prophets out of the academy and the laboratory, have taken their place; and for them the Word has now been swaddled in other words, the jargon of psychoanalysis, cybernetics, celestial physics, sociologistics, and so on, just as the various conflicting political and social ideologies during the Age of Faith had to assume the guise of religious dogma. *Olev hasholem* and/or *Sartor Resartus.*

Among these oracles the most celebrated at present are: Norman O. Brown, author of *Love's Body,* who has attempted to psychoanalyze Man himself, treating his entire history from the Pleistocene to the present as an ever-deepening neurosis; Dr. Timothy Leary, who has proclaimed a New Dispensary, with LSD as a more up-to-date Eucharist for ecstatic liquefaction and communion with OM; and, of course, Marshall McLuhan, the media man, who preaches the coming of a new electronic Age of Gold in which Man will be redeemed and transfigured. And of these three, it is McLuhan who has Made It most spectacularly, turned (or put) more people on, given the kaleidoscope a new shake.

One globe-eyed critic (*Zip-zap! Ten thousand volts!*) has compared him to Pavlov and Darwin, Freud and Einstein, and Sir Isaac Newton. His famous slogan "the medium is the message" (or "massage") has already become as proverbial as "nice guys finish last" or "history is bunk," part of American folklore. And though he disapproves of the medium of print, four of his books have become best sellers, while his theories have been expounded in universities and seminaries as well as on TV and the radio and in all the mass magazines. Most of the converts to McLuhanism came with minds already well equipped with the latest thought-saving ideas, from angst to Zen, and accepted it as a new and shinier intellectual gadget. But he has also found support among distinguished writers and professors and experts in various fields. And to many young McLuhanites, tired of squinting through the Freudian-Marxist bifocals of their elders, he seems to provide a periscopic view into the next millennium . . . though there are others, too, who think it's a rearview mirror image of the millennium before this one.

The germinal idea, or genesis, of the McLuhan gospel can be found in one compacted metaphor: "All media are extensions of some human faculty—psychic or physical," as the computer is to the mind, radar to the ear, the H-Bomb to the fist. To extend the metaphor, then, suggests that we are all members of a single hypostatized Man in whose body we have our being and in whose mind we participate. ("The godhead is broken," as Melville once wrote, "we are the pieces.") If one accepts Anselm's ontological proof of God—that the idea of Him necessarily implies His existence—then the existence of a "deified" Man can likewise be "proved." And, McLuhan adds, since the media are changing rapidly from the mechanical to the electronic and the nuclear, Man's faculties are also changing.

With only mynah variations, this repeats the French Catholic philosopher Teilhard de Chardin's conception of a planetary "noosphere"—the psychic layer of mankind above all other living things—and of a "noospheric brain, the organ of collective human thought," which result from the evolutionary "convergence" and "super-cerebralization" of human society. And yet, Teilhard asserts, "Man is only now, after a million years of existence, emerging from his embryonic phase." But the ultimate source of this idea may lie even deeper, in the Gnostic and Pauline vision of the "pleroma" (or "fullness of God"); and it also has affinities with Plotinus' "world-soul," Hegel's "Zeitgeist," Jung's "collective unconscious," and so on. Cosmic Man, in the guise of H.C.E. (Here Comes Everybody), has been celebrated as the hero of Joyce's *Finnegans Wake*.

No one would care to quarrel with so grand and utlimately poetic a conception of the human species, yet it does tend to exalt Man at the expense of ordinary men, whose lives are still as nasty, brutish, and short as ever. "Between the idea," wrote T. S. Eliot, "and the reality . . . Falls the Shadow." And when McLuhan, alas, brings his metaphor down to earth and applies it to the quiddities, the hard little facts, of existence, he sometimes stumbles into absurdity. Everybody nowadays believes the world is round, but no one wears arc-shaped shoes.

McLuhan, following Joyce, seems to believe that history repeats itself in a "commodious vicus of recirculation." In the mid-fifteenth century, then, a second fall of Man took place as the result of Gutenberg's fatal invention (the stuttering thunder of the printing press reiterated and gutenburbled by Joyce as "bababadalgharaghtakamminnarronnkonnbronntonnerronntuonnthunntrovarr . . . ," like pied type); after which Man was thrust out of the "sacred" oral and tribal culture of the past, where all his senses were in harmony, and into the "profane" and sensorily unbalanced mass culture we live in today, dominated by the eye with its fixed "point of view," thus causing our anxiety-ridden time sense, our robotized work schedules, and all our other woes. (Even the Bible says of the first fall: "And the eyes of both of them were opened. . . .") What T. S. Eliot and the old New Criticism in its heyday once characterized as a "dissociation of sensibility," between thought and feeling—which is supposed to have occurred sometime in the seventeenth century and to have led to our present schizophrenzied society—might have influenced McLuhan's own ideas here, since he is by profession a literary scholar. ("You wipes your glosses with what you knows," as Joyce said.) However, McLuhan affirms, now that the Electronic Galaxy has arrived to challenge Gutenberg's, the dominance of the visual will be broken, the human sensorium balanced once more, and Man himself retribalized and re-redeemed. A family today watching the flickering shadows on the TV screen would thus be reaching across the millennia to commune with savage ancestors squatting around a campfire. The "all-at-oneness" of the electronic media (according to McLuhan's weird parody of Scripture) is atonement for the Gutenbergian sin of "single vision."

Natheless, the mind boggles at the thought that the entire economico-technico-scientifico and social and cultural complex of society has been determined by the printing press, which is, after all, only its product. But McLuhan is fond of such metonymous *presto-changos*—viz., "the medium is the message." Granted that a medium such as TV affects us in its own way, for good or ill, there is also a message . . . from the Sponsor—commercial in the United States, political in the Soviet Union, but total, exclusive, and pervasive in both. (One might even say that it is for the sake of this "message" that the medium has been developed and sustained in the first place.) Again, in his chapter on "Roads and Paper Routes" in *Understanding Media*, McLuhan writes that "the use of papyrus and alphabet created the incentive for building fast, hard-surfaced roads," and, consequently, made possible the Roman Empire. How come, then, that the otherwise highly advanced Incan culture before the Conquistadores, had no alphabet, no means of writing—not even a vague surmise of what it might be—yet constructed hard roads and suspension bridges from one end of Peru to the other, which are considered by engineers to equal those of the Romans?

McLuhan's need to build his system and get his "massage" across—his own sin of "single vision—tempts him to overlook and to disparage the visual sense on every occasion. For instance, he insists on calling TV a "tactile-kinetic" (or sometimes an "audible-tactile") medium when it is, plainly, visual—as any late viewer with rectangular eyeballs can tell him. Though the eyes (as the blind John Milton complained) are "so obvious and so easy to be quenched," it is sight—not smell, hearing, touch, or taste—that is the prime human sense and source of knowledge, now and as in primitive times, and will remain such until the advent of ESP. ("You wipes your glosses with what, your nose?") Then again, why must the movies be labeled a "hot" medium (one that extends a single sense in "high definition") and TV a "cool one" when, after all, not only is the quality of the TV mosaic bound to be improved by technology (consider the dim, jerky, and scratchy movie image circa 1900) but also so much depends upon the individual's own far-, near-, or clear-sightedness, anyway? Men see through their eyes, not the Eye. . . . But 'twould require Occam's cleaver to hack one's way through some of McLuhan's wilder exfoliations. Like some medieval alchemist, he tends to regard symbols as somehow more real than what they symbolize and to transmute base facts into glittering half-truths. With so much mental smog around, why pollute the noosphere any further?

Since McLuhan prefers to consider himself an "explorer" ("Casting my perils before swains," as he tells us), and used to ranging at large through conceptual galaxies, a mere pedestrian critic has no right to carp if McLuhan sometimes loses his way in one universe of discourse or other. Nevertheless, as several of these ungrateful "swains" have pointed out, the medium he must use for these intergalactic explorations is words, words arranged in syntactic order and in uniform lines stamped out by the printing press. How, then, avoid the "single vision," "serial time sense," "fixed point of view," and all the other evils that Gutenbergian flesh is heir to? The philosopher Wittgenstein saw this paradox clearly: "Propositions cannot represent the logical form: this mirrors itself in the propositions. That which mirrors itself in language, language cannot represent. That which expresses itself in language, we cannot represent."

To unhoist himself, McLuhan has lately published a picture book (with Quentin Fiore), *The Medium is the Massage*, that strives for a "mosaic effect," the "simultaneity" of the electronic, with the words confined to a few slogans and cryptic remarks; more recently, he has even made a long-playing record for people who want to get the "massage" through their ears; and the next step may be a version in braille or even in a futuristic Des Esseintes-type taste & smell package, just to cover the whole sensorium.

But understanding McLuhan, unfortunately, still necessitates reading *Understanding Media*, no matter how onerous or old-fashioned the experience is; and if words fail him, think how he's failed them.

For all its idiosyncrasies, there is a curiously impersonal though shrill tone to McLuhan's prose, as if the intention were to harangue a crowd of readers rather than to persuade a single one. Certain key words and phrases, such as "audile-tactile," "single vision," "high intensity" and "low intensity," "tribalized" and "detribalized," and so on, recur throughout and are repeated insistently like Tibetan *mantras* or radio commercials; and should the reader's attention be lulled at times by the predictability and repetitiveness of the argument, he is liable to be jabbed awake by unexpected puns, some of them painful. It is a "hot" — to use McLuhan's term — rather than a "cool" style, somewhat reminiscent in its messianic fervor of Ezra Pound's and Wyndham Lewis' magazine *BLAST* during World War I. This sometimes causes him to overload and thus short-circuit his sentences, as in the following from *The Gutenberg Galaxy*: "The art and scholarship of the past century and more have become a *monotonous crescendo of archaic primitivism*" [my italics]. Or in this, from *Understanding Media* (which must have been intended solely for the eye, since no one could possibly mouth it): "Only the visceral and audile-tactile Teuton and Slav have the needed immunity to visualization for work in the non-Euclidean math and quantum physics." His two chief works (which are really integral) contain a number of such howlers and, in addition, stagger under a load of scholarly jargon as well as his own peculiar brand of academic jive, with hundreds of heavy tomes epitomized, so that in a way it is a kind of left-handed tribute to Gutenberg: Never has there been so bookish a book against books.

Actually, the secret of the printing press was discovered by Gutenberg (born Gensfleisch, meaning "gooseflesh") after he took part in a grape harvest in his native Rheinland, and suddenly saw that the wine press could also be applied to seals, or movable type, thereby producing his great invention. A bibulous bibliomania, endemic among writers and scholars of all sorts, may thus be traced back to the press itself, though McLuhan himself claims to have taken the pledge. Both Gutenberg and McLuhan, it turns out, have much in common. For the chief talent of the author of *Understanding Media* may lie not in weaving metaphysical systems but in compounding intellectual metaphors, rare bisociations of ideas, like Gutenberg's from seemingly unrelated fields.

Some of these metaphors, which abound in his work, may strike the reader as frivolous or even silly, such as this: "An army needs more typewriters than medium and light artillery pieces . . . suggesting that the typewriter now fuses the function of the pen and the sword"; or this: "What we call the 'French phone,' the union of mouthpiece and earphone in a single instrument, is a significant indication of the French liaison of the senses that English-speaking people keep firmly separate." But once in a while he comes up with something exceptional. One memorable example is his analogy between the medieval monk's private reading booth in the monastery and the contemporary phone booth.

As McLuhan indicates, the old illuminated manuscript, like our telephone directory, was bulky and hard to come by, and so it had to be chained to the wall; and since the monks could read only by reading aloud (for there were no punctuation marks in their books and no divisions of words), each monk had to have a separate nook, just as we need individual phone booths, so as not to disturb one another. (In synagogues today, incidentally, the Torah is still chanted aloud by the congregation.) But silent reading — which makes possible the public rooms of libraries — was a later development in the cultural history of mankind.

For a touch of the marvelous, the Argentine poet Jorge Luis Borges, in an essay entitled "The Cult of Books," claims to have found the exact time, A.D. 384, when this event took place. Borges cites St. Augustine's account in the *Confessions* (Book VI) of his teacher St. Ambrose reading in his cell in Milan:

> When Ambrose read, his eyes moved over the pages, and his soul penetrated the meaning, without his uttering a word or moving his tongue. Many times . . . we saw him reading silently and never otherwise, and after a while we would go away, conjecturing that during the brief interval he used to refresh his spirit, free from the tumult of the business of others, he did not wish to be disturbed, for perhaps he feared that someone who was listening, hearing a difficult part of the text, might ask him to explain an obscure passage or might wish to discuss it with him, and would thus prevent him from reading as many volumes as he desired. I believe that he read that way to preserve his voice, which was easily strained. Whatever the man's purpose was, it was surely a good one.

This feat by St. Ambrose — actually swallowing the biblical thunder, the Word, and allowing it to mutter away into silence inside him — which so astonished Augustine, marks a stage in the transit of mankind from what McLuhan terms the oral and "sacred" to the visual and "profane."

A profane reader can almost forgive the author for leading him up the garden path of his metaphysics when there are such real toads hopping about. Another step, though, and McLuhan would be out of the familiar everyday world (as Alice once passed through the Looking Glass) and into the noumenal realm of Art, or Imagination, which might be the proper medium for much of *Understanding Media*; yet for some reason, he holds back, teetering, and tries to stand on both sides of the Looking Glass at once. How he does this provides a valuable clue to McLuhanism, though it gets us there by labyrinthine ways.

There is a famous poem by Yeats, called "Fragments," which McLuhan cites in order to illustrate the "hypnotic trance induced by stepping up the visual component of experience until it filled the field of attention":

Locke sank into a swoon;
The Garden died;
God took the spinning-jenny
Out of his side.

If we unlock the symbols of this cryptic little poem, which compresses an entire cosmology into just seventeen words, its "meaning" can be paraphrased as follows: John Locke, the contemporary of Newton and celebrated Whig philosopher ("but what is Whiggery?" asks Yeats in another context. "A levelling, rancorous, rational sort of mind . . ."), denied and refuted the doctrine of innate ideas taught by the medieval schoolmen as well as the neoplatonists up to his time. (Plato's and Plotinus' system of Ideas rooted in the Mind was once regarded as the pagan counterpart of the Garden of Eden.) By advocating the experimental method in science, religious skepticism, and a broader political and social economy, Locke thus became the source (Adam) of the Industrial Revolution (the wicked Eve being the "spinning jenny" taken from Adam's side) and of modern democracy.

However, McLuhan follows relentlessly the gleam of his own "single vision," and interprets "The Garden" to mean "the interplay of all the senses in haptic harmony," though that is merely one of the posies in it. Yeats goes on to ask in the second part of the poem:

Where got I that truth?
Out of a medium's mouth,
Out of nothing it came, . . .

He got it from neither place, but (whether aware of the fact or not) from a poem similar in form by William Blake:

When Sr Joshua Reynolds died
All Nature was degraded;
The King drop'd a tear into the Queen's ear
And all his Pictures Faded.

Blake's quatrain was written in the margin of a copy of Sir Joshua Reynold's *Discourses*, next to an account in the Introduction of the painter's death in 1792. At his State funeral, attended by the royal family, King George himself is supposed to have wept. Reynolds was to Blake what Locke was to Yeats — a worshiper of the physical world of appearances

203

("Satan's wife, the goddess Nature," according to Blake), who denied the all-creating Spirit of the Imagination.

On another page of the *Discourses*, Blake wrote: "Mind and Imagination are above Mortal & Perishing Nature. Such is the End of Epicurean or Newtonian Philosophy; it is Atheism"; and then, further on: "Man is born like a Garden already Planted & Sown. The world is too poor to produce one Seed." Finally, next to an editorial footnote in the *Discourses* that the colors of certain pictures by Reynolds were fading, Blake comments: "I do not think the Change is so much in the Pictures as in the Opinions of the Public."

The status of Nature was thus diminished, or "degraded," by Reynolds' death. And if we recall that to Blake "tears" (like the tears shed at Reynolds' funeral) were mental ("For a tear is an intellectual thing / And a sigh is the sword of an Angel King" — "The Gray Monk"), then the literal-symbolic meaning of this druidic little poem becomes clear.

The prophetic vision of Blake — and, by seeing through his eyes, of Yeats — stems ultimately from the author of the book of Daniel in the Bible, who was the first to have comprehended world history symbolically as a divine drama moving toward some final consummation. The four great beasts in Belshazzar's dream — the LION with eagle's wings; the BEAR; the LEOPARD with four heads; and the unknown MONSTER with four heads — were interpreted by Daniel as emblems of "four kings which shall arise out of the earth." So also, the LOCKE and REYNOLDS imagined by the poets were not the actual physical beings Locke and Reynolds, but mythic characters who played great roles in the *theatrum mundi*. As personifications of historical forces and abstract human values, they seem to sustain the theory of the Greek philosopher Euhemerus, who held that the gods and demigods were merely the deified great men of a long-forgotten time.

Finally, after this long "commodius vicus of recirculation," to return . . .

The historical Gutenberg (or Gensfleisch), blown up by McLuhan's afflatus into GUTENBERG, who deranged the human sensorium and profaned the Word, takes his place alongside Blake's REYNOLDS and Yeats' LOCKE. But since this godling is contained neither in a religious myth nor a poem, but presented as a historical reality, then he must be judged as such; and in that case, what emerges is a spook, an hallucination bred from the fumes of literary scholarship, and of the sort beloved by those mystagogues described in Butler's *Hudibras*:

> Those busy, puzzling stirrers up of doubt,
> Who frame deep mysteries, then find 'em out.

McLuhan could have attempted a poem in the manner of Yeats and Blake, maybe something like this:

Gensfleisch pressed the Word like grapes;
Man's mind was pied;
Jehovah took His fatal law
Out on his hide.

Perhaps then all the evils attributed to the invention of printing might be more comprehensible.

When Blake later came to write his prophetic and symbolical works (*Jerusalem, The Four Zoas, Milton, The Book of Ahania*), such mythic personae as Los, Enitharmon, Albion, Urizen, and the rest were cast with Voltaire and Socrates, Milton and Abraham and Benj. Franklin, erasing the border between poetry and fact, for by then he had come to believe that Imagination was the sole reality. James Joyce, as well, expounding the dream of Earwicker in *Finnegans Wake*, unites the conscious and unconscious and so gives equal billing to Don Quixote and Cervantes, Hamlet and Shakespeare, Mutt and Jeff and Romulus and Remus, et al. in his cosmic drama. As a scholar and critic of Joyce, McLuhan has borrowed much from the Meister in his own glossolalia on the media. "We are following the track of the old Finn," he writes, "but wide awake this time as we re-enter the tribal night. It is like our contemporary consciousness of the Unconscious." The Joycean puns, the palimpsestic style, the cyclical recurrences — "vicious circles" — and cross-references of theme, all are present in McLuhan's own work . . . and also a propensity to forget that he is not supposed to be writing literature but social criticism. As a result, we have neither one nor the other, but a kind of Delphic gibberish, in which metaphors turn into facts and facts are transsubstantiated into symbols and symbols blur into myth . . .

In an essay on McLuhanism, Dwight Macdonald quotes the following: "The computer promises by technology a Pentecostal condition of universal understanding and unity. The next logical step would seem to be . . . to bypass language in favor of a general cosmic consciousness which might be very like the collective unconsciousness dreamt of by Bergson." Upon which Macdonald comments: "Only McLuhan would see the conscious as 'very like' the unconscious; in his case, the resemblance may be close." So be it. Freud's Olympian pronunciamento: "Where id was, there ego shall be," has here been strangely reversed.

And there's something else, too. McLuhan is well known as a convert to Catholicism (now teaching a course in Millenniary Ecstatics at Fordham);

therefore his bias in favor of the "oral" and so "sacred" medieval Church may have led him to anathematize Gutenberg and the Bible-reading Reformation he helped bring about. An old-fangled profane reader sometimes has the feeling that underneath the persiflage of print versus electronics, serial order versus instantaneous galaxies, "hot" versus "cool" media, and all that jazz, a weird allegory is being produced in which the Senses Five are personified as actors engaged in a struggle for the human psyche, with Sight finally exposed as an agent of Lucifer, racked up, and made to confess.

The Catholic Church, as it should, has responded nostalgically to this message, but also with its newly acquired electronic pep. (What hath Pope John wrought?) Among McLuhan's most fervent acolytes, spreading the good news about the media, are numerous priests. The Reverend John Culkin, S.J., Director of the School of Communications at Fordham, has proclaimed: "The linguists are doing it for languages. The anthropologists are doing it for culture. McLuhan is doing it for the media." The late Prophet Jones once said almost the same thing, though somewhat more eloquently, in praise of Father Divine: "I know that the chassis of your divine mind has been lubricated with divine lubrimentality." Should this new modernizing trend persist, it offers hope that the Church, which in time came to accept the Copernican system and the plurality of worlds, and now, it seems, has even made room for McLuhan's electronic galaxy, may someday find a little niche, so to speak, in its vast theological corpus, for the insertion of Mrs. Margaret Sanger's humble, but humane, device.

Outside the Church, McLuhan's disciples among the young have already started to build their own temples. These are the new stomp-and-salvation "intermedia kinetic environments," discotheques that provide a multisensory *schwärmerie,* the next thing to acid, in which to get McLuhan's massage. For those who don't, or who have tired blood, it's like being trapped inside a jukebox, an imploded Coney Island, and reduced to a state of zomboid catatonia. Perhaps they may serve a benevolent purpose—who knows?—as decompression chambers for the Orwellian future. Like they say, man, God's tripped out . . .

One engineering firm, called "Sensefex," that designs such places, has recently declared its faith: "Our three muses are Tim Leary, the Beatles, and McLuhan. In our daydreams we approach every project with: How many senses can we involve?"

The Beatles have their own daydreams to dream; but if we substitute the name of Norman O. Brown (cited at the start of this trip into McLuhanland), then our original trinity of mystagogues, all homooisian if not homoousian, will be complete. The author of *Love's Body* can jump from ergo to ergo to ergo with as much slippery facility, and has the same prestidigitational expertise with symbols as McLuhan himself. And as for Dr. Leary, the author of "Tune in! Drop out! Whack off!" has much in common with the inventor of "The Medium is the Massage." As McLuhan states: "In business as in society, 'getting on' may mean getting out. There is no 'ahead' in the world that is an echo chamber of instantaneous celebrity." *Ipso dixit.*

Their conclamant voices, amplified by all the media, Gutenbergian as well as electronic, proclaim:

If LSD can offer instant hallelujah, without any moral or spiritual effort required, why not just freak out? . . . If all social institutions are nothing but giant cribs to prevent us from enjoying our god-given rights to polymorphous perversity, why not rip them all down? . . . If the media can massage our heads with divine lubrimentality, at the expense of no mental exertion whatever, why read dull tomes by old fogies?

Having come so far around, we can now change the famous conclusion of Hume's *Enquiry Concerning Human Understanding* (which the philosopher had intended, ironically, to banish the smog of superstition) to read:

"If we take in our hand any volume, let us ask: *Will it help make me high?* No. *Will it help me make out?* No. *Will it help me Make It?* No. Then commit the book to the flames, for it can contain nothing but abstract and dreary reasoning or boring speculations on matters of fact and existence, and who the hell needs it?"

(1962)

Art & Life: A Menippean Paean to the Flea; or, Did Dostoevsky Kill Trotsky?

> On a huge hill
> Cragged, and steep, Truth stands, and hee that will
> Reach her, about must, and about must goe;
> And what the hills suddennes resists, winne so.

> — John Donne, "Satyre III"

1. "To Hold, as 'Twere, a Mirror Up to Nature"

Give him a long white forked beard — no, make that a black beard, for he was only 28 years old at the time. *Give* — no, why give him any beard at all, since he was both by descent and by temperament a Puritan and puritanical, a "Roundhead," so called, and therefore must have been close cropped and shaved. And yet without it, somehow, something seems lost in the spirit, his image fades. . . . No. *Give him* (as said before) *a long white forked beard*, a conical hat, and a star-spangled velvet coat to match, like one of Ben Jonson's or Brueghel's alchemists, but with a nimbus of radioactive photons glowing about his head; and then transpose him just like that, anachronized and hybridized, to some dungeon laboratory where all his absurd rube goldberg and/or sinister frankensteinian apparatus has already been set up; so that in this way, adjusting his image in the mind's eye between the uncanny and the futuristic, we may bring into focus, and thus conjure up, the spectral presence of Robert Hooke, Curator of Experiments for the Royal Society, on that April day in 1663 (to begin this roundabout trip at the beginning) as he is about to peer into what, at one time, might have been taken for a magic speculum but was, in fact, his

Originally published in the *American Review* (April 1974).

own newly devised compound microscope. So then, at last, now that the moment has come . . .

He struck a spark from his flint, thereby lighting a small lamp clamped to a movable brass arm screwed into a pillar fixed upon a pedestal, and then directed the flame so that it shone through "a pretty large Globe of Glass fill'd with exceeding clear Brine" connected on the same pillar to a second movable arm with numerous joints that could be stretched or swiveled this way or that way at will, to the end of which had been attached a deep convex lens in order to concentrate the rays of light streaming through the globe into a point upon a small iron pin where, like a sacrificial victim upon an altar, the tiny corpse had been reverently and ceremoniously laid out. That done, and taking care not to breathe too close to the pin in his excitement (for even the slightest draft in the room, or an ineluctable sigh or fart, might have blown all his labors into thin air), he bent his head down toward the instrument and socketed his left eye to the aperture, his bare right eye meanwhile remaining free to enable him, quill in hand, to sketch whatever might appear, while with his other hand he turned the brass adjusting ring of the tube — which tube had one lens fixed by means of wax at the base, with its convex side turned toward the iron pin, and a second lens at the top, with its convex side turned toward his eye, "the intervening spaces between these two Glasses fill'd with very clear water," so that the image coming through would really be the twice magnified image of an image — and thus vigilantly and patiently continued to align and to rectify the instrument until, out of the surrounding darkness, an amorphous gray cloud of unknowing slowly swam, or rather floated, into his ken, growing steadily more luminous, whereupon he gave the brass adjusting ring one last slight twist . . . and there, glittering into his eye, for the first time truly seen, it was: the Flea.

"The strength and beauty of this small creature," he wrote exultantly, "had it no other relation at all to man, would deserve a description." Which he then proceeded to give. Its strength, though prodigious for its size, Hooke duly praised and then quickly passed over, since (as he said) "the *Microscope* is able to make no greater discovery of it than the naked eye."

> But, as for the beauty of it, the *Microscope* manifests it to be all over adorned with a curiously polish'd suit of sable Armour, neatly jointed, and beset with multitudes of sharp pinns, shap'd almost like Porcupine's Quills, or bright conical Steel-bodkins; the head is on either side beautify'd with a quick and round black eye, behind each of which also appears

a small cavity, in which he seems to move to and fro a certain thin film beset with many transparent hairs, which probably may be his ears; in the forepart of his head, between the two fore-leggs, he has two small long jointed feelers, or rather smellers, which have four joints, and are hairy, like those of several other creatures; between these, it has a small proboscis, or probe, that seems to consist of a tube, and a tongue or sucker, which I have perceived him to slip in and out. Besides these, it has also two chaps or biters . . . shap'd very like the blades of a pair of round top'd Scizers, and were opened and shut just after the same manner; with these Instruments does this little busie Creature bite and pierce the skin, and suck out the blood of an Animal, leaving the skin inflamed with a small round red spot.

Hooke's graven image of the Flea—almost two feet in length and about half that as wide, large enough for at least 10^{10} real fleas to settle easily upon it—was first published in his MICROGRAPHIA *or Some Physiological Descriptions of Minute Bodies* in 1665.

Quilled like a porcupine, yet tusked and even dewlapped like a walrus, or maybe a lobster, fanged like a tarantula, clawed like a grizzly, and armor plated and imbricated all over like an armadillo, Hooke's ferocious "little busie Creature" might pass for a chimera, and a mechanical chimera at that, with all its clocklike working parts meticulously depicted and ticketed. Only a Maker could have made it, Hooke believed, and on the same principles that he himself had made his microscope. It seems to be staring fixedly, almost balefully, straight ahead into the future, with its powerful jointed legs fully extended and poised beneath its abdomen, as if about to leap across the intervening centuries. . . . Except, of course, that its vital spring was missing.

Howbeit, soon after investigating the Flea, Hooke placed under his microscope several of its distant but no less consanguine relations, such as the common domestic Black-Fly, the Grey Drone-fly, the amphibious Water-fly, the Blue-fly, the Dragon-fly, and the Brush-horn'd as well as "great Belly'd," or female, Gnat. And, as before, he described and depicted in exact detail their various parts, marveling especially at the radiant circumspection of their huge pomegranatelike eyes; the humming rapidity in flight of their delicate transparent wings, which were protected, as he observed, by "several joynted pieces of Armor" on their backs and sides; their gladiatorial stingers, suckers, and gnashers; their nimble yet prehensile feet that enabled them to walk upside down on glass or cling to a hair — these "stupendious [sic] contrivances," as he called them — and was so awed by the mechanical ingenuity of the Curator of Curators that he exclaimed: "And can any be so sottish as to think all those things the productions of chance?" A swipe, as he intended, at the materialist philosophers of his own age who had misplaced the faith due to Him in the bewildered atoms of Democritus and Epicurus. "Certainly," Hooke concluded, "either their Ratiocination must be extremely depraved, or they did never attentively consider and contemplate the Works of the Almighty."

But there was another, even more noxious, bugaboo he wanted to swat. This was the ancient but still virulent superstition which held that such bloodthirsty pests as gnats and fleas, miniscule draculae actually, injected their venomous needles into our flesh out of pure malice toward mankind; from which it followed a fortiori that they must have been sent to plague us — what other reason could there be for their existence? — by no one else than Beëlzebub ("Lord of the Fly") himself, commander in chief of Satan's legions. Though considered the lowliest of spear-carriers, insignificant curse-provokers, hardly worth a damn, in the ranks of ghouls and demons, nonetheless they were equally hellborn and allied with the rest in the abysmal, inner and outer, darkness where they all connive.

So then, to dispel this darkness by the light of reason, Hooke submitted himself to an experiment that, in a small way, anticipates the martyrdom of Dr. Walter Reed with the malarial anopheles mosquito (and, in an even smaller micro-mock-heroic way, recalls the self-sacrifice of the titan Prometheus, the Light-Bringer, compared to whose enormous bulk the eagle sent by Zeus to gnaw at his liver would have seemed no larger than a flea), by exposing his flesh to the bite of the "great Belly'd," or female, Gnat. As he relates:

> One of these Gnats I have suffered to pierce the skin of my hand, with its proboscis, and thence to draw out as much blood as to fill its belly as full as it could hold, making it appear very red and transparent; and this without any further pain, than whilst it was sinking in its proboscis, as it is also in the stinging of Fleas: *a good argument, that these creatures do not wound the skin, and suck the blood out of enmity or revenge, but for meer necessity, and to satisfy their hunger.* [My italics]

But after this gnat, one imagines, had finished gorging itself, and he too had thoroughly satisfied his own curiosity, being only human he must have crushed it, like superstition, with at least some vindictive pleasure, beneath his thumb, then drawn a rubric with its blood across the back of his hand, as if to underline that the issue had finally been laid to rest. Q.E.D. and/or Amen.

For, in that streaky, quasi-manichaean dawn of what, a century later, became known as the Age of Enlightenment, Hooke and his fellow virtuosi (so called) of the Royal Society conceived their mission to be as much religious as scientific. The society itself, which Hooke had served as Curator of Experiments since its inception in 1662, had evolved out of informal meetings at Oxford and London by natural philosophers (when it was dubbed the "Invisible College" by the chemist Robert Boyle), most of whom were either Puritan divines or else adherents of that high-minded but tight-sphinctered religious sect. With the same evangelical zeal that their fundamentalist brethren had once applied to the interpretation of God's Word in the Bible, these virtuosi now investigated God's Work, as revealed in His other "book," Nature, whose language was mathematics. Hence their motto: *Nullia in Verba* ("Nothing in Words"). "Why," asked Hooke in the preface to his MICROGRAPHIA, "should we endeavour . . . like *Rabbins* to find out *Caballisms* and aenigmas in the Figure, and placing of Letters, where no such thing lies hid: whereas in *natural* forms there are some so small, and so curious, their designed business so far remov'd beyond the reach of our sight, that the more we magnify the object . . . the more we discover the imperfections of our senses, and the Omnipotency and Infinite perfections of the Creatour." As evidence there were his own microscopical engravings, together with their "physiological descriptions," which commented upon them as sermons to texts from Nature.

In the minutes for the Royal Society, for July 6, 1663, there is the following entry: "The King's entertainment being taken into consideration . . . Mr. Hooke is charged to shew his microscopical observations in a book to be provided by him for that purpose." Accordingly, a large volume of the copper engravings made from Hooke's sketches, together with his commentaries, was then gathered and sumptuously bound in what else but puce-colored leather, with the arms of the Royal Society emblazoned upon it, to be presented to Charles II.

The king, who kept a bemused and quizzical eye on the latest whim-whams of his virtuosi, was himself something of a dabbler in chemical experiments and maintained a laboratory at Whitehall Palace for his own diversion. But that was as far as it went. Once, after attending a demonstration of Robert Boyle's discoveries about the nature of gases, he is said to have "mightily laughed" at the folly of such a cloud-cuckoo philosopher who spent all his time, as he put it, "only in weighing of ayre"; and it must have been with the same sovereign hilarity that he veiwed Hooke's engravings of (besides the Flea) dandruff, the teeth of snails, frozen crystals of urine, a louse, hog hair, mold, poisonous nettles, and so forth. The bathetic solemnity with which Hooke and his fellow virtuosi went about their ritual grubbing for facts, and their seemingly preposterous experiments and speculations, might even have reminded Charles (who had spent much of life exiled in France during the reign of the Puritan Commonwealth) of Rabelais's "quintessential Queendom of Whim," in *Gargantua and Pantagruel*, as if Her Whimsical Majesty's fantastic court of *Spodizators, Tabachniks,* and *Abstractors* had been transmogrified into the virtuosi of his own kingdom of England:

> I saw a young *Spodizator*, who very artificially got Farts out of a dead Ass, and sold 'em for five pence an Ell.
> Others made Chalk of Cheese, and Honey of a Dog's Turd.
> Another did putrifie Beetles. O the dainty Food!
> Others in a large *Grass-plat*, exactly measured how far the Fleas could go at a Hop, a Step, and Jump; and told us, that this was exceeding useful for the Ruling of Kingdoms, the Conduct of Armies, and the Administration of Commonwealths. And that *Socrates*, who first had got Philosophy out of Heaven, and from idling and trifling, made it profitable and of moment, us'd to spend half his Philosophizing time in measuring the leaps of Fleas, as *Aristophanes,* the *Quintessential*, affirms.

While there were among the clergy doomsayers who preached against them, warning that these new prophets of the Work would eventually undermine the authority of the Word, to most of the wits and wordlings of the age they seemed no menace but rather the butts of ridicule. The playwright Thomas ("MacFlecknoe") Shadwell, for instance, pounded them will bulls' pizzles in a burlesque entitled, simply, *The Virtuoso*; and they were also hudibrastically bethumped by Samuel Butler in his long satire *The Island on the Moon*. Even a half-century later, reflected in the Coney Island mirror of Swift's *Gulliver's Travels*, we can still recognize them as the mad professors of the Grand Academy of Lagado on the floating island of Laputa, who attempted "to extract Sunbeams from Cucumbers" and "to reduce human Excrement to its original Food." . . . Which is to say, the food of the gods.

Swift's coprophagous fantasy aside, however, the ambition of these early otherworldly scientists was in truth just that, out of this world. With what might be described as Luciferian *chutzpah*, or maybe Promethean

213

hubris, they sought nothing less than to extend and complete the work of the Creator on the great day when the light was first separated from the darkness. ("Where id was," spake Sigmund Freud, "there ego shall be.") Therefore, in an expansive moment, Hooke was to compare the mundane limitations of Alexander the Great, who wept that he had no further worlds to conquer, to the seemingly horizonless prospects open before him and his fellow virtuosi, with (as he put it) "every considerable improvement of *Telescopes* or *Microscopes* producing new Worlds and Terra-incognita's to our view."

Even at the time he was writing this, Anton van Leeuwenhoek in Holland had already succeeded in grinding lenses for a new compound microscope more than twice as powerful as Hooke's and 20 times more so than the first crude "Optick tube" devised by Galileo around 1610. Through this instrument, van Leeuwenhoek was now able to observe the metamorphosis from egg to worm to chrysalis to the bounding and (all too) familiar flea itself; and by so doing, helped to disprove the once widely held belief that all insects, being so nasty and insignificant, beneath the notice of the Creator, must have been spontaneously generated out of sweat, scurf, dust, drek, scum, lees, urine, and so forth, with each kind of vegetable rot or animal putrefaction breeding its own peculiar species. But what most expanded the consciousness of the age (and so pricked its metonymic fancy that the microscope became commonly known thereafter as a "flea glass") was his further discovery that the tiny pupa flea was upon the eye; while Newton, though wavering, as 'twere, between the two, decided on the latter as more consistent with the rest of the material universe. In their eyeball-to-eyeball confrontation over this issue, they might have been two tribal wizards trying to stare each other down, Newton's particles bombarding Hooke's advancing waves, a deadlock of opposing points of view that was not to be broken until our own time, with the advent of quantum mechanics, when it was determined that light was either-neither but somehow both together and at once.

As is well known, Newton, that godling of science, was in private life suspicious, cantankerous, puritanical, old-maidish even, puckered, an anally retentive and rectitudinous personality, hoarding his ideas as if they were secrets between himself and the Creator, to be shared only reluctantly with others. He did not publish the *Principia Mathematica*, in which his early discoveries were systematically worked out, until as late as 1687 at the age of 45; and even then he deliberately made the proofs as difficult as possible to follow, in order, as he said, "to avoid being baited by little smatterers in mathematics." (Most likely meaning Hooke, who, while not exactly a "smatterer," was comparatively deficient. In their mechanical ingenuity, however, they were more or less equal: Newton during his childhood is said to have made "a little windmill and put a mouse inside it to turn the sails"; while Hooke, though he never contrived a chain fine enough to yoke a flea, as a boy at school, so his friend John Aubrey relates in one of his *Brief Lives*, had already "invented thirty severall wayes of Flying.") Anyway, because of his own morbid suspicion and secretriveness, Newton found himself throughout his career embroiled in quarrels with rival virtuosi concerning priority — with Leibniz, for instance, over the invention of calculus, and again with Hooke, over the discovery of the inverse-square law of universal gravity — disputes in which he saw a conspiracy by his enemies to deprive him of his just claims. Paranoia reifies. The prodigious effort of concentration required to complete the *Principia,* during which he is said to have remained propped up in bed for weeks, immobile, in almost uninterrupted solitary confinement within his own thoughts, left him in the end physically and emotionally racked, suffering long afterward from an insomnia that prevented him from escaping the glare of consciousness. The breaking point, it seems, occurred in early 1692, when a fire in his house destroyed the notes and papers of 20 years of research in optics. About this time he accused his friend and benefactor, the philosopher John Locke, of scheming against his chastity, no less,

> Sir:
>   Being of opinion that you endeavour to embroil me with women and by other means, I was so much affected with it, as that when one told me that you were sickly and would not live, I answered, "'twere better if you were dead."

whereupon it became evident that the mind of Newton, the great Light-Bringer himself, had darkened.

Upon his recovery in mid-1693, he was again able to resume his scientific work; even engaged in high political intrigue as Master of the Mint; and, among other honors accorded him, was elected president of the Royal Society in 1703. But after that interregnum of madness through which he had passed, Newton was radically altered, or rather, looked at another way, became more than ever himself. During his youth he had conducted experiments at Cambridge in a search for the Philosopher's Elixir and had read deeply in occult and theosophical literature, for a time falling under the spell of the great German mystic Jacob Boehme. (Which led Boehme's 18th-century translator, the Quaker William Law, to assert that Newton "did but reduce to mathematical form the central principles of Nature found in Behmen [sic].") These arcane studies continued to obsess him in later life, so much so that, as he wrote in a letter to Hooke in 1679, he "grutched the time" spent at science "unless it be perhaps at idle hours sometimes for a diversion." Now, having already disclosed, he believed, the unalterable laws governing the cosmos, God's Work, his immense intellectual powers were henceforth to be focused upon God's Word, especially the mystical symbology contained in the books of Daniel and Revelation.

Newton had conceived the *Principia*, he declared in the preface, "with an eye upon such principles as might work with considering men for the belief of a deity." But what worked out instead was the reverse. For it became more and more plain to "considering men," even in his own time, that a hypothetical deity did not have to be feigned in order to uphold his system; the Cosmic Machine, being self-adjusting, could run along forever without Him; and besides, as Newton himself acknowledged, such "a god, without dominion, providence, and final causes, was nothing else but Fate and Nature." So who needed Him? And, to complete this dismal weltanschauung, just as Newtonian physics had banished all "occult qualities" from a universe composed uniformly throughout of irreducible and impenetrable particles, so its counterpart, the sensationalist psychology of John Locke

> For speculation turns not to itself
> Till it hath travell'd, and is mirror'd there
> Where it may see itself

was to fumigate the mind of all "innate ideas." Set adrift, as 'twere, in this abandoned universe, without a terminus a quo or terminus ad quem, Everyman was thus left to chart a course through absolute space and time by dead ratiocination alone.

Or so, at least, it must have seemed to many whose religious faith had been undermined by Newtonian science. But to the devoutly rational and/ or rationally devout Newton himself, for whom both the Word and the Work reflected the Supreme Intelligence, faith as well as reason joined in one hallelujah of an ergo: a divine Plan in nature meant that there was an equally divine Plot in history. It was a Plot, moreover, discerned in broad outline by the prophets, that subsumed all other sub-, side-, cross-, or counterplots, a Plot of plots, unfolding the destiny of mankind *in saecula saeculorum* as a religious drama with a beginning, a middle, and an eschatological cherry at The End. Concerning the prophet Daniel, especially, Newton wrote that "to reject his prophecies is to reject the Christian religion: for this religion is founded upon his prophecy concerning the

Messiah." He therefore searched for clues not only in Scripture but in gnostic and hermetic philosophy, alchemical traditions, Egyptian hieroglyphs, cabalistical gematria, and the geometry of Solomon's Temple, subjecting them all to the sustained and concentrated powers of analysis that had enabled him to hold a problem fixed in his mind for days while composing the *Principia*. (Yet when his correspondent Bentley accused him of "expounding the prophecies as he would demonstrate a mathematical proposition," Newton responded with indignation.) Characteristically, he published none of the results of this immense labor in his lifetime, though he did prepare, at the request of King George I's wife Caroline, a treatise, entitled *A Short Chronicle from the First Memory of Things in Europe to the Conquest of Persia by Alexander the Great*.

For his chronological sequence of historic and prophetic events, Newton relied mainly upon a highly influential tract published in 1627, *Clavis Apocalyptica*, by a Cambridge cabalist named Joseph Mede. Mede (along with the more famous Archbishop Ussher) had proclaimed that the light was first divided from the darkness, and the curtain raised on the universe, at the dawn of 4004 B.C. With that as a beginning, the rest of Newton's Plot was foreordained to turn into a farce, or phantasmagoria, of miscued exits and entrances: Noah's Flood, for instance, was dated at 2348 B.C.; 2,000 years of Egyptian history, with gods and pharaohs confounded, were pressed into a single generation; followed by a circus procession of heraldic beasts out of Nebuchadnezzar's dream interpreted by Daniel—the lion with eagle's wings (Assyria-Babylonia), the leopard with four wings and four heads (Macedonia), the chimera with iron teeth and ten horns, plus another "little horn" that sprouted eyes and a mouth (Rome and the kingdoms of Europe)—all treading closely on each other's dates; and so forth; the climax to occur in the year 2000, which would see the fall of the Papacy, the Second Coming, and a Day of Judgment, when the powers and principalities and rulers of the darkness of this world would be sent back where they came from.

Considering the dearth of knowledge about the ancient world at the time, and also the narrow tunnel vision of history derived from scripture, this scenario is more or less what might have been expected. But, Newton being Newton, at the bottom of the Plot he uncovered yet another "plot," a conspiracy that is, and one that had actually succeeded in deflecting God's will by corrupting the Word itself. Newton charged that at the worldwide Council of Nicaea in A.D. 325, when the crucial debate on the nature of the Logos, or Christ, the Son of God, took place—whether He was of the same substance as God (homoousian), as maintained by Athanasius, or else of a different though divinely begotten substance (homoiou-sian), as asserted by Arius — the villainous Athanasius had conspired with the Roman Emperor Constantine to forge and then insert into the Bible, I John 5:7: "For there are three that bear record in heaven, the Father, the Word [Logos], and the Holy Ghost: and these three are one," upon which the orthodox Catholic doctrine of the Trinity is based. As a Puritan ra-tionalist as well as convinced Arian, Newton argued that the Son must be of a different substance from the Father, for if they were one and the same then God would have had to create Himself, which is absurd.

Nonetheless, that the indubitable iota of difference between the homoou-sians and the homoiousians could so profoundly have altered the Plot of history, while also absurd, is still no more so than that the troubled dream of the sixth-century B.C. Chaldean king of Babylon, Nebuchadnezzar (sometimes called Nebuchadrezzar), became the source of the messianic view of history shared by both Judaeo-Christian theology and Marxist socialism; or, for that matter, no more absurd than that the flea, as the then unknown instigator of the plague, should have driven Newton to take refuge in Lincolnshire in 1665, at which time he made his great discoveries and, by so doing, changed the course not only of his personal life but of the destiny of mankind as well. For, in attempting to solve the Plot, Newton had left himself out of his own historical equations as the chief factor and/ or leading actor of the Enlightenment. ("What is called the spirit of the age," said Goethe, "is really one's own spirit in which the age is mirrored.") The Plot, then, would somehow be made up as it went along of a bewilder-ing multiplicity of sub-sub, crisscrossing, and counter-counter plots in endless ramifications, connected not by logical necessity but by chance coincidence — sometimes called "mere" or "sheer," "pure" or "simple" — that inevitably hardens, in retrospect, into the appearance of inevitability.

2. The Plot Thickens

. . . So all right, already, to get back to our own plot: enter, as promised and foreordained, the Flea. From its first manifestation under Hooke's microscope, it made a quantum leap across a century (how, who knows?) and was spontaneously re-generated, as 'twere, or metempsychosed, in the psyche of that wildly talented and most haunted poet of his age, Christopher Smart. It was a case, as we shall see, of what once would have been de-scribed as "diabolical possession," yet even nowadays must be considered uncanny. A modern British neurologist with the unlikely name of Dr. Brain has diagnosed Smart's mental illness as cyclothymia, symptomized by violently alternating roller-coaster peaks and troughs of exaltation and depression, which sometimes leads to blackouts of lost or mistaken identity. But this still does not explain his weirdly grotesque avatar.

While Smart was in residence during the 1740s as a Fellow at Cambridge University, where he acquired a reputation as wit and poet as well as roisterer at the local taverns, his colleague Thomas Gray, after observing in a letter to a friend that Smart had fallen heavily into debt and "takes Hartshorn from Morning to Night lately" (i.e. spirits of ammonia, or smelling salts, the equivalent nowadays of "popping ammies," which must further have steepened his ups and downs), made the prediction, in words incised like an epitaph, that "for his Vanity & Faculty of Lyeing . . . [he] must soon come to a Jayl, or Bedlam, & that without any help, almost without Pity." Gray's own grismal prophecy, however, might have been in retaliation for a jibe.

> For my talent is to give an impression upon words by
> punching, that when the reader casts his eye upon 'em,
> he takes up the image from the mould wch I have
> made.

from which he was still smarting, viz: "Gray walks as if he had fouled his small clothes, and looks as if he smelt it." *Soit*. Both poets, though born only a few years apart and nurtured by the same traditions, were temperamentally opposed. Gray, punning on his own name, once referred to the humor it so described as a "white melancholy"; while Smart's, in contrast, was of shades of melancholia the most melanistic,

> For black blooms and it is PURPLE.

and subsequently ripened into madness. Which, briefly occurred as follows:

In the summer of 1749, having already squandered a fairly substantial inheritance and been dismissed for his "irregularities" as a fellow, Smart left Cambridge to escape a plague of creditors and came to London. Then 27 years old, he had twice won the valuable and prestigious Seaton Prize for religious poetry at Cambridge, and his early translations from and into Latin had received the blessing of the reigning Pope, Alexander, whose say-so in literature was as great as Newton's had once been in science. Not long after his arrival, therefore, he was able to earn his livelihood as a free-lance contributor of essays and light verse to various magazines, pluming himself under such *noms* as "Chimaerius Cantabriensis," "Ebeneazer Pentweazle," "Miss Nellie Pentweazle, a young lady of 15 years," "Zosimus

Zephyr," and so forth; and, in addition, wrote the lyrics for several songs that were set to music by the celebrated composers Boyce and Arne and performed successfully at concerts and theatricals in Vauxhall Gardens. About this time, too, as a rising literary star, he was befriended by Dr. Samuel Johnson, and so became fixed, together with Garrick, Boswell, Goldsmith, Dr. Burney, Fielding, and the rest, within the Great Bear's constellation. Toward the close of 1750, at the height of his fame, he founded and edited a popular humorous digest, *The Midwife, or The Old Woman's Magazine*, producing along with it a series of vaudeville performances billed as "Mother Midnight's Entertainments, or The Old Woman's Oratory," in which Smart himself, dressed in drag as "Mother Midnight," appeared on stage as impressario.

The financial backer for these ventures was a self-made and self-important entrepeneur, Thomas Newbery, who had previously gained a fortune by hustling such favorite nostrums of the time as Dr. Hooper's Female Pills and Dr. James' Fever Powders. Smart, to complete his new-found prosperity, now paid court to Newbery's young stepdaughter Anna Maria Carnan. What he lacked in physical stature (for he was, incidentally, scarcely five feet tall, "round and stubbed," so the novelist Fanny Burney once described him, or, as another contemporary put it, "a little smart black-eyed man") he most likely made up for somewhat by his wit and vivacity. Anyway, his suit proved successful. In a poem written during their courtship, Smart paid tribute to Anna Maria's "adamantine innocence"; yet it must have shattered under the force of his abracadabra, for she is said to have been pregnant when they were secretly and hurriedly married sometime in 1752.

Shortly thereafter, the first symptoms of his madness appeared. Smart had always been a devout communicant of the Church of England, but now, God-struck, he took to praying almost incessantly, in public and in private, whenever and wherever the fit came over him,

> For I blessed God in St. James Park till I routed all the
> company.
> For the officers of the peace are at variance with me and
> the watchman smites me with his staff.

sometimes bursting into the homes of friends and acquaintances while they were at dinner, or seeking them out at coffeehouses and taverns, even prying them from their beds late at night, to compel them to get down on their knees with him and pray. The once pert and dapper homuncular Smart could now be seen wandering wigless, unkempt, and unwashed, through the streets like Tom Thumb o' Bedlam, praising the Lord with all his might, an offense to the public and a scandal to his friends and family. While this frenzy was upon him, Smart was of course incapable of working to support his wife and infant daughter; so that Newbery, alarmed as both his employer and father-in-law, prescribed dosing him heavily with his own patented Dr. James' Fever Powders. Miraculously these powders, which must have been loaded with laudanum, served to keep Smart under sedation until the "fever" (as they termed it) passed and he was able to function once more. To oblige his father-in-law he later composed a "Hymn to the Supreme Being, on Recovery from a Dangerous Fit of Illness," dedicated "In Gratitude to Dr. James," which humbugery Newbery then printed and distributed as a testimonial.

In this way, off and on, through the years, up and down, the cyclothymic roller coaster accelerating with ever dimmer and shorter periods of lucidity until what seemed a total blackout occurred in 1757. In May of that year Smart was finally committed by his family. He was sent to St. Luke's Hospital in London, a private asylum run by a highly respected, and for his time, not altogether inhumane practitioner named (yes!) Dr. Battie, whose therapy consisted mainly in applying corrective punishment as forcefully as possible to his patients

> For they work me over with their harping-irons, which is
> a barbarous instrument, because I am more unguarded
> than others.

and, as the name proclaims, literally attempting to beat these batties back into their senses. Also, in order to reduce the "fever" believed to be inherent in madness during that Age of Reason, the more stubbornly unreasonable patients were sometimes plunged into baths of ice water or chained naked outside in freezing weather. Failing to respond to this treatment, Smart was discharged within a year and sent home under the care and supervision of his wife. This proved too much for her to endure. Not long afterward she left him, taking their two children (another had been born in the meantime) with her to Dublin, where she opened a shop selling her stepfather's pills and powders; but to make her rejection of the fanatically anti-Papist poet more complete, and galling, she also became a convert to Roman Catholicism and sent the children to be educated at a convent. Newbery, following her departure, refused to support his son-in-law any longer, and so Smart's friends now had to come to his assistance.

Garrick, who was devoted to the poet, agreed to give a special subscription performance, billed as: "For the benefit of a Gentleman, well known in the Literary World, who is at present under very unhapy Circumstances." And for this occasion even Thomas Gray, perhaps feeling some remorse

221

now that his prophecy, like a curse, had been fulfilled, bestowed a guinea but not his presence. With the money thus raised, Smart was committed to the asylum of Shrewsbury House in Chelsea, and here, except for occasional visits by friends from the great "Literary World" outside,

> DR. BURNEY: How does poor Smart do, Sir; is he likely to recover? JOHNSON: It seems as if his mind had ceased to struggle with the disease; for he grows fat upon it. DR. BURNEY: Perhaps, Sir, that may be from want of exercise. JOHNSON: No, Sir; he has partly as much exercise as he used to have, for he digs in the garden. Indeed, before his confinement, he used for exercise to walk to the ale-house; but he was *carried* back again. I did not think he ought to be shut up. His infirmities were not noxious to society. He insisted on people praying with him; and I'd as lief pray with Kit Smart as anyone else. Another charge was, that he did not love clean linen; and I have no passion for it.

he was to remain in seclusion, almost forgotten, for the next four years.
　　While incarcerated in this madhouse, with no other close companion but a cat named Jeoffrey—my MAGNIFICAT," Smart called him—

> For I am possessed of a cat, surpassing in beauty, from
> 　whom I take occasion to bless Almighty God.

like another Saint Jerome and his lion in petto—he conceived and undertook a vast prophetic work, in form resembling an oratorio, by which he hoped to redeem the Chosen People of England. Smart's mania for prayer, fused with his poetic vision, inspired him to compose several of the oracular verses for this weird masterpiece each day for years until, just before his release from Shrewsbury, the ecstatic blast abruptly subsided and he left off while it was still unfinished. His last entry is dated January 13, 1763. The manuscript afterward came into the possession of certain friends and admirers of the poet William Cowper, whose mind had been similarly afflicted, and so was preserved by them not for its own sake but as a case study in poetic madness; from whom it descended into other hands and then floated, like a castaways' message in a bottle, unopened and unread, from generation to generation; until our own time, when it was rediscovered by chance, with more than half its pages missing and the rest often mutilated or illegible, by the literary scholar William F. Stead. Stead unjumbled and edited the remaining pages and then published it, in 1939, under the title *Rejoice in the Lamb (Jubilate Agno)*.

222

Since then, critical analysis has shown that Smart, in imitation of the antithetical syntax of the Psalms, had divided the entire work into two distinct but inter-related parts: a "Let" section, so called because each verse begins with that word, wherein a character whose name appears in scripture unites, as if it were his totem, with some animal, vegetable, or mineral to offer up a prayer to the Lord; and a section of verses beginning with "For,"

> For I have a providential acquaintance with men who
> bear the names of animals.
> For I bless God to Mr. Lion Mr. Cock Mr. Cat Mr.
> Talbot Mr. Hart Mrs. Fysh Mr. Grub, and Mr. Lamb.

wherein Smart himself responds antiphonally with a personal reference or moral insight drawn from his own experience. He most likely imagined a scene like the one described in Nehemiah 8:1-6:

> And all the people gathered themselves together as one man
> into the street that was before the water gate. . . . And Ezra the
> scribe stood upon a pulpit of wood, which they had made for
> that purpose. . . . And Ezra opened the book in the sight of
> all the people: (for he was above all the people); and when he
> opened it all the people stood up: And Ezra blessed the Lord,
> the great God. And all the people answered, Amen, Amen. . .

but with Smart himself as the prophet laying down the law. An oratorio so grandiose, and with a cast so huge, could only have been performed in a Canyon appropriately Grand, with banks of organs set into the cliffs and flocks of aeolian harps, like angels' wings, floating above an orchestra of thousands of violins, trumpets, and flutes, psalters, sackbuts and shofars, cymbals, glockenspiels, knuckle bells, dulcimers, and tinkles assembled there in the pit to accompany a choir of, say, 100,000,000 trained and Chosen voices on one side chanting the "Lets," and, on the other, the solo voice of Smart himself, rising above them all, responding with the "Fors." It was no doubt mad, but mad in excelsis, for within it were flashes and sometimes sustained visions of a numinous reality.

One line, especially, leaps up at us:

> Let Ethan praise with the Flea, his coat of mail, his
> piercer, and his vigour, which wisdom and providence
> have contrived to attract observation and to escape it.

But there it inescapably is, Hooke's own heroic Flea observed (or rather envisioned, for how could it have been seen so closely with the naked eye?)

even down to the "coat of mail" which the author of the MICROGRAPHIA had described metaphorically as "a curiously polish'd suit of sable Armour." A new edition of Hooke's famous work had appeared as late as 1745, while Smart was still at Cambridge, so it is highly unlikely that the poet, who had a naturalist's curiosity and a passion for odd bits of lore about God's creatures, would have been unfamiliar with it. The Flea, then, entered Smart's imagination already armored by Hooke's metaphor. As for Ethan (a name meaning "strong" in Hebrew), he is mentioned in the Bible, surnamed "the Ezrahite," as author of the militantly Jahvistic Psalm 89, and also (in I Kings 4:31) as a sage whose wisdom was worthy of comparison with Solomon's. Since Ethan and the Flea, therefore, were both valiant as well as wise, Smart "Let" them pray together in his totemic congregation.

And then, with Smart's own responsive "For"—or rather the verse I choose, out of the MS. mishmash of possible choices, to take as his response—what up to this point might have seemed merely grotesque now shades into the uncanny:

> For Agricola is SAINT GEORGE, but his son Christopher
> must slay the Dragon with a PHEON'S head.

By a further transubstantiation, it appears, Saint George the Dragon Killer, patron saint of England, has also been joined with the Flea (each with his "piercer" and his "coat of mail"), along with Ethan the Ezrahite, Agricola, and "his son Christopher"—i.e. Smart himself—a quincunx indissolubly homoousian, one for all and all for one. It is as if we had been able to descend, by way of Smart's undermind, into the magical Dream Time of those prancing sorcerers with animal masks depicted on the walls of caves 20,000 years ago, when such theriomorphic presto-changos actually took place. But to understand the process whereby all the personae in this verse are fused, we have to hold up, as 'twere, a kind of psycho-historico-anthropologico-theologico analytical ophthalmoscope (no less) to see through and behind his eyes into the workings of his imagination.

To begin with "Agricola is SAINT GEORGE . . ." By thus confounding Agricola, the Roman general who conquered and ruled Britain in the first century A.D., with the legendary Saint George, Smart regressed to an atavistic way of thinking wherein names and images, according to the principle of *pars pro toto*—or even a part-of-the-part standing for the whole—possessed miraculous powers. The philosopher of *Symbolic Forms*, Ernst Cassirer, remarks on this dominant trait of savage consciousness: "The 'image' [or name] does not represent the 'thing,' it *is* the thing; it does not merely stand for the object, but has the same actuality. . . ." In such a

Once-upon-a-time Time, or Dream Time, shared by children (*Rumpel-stiltskin!*) as well as by certain types of schizos (Cassirer, incidentally, mentions one case in which a patient believed that if the word *chaos* were broken apart the pieces would each fully express its meaning), all that is, real or imagined, exists on a single "cubist" plane of being. If that's the way it seems

> For the phenomenon of the horizontal moon is the truth —
>   she appears bigger on the horizon because she actually is so.
> For the moon is magnified in the horizon by Almighty
>   God, and so is the sun.

that's the way it is. So then, since both the Latin *agricola* and the Greek γεοργος, our George, mean *farmer*, it follows for Smart that "Agricola is SAINT GEORGE."

"... but his son Christopher," Smart himself, now enters the picture. As the self-anointed champion and redeemer of the Anglican Chosen, albeit temporarily confined

> For I am under the same accusation with my Saviour — for
>   they said, he is besides himself.

in a madhouse, Smart claimed (or so imagined, which for him was the same) to be the incarnate "son" of Agricola-SAINT GEORGE

> For I am descended from the steward [Agricola] of the
>   island, blessed be the name of the Lord Jesus king of England.

called upon by the Almighty "to slay the Dragon with . . ." *What?* With "the PHEON'S head," of course — a pheon in heraldry being a dart or the barb of an arrow — which choice of weapon can be explained genealogically. Smart's family traced its descent from a Sir John Smart, Garter Knight of Arms to Edward IV, during whose reign (1461-83) Saint George became patron saint of England, thus entitling the poet to bear arms, viz.: "Argent a chevron between three pheons sable." Having thus unsheathed his vorpal pheon (*pen? piercer? penis?* . . . since the penis itself, by a similar sort of free-associational word magic, has been befreuded into a phallic symbol), and clad in his Flea "coat of mail," the armor of righteousness, Smart could now go forth

> With a heart of furious fancies
>   Whereof I am commander
> With a burning spear and a horse of air
>   To the wilderness I wander

on his holy mission "to slay the Dragon."

And the Dragon, it so happened, was none other than Newton himself. Not, to be sure, the historic and mortal Newton (1642–1727) we know, but NEWTON sub specie aeternitatis as transfigured in his imagination; just as Smart's own tutelary spirit of a Flea was no nameless and insignificant bug, such as might have sprung from the fur of his cat Jeoffrey or from his own none too clean linen, but the "mental vision" of a Flea, a quintessential Flea of fleas, if you please, with a noumenal existence more Real than real.

Newton's mechanistic world view revealed by his theory of light Smart condemned as blasphemy against the Word and a desecration of the Work.

> Newton is ignorant, for if a man consult not the WORD
> how should he understand the WORK?

Against it he opposed his own faith in the mystical nature of light, first envisioned by neoplatonism and then embodied by the Church Fathers in the doctrine of the Trinity, that God begat the Son, or Logos, as the consummation of His thoughts, which surround and radiate from Him

> Hail, holy Light, offspring of Heaven first-born!
> Or of the Eternal coeternal beam
> May I express thee unblamed? since God is light,
> And never but in unapproachéd light
> Dwelt from eternity—dwelt then in thee,
> Bright effluence of bright essence increate!

(so Milton saw) as the *logoi spermatikoi* of ideas impregnating and so giving form to Nature. These seminal ideas would thus be voided and rendered sterile in the reduction of light to mere "particles" by materialist science. And it followed, too, that since Newton was blind to the "inner light," he must be equally color-blind, because to Smart colors were no mere "secondary qualities" of things, or "phantasms," or "agitations within the sensorium," but irreducible psychic facts

> For Newton's notion of colours is αλογος unphilosophical
> For the colours are spiritual. . . .
> For the next is GREEN of which there are ten thousand
>   distinct sorts.
> For the blessing of God upon the grass is in shades
>   of Green visible to a nice observer as they light upon the
>   surface of the earth.

226

> For the next is YELLOW wch is more excellent than red,
>   tho Newton makes red the prime.
> For Red is the next working round the Orange.
> For Red is of sundry sorts till it deepens to BLACK.
> For black blooms and it is PURPLE.

in a spiritual spectrum as self-evident as the primal cries "ugh" or "ah" or "oo" or "oi" are self-expressive.

The only good word Smart had for Newton was to praise him for his "chastity." But the philosopher John Locke, whom Newton during his own derangement had accused of being his tempter, came in for the full thrust of the pheon:

> For Locke supposes that an human creature, at a given
>   time, may be an atheist i.e. without God, by the folly
>   of his doctrine concerning innate ideas.

The Word explicitly saith: "So God created man in his own image in the image of God created he him," without *and* within, so how could the mind, as Locke supposed, be a tabula rasa? The Word itself would then be erased as merely another word among words, with no intrinsic value except that assigned by custom. And man, who as Adam had once named and thus "known" intuitively the God-implanted Ideas of the Garden of Eden,

> For there is a language of flowers.
> For flowers are musical in ocular harmony.
> For the right names of flowers are yet in heaven. God
>   make gardners better nomenclators.

would again be expelled — "Locked-out," — into a world devoid not only of occult qualities but of meaning as well. But 'twas not so. Though words, declared Smart, may have their roots in the material world, as manifestations of the Word they bloomed only in the spirit.

More than a century later, when Robert Browning first came across Smart's *A Song to David* in a dusty anthology of poems, and instantly recognizing it as a masterpiece rescued the poet from oblivion, he wrote that of "the throngs between / Milton and Keats," it was solely Smart who *"pierced the screen / 'Twixt thing and word."* [My italics] He was able to pierce it, as we know, because for him there was no screen, a screen placed there by reason, but a clear transparency in which things were magically spelled out and words were substantially what they stood for. Smart's

227

atavistic regression during his madness to a savage foretime when such word magic was universally accepted and practiced, along with his own profound religious mysticism derived from a lifelong study of cabalist and hermetic literature, no doubt consciously and subconsciously sustained and reaffirmed each other. But in his time, living as he did when the shadows cast by the declining sun of the Enlightenment were already growing longer, the moral and intellectual stigma attached to madness was enough to deny him acceptance. Even that great Noah's Ark of a poem, *A Song of David*, which he began while still at Shrewsbury and published soon after his release, ran aground on the ignorance and stony indifference of critics. Dr. Johnson, for instance, when asked to judge between Smart's poetry and the now forgotten drek of a versifier named Samuel Derrick, came up with this astonishingly apt (for our purposes) yet also remarkably obtuse comment: "Sir, there is no settling the point of precedency between a louse and a flea." What he might have said if confronted with the *Jubilate Agno*, with its ascending tiers on tiers of metaphorical argument and reechoing eurekas and hallelujahs, the shrieking interior, so to speak, of Smart's own mind, like one of Piranesi's gigantic imaginary prisons, though "a puzzling Question" (as Sir Thomas Browne once put it) "is not beyond all conjecture."

Following his release from Shrewsbury, in 1763, Smart survived for eight more years and wrote some of his best poetry. His bizarre religious mania was now apparently pronounced harmless or else under control. But it must be the characteristic fate of all such prophets to be improvident; and, in the end, the strain of having to ply his pheon as a Grub Street drudge finally undermined his health, and so reduced him to poverty and bankruptcy. This time neither his family nor friends from the great "Literary World" came to his assistance. He was arrested and brought to trial by his creditors, then sentenced for an indefinite term to King's Bench Prison in London, where he remained, suffering from sickness as well as hunger despite desperate appeals outside for help,

> Sir:
> Being upon a recovery of a fit of illness, and having nothing to eat, I beg of you to send me two or three shillings, which (God willing) I will return, with many thanks, in two or three days.

until he died in May of 1771.

Gray's grismal prediction made 25 years earlier — that he "must come to a Jayl, or Bedlam" — thus proved true on both counts. Actually, however,

Smart was never committed to Bedlam itself (which was the generic name, a corruption of "Bethlehem," for all madhouses at the time and also the famous public institution located at Moorfields), but rather, as we know, to privately endowed asylums for insane gentlemen. This is a curious but in no way captious point. For had he been confined instead to Bedlam, then Smart, in his totemic role as Flea in his own oratorio, would have passed, or "pierced," as 'twere, through an Alice in Wonderland mirror and entered behind the scenes of the weird and weblike "plot" in which he was caught. For it was Hooke, Robert, this time in his official capacity as Architect of London, appointed together with Christopher Wren after the Great Fire of 1666 that followed the Great Plague of 1665, who had himself designed and supervised the construction of the Moorfields Bedlam.

Of course this can only be "pure" coincidence, though perhaps purer than most, but I am not making it up: except in the same way that Umpire "Jocko" Conlon, who stood behind the plate calling balls and strikes for 30 years, must have had in mind when he said: "It ain't nothing till I call it." To make sense of such quirky yet meaningful coincidences we might conjure up Aristotle, who in his own bafflement leaves us with the poet Agathon's gnomic remark: "Art loves chance, chance loves art"; or else the philosopher Lao-tzu, from the sixth century B.C. in China, who explains chance occurrences by a magical taoist correspondence and sympathy underlying the "shapes without shape, forms without form, vague semblances," which make up Things As They Are and/or Seem To Be; or else, closer to our time, the psychologist Carl Jung and the quantum physicist Wolfgang Pauli, who collaborated on a theory of "acausal orderedness," or "synchronicity," thus reviving the doctrine of "pre-established harmony" once posited by Leibnitz, to deal with the parapsychology of everyday life; or else, to pull up the Idea of coincidence by its roots, Arthur Koestler, who recently formulated the hypothesis of "confluential events" occurring in a psychomagnetic field, as if all minds were part of one Mind. . . . The fact, nonetheless, remains: Hooke's Bedlam.

An immense structure, with a facade 540 feet long, it was ornamented above its gate with twin colossal stone statues of lunatics (one manic and raving, with his hands and feet in shackles, and the other depressive, slumped in a catatonic stupor), and was much admired in its time for the grandeur of its architecture. Besides serving as a hospital, it was also a sort of human zoo, or freak show, visited for a penny admission by thousands of sightseers each year. The building remained standing until 1815, when it was torn down and replaced by an even larger asylum in southeast London bearing the same name.

And it was in this new Bedlam—the *name*, not the place—that Smart and the poet most closely allied with him, William Blake, his successor as champion of the Word, who picked up the pheon

> I come in Self-annihilation & the grandeur of Inspiration
> To cast off Rational Demonstration by faith in the Saviour
> To cast off the rotten rags of Memory by Inspiration,
> To cast off Bacon, Locke & Newton from Albion's covering,
> To take off his filthy garments and clothe him with
>   Imagination,
> To cast aside from Poetry all that is not Inspiration,
> That it no longer shall dare to mock with the aspersion of
>   Madness
> Cast on the Inspired by the tame high finisher of paltry Blots . . .

where Smart had let it fall, can be said to have "met" in spirit. What brought them together, it goes without saying, was the Flea. . . .

In 1833 an anonymous French journalist for a magazine published in Paris contributed a sensational and trumped-up article, headed "*Hôpital des Fous à Londres,*" in which he pretended to have visited Bedlam and while there to have conversed in his cell with "*Blake surnommé le Voyant.*" Blake, as it so happened, had already been dead for five years when the interview supposedly took place. This spectral Blake, described by the journalist as "*un homme grand et pâle*" (his elongated shade, no doubt, for Blake alive had been ruddy and short), stooped obligingly to discuss his own visions with the intruder, and even showed him several sketches of the ghosts of Semiramis, Moses, Marc Antony, Richard III, et al., who he claimed had risen from the spirit world to pose for him. A false ghost claiming to have seen real ghosts, which *were* real, is the sort of involuted ghost story that would have turned Blake himself around. But then—and yes, here it comes again—the journalist added: "*When I entered his cell he was drawing a flea whose ghost, he asserted, had just appeared before him.*" [My italics] For of all the prophetic and visionary works of Blake, his famous drawing of *The Ghost of a Flea* had seemed to contemporaries clinching proof that he was indeed mad, and so, most likely, had also misled the author of the article to assume that he had been confined in Bedlam.

Fortunately, there exists a full account of the circumstances under which the drawing was actually produced.

Blake, during his later life, used to hold regular 9–5 A.M. visitation hours at night for any spirit who might wish to appear; at which time he would sit poised and waiting before his drawing board, pencil in hand, ready to sketch their portraits. On several occasions his young friend John Varley, a painter and devotee of astrology who believed in Blake's occult powers, kept vigil beside him, thereby coming into possession of a number of these portraits. One evening years afterward, while entertaining at his own home another admirer of Blake, the writer Alan Cunningham, Varley showed them to him; and then (as Cunningham relates in his memoirs), "taking out a small panel from a private drawer," Varley revealed "his greatest curiosity," and asked Cunningham what he saw:

> "I see," said I, "a naked figure with a strong body and a short neck—with burning eyes which long for moisture, and a face worthy of a murderer, holding a bloody cup in his clawed hands, out of which it seems eager to drink. I never saw any shape so strange, nor did I ever see any colouring so curiously splendid—a kind of glistening green and dusky gold. . . . But what in the world is it?" "It is a ghost, Sir—the ghost of a flea—a spiritualization of the thing!" "He saw this in a vision then," I said. "I'll tell you all about it, Sir. I called on him one evening, and found Blake more than usually excited. He told me he had seen a wonderful thing—the ghost of a flea! And did you make a drawing of him? I inquired. No, indeed, said he, I wish I had, but I shall, if he appears again! He looked earnestly into a corner of the room, and then said, here he is— reach me my things—I shall keep my eye on him. There he comes! his eager tongue whisking out of his mouth, a cup in his hand to hold blood, and covered with a scaly skin of gold and green;—as he described him so he drew him."

It was, of course, Hooke's own Flea redivivus, the spitting image: from the "tongue or sucker" that the Curator had perceived under the microscope "to slip in and out," described by Blake as "eager" and "whisking," down to the "curiously polish'd suit of sable Armour, neatly jointed," now envisioned as a "scaly skin of gold and green." But what Hooke had seen, as 'twere, through a glass darkly, Blake saw face to face.

> The Microscope knows not of this nor the Telescope: they alter
> The ratio of the Spectator's Organs, but leave Objects untouched.

Across the proscenium of what appears to be a narrow curtained stage suspended in the night sky, and against a scenic backdrop of stars and a gigantic onrushing comet (which might be a spiral nebula viewed obliquely, if the existence of such galaxies had been known or suspected at that time), this Ghost of a Flea moves on tiptoe—or does it move?—rather it stands there transfixed, half-turned in a sort of arabesque, and stares balefully into a huge but apparently empty bowl (of blood?) held in the talons of its left hand, while with its right, thrust far behind its back, it pinches between thumb and forefinger some mysterious two-horned object. Behind him the curtain (or is it a curtain?), shaped like a monstrous leg, drops flat-footed down to the floor, as if another and even stranger apparition were following in pursuit.

> A MEMORABLE FANCY: An infernal laboratory somewhere in Hell where Hooke himself, socketing his eye ("an eie," so John Aubrey informs us, "full and popping, and not quick; a grey eie") to the tube of a diabolical speculum, waits for the cloud of unknowing to clear up, and then gazes, with a certain prickly and, as 'twere, creepy horripilation of awe and dread, at Blake's Ghost of his own Flea gazing back at him.

In Varley's astrological treatise entitled *Zodiacal Physiognomy,* where he cast Blake's horoscope, he adds this to what we know of the Flea's visitation: "During the time occupied in completing the drawing, the Flea told him [Blake] that all fleas were inhabited by the souls of such men as were bloodthirsty to excess, and were therefore providentially confined to the size and form of insects; otherwise, were he himself, for instance, the size of a horse, he would depopulate a great portion of the country." The ancient Vedic myth of karmic retribution and the transmigration of souls—adapted, by way of Plato's *Timaeus,* into neoplatonist doctrine and thence into Blake's own mystique—the souls of the blessed and enlightened after their death become birds; the souls of the worldly and ambitious, bees or ants; and so forth; but the souls of the cruel and warlike (as the Ghost so informed Blake) become such vicious pests as fleas and gnats. Compared to Smart's heroic little knight in shining armor, Blake's was indubitably diabolical, a spear-carrier for Bëelzebub.

The question, however, can't be helped: Did he really see it, the Ghost, or did he imagine it? But to ask that is to confound our own "Locked-in" and Cartesian way of seeing

> Two Horn'd Reasoning, Cloven Fiction,
> In Doubt, which is Self contradiction

with Blake's, for he was a "literalist of the imagination," just as Smart was a fundamentalist of the Word. "I question not," Blake wrote, "my Corporeal or Vegetative Eye any more than I would question a Window concerning a Sight. I look thro' it & not with it." So, then, he did see it, for he was a "seer"; and besides, as Ipse dixit, "to converse *in* the spirit is to converse *with* spirits." [My italics] For if ever anyone can be said to have been gifted with "second sight" it was surely Blake. From early childhood, apparently, he had discovered and cultivated within himself the astonishing power (what the parapsychologist, F. W. H. Myers once described in the chomping phrase "psychorrhagic diathesis") of envisioning images of such intensity that they were projected before him as apparitions. He could as soon have doubted their real existence as, say, anyone could doubt the reality of his dreams in the course of dreaming them. "What seems to Be," he wrote, "Is, To those to whom / It seems to Be." This was of course Blake's own conscious poetic re-vision of Bishop Berkeley's idealist conception of being: esse est percipi ("to be is to be perceived"); but it was also, it seems to us, a reaffirmation, independently and unconsciously arrived at, of Smart's primitive "cubist" point of view.

By Blake's time, however, the idea of ghosts lingered on only as the ghost of an idea that had already been exorcised by reason, no longer worth considering, though it still might haunt the minds of religious cranks and/ or lunatics. Which is how Blake was in fact regarded by many of his contemporaries. The poet Robert Southey, for instance, after meeting him for the first time, recalled 20 years afterward that "his madness was too evident, too fearful. It gave his eyes an expression such as you would expect to see in one who was possessed." Wordsworth, too, though he recognized the poetic genius of the author of *Songs of Innocence and of Experience*, remarked after reading it, "There is no doubt this poor man was mad . . ." (To these and other such "aspersions of madness" cast upon Blake by "tame high finishers of paltry blots," the painter Samuel Palmer, who had known and revered the poet in his youth, was to reply, "If Mr. Blake had a crack, it was a crack that let the light through.") Once, commenting on Smart's own religious mania, Dr. Johnson observed: "Madness frequently discovers itself merely by unnecessary deviation from the usual modes of the world." For, after all, it *was* "mad" of Blake to have believed he could talk familiarly with ghosts, and to claim that his poems had been dictated to him by spirits, and yet not be condemned by the public as mad. Viewed in the open light of reason, his own "inner light"

> That dark lanthorn of the spirit
> Which none see by but those who bear it

was only an ignis fatuus of the mind, an * with no visible reference in reality.

In a book by one J. G. Spurzheim, *Observations on the Deranged Mani-*

festations of the Mind, or Insanity, published in 1817, Blake came across the following: "Religion is another fertile cause of insanity. . . . Hence the primitive feelings may be misled and produce insanity; that is what I would contend for, and in that sense religion often leads to insanity." He then wrote in the margin:

> Cowper [the poet (1731–1800) whose own religious mania had indirectly resulted in the preservation of Smart's MS.] came to me and said: 'O that I were insane always. I will never rest. Can you not make me truly insane? I will never rest till I am so. O that in the bosom of God I was hid. You retain health and yet are as mad as any of us all – over us all – mad as a refuge from unbelief – from Bacon, Newton & Locke."

Against this spectral triumvirate who, by force of reason, had beguiled mankind into worshiping "Satan's Mathematic Holiness, Length, Bredth & Highth," Blake, like Smart before him, tilted his own more formidable pheon:

> I must create a system or be enslaved by another Man's.
> I will not Reason & Compare: my business is to Create.

What sort of "System"? Not one to rival theirs, certainly, but rather an anti-System; or, as he put it, "Striving with Systems to deliver Individuals from those Systems." His immense "prophetic books," from *Thel*, written in 1789, to *Jerusalem* in 1820, comprised an "Intellectual Allegory," so called – broadly similar to Claude Lévi-Strauss's description of primitive thought as "a system of concepts embedded in images" – which was as self-consistent and self-evident as a dream or a weltanschauung would appear to the dreamer or the inhabitant of that welt. Newton's equations and his laws were Blake's eidolons and his metaphors.

The rivalry between these two almost mythic antagonists, the system-forging scientist NEWTON and the spellbinding poet BLAKE, might almost have had its genesis at the time the book of Genesis itself was composed. *In illo tempore* – or Once Upon a Time – as Mircea Eliade, the author of *Shamanism,* relates, at the dawn of the age of metallurgy, there occurred a worldwide struggle for power in the tribes of mankind between the shamans and the smiths. Both were regarded with awe as magic-working professions, masters over fire, whose closely guarded secrets and techniques were passed on from generation to generation only after a long and arduous apprenticeship. At first, throughout the period when our own religious myths were formed, the power of the shamans must have prevailed. Evidence of their triumph is still preserved in the iconology of angels, who are depicted with birds' wings and feathers in the same ornithomorphic guise that shamans once put on in order "to fly"; and, conversely, in the depiction of Satan's host of devils and demons, cast out of heaven

> . . . flaming from the ethereal sky
> With hideous ruin and combustion, down
> To bottomless perdition, there to dwell
> In adamantine chains and penal fire

after their rebellion against the Almighty, as soot-blackened and fire-breathing smiths. But by the time of BLAKE and NEWTON — to pass, or rather "to fly," over the intervening ages — the shamans' power had been broken by the heirs of the smiths, scientists who learned to bind the forces of nature with mathematical laws and formulas:

> A mighty Spirit leap'd from the land of Albion,
> Nam'd Newton; he siez'd the trump and blow'd the enormous
>   blast!
> Yellow as leaves of Autumn, the myriads of Angelic hosts
> Fell thro' the wintry skies seeking their graves,
> Rattling their hollow bones in howling and lamentation

By such a cataclysmic reversal in image, the once damned and denigrated smiths were now exalted; while the shamans and their heirs, prophets and poets, visionaries, necromancers, occultists, and abracadabrists of all sorts, collectively labeled "crackpots," became not heavenly (for the place itself was abolished) but social outcasts.

Of course Blake in his time could have known nothing of shamanism, as Smart, too, knew nothing of totemism, since they were not as yet even names. But in his quest for the one true proto-religion he did discover, and transform into his own private mythology, ideas then current among antiquarians about the mysterious cult of the Druids. Blake imagined the builders of Stonehenge as a pre-Adamic race of beings with miraculous spiritual powers, the founders of the "One Religion" (as he called it), whose later descendants included the Hebrew patriarchs as well as Jesus and the prophets. What's more, so he declares in the last and greatest of his visionary poems, *Jerusalem*, the Druids themselves sprang from the Divine Body of the primordial God-Man, Albion, "who anciently contained in his mighty limbs all things in Heaven & Earth." Blake most likely adapted his conception of Albion from the symbolical anthropos Adam Kadmon in the cabala, where he is described as the first manifestation of God's own inner light; and it was this idea, following the gleam, that provided him with an even more astonishing insight. For if the Druids were the children of Albion, and the patriarchs and prophets were themselves lineally descended from the Druids, ergo Britain must be "the Primitive Seat of the Patriarchal Religion." The implosive force of the intellectual ergs released by this ergo overwhelmed him. "Can it be? . . ." he asks himself incredulously; and then, in self-confirmation, gives three cheers, two in Hebrew and one in English: "Amen! Huzza! Selah!" Blake chose to be Chosen, but only as a loyal son of Albion.

Apropos this symbolical anthropos Adam Kadmon, alias Albion, there is another notion in the cabala related to it, a kind of conundrum, but one that Blake would immediately have recognized as self-evident by holding, as 'twere, up a mirror: viz., that there exist 600,000 "faces" of the Law, as many as there were Chosen People at Sinai who shared the revelation with Moses, so that each one present had his own way of interpreting it, according to "the root of his soul." Yet the law, paradoxically, is the same for all. Thus, to encircle the argument and box the paradox, Blake could declare himself in the preface to *Jerusalem* to be a "true Orator": that is, a single voice inspired by the Almighty to speak as the Voice of all. The feathered costume of the shaman, turned inside out, became for him the mantle — or hairshirt — of the prophet.

Blake's own life was thereby transfigured, *pars pro toto*, into the life of Everyman, or Adam Kadmon, or Albion, or Finnegan. . . . "The series of men," wrote Pascal, "may be considered a single man, living forever and continuously learning," from the uroboric alpha of our ancestral Dream Time to the omega point of the noosphere in some future Space-Time; for Blake, however, it was not men or man in the abstract but the unique historical and biological person, suffering and dying, who was (as Paracelsus described him) both microtheos and microcosmos. In Blake's prophetic books, conceived over a span of decades as a single Book, people who played even minor roles in his life appear under their own names on the same exalted stage as biblical or legendary or mythical personae, for all of them, as envisioned by and through him, were also specters and emanations of the 6,000-year-old dream of Albion:

> Then those in Great Eternity met in the Council of God
> As one Man, for contracting their Exalted Senses
> They behold Multitude, or Expanding they behold as one,
> As One Man all the Universal family . . .

The screen that had been imposed between material and mental reality by Newton's "single vision"

> We are led to Believe a Lie
> When we see not Thro' the Eye

and creeping and peeping "Two Horn'd" reasoning was thereby dissolved; for *all* was spirit: the snail, the spiral nebulas, and the concept of the Spiral itself.

Because it denied spiritual agency, Newton's foreordained historical "Plot," though spun out of Daniel and Revelation, would have been seen "Thro' the Eye" of Blake as materialist determinism in another guise. In 1795 Blake did a famous series of pictures in tempera, one of which shows Newton sitting naked upon a stone at the bottom of the sea, crouched so far forward that his back is almost parallel to the ground, and staring with almost catatonic fixity at a diagram inscribed upon a snail-like scroll at his feet, then, a picture of Nebuchadnezzar, the Babylonian king whose dreams Daniel had interpreted (which interpretation Newton had then reinterpreted), here shown in his madness grazing like an ox on all fours, staring back wild-eyed at the viewer. The pictures were meant to be conjoined, since Newton-Nebuchadnezzar personified for Blake dual aspects of materialism: the "vegetative" degradation of sense and feeling and the disassociation of reason from the imagination. Blake's "business," as he put it, being not to "Reason & Compare," but "to Create," employing symbols and metaphors rather than formulas and equations, he imagined that the "Divine Imagination" might deliver man from the systems that enslaved him.

As a poet he thus metaphorically equated the Newtonian system with the once dominant poetic form of the Age of Reason, the heroic couplet, within whose narrow double-barred cell the spirit had been forced to pace, ten paces up and ten paces down, for over a century. And for Pope, therefore, as Newton's alter ego, he prepared an elegant jacobin contraption of an epigram, "Imitation of Pope: A Compliment to the Ladies":

> Wondrous the Gods, more wondrous are the Men,
> More Wondrous Wondrous still the Cock & Hen,
> More Wondrous still the Table, Stool & Chair,
> But Ah! More wondrous still the Charming Fair.

In this mock "mock-heroic" so-called "imitation," the shimmering equilibrium of Pope's precisely scaled and measured style (the social scale of

237

The Rape of the Lock and the ontological scale of the *Essay on Man*) has been presto-chango tilted upside down. But still more wondrous, the materialist reduction of all that is to "particles," or atoms (enabling Blake with a straight face to "personify" persons) has itself undergone a reductio — or rather elevatio — ad absurdum, since the blade of the guillotine in the last line has to be raised higher and higher, ever more wondrously wondrous, before it finally descends on the "Charming Fair."

Both Pope and Newton, as Blake envisioned them, did not represent in the 18th century any nebulous "spirit of the age," but *a* Spirit, namely Urizen (yours & mine), who controls this "Hermaphroditic Satanic world of rocky destiny." What the power of Urizen meant in his own time he perceived with prophetic insight. In a famous passage in *Jerusalem* he describes

> . . . the Loom of Locke, whose Woof rages dire,
> Wash'd by the Water-wheel of Newton: black the cloth
> In heavy wreathes folds over every Nation: cruel works
> Of many Wheels I view, wheel without wheel, with cogs tyrannic
> Moving by compulsion each other

in a dreamlike fusion of images (also "moving by compulsion each other") that connects the starry wheels of Ezekiel with the shuttles of the weaving Fates and evokes, as a shadowy afterimage, the "dark satanic mills" of the early Industrial Revolution. These were the same mills, of course, that Karl Marx some 50 years later was to study in depth, dredging through mounds of official government blue books and statistical reports in the British Museum, to make his own arraignment of them in *Das Kapital*. And yet, for all the enormous suffering caused by what he termed "primitive capitalist accumulation," Marx believed it to be a necessary and "higher" stage in man's progress toward the socialist millennium. Himself tormented by boils and a griping liver (like a Prometheus-Job) while he labored on *Das Kapital*, Marx sought his own redemption as the discoverer of the "laws" of history that would some day redeem mankind. But for Blake, to whom these laws and statistics were human blood and tears, the dialectical interpretation of history would have seemed no more than a "Delusion Of Ulro" (the materialist cosmos), and Marx himself a mere "reasoning historian, turner and twister of causes & consequences."

> And every Natural Effect has a Spiritual Cause, and Not
> A Natural; for a Natural Cause only seems: it is a Delusion
> Of Ulro & a ratio of the perishing Vegetable Memory.

238

Humanity, misled and enslaved by "the blind world rulers of this life," was perishing for lack of vision; and without vision—the "Divine Imagination"—Blake perceived history itself as a kind of slow Auschwitz in which generation after generation of the Children of Albion would be consumed. . . . Which has made him, of course, a witness for our own age.

Among the many oracular insights for which Blake has sometimes been taken as a precursor of Freud ("He who desires but acts not, breeds pestilence") or of Nietzsche ("One Law for the Lion & Ox is Oppression") or even of Timothy Leary & Co. ("If the doors of perception were cleansed every thing would appear to man as it is, infinite"), there is one, from his *Jerusalem*, that might be said to have anticipated the so-called "Uncertainty Principle" of Heisenberg underlying quantum theory: "And Accident & Chance were found hidden in Length, Bredth & Highth."

The revolution in our perception of reality achieved by quantum physics,

> For the Eye altering alters all;
> The Senses roll themselves in fear
> And the flat earth becomes a Ball

whereby the idea of chance, as the "grace" of materialism has rendered uncertain what were once regarded as immutable laws of nature, itself seems to have come about by chance. According to Heisenberg, the flash of insight occcurred during a conversation with Einstein, when he let drop a casual but seminal remark: "It is the theory which decides what we can observe." ("What is now proved," said Blake, "was once only imagined.") Following Heisenberg, with the further development of quantum theory by physicists, light was seen to be neither waves nor particles but somehow both simultaneously. For Einstein, whose God, like Newton's, did not "play dice," the irruption of "Chance & Accident" in "Length, Bredth & Highth" was unsettling enough; but for light to have become "schizophrenic,"

> —The Flea! What's happened to the Flea! Don't forget the
> Flea!
> —Hang in there! I'll not tarry long, for I am always with
> thee.

was to him an offense against reason itself. Throughout the rest of his career, as we know, he attempted to devise a "Unified Field Theory" to reconcile this split. But if the light of reason hath lost its luminosity with what shall he illuminate it?

"The dream of reason," as Goya prophesied, "produces monsters." For it is in our own haunted universe—a *mysterium tremendum* that steadily grows more tremendous and mysterious—that modern physics has conceived such certified scientific apparations as, say, pulsars, "black stars" that ultimately collapse, under their own weight of billions of tons per cubic inch, into hellholes in space (which we needn't go into now), but whose density is so great that even light can't escape their gravitational pull; or those elusively infinitesimal neutrinos, whose shadows have been seen fleetingly in cloud chambers, that pass to and fro across the "margin of nonentity"; or antimatter, for that matter, the mutually annihilatory mirror image, as 'twere, of material creation; and so forth. It is a universe closer to the "meontic Unground" envisioned by the mystic Jacob Boehme (who cast his spell on Blake as well as on Newton) than to the erector-set cosmos formulated and regulated a century ago by positivist science. And perhaps even closer in spirit to the magical universe of our Dream Time ancestors. . . .

So then, if the Flea were to leap into the present, its latest avatar would have to be seen "Thro' the Eye" of someone whose consciousness had been formed by such a science-fiction and/or Dream Time reality. As it so happened: in the by now famous account by the anthropologist Carlos Castaneda of his initiation into shamanism by the Yaqui Indian *brujo* Don Juan. What's more, Castaneda attained his vision by means of the same drugs

> To see a World in a Grain of Sand
> And a Heaven in a Wild Flower
> Hold Infinity in the palm of your hand
> And Eternity in an hour

that shamans also employed in bygone eons for their own ecstatic flights.

The event, described in *A Separate Reality,* took place on November 9, 1968, when Don Juan added to Castaneda's "mixture of fear, loneliness, and expectation" a psycheful of his own hallucinogenic smoking "mixture": peyote ("Mescalito"), jimson plant ("Devil's Weed"), and the mushroom psylocibin ("Little Smoke"). By taking it, Castaneda hoped to attain the power to "see" — *what?* — "the guardian, the keeper, the sentry of the other world," which would reveal itself in the totemic form of a personal spirit "ally." Don Juan then advised him that, when the "ally" appeared, he should look at it with only one eye, the left eye:

"'Puff, puff,' he ordered me gently. 'Just one bowl this time.' . . . When I had taken the last puff I felt that the entire inside of my body was coated with a peculiar sensation of cold warmth."

And then it happened:

> At a certain moment . . . I noticed a gnat flying in front of my
> eyes. I came very close to me, so close that my visual percep-

tion blurred. And then, all of a sudden, I felt as if I had stood up . . . and what I saw shook up the last fiber of my being. . . . Right there facing me, a short distance away, was a gigantic monstrous animal. A truly monstrous thing! . . . Its body was covered with tufts of black hair. It had a long muzzle and was drooling. Its eyes were bulgy and round, like two enormous white balls. . . . It circled twice in front of me, vibrating its wings, and whatever was drooling out of its mouth flew in all directions. Then it turned around and skidded away at an incredible speed until it disappeared in the distance. . . . An instant later the gigantic beast was circling again at full speed in front of me. Its wings cut closer and closer to my eyes until they hit me. . . . I yelled with all my might in the midst of one of the most excruciating pains I have ever had.

All right, sure I know it's the wrong bug: but "seen" close up, and through the freaked-out Castaneda's left eye alone, it would be hard to tell a 100-foot gnat from a 100-foot flea. About a year later, however, on January 18, 1969, his guardian spirit paid him a return visitation; and on this trip, seen through both eyes and in the flash provided by Don Juan's psychedelic mixture, it was, unmistakably, a descendant of Hooke's own chimera of a Flea:

"Its front," wrote Casteneda, "was covered with long, black, insidious hair, which looked like spikes coming through the cracks of some slick, shiny scales. . . . It had two white, bulging eyes and a long muzzle. This time it looked more like an alligator. It seemed to have long ears, or perhaps horns, and it was drooling." And when it turned around, he added, "Its back looked *like brilliantly colored armor*. . . . [My italics]

Blake's ferocious Ghost, who threatened that if he were "the size of a horse he would depopulate a large portion of the country," would have recognized his blood brother in Castaneda's gigantic "ally." But Blake's was a monster envisioned out of 18th-century Gothic horror stories, Castaneda's out of science-fiction movies by way of hallucinogens. Each took the form it had to take in order to "pierce the screen" of consciousness; or, as Blake himself put it, "Every Eye sees differently, As the Eye, Such the Object."

Right after each of Castaneda's trips into the spirit world, Don Juan had to dunk his overheated disciple into a ditch or a cattle trough to cool him off. Castaneda submitted meekly, even gratefully, to this humiliating treatment, as it figured he would. The one-way give-and-take between sorcerer and apprentice, Zen master and monk, guru and gull ("For many are gulled but few are chastened"), shaman and schnook, and for that matter, between Jehovah and his prophets Jonah and Job, has always been inherently and ritually slapstick, as exemplified by the sort of blackout shenanigans and practical jokes played on Castaneda's ego by the *brujo* Don Juan. Actually, his hazing was mild, hardly more severe than what Don Juan himself, as plain Juan Matus, a Yaqui Indian from Sonora, might have been put through had be been hired on as a cotton-picking wetback by a plantation in Texas or as a greenhorn roustabout by an oil-rigging crew. However, among hunting tribes in remote parts of the world where shamanistic traditions still survive, anthropologists report that youthful candidates like Castaneda, to prove their mastery over fire, may be compelled to walk barefoot over burning coals; dive naked through nine (9) holes cut in the ice when the ocean is frozen over in the Far North—into the first hole, out the second, into the third, and so on; dry wet sheets, draped over their bodies in sub-zero weather, by their own "inner heat"; and, to bring them out of an ecstatic trance, in certain South American tribes they are not merely dunked into a trough of water, but covered with a woven mat, called a *maraque*, swarming with a species of large, fierce-biting, poisonous ants. Only after such an initiation are they considered qualified to see visions and interpret dreams, perform miraculous cures, commune with the dead, or fly to heaven.

Those savage bands of Asiatic hunters some 20,000 or so years ago, at the close of the last Ice Age, who pursued the dwindling herds of mammoth, reindeer, and musk-oxen through Siberia into Alaska, then across the Bering Straits land bridge into America, brought with them their shamanistic traditions. As their 20th-century descendant and heir, the Indian *brujo* Don Juan may thus be considered a living social fossil. But if (as anthropologists such as Carleton Coon maintain) "shamanism may be nearly as old as human speech," then long before the Paleolithic era it must already have developed an elaborate mythological and ritual syntax. Man's development having occurred over a period of about 1.5 million years, roughly coeval with the Ice Ages of the Pleistocene, certain symbolic traces, or archetypes, the afterimages of that long Dream Time, may still remain rooted in his psyche. Once again Blake:

> Man is Born Like a Garden ready Planted & Sown.
> . . . Innate Ideas are in Every Man, Born with him;
> they are truly Himself.

In primitive societies throughout the world that (as Mircea Eliade puts it) "still live in the paradise of archetypes and for whom time is recorded only biologically without being allowed to become history," we can observe these archetypes ritualized in the everyday life of Everyman . . . and also, even in our own technological culture, in the everyday lives of children, for whom time is also "recorded only biologically."

3. "Life's Nonsense Pierces Us with Strange Relation"

On that cue, therefore, let me now unmuffle myself from the mask of impersonality and come forward, skull in hand, to soliloquize briefly, as follows:

Way back then, *in illud tempore,* during my own Once-upon-a-time Time, all those symbols and motifs that ethnologists such as Eliade describe as belonging to the shamanistic tradition — such as the Descent to the Underworld & the Ascent to the Heavens, the Cosmic Mountain, the "Difficult Passage," the Ladder (or *Klimax*), and so forth — figured in rites of initiation — for myself and the rest of the kids on the block. My best friend, about a year older but in my class, was a fellow of infinite jest named Jacob Itzkowitz, so of course everybody called him "Itchky." After school was out, if nothing happened to be happening on the block, Itchky and I would spend the long afternoon hanging around the back of the candy store, which was run by a Stalinoidal and irascible man named Mr. Fliegel (what else?), who suspected us of swiping his candy and leaving dirty fingerprints on his comic books, and would usually kick us out after a while. But most of the time — and this is what I've been leading up to — there would be enough kids outside for us to be able to choose up a game of kick-the-can or Johnny-on-the-pony or maybe ringelevio; and then the whole block would become, as 'twere, a cosmos, where we'd chase each other down to the basement underworld of buildings and up to the roofs, and from roof to roof, in flying leaps, climbing up fire-escape ladders, squeezing through narrow passages in alleyways, the more narrow and difficult the better, and so forth; and in the winter, after a heavy snowfall, we'd all pitch in and build a sort of Cosmic Mountain of snow, pour enough water on it till it became slippery ice, then play king-of-the-hill. . . . You get the picture.

On similar high and therefore sacred places in Israel during Biblical times, the local heathens would erect temples to their gods, those "baals" (or lords) anathematized by the prophets. Beëlzebub ("Lord of the Fly") was originally such a hilltop deity, one of many worshiped by the Canaanites; but somehow Beëlzebub rose to such "bad eminence" that, for the chosen people, he came to represent, along with Satan himself, the very principle of evil. At the first crack of the Cosmic Egg, out he crawled, dripping with yolk. Beëlzebub, as it happened, had a shrine and oracle near the city of Ekron, perhaps also at Ascalon, where, some centuries later, the crusading knights first discovered scallions (hence the name) and then introduced them into the European diet, without which the chopped eggs and chicken livers my mother once prepared for us with schmaltz and love in her kitchen would have lacked savor. "For" . . .

Having gone about and about in pursuit of the bounding Flea, what else remains but to pick up the pheon myself? But before anyone points a revolving forefinger at my own head, let me try to explain what led me up here in the first place.

My own involvement, which I have come to regard as no less than a *"participation mystique,"* began some years ago, in the mid-'50s, though at the time I wasn't fully aware of what it all meant.

To help me escape if not a plague, at least a miasma, of debts, a friend of mine, the late poet Delmore Schwartz, suggested that I write something for a magazine called *The Reporter*, published and edited by Max Ascoli. So then, I went up to see the editor; and among other ideas for possible articles, he came up with one that appealed to me immediately for its surrealism. This was to investigate and write about a publication called CLASSICS *Illustrated*, which I had already observed on the rack in candy stores side by side with *Superman, Bugs Bunny, Flash Gordon,* and the rest, and which transformed such literary masterpieces as *The Iliad* and *Hamlet* into comic books. At the time, coincidentally, I had been struck by the eureka that the enclosed form of the heroic couplet, after a morphogenesis as astonishing as the metamorphosis of a flea in its life cycle, had evolved into the boxes of comic strips. How such a chimera as a comic-book *Iliad* or *Faust* could be conceived and "Made in the U.S.A." seemed to me, therefore, well worth finding out.

At the offices of CLASSICS *Illustrated*, where the president of the firm explained its operation and showed me around, it became apparent that this was no piker enterprise. Millions of copies were sold per year, with more than 200 different titles translated into almost every language in the world, including Swahili, Tagalog, Urdu, Kurdish . . . but not, however, into Russian or any other language spoken behind the Iron Curtain. The president then confided that, soon after World War II, when relations between the U.S. and the U.S.S.R. had not yet grown cold, he had asked the former head of the American Communist Party, Earl Browder, to help persuade the Russians to open up their market to CLASSICS *Illustrated*. Browder, who was then serving as a go-between for American business interests and the commissars, transmitted his offer, but it must have been laughed out of the Politburo; however, the president informed me, Stalin himself had made a counteroffer that CLASSICS *Illustrated* produce a series of comic books on the history of the C.P.S.U. *Das Kapital,* and the COMMUNIST MANIFESTO *Illustrated,* the life of Lenin, and so forth, for distribution in both the U.S. and the U.S.S.R., but it was indignantly and, of course, patriotically refused.

When I got home to recollect in tranquillity, the mock-heroic bathos of the whole affair seemed to me so "wondrous"

> Wondrous the Gods, more wondrous are the Men,
> More Wondrous Wondrous still the Cock & Hen

that I decided to imp things along somewhat (after all I was a reporter for *The Reporter*) by phoning Earl Browder for his version. Browder by this time, having been expelled and damned by the Party as a "bourgeois revisionist," was living under guard on a remote farm in New Jersey, in fear for his life, and cooperating with the FBI in exchange for saving his Russian-born wife from deportation. His phone, it figured, must have been tapped. But getting his unlisted number from *The Reporter* proved no problem; and after I dialed it, lo! like rubbing a lamp for a genie, within three rings his voice, unmistakably and uncannily Browder, *pars pro toto,* flat, twangy, and adenoidal, came over the line: *"What can I do for you?"*

Entranced by that voice, I tried to make my own sound journalistically crisp and efficient down the line, and the story I told him of what the president of CLASSICS *Illustrated* had told me of his mission to Moscow sounded less preposterous than it had struck me in the telling, but I kept mixing up, repeating and then garbling the facts, for my mind really wasn't with it or on it. Instead, it had flown far back in memory to a night long ago, *in illud tempore,* when I had first heard that voice, Browder, speaking at a Communist rally at the Velodrome in Coney Island. . . .

My best friend Itchky, of course, had gone along with me that night. After being kicked out of Fliegel's candy store, and having nothing to do, Itchky had come up with the idea of sneaking into the Velodrome. It was a "difficult passage" but not that difficult, one we had managed many times before, requiring merely that we squeeze through a hole ripped at a certain place in the wire mesh screen, then creep around in the shadows past a tin shack where the watchman sat outside beneath an arc light, reading the *Daily News,* too self-absorbed to notice us, and keep on going till we got to the catacombs under the stands, dodging from pillar to pillar to the back door of the ladies' room, always left slightly ajar, and then, as soon as the coast was clear, charge on through inside without being seen. The rally had already been on for hours and was at a crescendo by the time we made it and raced up the back stairs into the bleachers. On a stage flanked on each side with huge poster pictures of Lenin & Stalin and Marx & Engels, and draped from end to end with an enormous red-white-and-blue banner reading: "COMMUNISM IS TWENTIETH-CENTURY AMERICANISM," a scowling, sturdy-looking man with a moustache, respectably dressed like a Kansas farmer on Sunday, Browder himself, harangued the crowd. Close to the end of his speech, he was laying down the line in sentences pithy as slogans, to which the crowd (almost like Smart's own convocation of the Chosen, come to think of it) responded antiphonally and in unison with the prescribed counterslogans. Though I was then only 13 or so years old, and had only recently grown self-conscious and hair, I was still pretty worldly-wise politically for that age, having listened from childhood on to dialectical wrangles over Marxist dogma that could not have been an iota less finespun or impassioned than the disputes between homoousians and homoiousians in fourth-century Constantinople.

> If you want a man to change a piece of silver, he tells you in
> what way the Son differs from the Father; if you ask the price
> of a loaf of bread, you are told by way of reply that the Son
> is inferior to the Father; and if you inquire whether the bath
> is ready, the answer is that the Son was made of nothing.

(as a contemporary, Gregory of Nyasa, relates); and so, of course, I was in no way surprised by the holy political rapture seething all around us. For in those days of Hitler and Stalin, the war that everyone knew was coming was coming closer, had already come in fact to Europe and Asia. . . .

Browder, finishing his speech, jerked his fist-clenched right hand up in the Popular Front salute, and then the whole crowd rose to applaud and burst out singing, "Browder is our leader, we shall not be moved . . ." *Jus' like a treeee that's standin' by the waw-aw-tuhhhh.* . . . Kooky Itchky, I might have known, had started singing along in falsetto; we might easily have been thrown out; but even so, people in the stands nearby turned around and gave us dirty looks. Among those who turned (*and am I imagining this now or actually seeing it as it was in memory?*) I caught sight of my cousin Robert, the one who had fought in the Spanish Civil War; and there was Mr. Fliegel, swart and squat, no doubt about it, but somehow seeming different without a chocolate-stained apron around his middle; and my own arithmetic teacher, Miss Himmelfarb, her spectacles glittering right through me, who nudged the arm of a tall dark man in a raincoat standing beside her and pointing toward us. . . . But before anything could happen, the lights on the stage below suddenly blazed up, and then, from the rear of the stadium, came a parade of delegations to the rally down the center aisle carrying posters and flags and totemic banners to identify themselves — cell members of trade unions and student front groups; fellow-traveling phratries of doctors, lawyers, dentists; Young Communist Leaguers; emissaries from clans as far off as New Jersey and the Bronx; even a lost battalion of veterans from the Abraham Lincoln Brigade ("pale warriors, death pale were they all") from the doomed war in Spain, some wearing their old uniforms and berets, a few with missing limbs, hobbling on crutches, even a couple being pushed along on wheelchairs; and many more — 'throngs of them, people from that vanished time, dimly familiar and grayed in memory, people I must have seen handing out leaflets, walking picket lines, debating late at night in cafeterias, singing the "Internationale" with all their might as they mounted the 999 steps of the pyramid of Quetzalcoatl with bared breasts up to the stage where Chairman Browder and the other leaders waited to greet them. . . .

"Naw . . ." It was Browder himself, right in my ear, a labyrinthine echo tolling me back, for I'd almost forgotten what I had asked him about Stalin's counteroffer to CLASSICS *Illustrated.* "Naw," he repeated, "that's just a slice of . . . cow pie." And hung up.

Afterward, when the mood I had fallen into was somewhat dispelled, I started to glance through a few copies of CLASSICS *Illustrated.* They were something else again, but as such not bad at all. *The Iliad,* for instance, was certainly not as classical as in Pope's elegant translation, but Homer's childsight simplicity and boldness of outline seemed almost at home in comic strips; and *Moby Dick,* too, with Melville's metaphysics and Jonah-like angst cast overboard, had been reduced to a parody, full of sound and fury, of his own great parable of the absurd, but signifying the same thing.

There was the proud but wretched Raskolnikov, Dostoevsky's psyched-out hero, shown sprawled upon his cot in the garret of a fleabag rooming house in Saint Petersburg and brooding about the rent. The artist, to emphasize his evil nature, has depicted him with a haggard, villainous-looking face set off by a suit colored venomous green, and he is wearing a kind of fez or beanie, maybe even a yarmulka, on his head. So far fine, what one would have expected. But a page or two later, when he visits the old hag pawnbroker in her apartment and contrives his plan to murder her, an eerie sense of foreboding came over me, of what I couldn't say, reading on, though, it gradually took shape in the back of my mind, a dark cloud of unknowing that became more and more luminous as I focused my memory—*or was it only my imagination*?—upon it until, out of the surrounding darkness, the intuition blazed into consciousness.

Right under my eyes, in that serio-comic comic-book version of *Crime and Punishment*, I saw revealed the method and even the very scene of the murder of Leon Trotsky in Mexico in 1940.

I'll be brief. The man who assassinated Trotsky, later identified by the police as a Spanish-born NKVD agent, Jaime Ramón Mercader, employed as his murder weapon an ice axe, or *piolet,* with a steel head, balanced at the haft, about seven inches long from tip to tip, one end of which had a proboscis as sharp as a stiletto and the other a forked hammer claw used by mountain climbers to split blocks of ice. The handle had been cut down to about a foot, so that it could easily be hidden in a pocket of his raincoat, where it was attached by a cord.

Now, as Dostoevsky relates in his novel, Raskolnikov also used an axe and concealed it in a similar way:

> As for the noose, it was a very ingenious device of his own; the noose was intended for the axe. It was impossible for him to carry the axe through the streets in his hands; and if hidden under his coat he would still have to support it with his hand, which would have been noticeable. He had only to put the head of the axe in the noose, and it would hang quietly under his arm on the inside. Putting his hand into the coat pocket, he could hold the end of the handle all the way so that it did not swing.

Before committing the crime, Raskolnikov, under the pretext of pawning his watch, pays a visit to the apartment of the old woman to survey the scene, promising to return again with a more valuable pledge. But in the days that follow he is filled with such self-revulsion that he almost gives up his plans; until a series of chance encounters and quirks of circumstance propel him not only to keep his appointment with fate but even fix the time. ("The traces of superstition remained in him long after," wrote Dostoevsky, ". . . and in all this he was always disposed to see something strange and mysterious, as it were the presence of some peculiar influences and coincidences.") For the actual murder, which now seemed to him foreordained, he brought with him a small but tightly wrapped and intricately knotted package, containing what he said was a silver cigarette case. It was meant to occupy her attention in opening it while he stole behind and bludgeoned her with the axe.

Likewise, Mercader—or "Jacson," the alias by which he was known to Trotsky—arranged a dress rehearsal of the murder several days earlier. At that time, August 17, 1940, clutching his raincoat with the concealed ice axe inside close to this body, he was allowed into Trotsky's fortresslike villa at Coyoacán and then admitted by Trotsky himself into the heavily guarded inner sanctum of his study. There he showed Trotsky an article on Occupied France he had been writing, the "pledge" of his sincerity, that criticized the heretical theories of James Burnham and Max Shachtman, two once faithful American Trotskyites who had begun to question the political infallibility of the "Old Man." Trotsky's suspicions were aroused by the nervous behavior of his visitor, but not sufficiently so. On August 20, returning with a corrected version of his article, Jacson entered the yard of the villa, where Trotsky was feeding his pet rabbits, and again the murdered man had a premonition of what was to come, but led him to his study as before. While Trotsky, seated at his desk, bent his head down to untangle the no doubt intricately knotted arguments in the piece, Jacson remained standing above him.

What then happened was described by the murderer a few hours later in his confession to the police:

> I put my raincoat on the table on purpose so that I could take out the ice axe which I had in the pocket. I decided not to lose the brilliant opportunity which was offered me, and at the exact moment when Trotsky started to read my article, which served as my pretext, I took the *piolet* out of my raincoat, took it in my fist and, closing my eyes, I gave him a tremendous blow on the head. . . . The man screamed in such a way that I will never forget it as long as I live. His scream was *Aaaaaaaaa* . . . very long, infinitely long, and it still seems to me as if that scream were piercing my brain.

In Trotsky's own brain the sharp point of the ice axe had penetrated to a depth of nearly three inches, breaking through the right parietal bone and meninges and destroying part of the brain substance. Yet he still managed to fight off his assassin and, when his guards rushed in meaning to kill Jacson on the spot, retained enough self-possession and strength of will to prevent them, hoping that he could be made to talk and thus expose the hand of Stalin. But unlike Raskolnikov, who was driven by the "agenbite of inwit" and a festering conscience to purge himself, Jacson maintained silence throughout the 20 years he spent in a Mexican prison about his real identity and his role in the worldwide plot to kill Trotsky. That was to emerge in full only after revelations made by defecting Soviet agents and Communist party officials.

To get back for a moment. Of course I had read Dostoevsky's novel long before, and so the description of the murder of the old pawnbroker must already have been subsconsciously present as a faded palimpsest in memory; but only after seeing his classic *Illustrated*, boxed into comic strips, could I envision the scene with and also "Thro' the Eye," at which point the synaptic = between Raskolnikov and Jacson clicked into place. Trotsky's murderer, accordingly, may or may not have consciously based his own stratagem on Dostoevsky; yet it hardly matters; for the crucial scene of the novel was by then "in the air," a free-floating eidolon in the mind of Everyman, a cloud in the noosphere, as 'twere, in which case the scheme might have entered into Jacson's imagination without his ever being aware of its source. Freud (in his *Jokes and Their Relation to the Unconscious*), after making the observation that joking—and any other *consciously creative* process, for that matter—and dreaming are both characterized by "condensation, displacement and indirect representation," then asks the question: Does not this agreement suggest the conclusion that joke-work and dream-work must, at least, in some essential respect, be identical? No doubt "at least." But there's also this to be considered: Jacson's own plot was only the culminating point—the entering wedge, as 'twere, that "pierced the screen"—in a series of other sub- and cross-plots in the larger Plot—in Newton's sense—whose success ultimately depended on innumerable quirks of personal and historical circumstance, coincidences that no one could have controlled or even imagined. For all these coincidences to coincide, the Three Fates and the Nine Muses had to join hands to form a clock that struck at that precise hour on August 20, 1940.

To begin with (though there might have been x^2 beginnings), an intense 28-year-old intellectually bespectacled and whey-faced social worker in N.Y.C. named Sylvia Ageloff, known to be a Trotskyite entrusted as a courier with confidential missions, quits her job in the summer of 1938 and makes plans for a trip to Europe. This news by subterranean ways reaches the NKVD in Moscow; the web trembles; and Louis Budenz, then managing editor of the *Daily Worker*, receives an important assignment. As he later disclosed before a congressional committee, he recruited an old friend of Sylvia's from childhood, Ruby Weil, who had since become a member of the Communist party, and gave her a sum of money to accompany Sylvia to Europe. In Paris, Ruby introduces her to a mysterious woman named Gertrude, who in turn introduces her to . . . Frank Jacson. Only he did not call himself "Jacson" at that time, but Jacques Mornard, and claimed to be the scion of a wealthy and aristocratic Belgian family, working as a sports correspondent for a newspaper syndicate. The handsome, dapper Belgian aristocrat wooed and easily seduced the plain and dowdy Trotskyite from Brooklyn. Though she had studied philosophy under Sidney Hook, and had a master's degree in psychology yet, all this wisdom proved of no avail against the obfuscations of love. When she returned to the U.S. in early 1939, soon after World War II broke out in Europe, he followed a few months later under a Canadian passport, persuading the smitten Sylvia that he had done so in order to be at her side and to escape the draft in Belgium.

This passport, issued under the name he then adopted, "Frank Jacson," had been taken by the NKVD from the body of a deceased Canadian volunteer to the International Brigade in Spain; but the Russian agent who prepared it, though intending to give him an inconspicuous name, evidently did not know that "Jackson" is spelled with a "k," a clue which subsequently proved important in tracing the killer's identity.

(Meanwhile, back at the Kremlin, the unfolding of this infraplot was being watched closely by Stalin ((for the assassination of Trotsky was for him part of a larger political plot in which, after the World War triggered by his recent pact with Hitler had decimated Europe, he hoped without any interference from his great antagonist to seize control of the revolution that must inevitably take place)), and this plot in turn was subsumed by one still larger ((the plot of history involving the domination of the world by Soviet Communism)), and this again by a metaphysical plot in which the destiny of mankind was at stake . . . and so forth, comprising a series of seemingly disconnected "sets" parenthetically enclosing each other so that the infraplot has gradually spread out and thinned into Fate and the scene of the crime become a circle whose circumference is nowhere and whose center is everywhere.)

All right, then, as we know, Jacson now proceeded to Mexico City where, he assured Sylvia, he had been offered a job by an import-export firm. High officials of the NKVD, including his own mother Caridad Mercader and her consort Col. Leonid Eitingon, who had served as Stalin's chief hatchet man in Spain under the alias of General Kotov, were already there waiting for him and preparing the denouement. Sylvia, having been supplied with funds by her lover, soon joined him. Her credentials as a devoted and trusted follower of Trotsky enabled her to visit him frequently at nearby Coyoacán to contribute her services as a secretary. This was what the conspirators from Moscow to New York to Mexico City had hoped and planned for the past two years. Jacson, Sylvia Ageloff's prospective husband, by waiting for her outside the villa each day, soon became a familiar sight to the guards and so, like Smart's flea, he "contrived to attract observation and to escape it." Eventually he was introduced to the Old Man himself; after which, as we know, he was able to pierce the screen into Trotsky's inner sanctum, with his alpine pheon hidden under his coat of rain, and commit the murder.

In Isaac Don Levine's psycho-socio-analytical investigation of Jacson-Jacques Mornard-Mercader's role in the plot, *The Mind of an Assassin*, he surmises that the killer might have gotten the idea for his modus operandi from the then head of the NKVD, Lavrenti Beria. Beria, it seems, had once assigned an agent of great physical strength to the task of killing a Soviet ambassador, suspected by Stalin of being a traitor, by striking him from behind with a short iron bar that could be hidden under his clothes. But this theory merely displaces the Freudian "joke-work — dream-work" of Raskolnikov from the conscious or unconscious mind of Jacson into that of Beria; and besides, the scene as it actually occurred is more "sharply" detailed, as 'twere, in Dostoevsky's imaginary axe murder. Levine also characterizes Trotsky's assassin as a "philosophical executioner . . . the product of the Age of Reason at its dead end." For Jacson, evidently, did not sacrifice his own life out of personal hatred of Trotsky or passion or hope of reward, but for a coldly political purpose; nor did he even strike with his axe at the sick and haunted yet indomitable "Old Man," Lev Davidovitch Trotsky, born Bronstein in Bobrinetz, Russia, but at an abstraction, TROTSKY, the demi-demiurge, along with Lenin, of the Russian revolution, and for this reason the greatest and most dangerous political enemy of his master, Stalin. (Jacson, come to think of it, did receive a reward, the Order of a Hero of the Soviet Union, in absentia, while his mother, for her labor pains, had the Order of Lenin hung around her neck by Stalin himself.) But here again, however, the literary prototype of this "philosophical executioner" is not, as Levine suggests, the zomboid protagonist of Albert Camus' *The Rebel*, but the intellectual Raskolnikov, who rationalized his murder of the old pawnbroker by persuading himself of all the good he might do for others with her money ("One death and a hundred lives in exchange — it's simple arithmetic"), Q.E.D., from which it followed, he believed, that "his reason and will would remain unimpaired at the time of carrying out his design, for the simple reason that his design was 'not a crime.'"

During the years 1865–66, when Dostoevsky under great emotional and financial stress wrote *Crime and Punishment*, he also suffered from frequent attacks of epilepsy. "The sight of a man in an epileptic fit," as he once described it, "fills many others with absolute and unbearable horror which has something mystical about it. . . . A quite incredible bloodcurdling scream breaks from the chest; in that scream everything human seems to be suddenly obliterated, and it is quite impossible, at least very difficult,"

> The man screamed in such a way that I will never forget it as long as I live. His scream was *Aaaaaaaaa* . . . very long, infinitely long, and it still seems to me as if that scream were piercing my brain.

"for an observer to imagine and to admit that it is the man himself who is screaming. One gets the impression that it is someone inside the man who is screaming." We know too, from the voluminous notebook kept by Dostoevsky during those years, that he had originally planned his novel as a narrative in the first person, with Raskolnikov as "I." By so closely identifying himself, from the inside out, with the "philosophical executioner" Raskolnikov, Dostoevsky might have intended *Crime and Punishment* as further expiation of the radical nihilism of his own youth, a "crime" for which he had already been punished in 1849 by a sentence of four years' hard labor in Siberia. Raskolnikov's almost megalomaniacal "I" exalted above the herds of "them," who are yoked by law, leads him at one point in the novel to compare himself with Napoleon: "I asked myself this question — what if Napoleon had happened to be in my place, and if he had not had Toulon nor Egypt nor the passage of Mont Blanc to begin his career with, but instead . . . there had simply been some ridiculous old hag, a pawnbroker, who had to be murdered to get money from her trunk? . . ."; and, at another, with Isaac Newton: "I maintain that if the discoveries of Newton could not have been made known except by sacrificing the lives of one, a dozen, a hundred, or more men, Newton would have had the right, would indeed have been in duty bound . . . to *eliminate* the dozen or the hundred men. . . ." And what if, according to this "Two Horn'd" reasoning, the stake were even larger than the careers of Newton and Napoleon, namely, the destiny of Man himself, then how many dozens, or hundreds, or myriads, or hundred dozen myriads of mere men would have to be eliminated, liquidated, exterminated, "cast into the dustheap of history" (to "make it perfectly clear") as an acceptable "sacrifice"?

Yet it was on the two horns of just such a moral-political dilemma that Trotsky, following the anarchist mutiny against the Soviet state by the seamen at the naval fortress of Kronstadt in 1921, was caught and forced to assume the role of "philosophical executioner." (Make of this what you will: but in the revolutionary years before the slaughter at Kronstadt, when these seamen had been Trotsky's most loyal comrades in arms, they were led by a commander named . . . Raskolnikov.) Of Trotsky, an admirer once wrote that his "entire behavior is dominated by his Ego, but his Ego is dominated by the revolution." He believed, and with the fervor of an Old Testament prophet, that the panspermic Word had come, from Marx however, and that the advent of the socialist millennium was a scientific certitude inherent in the nature of things, to be brought about by a chosen class of people living at a chosen time, which also happened to be his own time. Even at the age of 21, in 1900, he could write: "As long as I breathe, I shall fight for the future, that radiant future, in which man, strong and beautiful, will become master of the drifting stream of history and will direct it toward the boundless horizons of beauty, joy and happiness." The End. At the height of his powers and power (though about to fall), in 1923, when he wrote *Literature and Revolution*, he was still dreaming the old apocalyptic dream of Daniel:

> *Homo sapiens*, now stagnating . . . will treat himself as the object of the most complex methods of artificial selection and psycho-physical training. . . . Man will not have ceased to crawl before God, Czar and Capital only in order to surrender meekly to dark laws of heredity and blind sexual selection. . . . The average man will rise to the stature of Aristotle, Goethe, Marx. And above these heights new peaks will rise.

But for all of us nowadays, who live in that "radiant future" he dimly imagined 75 years ago, such "complex methods of artificial selection and psycho-physical training" falling into the hands (dread prospect) of another Hitler or Stalin, would produce not the socialist utopia but what George Orwell once described as "a world of rabbits ruled by stoats." Still, he meant well: an end to wars, poverty, oppression, ignorance, alienation, disconnections, wrong numbers, insufficient postage . . . *Ah Bartleby! Ah, Humanity! Whither have all the foregone conclusions gone?*

In 1904, however, after attending the Russian Social-Democratic Congress in Brussels, at which the fateful split between the Bolsheviks (or majority faction, and by a mere two votes) and Mensheviks took place, Trotsky wrote an impassioned attack on what he then considered Lenin's authoritarian methods. And with clairvoyant political insight he predicted the future course of Russian Communism:

The caucus substitutes itself for the party; then the Central Committee for the caucus; and finally a dictator substitutes himself for the Central Committee.

Pars pro toto. At the time the dictator was merely a shadow with a name unknown, Dzhugashvili, a Georgian terrorist and/or Czarist police agent, by turns, his features becoming more and more distinct, solidifying himself in power, from stage to stage, until just as Trotsky had foreseen (yet appeared taken by surprise when it actually happened), he emerged as the demi-deified Stalin. This former shadow, now become the prickly and prepotent ithyphallic leader, STALIN, a figure in the same ageless mold as Osiris, "the mummy with the long member who cannot die," was to cast his shadowier shadow over the world of my childhood, and beyond, until he was killed by a stroke, of luck too,

Dear Itchky:
Bewhiskered, bulbous, pugnacious
Old Fliegel who used to chase us
Out (*"Raus!"*) from his lousy store, that Beëlzebub
Of sticky jujubes, licorice, and syrupy glub—
Forever wiping, wiping, twitching and wiping,
With eyes, believe it, in back of his head
To catch us both nibbling, licking or swiping—
Well, Itchky, Mr. Fliegel—he dead. . . .
Last night asleep I heard a steady *thump, thump, thump*
Upon my mind (*"Who's there?"*) and right outside
The screen a snot-sized fury clung, flipped, fell like a lump,
Then buzzed and wobbled, hummed, lay down and died.

for he was then, as witnessed by Khrushchev and others, constantly doodling wolves on the margins of documents, plotting once more to turn his paranoid fantasies into reality, and drawing up lists of victims for show trials and purges on a scale greater than any in the past. "Projections," wrote Jung, "change the world into the replica of one's own unknown face."

For Trotsky the recognition that the Soviet Union, which he as much as anyone else had helped to create, had evolved into a Moloch state devouring its own people, was slow and bitter in the coming. Yet it came nevertheless. During the last years of his life, many of his political followers had begun to question the Marxist dogma that the expropriation of the means of production by a revolutionary socialist party, acting in the name of "the workers," would ipso facto bring about a free and classless society; but this had already occurred in the Soviet Union; and look . . . a new class of Byzantine bureaucrats, commissars of industry, military chieftains, thought controllers, and secret police had sprung up. With the signing of the pact between Hitler and Stalin in 1939, a kind of homoousian-homoiousian controversy took place within Trotsky's Fourth International: whether the Soviet Union should be considered a degenerate but essentially "workers' state," capable of being reformed and redeemed, as Trotsky maintained, or else something other and far more sinister. The sects led by James Burnham and Max Shachtman in the U.S. played for Trotsky, himself now cast into the dung heap of history, the roles of Job's cold-comforters and his wife who urged him "to curse God and die." Still he resisted almost to the end ("Yea, though He slay me yet shall I believe in Him"), until finally the following admission, based on the possibility of World War II might not produce a revolution after all throughout Europe and the U.S.S.R, was wrenched from his soul:

> Then it would be necessary to establish in retrospect that . . . the present U.S.S.R. was the predecessor of a new and universal system of exploitation. . . . However onerous this perspective may be, if the world proletariat should actually prove incapable of accomplishing its mission . . . nothing else would remain but to recognize that the socialist programme, based on the internal contradictions of capitalist society, had petered out as a Utopia.

That was his *"Eli, Eli, lama sabachtani."* . . .

So then, long before the flealike Jacson, Dostoevsky's apparitional Raskolnikov, had "pierced that screen," the defences of Trotsky's own ego had been shattered. His plight, after being cast into inner and outer darkness, thus bears an uncanny resemblance to that of an exiled member of a primitive tribe who has been sentenced to death by shamanist rites and spells. According to Lévi-Strauss, an individual condemned by such sorcery, "brutally torn from all of his family and social ties and excluded from all functions and activities through which he experienced self-awareness, then banished by the same forces from the world of the living . . ." becomes as the result of this "sudden total withdrawal of the multiple reference systems provided by the support of the group . . . dead and an object of fear, ritual and taboo." To the bafflement of modern medical science, the victim often withers away and dies for no ascertainable physiological reason. As a possible explanation, Lévi-Strauss cites the theory (by W. B. Cannon) that the sympathetic nervous system of the individual under taboo may be traumatized — "The efficacy of magic implies a belief in magic" — so that no lesion is observed afterward on his body. "Physical integrity," he concludes, "cannot withstand the dissolution of the social personality."

A clan member of a primitive tribe, therefore, for whom shamanism was an existential reality, would have considered Trotsky already doomed after his exile and execration by the Soviet Union; and as for Jacson, he too would have been regarded only as the means by which the sorcery against him was fated to be carried out. And so, perhaps, would Dostoevsky himself. Though the socialist utopia seemed to him merely a mechanized Cockayne, where man would lose his soul and his freedom, he did believe ambiguously in ghosts. For they themselves became manifest only in a twilit ambiguity, screened by coincidence, and thus were invisible under the light of reason. In the notebook for *Crime and Punishment*, the sinister Svidrigaylov, himself almost a ghost, expressed this idea as follows:

> The fact that ghosts do not appear to healthy people is understandable: nature herself stands in opposition to ghosts, because for order and fulness . . . it's necessary that we live one life and not two. . . . As soon as our organism breaks down a bit, we become capable of coming in contact with ghosts (and with other worlds). So that it is true that the appearance of ghosts is a sign of a sick organism, from which, however, it is completely impossible to conclude that ghosts do not exist.

His own organism, as we know, was a prey to the "falling sickness," or epilepsy, that mysterious disease of the old brain in which the one afflicted, uttering animal cries and raving in a delphic gibberish, enspasmed in oblivion, seems possessed by demonic forces. "The only difference between a shaman and an epileptic," delcares Mircea Eliade, "is that the latter cannot deliberately enter into trance." And he points to the extreme cold of Arctic regions, the long nights and glacial solitude, the lack of fats and vitamins in the diet, and the sense of cosmic oppression felt by the inhabitants as "giving rise either to mental illnesses (Arctic hysteria) or to the shamanic trance." Yet that trance perhaps may lie at the bottom of the Dream and at the beginning of the Plot.

For it was under similar climatic conditions, when the earth was alive and the four great Ice Age trolls — Gunz, Mindel, Russ, and Würm — stalked up and down the Pleistocene, that the unkillable fire-eyed elves, who are Everyman, first emerged gripping their flint-axe pheons, hiding out in caves and in the bosky interstices of glacial valleys, and so survived from day to day and from millennium to millennium until the present. The worst plots, thought Aristotle, are the episodic, except those that go around in a circle. After all our hypothetical leaps and bounds in pursuit of the metaphorical Flea — *there it is!* — perhaps that's what it was foreordained to come to in The End:

> *MAN like a Flea shall*
> *jump from star to* *

(1974)

FOUR

The Descent of the Muse

Every time I turn on the light, every time I try to say what I mean, the words scatter like cockroaches. Away from me in a radiating panic of angular jerks and sprints, feints, dead-stops, sudden swerves and sidelong plunges under the sink, up the wall, down the drain, they all go into the dark. And there they hide inside themselves, swaddled in other words, in darkness, if you know what I mean.

Since that's the way it is, I shut my eyes. I pull down all the blinds, making the darkness without equal to the darkness within, an absent space neither here nor there where nothing goes but echoes, mirages, memories, after-images and dead stars, ghosts of departed qualities. . . . And then I brood, thinking of nothing, or something far more deeply interfused. Suddenly, just as I thought, one bolts out of nowhere like a forgotten phone number, perfect in all its joints; another, another, and still another, until the room is full of them, waving their filaments and peering about with a wild surmise.

> I know them all as well as my own name:
> There's *Moon*, there's *Spasm*, and there's *Fire*
> With brilliant *Flame* (my favorite);
> And there, with his snout in the air,
> That dirty little *Shit* who lords it everywhere;
> There's *Love*, behind the sink;
> There's *Truth*, who takes to drink;

Originally published in the *Hudson Review* (Winter 1955).

261

> There's *Beauty*, teetering on the brink;
> And there's that pompous *I* who thinks he's *Me*
> Or *You* or *Who-Knows-Who-Knows-Who-Is-Who?*
> And there, way up, way up the wailing wall —
> O *Life* O *Death* O *Time*
> Whose petty pace doth climb and climb —
> That sad, old, bad, bold *Nobodaddy* of them all.

What a sight that was! Multitudes were walking and skittering on the floor with little graph-like movements up and down, a pedestrian mob of the sort you can find anywhere; but, here and there, as if in a trance, a few stood alone and introverted with their antennae lifted in attitudes of prayer; others were rolled over on their backs, thrashing and kicking up their legs in playful copulation; some were mounting one another in a ring, a sort of circus posy of tiny acrobatic hippopotami or segmented sillabubs with shiny armored dewlaps; others were creeping along, precious and aloof, even a little bored, with long delicate trembling wands and Hamlet-like refinements of indecision; and some were there of a dark and foreign aspect, intruders from a distant apt. or evil neighborhood, maybe Arabian berbers or Delphic gibberers —

> They mince apart upon tip-toe
> Eeny, Meany, Miny & Moe
> Mene, Mene, Tekel Upharsin:
> O MANY ARE TAKEN IN THEIR SIN.

And I, still I stood there, a blind lighthouse watching and waiting. The irregular heart of the refrigerator began to beat and shake. Then, from the depths of the sink, came a long, lonely, agonized squawk like the horn of some ghost ship lost in the coils, a sound that steadily rose eeking and eeking from a wild Wallala leialala to a far gray wailing Eli Eli and a high aiyaiyai too pure and thin to be heard. The time was near at hand.

Through the open window, a breeze came and and blew the curtains back into the room, spreading and fluttering like the wings of a great lunar moth, an aerial image that danced in my eyes, blurred, dipped and wavered in the darkness slowly toward the lamp, hung there for a split second, passed under the shade, and slipped, just as I thought, inside the bulb at last. The room lit up! Everything was made clear in one magnesium burst of revelation!

And there they go! Away from me in a radiant panic!

(1955)

W.B.⁴: or, The Seer Seen by His Own Vision

In *The Marriage of Heaven and Hell,* celebrated in 1793 as both holy sacrament and revolutionary manifesto, Blake engraved and etched upon "the minds of men" with the "corroding fires" of his infernal acid these apocalyptic sentences:

> If the doors of perception were cleansed every thing would appear to man as it is, infinite.
> For man has closed himself up, till he sees all things thro' narrow chinks of his cavern.

Thro' such "narrow chinks" we still peep out, even at Blake's words themselves, blearing them o'er with the pale cast of cant as merely vaguely and generally referring to a Higher Truth, to which we assent while nodding. And then rest assured, as before, within the Sleep of Reason. For it is not, so Blake insisted, by mathematical abstractions or metaphysical generalities, but only in what he called "minute particulars," specific and irreducible nitty-gritty quiddities, that the "infinite," as it itself is, can be perceived.

And to make it still more specific, such perception must be personal. Whatever the seer sees — whether envisioned in a religious trance, or in a poetic or prophetic rapture, or even, as nowadays, in the spell of "psyche-

Originally published in the *American Review* (October 1976). From *William Blake: The Seer and His Visions*, by Milton Klonsky. Published 1977 by Harmony Books, a Division of Crown Publishers, Inc. Reprinted by permission of Harmony Books, a Division of Crown Publishers, Inc.

delic" drugs—has to be seen by himself alone. There can be no other eyewitness.

For better or for worse, Blake's words from *The Marriage of Heaven and Hell* were deeply etched upon my own mind one day about ten years ago, at a beach on Fire Island, N.Y., when for the first (and also the last) time I was turned on to LSD. From the start I had been forewarned not to expect any instant hallelujuah or Jekyll-into-Hyde metamorphosis; but after what seemed an endless minute-by-minute countdown, during which I felt nothing but a slight tilt of vertigo, my initial dread slowly gave way, I admit, to relief that the acid had apparently been cut too thin to take effect. In this still queasy and uncertain mood I detached myself from my friends, who had kept vigil around me like Job's comforters, and wandered out alone to the beach.

The sun was then at its height, blazing down upon the dunes from a bare blue sky without a wisp of cloud for shade. As far as I could see on either side no one else was there—I had the whole beach to myself—and for good reason: it was so hot that the sand, reflecting the sun's rays from innumerable diamond-faceted particles, "boundless as a nether sky," seemed to glow and kindle here and there with sparks of real fire. Some lines of Blake, dimly remembered, came to mind:

> Turn away no more;
> Why wilt thou turn away?
> The starry floor,
> The wat'ry shore,
> Is giv'n thee till the break of day.

For by then, twisting and turning, as if on a spit, from side to front to side to back to side again, to keep from being scorched, I had become increasingly aware that a similar kind of corrosive scorching was gonig on inside me, "melting apparent surfaces away," as Blake put it, "and display-ing the infinite which was hid." Flayed, that is, from within and without, in a panic I got up and ran, stumbling at times and staggering headlong, then even crawling, unable to stand up again, on all fours until I reached the surf.

The first cold shock of the water went through me tingling with such ecstatic, such baptismal, joy—or was it anguish?—that I felt as if reborn. The ocean, which had appeared from a distance to be a clear, translucent emerald-green, now that I stood inside it and looked closer seemed like a soup, almost a stew, in which floated scraps and pods of rubbery brown seaweed, tassels of hairy-looking filaments, odd calcareous fragments, maybe the bones of fish, maybe broken shells or teeth, bits of shredded cork, micalike scales, flecks of spume or phlegm, unnameable jellies, and brimming throughout with swarms of evanescent infinitesimal motes, but whether light or plankton, organic or inorganic, real or illusory, hardly mattered, for everything in that soup, I knew, would ultimately be dissolved and annihilated. From the horizon, swelling out, an endless succession of waves, waves salaaming waves salaaming waves salaaming waves, uplifting me momentarily as they went by, one after the other, prostrated themselves upon the shore. Their pulse, rising and falling, became indistinguishable from my own. How long I remained there, without will or consciousness, spellbound in that jump-rope rhythm, I can't say, but long enough so that when I did leave, my teeth had already begun to chatter and my body felt numb with cold.

It was while I lay sprawled out once more on the beach, this time basting myself with handful after handful of hot sand, shivering uncontrollably, that it happened. The loneliness of my self-inflicted ordeal was so intense that, just to hear the sound of a human voice, even if only my own voice, I recited aloud what had to be, under the circumstances, Blake's inevitable lines:

> To see the world in a grain of sand
> And heaven in a wild flower . . .

and then stopped. No, I thought, that wasn't right . . . and a pulsebeat later the words flashed back — it was *a* world, *a* heaven — expanding inside my mind:

> To see a World in a Grain of Sand
> And a Heaven in a Wild Flower,
> Hold Infinity in the palm of your hand
> And Eternity in an hour.

The "blue Mundane Shell" (as Blake imagined it) of the sky — a "hard coating of matter that separates us from Eternity" — cracked open for me at that moment, and I perceived the sun with acid clarity as *a* star, one of billions, so many that the grains of sand I then held in my palm would comprise only a handful; and in the same split second the shell of my own time-hardened and encrusted ego, of which the material universe, as Blake thought, was merely the sensual reflection, also cracked, and something within me but not quite me — Ka, or Atman, or Spirit, or Pneuma, or whatever — that had been brooding coiled up in itself, stirred awake. Of course I had always believed that the sun was a star, but now I saw it as if for the first time in its "minute particularity." In its next-to-nothingness as well, and on that scale my own life, not only mine but all life, seemed so paltry, so drained of purpose, value, or significance, that I actually began to cry, without shame or self-restraint, the way I used to cry as a child.

Within a few minutes—the sun was that intense—I had switched once more from freezing to burning. Only now, instead of quenching myself in the surf, I decided to get back, and as quickly as possible, to my friends and whatever cold comfort they had to offer. My "trip," I knew, would last from five to six hours, depending on how long the acid inside me could be "stopped out"; but suppose it were to take 50 years, 60, a whole lifetime? What then? As if existence itself were another more subtly corrosive kind of acid, consuming and flaying us, almost unawares, from within and without, to whose pangs we gradually become accustomed until the end. It occurred to me then, as I lurched and staggered off the beach, that this is what Blake must have meant when he wrote: "Time is the mercy of Eternity; without Time's swiftness / Which is the swiftest of all things, all were eternal torment."

. . . Naturally (as said before) it had a stop, some ten years ago. Looking back now I can recall neither visions nor apparitions, no disembottled genii or spirits out of the vasty deep—unless, perhaps, that of Blake himself, whom I invoked to preside over the scene. What I saw instead ("As the Eye," said Blake, "such the Object") was the world as I had always conceived it to be, the only "real" reality of matter reduced to minuter and minuter particles in a space-time expanding to infinity-eternity, no more or less, according to the scientific dispensation of Newton & Einstein, but which I had never perceived so "im-mediatively" and "into-it-ively" until then. In sum:

> . . . the very world, which is the world
> Of all of us—the place where, in the end,
> We find our happiness, or not at all!

as Wordsworth once described it. Whether the doors of perception be open of shut, our common world, in that sense, which is the world of common sense, was "the very world" Blake lived in as well . . . and yet not entirely.

For he also—or so he claimed—saw visions and spoke face to face with spooks . . . and what can we make of *that*? Starting in early childhood, at the age of four, when God (who even then must have had for him the ghastly visage of Urizen) poked his head through a nursery window to set

266

him screaming with terror, and continuing throughout his life, into his old age, when he would keep regular 9 to 5 A.M. visitation hours for any ghost who might care to chat for a while or pose for his portrait, Blake lived on familiar terms with the spirit world. Invisible to anyone else yet visible to him, as numinous presences, he observed and described them in their "minute particularity." "Spirits," he wrote, "are not as the modern philosophy supposes, a cloudy vapour or a nothing: they are organized and minutely articulated beyond all that the mortal and perishing nature can produce." Being by definition incorporeal, their presence cannot be perceived with or in the "vegetative and corporeal" eye, as he put it, but only with-in the imagination "heightened to Vision" . . . and never evident except when "self"-evident. Like the leptons and muons, quarks and antiquarks, "strange" or "charmed," of nuclear physics, they were mind-stuff, the stuff that dreams and concepts are made of, close to the margin of nonentity, and crossing over from time to time.

A literary journalist and barrister named Henry Crabb Robinson, who came to know Blake intimately in his last years and kept a detailed record of their conversations, attempted to cross-examine him on his beliefs. Robinson relates: "At the same time that he asserted his own possession of this gift of vision, he did not boast of it as *peculiar* to himself; All men might have it if they would." Blake was merely reaffirming the reply made by Moses himself (in Numbers 11:29) upon being told that two lowly upstarts, named Eldad and Medad, had dared to prophesy in the camp of the Israelites, and was asked to forbid them: "Would God that all the Lord's people were prophets, and that the Lord would put his spirit upon them!" The down-to-earth lawyer, however, remained unconvinced, and wrote in his Diary: "Shall I call him Artist or Genius — or Mystic or Madman? Probably he is all."

Blake's visions and visitations have sometimes been explained (though not explained away) by reference to his own rare poetic faculty, cultivated by him since childhood, for envisioning images of such intense cathectic power that they were projected before his eyes as apparitions. Their actual presence could no more be doubted by Blake

> He who Doubts from what he sees
> Will neer Believe do what you Please
> If the Sun & Moon should doubt
> Theyd immediately Go out

than, say, a dreamer, without waking up, could doubt his own dreams in the course of dreaming them. What Blake "saw," in any case, were not

267

hallucinations, for he was always aware of the distinction between his own self-inspired visions and the delusions of sense-perception.

In a letter in verse to his friend and patron Thomas Butts, in 1802, Blake made this explicit:

> A frowning Thistle implores my stay.
> What to others a trifle appears
> Fills me full of smiles or tears;
> For double the vision my Eyes do see,
> And a double vision is always with me.
> With my inward Eye 'tis an old Man grey;
> With my outward a Thistle across my way.

Had he mistaken the thistle by the roadside for "an old Man grey," that would have been the sort of twilight garden-variety hallucination with which we are all familiar, but clearly Blake saw it for what it was. Only in his imagination, "heightened to Vision," did that frowning and thistlelike old man exist. Further on in the letter Blake proceeds to illuminate his compound visionary credo:

> Now I a fourfold vision see,
> And a fourfold vision is given to me;
> 'Tis fourfold in my supreme delight
> And threefold in soft Beulah's night
> And twofold Always. May God us keep
> From Single vision & Newton's sleep.

His "soft Beulah's night," where vision, because annealed by passion, becomes threefold, is Blake's erotic realm of the creative unconscious, presided over by the Daughters of Inspiration. Twofold vision, with him "Always," we have already encountered in the personification of the thistle; and single vision, exemplified by the hypnosis of Newtonian science, occurs when we see with, not thro', our eyes. But fourfold vision, his "supreme delight," is only attained when the phenomenal world has been transcended by the Divine Imagination and reunited with spirit.

Taken all together, Blake's fourfold method of envisioning reality seems to reflect, mirrored within his "inner eye," the fourfold hermeneutics devised by both cabbalists as well as scholastic commentators upon the Bible, whereby the literal-historical, the allegorical, the tropological (or moral), and, finally, the anagogical (or spiritual) levels of meaning in Scripture are successively revealed. And, upon further reflection, there's something else too: the various cabbalist and neoplatonist and alchemical mystagogues, from strands of whose doctrines Blake largely spun his own mythopoeic system, held that God's Word (Scripture) was not only prior to his Work (Nature), but had formed it and lay concealed within its outer material husks as essential "ideas" or divine "sparks." Nature, sometimes referred to in this sense as God's "other" Book, was thus conceived as a vast rebus of image-ideas that reflected, and reflected upon, one another in multiple facets of meaning. Moreover, the "word" of man, as in a poem, say, was a particle of *the* Word of God, and so, *pars pro toto*, shared in its sacredness, just as a picture, like a talisman, images his Work, and is likewise sacred.

Based on this mystical cosmology, there emerged during the Renaissance the tradition of picture-poetry — or "Emblem poetry," as it came to be called — and it is to this tradition that Blake, with his fourfold visionary aesthetics, squarely belongs. But to his own age, the Age of Reason, Emblem poetry had come to seem in itself emblematic of the superstition and obscurantism of a benighted past. What had intervened, inexorably and, it appeared, permanently, was the science of Newton and its philosophical wedge, the dualist psychology of Locke and Descartes,

> Two Horn'd Reasoning, Cloven Fiction,
> In Doubt, which is Self contradiction,

cleaving existence between the mind within and the world without, and thereby annulling the unified mystical world-view upon which picture-poetry had been based.

Against Newton's mechanist universe, ruled by Urizen, Blake opposed the Divine Imagination, personified and apotheosized by him as the God-Man Albion:

> That might controll
> The starry pole,
> And fallen, fallen light renew!

As Englished by Blake, Albion, "in whose Sleep, or Chaos, Creation began," was his patriotic counterpart to the Hebrew Adam Kadmon of cabbalist legend. At the beginning of *Jerusalem* (subtitled *The Emanation of The Giant Albion*) Blake wrote "To the Jews": "You have a tradition, that Man anciently contain'd in his mighty limbs all things in Heaven & Earth: this you recieved from the Druids." But if so, Blake received it back again, and much more besides, from the cabbala. He was undoubtedly familiar with its nuclear ideas and symbols as adapted by Jakob Boehme and Robert Fludd and Paracelsus, among others; but a bill of "minute particulars"

269

might be drawn from his own works to show that he was also acquainted, perhaps at first-hand, with the most famous version of the cabbala, the 16th-century *Zohar* (literally, "Radiance").

"In every word [of Scripture]," states the *Zohar*, "there are many lights." Specifically, every word has 70 "facets," corresponding to the 70 known languages of the 70 nations of the earth; and every separate letter of every word also has 70 "facets"; and, furthermore, for each of these 70 x 70 light-revealing "facets" in every word there are 600,000 "entrances," or possible interpretations, a number equivalent to the 600,000 eyewitnesses said to have been present at Sinai with Moses when the Word was first revealed, and so were able to see for themseles, according to their own "inner light." ("As a man Is," wrote Blake, "so he sees.") Finally, the entire body of Scripture, the words, the letters, and even the shapes of the letters, comprised the secret name of God, not a tittle of which could be altered or removed without tearing a hole in the material fabric of the universe.

"As Poetry admits not a Letter that is Insignificant," Blake insisted, "so Painting admits not a Grain of Sand or a Blade of Grass Insignificant — mush less an Insignificant Blur or Mark." For to him any picture, or picture-poem, if inspired by the Divine Imagination, was as holy as holy writ. Thus, in *Jerusalem*, the cabbalist vision of the multiplicity of possible entrances into the infinite, was refracted by Blake and revealed in its "minute particularity":

> There is a Grain of Sand in Lambeth that Satan cannot find,
> Nor can his Watch Fiends find it; 'tis translucent & has many
>   Angles,
> But he who finds it will find Oothoon's[1] palace; for within
> Opening into Beulah, every angle is a lovely heaven.

Through the Blakean dispensation, all men, not just the 600,000 eyewitnesses at Sinai, even we ourselves, can find the way by our own "inner light" to Oothoon's palace, see visions, dream dreams, converse with spirits. . . .

Should there be any doubt, we need merely conjure up the spirit of Blake himself (as "Memorable Fancy") and present him seated centerstage in the Imagination before us, arms of course akimbo, and with one knee folded, or crossed — 4-fold, that is — over a leg planted firmly on the ground, and allow him to speak out, ex cathedra, as follows:

> I assert foy My Self that I do not behold the outward Creation
> & that to me it is a hindrance & not Action; it is as the dirt

upon my feet, No part of Me. "What," it will be Questioned, "When the Sun rises, do you not see a round disk of fire somewhat like a Guinea?" O no, no, I see an Innumerable company of the Heavenly host crying, "Holy, Holy, Holy is the Lord God Almighty." I question not my Corporeal or Vegetative Eye any more than I would Question a Window concerning a Sight. I look thro' it & not with it.

Blake was (in Marianne Moore's phrase) a "literalist of the imagination," though not in any cross-eyed sense of envisioning "imaginary gardens with real toads in them," for both gardens *and* toads were to him imaginary . . . and thereby more, not less, "real." "What seems to Be," he wrote, "Is, To those to whom / It seems to Be."

It all depends, of course, on what seems to be to whom. And to many of Blake's contemporaries, his visions and visitations seemed unmistakable proof of madness. The poet Robert Southey, for one, recalling his first and only meetig with Blake, which occurred in the summer of 1811, declared that "his madness was too evident, too fearful. It gave his eyes an expression such as you would expect to see in one who was possessed." Not long afterward, Southey related his observations to Crabb Robinson, who duly noted them at the time in his Diary, apparently in full agreement. But a quarter century later, when Robinson came to know the "fearful" madman personally, he wrote: "In the sweetness of his countenance & gentility of his manner he added an indescribable grace to his conversation"; and, further, that his "observations, apart from his visions and references to the spiritual world, were sensible and acute."

Still, it was not these "sensible" views, whatever they were, but his visions and, especially, his "references to the spiritual world," which so fascinated Robinson, and to which he returned again and again in his relentlessly rational cross-examination. Blake was then about 68 years old, within a year of joining that world himself, and no longer attempted to rationalize what could only be witnessed — but never proved or demonstrated — by the witness alone.

"As he spoke of frequently Seeing Milton," Robinson writes in his Diary, "I ventured to ask, half ashamed at the time, which of the three or four portraits in Hollis's *Memoirs* [of Milton] is the most like. He answ[d], 'They are all like, At different Ages. I have seen him as a youth And as an old man with a long flowing beard. He came lately as an old man.'" Blake, in Robinson's account, then tells what happened:

271

He came to ask a favor of me. He said he had committed an error in his Paradise Lost, which he wanted me to correct, in a poem or picture; but I declined. I said I had my own duties to perform. "It is a presumptuous question," I [Robinson] replied. "Might I venture to ask — What that could be?" He wished me to expose the falsehood of his doctrine, taught in the Paradise Lost, That Sexual intercourse arouse [sic] out of the Fall. Now that cannot be, for no good can spring out of Evil.

On another occasion, a few days afterward, Blake described a similar encounter with the spirit of Voltaire, informing Robinson:

I have had much intercourse with Voltaire. And he said to me, "I blasphemed the Son of Man and it shall be forgiven me, but they (the enemies of Voltaire) blasphemed the Holy Ghost in me, and it shall not be forgiven to them." I asked him in what language Voltaire spoke. His answer was ingenious and gave no encouragement to cross questioning. To my sensations it was English. It was like the touch of a musical key — he touched it probably French, but to my ear it became English.

The detail about the "musical key" that nonplussed Robinson, who had thought to trap him by questioning his knowledge of French,

The Questioner, who sits so sly,
Shall never know how to Reply.
He who replies to words of Doubt
Doth put the Light of Knowledge out.

was a neat thrust, most likely inspired by some spirit on the spot — jabbing this pointed detail, like a bare bodkin, into his solidly planted and down-to-earth meaphysical fundament . . . Just to get a rise out of him.

"He who does not imagine in stronger and better lineaments," wrote Blake, "and in stronger and better light than his perishing and mortal eye can see, does not imagine at all." He must previously have told the tale of Voltaire's visitation to others besides Robinson, reimagining it afresh each time in the telling and, as in this case, touching up the lineaments to make them "stronger and better."

But even if imagined, and therefore "imaginary," these emissaries from the far-out peripheries of the visionary fourth-dimension would not (as said before) have made them any less "real" to Blake. "And as all of us on earth are united in thought," he wrote as long ago as 1788 (in his annotations to Lavater's *Aphorisms)*, "for it is impossible to think without images of somewhat on earth — So it is impossible to know God or heavenly things without conjunction with those who know God & heavenly things; therefore all who converse in the spirit, converse with spirits." (That *therefore!*) In his mental realm, where seeming is being and art & life confabulate, they have a marginal existence; though how they might then differ, if at all, from the mythic personae and "Giant Forms" of his prophetic books, such as Los or Urizen or Enitharmon or Luvah, his Questioner forgot to question.

"I never in all my conversations with him," wrote Blake's friend, the artist Joseph Linnell, some three years after his death, "could feel the least justice in calling him insane; he could always explain his paradoxes when he pleased, but to many he spoke so 'that hearing they might *not* hear.'"

What Robinson heard, *sans doute*, was what he had told himself . . . he would hear; yet it was also, paradoxically, the case. In another letter addressed by Blake to Thomas Butts (dated April 25, 1803), he speaks of having "composed an immense number of verses on One Grand Theme [possibly his *Milton* or *Vala*], Similar to Homer's Iliad or Milton's Paradise Lost, the Persons & Machinery intirely new to the Inhabitants of Earth. . . . I have written this Poem from immediate Dictation," he continues, "twelve or sometimes twenty or thirty lines at a time, without Premeditation & even against my Will; the Time it has taken in writing was thus render'd Non Existent, & and immense Poem Exists which seems to be the Labour of a long Life, all produc'd without Labour or Study." Since all who converse *in* the spirit, as he said, converse *with* spirits, the 18th century poetic device of Personification was for him no "mere" figure of speech. As a mystical poet-painter — that is, clairaudient as well as clairvoyant — while under the spell of creation he would first hypostatize ideas into real entities, which were then personified, a hypertrophy of the trope, as 'twere, so that to be inspired was, literally, to be inspirited. The ideas themselves might have been "mad" — or the spirits that personified them — but not Blake. Judging, moreover, from the many deletions and revisions in the surviving ms. of *Vala*, which was never published, these spirits, like mortal and corporeal authors, must have had second thoughts, and then seconded their second thoughts, before leaving well enough alone.

"I am under the direction of Messengers from Heaven," he told the faithful Butts, "Daily and Nightly." But what sort of "Messengers? Were they, for instance, like the seraphic scouts of Jehovah through whom, in the old days, he despatched his communiqués to the prophets? Or did they resemble instead the personal *daimon* of Socrates, the warning voice that, so he claimed, had attended and guided him throughout his life? They must have shared the characteristics of both. But if more like the latter, then what Blake envisioned was not one but legions, a pandemonium of such *daimons*, innumberable as motes within the beam of his own inner light, whose imagined actions were his thoughts. Speaking for themselves, they declared in *Vala* that "in the Brain of Man we live & in his circling Nerves / . . . this bright world of all our joy is in the Brain of Man." However, the "Brain," hypostatized and capitalized, was not Blake's alone but Everyman's — or Albion's — for we are all one in spirit as well as one Spirit. "Man is All Imagination," he wrote. "God is Man & exists in us & we in him."

To which pledge of spiritual allegiance, one for all and all for one, Crabb Robinson himself might have piously assented; but, as a lawyer, he could not help but balk at the enormous consequences concealed within the small-print minutiae. "We who dewll on Earth," wrote Blake in *Jerusalem*, "can do nothing of ourselves; every thing is conducted by Spirits, no less than digestion or sleep"; and further, but in a different context, "For every Natural Effect has a Spiritual Cause, and Not / A Natural; for a Natural Cause . . . is a Delusion of Ulro [materialism] & a ratio of the perishing Vegetable Memory." But, if so, this would merely invert the materialist determinism of Newtonian science, replacing it with an equally binding, though spell-binding, spiritual determinism, and thus reanimate the once haunted animist universe of our savage ancestors. No wonder Robinson, baffled in his attempt to rationalize Blake's ideas, kept pointing a revolving forefinger at his head. "He incidentally denied [physical] causation," he notes in his Diary, "Every thing being the work of God or Devil." Yet Blake was no predestinarian or zomboid fatalist either, for the impulses that lead us to act one way or the other, like the improvisations of art, he believed to be freely inspired. As seemed self-evident . . .

He appears to us now (if such can be imagined) a kind of existential hieroglyph, a figure in whom the ancient prayer of Socrates, that the inner and outer man be one, has been realized. He not only believed but lived his visionary ideas, and as he saw himself so can he be seen thro' by us. For Blake to have become Blake, that is, the chance coincidences of his life, like the "minute particulars" of his poems and pictures, could not have been otherwise. "Look over the events of your own life," he suddenly confronts the reader (in his marginalia to Watson's *Apology*), "& if you do not find that you have done such miracles & lived by such you do not see as I do."

Of all these seemingly miraculous coincidences the most crucial, as it turned out, was the date of his birth: 1757. For that was the year in which the mystical theologian Emanuel Swedenborg claimed to have been transported to heaven in a vision, and while there to have personally witnessed the commencement of the Last Judgment, as foretold by the book of Revelation. In 1771 Swedenborg, in his corporeal being, traveled to London to organize a branch of his church, dying there a year later at the age of 85. Though none of his works was translated into English until 1788, Blake must have learned, long before then, that the beginning of Swedenborg's millennium coincided with the date of his own birth. It was a "fact that would have aroused anyone's sense of wonder, but especially Blake's. When the London branch of Swedenborg's New Church was founded, again in 1788, he and his wife attended several of the meetings, though they never became members. Among other things, Blake ridiculed Swedenborg for his pious orthodoxy in accepting Good and Evil as static and eternally opposed, rather than dynamic and conjugally united. As he wrote in his *Milton*:

> O Swedenborg! strongest of men, the Samson shorn by the
>   Churches,
> Shewing the Transgressors in Hell, the proud Warriors in Heaven,
> Heaven as a Punisher, & Hell as One under Punishment . . .

And besides, he once told Crabb Robinson (no doubt with a sidelong glance), Swedenborg was "wrong in trying to explain to the rational faculty what the reason cannot comprehend."

But of the truth of Swedenborg's prophecy, that the Kingdom of God was at hand, Blake remained convinced. In further confirmation, another mystical author, Jakob Boehme, whom Blake revered, had also predicted that a seventh "Enochian Age"—from Adam to Seth to Enos to Cainan to Mahalaleel up to Enoch, the so-called "Prophetical Mouth"—would see the fulfillment of the Word . . . and this age Blake identified with his own. In the American War of Independence and the overthrow of the monarchy in France, Blake saw signs and portents of still greater things to come in the spirit world.

The Marriage of Heaven and Hell (even the title parodies Swedenborg's most famous book, *Heaven and Its Wonders and Hell*) was conceived in, and by, this confident expectation of world revolution and divine revelation. Though not published until 1793, it was apparently composed in 1790, when he wrote: "As a new heaven is begun, and it is now thirty-three years [the lifespan of Christ, and Blake's own age in 1790] since its advent, the Eternal Hell revives. And lo! Swedenborg is the Angel [of the Resurrection] sitting at the tomb: his writings are the linen clothes folded up. Now is the dominion of Edom, & the return of Adam into Paradise. See Isaiah xxxiv & xxxv Chap." Instead, as we know, the Second Coming never came (or kept on coming as always), and the growing threat of revolutionary France brought about the suppression of radical political and religious dissent in England, with the imprisonment or deportation of its Jacobin sympathizers.

Not long after the celebration of *The Marriage*, however, something astonishing, almost uncanny, did occur, which must have reminded Blake that the ways of the Lord surpasseth the understanding even of prophets. For there then appeared in London, proclaiming himself a "nephew of God" and "Prince of the Hebrews," a strange, demented, tragic figure named Richard Brothers. A former naval officer, he had resigned from his commission in 1792 to protest the war being organized against the French republic, after which he sent urgent letters to the king and his ministers appealing to them to repent and desist. This war, he prophesied, would be the final conflict between Good and Evil foretold in Revelation 19:19: "And I saw the beast [with 'seven heads and ten horns,' representing the crowned heads of Europe, one of them, presumably, on the neck of George III], and the kings of the earth, and their armies, gathered together to make war against him that sat on the horse [the Word of God], and against his army." By 1794, with the war already underway, he began to preach among the people that the apocalyptic Day of Wrath was at hand, and also published a tract, entitled *A Revealed Knowledge of the Prophecies and Times*, in which he predicted the imminent destruction of the British and all other empires. This was to be succeeded by a new political-religious dispensation, when the Jews both "visible" and "invisible" (those who identified themselves as such and others who, unknown to themselves, were descendents of the ten lost tribes) would return to the Promised Land. A universal brotherhood — led, naturally, by Brothers — would then be established on earth, with its capital in Jerusalem.

By the charismatic force of his own self-persuasion, turned outward, Brothers gathered a large and enthusiastic following — including Blake's friend, the engraver William Sharp, a former Swedenborgian — and persuaded them that he was the prophet chosen by the Lord to blow the shofar for year 1 of the millennium. When, for instance, he warned his brotherhood in the summer of 1794 that an earthquake was about to devastate London, crowds are reported to have fled the city in panic. The authorities, by this time, came to regard him as a social as well as political menace. Arrested in March of 1795, on the charge of disturbing the peace and making "fond and fantastical prophecies," he was pronounced insane and sentenced to be confined in a lunatic asylum, remaining there for 11 years until his release in 1806, by which time he was almost forgotten.

In Brothers, Blake must have recognized, with a double take, his own spiritual doppelganger; and this in turn, upon further reflection, would have been redoubled thro' his eyes — becoming fourfold, that is — with the realization that Brothers, too, had been born in the annus mirabilis of 1757. His fate must also have seemed to Blake as a warning by the spirits. Three years after Brothers's imprisonment, Blake wrote gloomily: "To defend the Bible in this year 1798 would cost a man his life. The Beast & Whore [of Revelation] rule without control"; and further down (on the back of the title page of Bishop Watson's *Apology*, which he was then annotating), Blake added: "I have been commanded from Hell not to print this, as it is what our Enemies wish." As he knew, his own "prophecies" might be regarded as no less "fond and fantastical" by the authorities had they wished to do so — or had they heard about them, for Blake's very obscurity here protected him — and he too had often been stigmatized as mad. From 1795 to 1808, a gap of 13 years, Blake was to publish no more of his "prophetic" books.

In a letter sent in 1800 to the sculptor John Flaxman, a devotee of Swedenborg, he relates how

> . . . terrors appear'd in the Heavens above
> And in Hell beneath, & a mighty & awful
> change threatened the Earth.
> The American War began. All its dark horrors
> passed before my face
> Across the Atlantic to France. Then the
> French Revolution commenc'd in thick clouds,
> And My Angels have told me that seeing such
> visions I could not subsist on the Earth . . .

The Blake who had once plumed himself with the red cockade of revolution on the streets of London was to choose, a decade later, as an epigraph for *Vala*, this quotation from Ephesians (6:12): "For our contention is not with the blood and the flesh, but with dominion, with authority, with the blind world-rulers of this life, with the spirit of evil in things heavenly."

Those "blind world-rulers" ("blind" to us because we are blind to them) exist within the mind of Everyman — and any one man — as moral commandments; as historical forces within society; and as eternal decrees within the realm of the spirit. Old Nobodaddy *is* King George III *is* the superego dominating our lives. "Are not Religion & Politics the Same Thing?" he asks (in *Jerusalem* 57:10), a truism as self-evident to him in 18th-century London as it had once been to the prophets in ancient Israel. Since, as he thought, "Thought is Act"—and reciprocally, in such a mental universe, Act must be Thought—the politics he envisioned was not that of "the reasoning historian, turner and twister of causes and consequences, such as Hume, Gibbon and Voltaire," but a spiritual politics, in which (as he declares in *A Descriptive Catalogue*) "Acts themselves alone are history. . . . Tell me the Acts, O historian, and leave me to reason upon them as I please . . ." and concludes: "His opinions, who does not see spiritual agency, is not worth any man's reading; he who rejects a fact because it is improbable, must reject all History and retain doubts only." Peering through the narrow chinks of "single vision," these squint-eyed rationalists "cannot see either miracle or prodigy: all to them is a dull round of probabilities and possibilities; but the history of all times and places is nothing else but improbabilities and impossibilities; what we should say was impossible if we did not see it always before our eyes."

. . . Yet, as we know, one man's undoubted "miracle" may be another's seeming "coincidence." Looked at thro' our own eyes, what strikes us nowadays as almost miraculously coincidental is the close resemblance between Blake's views denying physical causation (for which he was deemed mad) and the theory of "acausal synchronicity" devised by Carl Jung, in collaboration with the physicist Wolfgang Pauli, to explain certain age-old but still baffling psychic phenomena. Jung's and Pauli's abstract principle has merely been personified by Blake into spiritual agency, in accord with the poetic conventions of his time; and the same may be said of Jung's "archetypes" as Blake's "Giant Forms," Jung's "collective unconscious" as Blake's "Divine Imagination." Toward the end of his life Jung came to believe that "Meaningful coincidences—which are to be distinguished from meaningless chance-groupings—seem to rest on an archetypal foundation"; and to this too, after transmuting Jung's psychological into his own occult and spiritualist terms, Blake would have agreed as self-evident. Finally, the concept of a "group-mind," postulated by some modern biologists to account for the highly complex and coordinated social activities among various species of insects and marine rhizopods, in which each member seems to share a "psychic blueprint," and, by extension, has been cited by parapsychologists to advance the possibility of ESP and telepathy and precognition among humans, obviously corresponds to Blake's own conception of man as microtheos, sharing in the mystical body of the collective God-Man, Albion. "What is now proved," he wrote (as one of the infernal proverbs of *The Marriage of Heaven and Hell*), "was once only imagin'd."

Looking over the events of his own life, there is one, at the outset of his career, that has sometimes been seen as objective proof that he must have been gifted with precognition; though Blake, who necessarily viewed it from the inside, subjectively, would have declined any such gift, and attributed the event instead to his tutelary spirits. Whichever, through its prism, we can observe in retrospect the young Blake in the act of realizing — or, rather, "imagining" — himself as an artist.

At the age of 14, in 1772, he was taken by his father, who owned a small business as a hosier in London, to be apprenticed to the once celebrated engraver William Wynne Ryland. Blake had been enrolled four years earlier at one of the conventional art schools of the period, where he was taught how to draw by sketching plaster casts of antique statuary and copying prints of old masters. But his father had become alarmed, as well as somewhat spooked himself, upon being told by his son of how, while walking about the countryside alone, he had encountered seraphic beings flitting through the hayfields and perched up in the trees, "their bright angelic wings bespangling every bough like stars." If he were accepted as an apprentice by Ryland, so his father hoped, these apparitions might fade in time from his mind, and meanwhile he would be able to practice his art and learn the profitable trade of engraving besides.

Right after his first interview with Ryland, however, Blake peremptorily refused to join his workshop, telling his father that the man had a "hanging look," and was doomed to die one day on the scaffold. Ryland was then official engraver to King George III, a social as well as artistic favorite at the court, and such a fate seemed highly unlikely. Yet some ten years later, just as the young Blake had foretold, Ryland was convicted of forging banknotes on the East India Company, denied a pardon by the angry king, and hanged. How Blake responded to this fulfillment of his prophecy is not recorded; but in 1798 (in his annotations to Watson), he wrote: "Every honest man is a Prophet; he utters his opinion both of private & public matters. Thus: If you go on So, the result is So. He never says, such a thing shall happen let you do what you will. A Prophet is a Seer, not an Arbitrary Dictator." The warning voice of his own *daimon*, he must have imagined, had whispered Ryland's fate into his inner ear.

Had Blake been apprenticed to him at so early an age, he would have been trained in Ryland's highly, fashionable style of mezzotint engraving by "stipple," or dots, which reproduced the syrupy tones and twilight shadings of chiaroscuro ("that infernal machine called Chiaro Oscuro,"

Blake so abominated) in paintings by Sir Joshua Reynolds, Cipriani, Angelica Kauffmann, et al., for prints meant to be framed in the elegant drawing rooms of the period above the Chippendale & Sheraton. But such a modish and rococo "Blake" could never of course have become our Blake. Instead, after his father had paid the requisite sum of 50 guineas, he was taken on as apprentice by the old-fashioned engraving firm of James Basire and sons (I, II & III) for a span of seven years, from 1772 to 1779. Though Basires provided engravings for various publishers of that time, it was chiefly employed as official engraver to the Society of Antiquaries as well as the Royal Society of London, for whom precision and clarity of line, rather than tonal values, were most important. This severely linear style, while outmoded, was in accord with Blake's own precocious enthusiasm for the prints and drawings of Albrecht Dürer, Marcantonio Raimondi (the engraver of Raphael), Hendrik Goltzius, Giulio Romano, Michelangelo — especially Michelangelo — and from it he never deviated. "Nature has no outline," he later declared, "Imagination has."

During his second year at Basires a quarrel erupted between two newly enrolled apprentices and the feisty, cocksure, and disputatious redheaded adolescent who was Blake. Once more, we can discern in this the fine hand of his attendant spirits; for, as a result, Basire decided to restore peace in his workshop by sending him off alone to Westminster Abbey, there to make preparatory sketches for a book on the *Sepulchral Monuments of Great Britain*. Up to the end of his life he was to recall the time (was it nine months?) spent there alone, sketching and meditating amid the Gothic vaults and tombs and effigies, as sacred, a religious as well as artistic second birth.

It was then, he declared, that he was revealed "the simple and plain road to the style at which he aimed, unentangled in the intricate windings of modern practice." Both the 16-year-old and the 60-year-old Blake saw this vision of the Gothic thro' the same eyes: "Grecian is Mathematic Form: Gothic is Living Form, Mathematic Form is eternal in the Reasoning Memory: Living Form is Eternal Existence" (commenting *On Virgil* in 1820). Coincident with this discovery must have come the further revelation, in medieval illuminated manuscripts, of the flamboyant and self-expressive, even self-willed, Gothic line, which was to germinate over the years into the luxuriant exfoliations of his own picture-poems. A firm and determinate "bounding line" (so to speak) was then drawn in his mind between the prevailing 18th-century conception of art as "imitation," ruled by the repressive and backward-looking daughters of Memory, and art as "inspiration," released by the prophetic agents of the Divine Imagination.

About this time, as it happened, Blake made still another discovery — actually a self-discovery — that was to prove as important to him as a poet as the Gothic had been to him as an artist. Once his work on the *Sepulchral Monuments* was finished, Blake was assigned by Basire to do certain of the illustrations for Jacob Bryant's *A New System, or An Analysis of Ancient Mythology*, a book that sought to trace the descent of the gods and demigods of the ancient world to the survivors of the Deluge in Noah's Ark. Though Bryant's fantastic chronology, which relied mainly on the murky genealogical system of dating in the Bible, was by modern standards no more than guesswork, a shot in the "dark backward and abysm of time," his analysis of the common motifs underlying the pantheons of Egypt and Greece, India and Babylon and Scandinavia, anticipated in the 18th century the comparative mythology of Frazer's *The Golden Bough*.

For the young Blake, reared in the bibliolatry of a fundamentalist Baptist household, Bryant's book came as an eye-opener. More than three decades later (in *A Descriptive Catalogue*), he wrote: "The antiquities of every Nation under Heaven, is no less sacred than that of the Jews. They are all the same thing, as Jacob Bryant and all antiquaries have proved. . . . All had originally one language and one religion: this was the religion of Jesus, the Everlasting Gospel." And to this belief in a perennial and primordial religion, with his usual patriotic fervor he came to add the notion (which was shared, incidentally, by Brothers) that the Druids, who had built the mysterious temple of Stonehenge on the plains of Salisbury, were none other than that chosen and original race descended from the ten lost tribes of Israel. From which it followed ("Can it be?" he asks in self-bemused astonishment in *Jerusalem*, "Is it a Truth that the Learned have explored?") that Britain was "the Primitive Seat of the Patriarchal Religion." When, in his Preface to *Milton*, he vowed:

> I will not cease from Mental Fight,
> Nor shall my Sword sleep in my hand
> Till we have built Jerusalem
> In England's green & pleasant Land.

he meant it literally, allegorically, morally, and anagogically.

That "Mental Fight" had in fact already begun while he was still an apprentice. In his marginalia — notes & comments, inscribed throughout his life in the books he considered important, that were sometimes asides addressed to the reader, or to the world at large, or to his attendant spirits, or else a retort direct to the author, as if all were present at the same time

281

looking over his shoulder — he wrote around 1808 on a page of Reynold's *Discourses*:

> I read Burke's Treatise [on the Sublime] when very Young; at the same time I read Locke on Human Understanding & Bacon's Advancement of Learning, on Every one of these books I wrote my Opinions, & on looking them over find that [they] are exactly Similar. I felt the Same Contempt & Abhorrence then that I do now. They mock Inspiration & Vision. Inspiration & Vision was then, & now is, & I hope will always Remain, my Element, my Eternal Dwelling Place.

The ideas he held then, engraved into his being, never really changed, but were only etched deeper by time; and in discovering them at so early an age he was, simultaneously, uncovering his own essential lineaments. Like Blake's mythic alter ego, the poet-engraver Los, "he became [as he wrote in *Vala*] what he beheld: He became what he was doing: he was himself transform'd." Basires, in that sense, was for him the sort of infernal "Printing house," described in *The Marriage of Heaven and Hell*, "in which knowledge is transmitted from generation to generation," and where "Unnamed forms" (later to be named as the "Giant Forms" of the prophetic books) "cast the metals into the expanse" of corrosive acid. The seven years he spent there had the effect, within and without, of "melting apparent surfaces away, and displaying the infinite which was hid."

The 22-year-old engraver who finally emerged in 1779 from his long apprenticeship was unmistakably Blake. For a time he enrolled at the Royal Academy as an art student, meanwhile supporting himself by doing commercial engravings on a free-lance basis for various publishers. The two English artists he then most admired and emulated were the Irish-born enthusiast James Barry, reputed like himself to be a seer of visions, and J. H. Mortimer, a historical painter in the grand style of medieval subjects, both of whom worked outside the official canons of taste decreed by Sir Joshua Reynolds. And for that reason alone would have appealed to Blake's rebellious spirits. In 1782, against his father's wishes, he got married "beneath him" — and "on the rebound," it was rumored — to the illiterate daughter of a greengrocer, Catherine Boucher, or Butcher, who signed the marriage register with an "X," but was subsequently trained and educated by Blake well enough to assist him at his work, becoming the Enitharmon to his Los.

Upon his father's death, in 1784, Blake received a small inheritance, and with it he went into partnership with a former fellow-apprentice at Basires,

James Parker, to open an engraver's and print seller's establishment on the same street as the family hosiery business. But the living was meager, and besides, his spirits had other plans for Blake. Sharing the same quarters with him and his wife at the time was his beloved younger brother Robert, whom he was teaching to paint and engrave. And when, in 1787, Robert fell sick and died of consumption at the age of 19, Blake dissolved his partnership with Parker and moved with his wife to a house in another neighborhood. The business that had begun as a direct result of a death in the family thus also ended with one, and Blake was afterward to refer with revulsion to the interim years, when he worked "as a slave bound in a mill among beasts and devils."

During the early 1780s he formed what turned out to be lifelong friendships with several other artists: the sculptor John Flaxman, the Swiss painter Henry Fuseli, the portrait painter George Romney (who thought Blake's "historical drawings rank with those of Michael Angelo"), and the engraver Thomas Stothard. Through Flaxman he was introduced into the intellectual salon run by the bluestocking wife of the Revd. Anthony Mathew. At a few of these gatherings Blake is said to have recited — or crooned, rather, to tunes of his own devising — the early poems assembled under the title "*Poetical Sketches*, by W. B." It was the Revd. Mathew, together with Flaxman, who sponsored the printing in 1783 of this volume of juvenile verse, which, though never offered for sale, was the only book by Blake ever to be printed commercially during his life.

At the time of his brother Robert's death, Blake was almost entirely unknown to the public, either as poet or painter, and seemed likely to remain so. His self-realization as both at once, in the picture-poems of the *Songs of Innocence and of Experience* and the prophetic books, had to await the invention of so-called "illuminated printing." The secret of this process, he claimed, was revelaed to him in a vision by the spirit of his deceased brother. Though some doubt exists about priorty (for a similar method was discussed by Blake's friend, the engraver George Cumberland, in correspondence dated 1784), Blake was the first to apply it successfully, in 1788, in the tiny plates for the tracts *All Religions Are One* and *There Is No Natural Religion*. And there is a passage in *An Island in the Moon*, written between 1784 and 1787, which suggests, that even without supernatural revelation, most of the technical problems had by then already been solved. Following a break in the text, with one or more missing pages apparently torn out by Blake himself to protect his secret, it continues:

"—thus Illuminating the Manuscript."

"Ay," said she, "that would be excellent."

"Then," said he, "I would have all the writing Engraved instead of Printed, & at every other leaf a high finish'd print—all in three Volumes folio—& sell them a hundred pounds apiece. They would print off two thousand."

Which would add up to a weighty 200,000 pounds of pie-in-the-sky—ironical, but also pathetic, considering that from 1802 to 1827, the year of his death, by Blake's own accounts he earned from all his illuminated books and the sale of pictures between 50 and 100 pounds a year, in toto about 1,531 pounds for a lifetime's effort.

In a *Prospectus to the Public*, issued in 1793, Blake first announced his new method of printing, "in a style more ornamental, uniform, and grand, than any before discovered . . . which combines the Painter and the Poet . . ." And he also remarks: "The Labours of the Artist, the Poet, the Musician, have been proverbially attended by poverty and obscurity . . . owing to a neglect of means to propagate such works as have wholly absorbed the Man of Genius. Even Milton and Shakespeare could not publish their own works"; but, he adds, now that a way has been found to do so," . . . the Author is sure of his reward." In this *Prospectus*, Blake offered his *Songs of Innocence* ("with 25 designs") and *Songs of Experience* (also "with 25 designs") for 5s apiece; *The Marriage of Heaven and Hell* ("with 14 designs") for 7s 6d; and *The Gates of Paradise* ("a small book of Engravings") for 3s. Each "highly finish'd" print, moreover, reproduced on "the most beautiful wove paper that could be procured," was to be illuminated by the artist in several colors.

Yet for all that—and at that price—there were few takers. By 1818, when the cost of a copy of *Songs of Innocence*, for instance, had risen over the years to 3 pounds 3s, Blake ruefully advised a potential patron that producing illuminated books was "unprofitable enough for me, tho' Expensive to the Buyer." Whatever else his spirits had going for them, they weren't very good at business. As Crabb Robinson observed in 1826, when he ordered a copy of the *Songs* for 5 guineas, "He spoke of his horror of money and of turning pale when it was offered him. . . . And this was certainly unfeigned."

For he knew its weight. Blake, to survive, had had to push that Sisyphean boulder uphill all his life, starting anew at the bottom of failure time after time. But especially during his early years, when the patronage of art in England was under the sway of Sir Joshua Reynolds, he must have found the going steep and rough. Writing in 1808 (in his marginalia to Reynolds's *Discourses*), he recalls having "spent the Vigour of my Youth & Genius under the Oppression of Sr Joshua & his Gang of Cunning Hired Knaves Without Employment & as much as could possibly be Without Bread . . ."; and when, further on, he says of the two visionary English artists whose work he had most admired in those days, that "Barry was Poor & Unemploy'd, except by his own Energy; Mortimer was call'd a Madman . . ." he might have been talking not only about, but to, himself. In the degradation of art — and artists — by money he saw the debasement of Albion.

An anonymous friend of Blake's, cited by Alexander Gilchrist in his *Life*, tells of his receiving a contemptuous rebuff during his youth from Sir Joshua himself:

> Once I remember his talking to me of Reynolds, [and] he became furious at what the latter had dared to say of his early works. When a very young man he had called on Reynolds to show him some designs, and had been recommended to work with less extravagance and more simplicity, and to correct his drawing. This Blake seemed to regard as an affront never to be forgotten. He was very indignant when he spoke of it.

The wound continued to fester, especially since he was reminded of it over the years by the rankling criticism, repeated and parroted so often that it came to be taken for granted, that his technical skills as an artist-engraver were inferior to his designs and conceptions.

"I know," he declares (in his *Public Address* of 1810), "my Execution is not like Any Body Else. I do not intend it should be so; none but Blockheads Copy one another." And then: " . . . the Lavish praise I have received from all Quarters for Invention & drawing has Generally been accompanied by this: 'he can conceive but he cannot Execute'; this Absurd assertion has done me, & may still do me, the greatest mischief."

What Blake chiefly resented was the critical disparagement of the severely linear style of engraving he had learned at Basires and still "religiously" practiced. This style, employed by Dürer and Giulio Romano and Marcantonio, which rendered tones by means of parallel lines of varying thickness and by elaborate webs of cross-hatching, had long been superseded by the method of engraving in mezzotint (and the more modern aquaint) known internationally as *la manière anglasie*, Its most successful exponents in England during Blake's youth were the celebrated William Woollett (1735–85) and Sir Robert Strange (1721–92).

"What is Call'd the English style of engraving," he writes, "such as proceeded from the Toilettes of Woolett [sic] & Strange (for theirs were Fribble's Toilettes) can never produce Character & Expression. I knew the Men intimately from their Intimacy wth Basire my Master & knew them both to be heavy lumps of Cunning & Ignorance. . . ." Against Woollett, especially, then 25 years dead, his rage and scorn were obsessive: "Woollett I know did not know how to grind his graver," he writes. "I know this . . ."

It is that stutteringly reiterated and apodictic "I know . . . I know . . ." that certifies for us that what he knows he knows for a certainty by the glow of his own inner light. With the prophetic fury of a cockney Ezekiel or Jeremiah, as weirdly anachronistic in his time as in ours, he denounces all the works of the blasphemous mezzotinters and no less perfidious tribe of aquatinters as "slobberings," "bunglishness," "blundering "blurs," "Venetian & Flemish ooze," "paltry blots," and more besides. Their sins in denying outline, as he saw them, were sins against the Divine Imagination; for to Blake art and morality, good works and good deeds, were inseparable and interchangeable. In the *Descriptive Catalogue* he makes this explicit:

> The great and golden rule of art, as well as of life, is this: That the more distinct, sharp, and wirey the bounding line, the more perfect the work of art; and the less keen and sharp, the greater is the evidence of weak imitation, plagiarism and bungling. . . . What is it that distinguishes honesty from knavery, but the hard and wirey line of rectitude and certainty in the actions and intentions? Leave out this line, and you leave out life itself; all is chaos again, and the line of the almighty must be drawn out upon it before man or beast can exist.

But in stressing "the bounding line" *in* art as *in* life, yet erasing the "keen and sharp" distinction between them, as it exists in this very world, Blake's paradoxical "golden rule" was regarded instead as the measure of his own madness.

The *Descriptive Catalogue*, though it had the opposite effect, was intended mainly to refute just that charge, that he himself was insane and his works "but an unscientific and irregular Eccentricity, a Madman's Scrawls." He now appealed directly to the public from "the judgment of those narrow blinking eyes, that have too long governed art in a dark corner." As pamphlet of some 38 pages, along with several related leaflets and handbills, it was given away free as part of the 2s 6d admission charge to an exhibition, held in the summer of 1809, of 16 "Poetical and Historical Inventions, painted by William Blake in water colors, being the ancient

286

method of fresco painting restored." These pictures had previously been refused for its annual show by the Royal Academy, a rejection in which Blake perceived the dead hand of Sir Joshua still raised against him from the spirit world. Accordingly, the *Descriptive Catalogue* — more a polemic than a catalogue, and less a description of the pictures than a religious and philosophical tract — criticizes throughout those artisits most esteemed by Reynolds, such as Titian and Rubens and Correggio, and even condemns oil painting itself, which (he declares) "deadens every colour it is mixed with . . . and in a little time becomes a yellow mask over all it touches." (Further on, he adds: "This is an awful thing to say to oil Painters; they may call it madness, but it is true.") One idea in the *Descriptive Catalogue* suggests another, sometimes only distantly or even metaphorically related, which immediately raises its voice above it, and then, in turn, may be drowned out by a following idea, before the first can be heard again. Written in the ejaculatory style of his Marginalia, but now across the whole page of everything he believes and knows, it is as though the conclamant and sometimes discordant voices of all his attendant spirits were alternately haranguing, explaining, protesting, denouncing, scolding, cajoling, lecturing, pleading, and prophesying.

The exhibition itself (not one painting was sold), like the *Descriptive Catalogue* that accompanied it, turned out to be a fiasco. One irate reviewer, writing about the show in September 1809, described Blake as "an unfortunate lunatic, whose personal inoffensiveness secures him from confinement," and went on:

> The poor man fancies himself a great master, and has painted a few wretched pictures, some of which are unintelligible allegory, others an attempt at sober characters by caricature representation, and the whole "blotted and blurred," and very badly drawn. These he calls an Exhibition, of which he has published a Catalogue, or rather a farrago of nonsense, unintelligibleness, and egregious vanity, the wild effusions of a distempered brain. . . .

In Blake's *Public Address* of 1810 (which was never made public), he refers bitterly to this article, complaining To-Whom-It-May-Concern that "the manner in which my Character has been blasted these thirty years, both as an artist & a Man, may be seen particularly in a Sunday Paper cal'd the Examiner," then passes without a break, and in the same sentence, to his other grievances, the ingratitude of friends and the contumely of patrons, the spite of his rivals, the decline of honest drawing in favor of spurious color in art, English engravers vs. European, puffed-up reputations in newspapers . . . which reminds him, and he suddenly erupts once more: "*It is very true, what you have said for these thirty two Years. I am Mad or Else you are so; both of us cannot be in our right senses. Posterity will judge by our Works.*" (My italics)

And in that, of course, he was right: "Posterity" (meaning ourselves) has done even better and made his works into a touchstone by which we judge our own works. The aspersion of madness against him, though it still persists, has come to seem increasingly beside the point. No doubt, among the heterogeneous swarms of spirits attending him he must have had (and who hasn't?) one or two or even more with a bit too much white around he eyeball; but to call an ecstatic and visionary artist such as Blake "mad" would be like saying of an accountant that he was "calculating."

Yet even with that in mind, the virulence of his hatred against all those whom he considered "spiritual enemies," especially Reynolds, sometimes teeters on paranoia. In the case of Sir Joshua—that "doll" (as Blake dubbed him) of the king and nobility—he continued to stick pins into his effigy long after the man himself had died in 1792. Around 1808, a year before his exhibition, Blake conjured up the spirit of Reynolds for a "mental fight," head-to-head and with no thoughts barred; when he came to annotate the *Discourses.*

Dr. Johnson had once remarked of Reynolds that he was "the most invulnerable man he knew; whom, if he should quarrel with him, he should find the most difficulty how to abuse"; but Blake, no respecter of persons— least of all Sir Joshua's—refers to him throughout as "hypocrite," "liar," "villain," "Damned Fool!" "sly dog," and so forth. On the title page, he states flatly: "This Man was Hired to Depress Art"; and then, should there be any doubt, adds: "This is the Opinion of Will Blake: my Proofs of this Opinion are given in the following Notes." Next to a passage in the dedication "To the King," where Reynolds declares that it was his duty for years "To give advice to those who are contending for royal liberality," Blake exclaims, "Liberality! we want not Liberality. We want a Fair Price & Proportionate Value & a General Demand for Art." Elsewhere, of a statement by Reynolds (in *Discourse* III) that "the whole beauty of the art [of painting] consists . . . in being able to get above all singular forms, local customs, particularities, and details of every kind," Blake pounces, "A Folly! Singular & Particular Detail is the Foundation of the Sublime"; and again, a bit further on, where Reynolds mentions "a rule, obtained out of general nature," he asks, "What is General Nature? is there Such a Thing? what

288

is General Knowledge? is there such a Thing? Strictly Speaking All Knowledge is Particular."

The *Discourses*, in fact, served as a foil for him to set off the "minute particulars" of his own ideas and, at the same time, to respond to Reynolds's old charge, unforgotten and unforgiven, that he was lacking in skill as an artist. From the start, though attached to no statement by Reynolds in his Introduction, this is blazoned upon the page as a kind of heraldic philosophic device: "Invention depends Altogether upon Execution or Organization; as that is right or wrong so is the Invention perfect or imperfect. Whoever is Set to Undermine the Execution of Art is set to destroy Art. Michael Angelo's Art depends on Michael Angelo's Execution Altogether." And later on (to *Discourse* IV), and again without reference to any one remark by Reynolds, he asserts: "I know"—that incandescent gleam of certainty!—"that The Man's Execution is as his Conception & No Better." For how, in Blake's mental realm of being, where "Thought is Act," could it be otherwise? Just as a dream may be said to be fully realized and enacted in the dreaming, so any work of the imagination is already realized in the imagining.

Elsewhere, in the very process of commenting, on the *Discourses*, Blake exhibits this thought (about the identity of thought and act) itself in action. Next to an editorial footnote that the colors in certain of Reynolds's pictures were fading, he remarks sarcastically, "I do not think that the Change is so much in the Pictures as in the Opinions of the Public"; and then, next to an account of Reynolds's death and state funeral, which was attended by the king and queen and all the potentates of England, Blake distilled the rage and resentment of a lifetime into a drop, no larger than a tear, of venom:

> When Sr Joshua Reynolds died
> All Nature was degraded;
> The King drop'd a tear into the Queen's Ear
> And all his Pictures Faded.

The alchemical ingredients of this verbal sorcery may be analyzed as follows: Nature, "mortal & perishing," as Blake saw it, though be-all and end-all to the "single vision" of Reynolds, was of course diminished, or "degraded," by the death of the man who had worshipped her in his art as a goddess. The tear ("For a tear," wrote Blake in *The Gray Monk*, "is an intellectual Thing") shed by the king into the queen's ear—a sort of mock Annunciation in which the demented George III plays the part of the Holy Ghost — suffices to wash out all the pictures of Reynolds from her mind.

Any work of the imagination, such as a poem or a picture, must necessarily be composed of mind stuff, but Blake saw the larger creation as well, this very world, as no different in kind. The acts that made up the lives of the prophets, in the Bible and in the world, spoke through them as thoughts, miming the voice of God. Ezekiel and Amos, Hosea and Isaiah, had been "set as a sign" by God to reveal, and so impose, by a kind of magic-working charade, His judgements upon the people. The Word & the Work, as thought & act, interpenetrate.

So then, to get back: the "Sr Joshua Reynolds" whose name has also been "set as a sign" and magically spelled out by Blake, once existed as the flesh-and-blood Reynolds, Joshua (1723–1792); but within the context of the poem he has been transfigured into a mythic character on the same transcendent plane as Orc, say, or Tiriel and Zazel, Tirzah and Rahab, and all the rest. At the time Blake came to annotate the *Discourses*, he had already begun the immense "Intellectual Allegory" (as he called it) of *Milton* and *Jerusalem*. In conception and execution the gnomic epigram he improvised on Reynolds is related to these as micro- to macrocosm, a bit of moon rock brought down to earth by means of which we can assay the moon itself.

Side by side with his pantheon of "Giant Forms" in the prophetic books, Blake introduced as well a set of historical personae, such as Milton & Newton & Bacon & Locke, and even, under their proper or fictious names, various minor characters whose sole importance was that they had once played a part in his own life. All of them act and react with one another, unite with or annihilate one another, shift identities and become one another like the phantoms of a dream, yet a dream within a larger dream, his own expanded into the 6,000-year-old dream of Albion. Mundane events in his personal life thus became symbolic of cosmic events in eternity. Blake himself may suddenly appear among his own creations, as in *Vala*, when he and his wife Catherine, apotheosized as Los and Enitharmon, are glimpsed in a domestic scene at work together:

> And first he drew a line upon the walls of shining heaven,
> And Enitharmon tinctur'd it with beams of blushing love.

Or in *Milton*, when he becomes Palamabron (one of the four sons of the fourfold Los) and resumes his quarrel with a quondam benefactor, Benjamin Hayley, there cast as Satan, whom Blake regarded as a "corporeal friend" but "spiritual enemy":

Then Palamabron, reddening like the Moon in an Eclipse,
Spoke, saying: "You know Satan's mildness and his self-
   imposition,
Seeming a brother, being a tyrant, even thinking himself a
   brother
While he is murdering the just . . ."

By his envisioning of himself in this way, as the blake-smith and poet Los, we can thus see him as he saw himself thro' his own eyes.

As his spiritual ancestor and predecessor in such a self-transubstantia-tion, there was the half-mythic patriarch and prophet Enoch, seventh in descent from Adam, who (as it says in Genesis 5:24) "walked with God: and he was not: for God took him." According to cabbalist tradition, Enoch (like Jakob Boehme) was a shoemaker by trade. With each stitch of his awl, joining uppers and lowers — symbolizing heaven and earth — he meditated upon a spirit that he had seen in a vision, the Archangel Meta-tron. His last stitch-thought was made at the age of 365 (one year for each day of the solar year, so that Enoch has often been identified with the Babylonian sun god Enmeduranna), at which time he was taken up alive by God to heaven and transformed into the Archangel Metatron he had envisioned during his labors on earth.

In the manner of Enoch the shoemaker, Blake as an engraver also com-bined "uppers and lowers," relief and intaglio, on copper plates that were etched and then printed in black and white. But which, relief or intaglio, was black, which white? He could, and did, engrave them either way, sometimes using black line in relief, etching away the whites, as in the designs for *Songs of Innocence,* sometimes using white line on a black ground (similar to the wood engravings of his contemporary, Thomas Bewick), as in the quicksilvery illustrations for *Jerusalem.* But the choice, in either case, was as much mystical as aesthetic. For Blake (as said before) not only believed but lived and enacted his ideas, reaffirming them within and without in each line he engraved. As Enoch became Metatron, he became Los.

Still another cabbalist tradition, of which Blake must have been aware, holds that the sacred Torah, containing the name of God, had originally been burned into being with "black fire upon white fire" . . . but in reverse, as in an engraving, so that the "white" is really the written Torah and the "black" the oral Torah transmitted from generation to generation. Con-cerning this, the author of *On the Kabbalah and Its Symbolism*, Gershom Scholem, remarks:

291

> Everything that we perceive in the fixed forms of the Torah,
> written in ink on parchment, consists, in the last analysis, of
> interpretations or definitions of what is hidden. *There is only
> an oral Torah*: that is the esoteric meaning of these words, and
> the written Torah is a purely mystical concept. It is embodied
> in a sphere that is accessible to prophets alone. . . . The mystical
> white of the letters on the parchment is the written Torah, but
> not the black of the letters inscribed in ink.

So Blake, in that incantatory and repetitive mantra of a poem, *The Everlasting Gospel*, written about 1818, contrasts in opposing visions the ex-
oteric black and the esoteric white:

> Thine loves the same world that mine hates,
> Thy Heaven doors are my Hell Gates. . . .

> Both read the Bible day & night,
> But thou read'st balck where I read white.

If we read the "black" of Blake, in the above, as self-evident, taking him
at *his* word, then to see it as he saw it we would have to read the Word-
within-the-Word of the Bible as "white," or (as he had already stated some
25 years before, in *The Marriage of Heaven and Hell*) "in its infernal or
diabolical sense."

What that "sense" was, in its Manichean black-white opposition to things-
as-they-are, he must have discovered, possibly while still quite young, in
the cosmogonic myths devised by the gnostic heretics of the 2nd and 3rd
centuries. Though none of the once widespread gnostic texts has survived,
Blake would have found a description of them in books of that era by
their Catholic adversaries, especially in the church father Irenaeus's *Against
Heresy*. But from whatever source, their mystical nihilism became etched
upon his mind, shaping his own essential and existential lineaments. Once
more (but for the last time) enter Crabb Robinson:

> On my obtaining from him the declaration that the Bible was
> the work of God, I referred to the commencement of Genesis:
> "In the beginning God created the Heaven & the Earth." But
> I gained nothing by this, for I was triumphantly told that this
> God was not Jehovah, but the Elohim, & the doctrine of the
> Gnostics repeated with sufficient consistency to silence one so
> unlearned as myself.

Blake is often ambiguous in his references to Jehovah, but in many of the gnostic myths the jealous and tyrannical God of the Jews, as they considered him, was identified with their own evil demiurge, called Ialdaboath, who created the world in his own image. Above and against Ialdaboath they elevated the Son of Man, Christ, as the saviour who would "raise the sparks" of divinity once again in mankind, or, as Blake put it, "fallen, fallen light renew!"

"Thinking as I do," he wrote, in his *Vision of the Last Judgment*, "that the Creator of this World is a very Cruel Being, & being a Worshipper of Christ, I cannot help saying: 'the Son, O how unlike the Father!' First God Almighty comes with a Thump on the Head. Then Jesus Christ comes with a balm to heal it."

Blake's misanthropic "Old Nobodaddy," Urizen, who appears in *Jerusalem* "muttering low thunders" and boasting, "Now I am God from Eternity to Eternity," has as a prototype the gnostic archon Ialdaboath; and his mysterious Eno, described as a Daughter of Beulah, or Inspiration, who

> . . . took a Moment of Time
> And drew it out to seven thousand years with much care
>   & affliction
> And many tears, & in every year made windows into Eden,

has for hers the gnostic aeon Ennoia (or Sophia Prunikos), the first emanation of the true God, the Nameless One. It was Ennoia, in the gnostic account of creation, who gave birth to Ialdaboath in thought, and afterward regretted her act. As related by Irenaeus, "He [Ialdaboath] boasted . . . and said, 'I am Father and God and there is none above me.' To which his mother [Ennoia] retorted, 'Do not lie, Ialdaboath; there is above thee the Father of all, the First Man, and Man the Son of Man.'" So Blake, in his *Milton*, tells of how this "King of Pride"

> . . . making to himself Laws from his own identity,
> Compell'd others to serve him in moral gratitude & submission,
> Being call'd God, setting himself above all that is call'd God; . . .

In rejecting this jealous and self-justifying deity Blake also rejected the authoritarian fiat that compels us, by reason, to accept the laws of creation as the only possible laws, to see the sun, that is, only by its own light. Instead he envisioned other creations with other laws, and saw the sun not with, but thro', his eyes, and by his own "inner light."

Where that led him, following the gleam, we already know: to the visionary perception of Old Nobodaddy–Urizen–Ialdaboath enthroned within

293

each individual as conscience and superego, and within society as judge and executioner, an all-pervasive monodeism with

> One command, one joy, one desire,
> One curse, one weight, one measure,
> One King, one God, one Law,

(as he described it in *The First Book of Urizen*), his ill-will being done on earth as it is in heaven. In his own time, having proclaimed himself as prophet of the Divine Imagination, Blake suffered the usual fate of prophets. His epic myths of creation, opposing creation itself, were almost entirely ignored, or else scoffed at, as mere delphic gibberish; his apocalyptical religious politics as crackpot either way, an offense to the right and a scandal to the left; his picture-poems, except for *Songs of Innocence and of Experience*, as inspired but formless and flawed in technique. Many of his works were destroyed after his death or allowed to disappear; *Vala*, for instance, remained in manuscript and unpublished until it was rediscovered by W. B. Yeats in 1889. Not before our own apocalyptic age, in fact, following World War II, has Blake's faith in his vision come to seem justified.

Writing in 1920, T. S. Eliot criticized Blake's "crankiness" and "eccentricity," while conceding that, for its "naked honesty," his work had "the unpleasantness of great poetry." And then concluded: "What his genius required, and what is sadly lacked, was a framework of accepted and traditional ideas which would have prevented him from indulging in a philosophy of his own, and concentrated his attentions upon the problems of the poet." But whatever the "problems" he had in mind, Blake's were not Eliot's; and, in any case, the man who once declared himself to be royalist in politics, Anglo-Catholic in religion, and classicist in literature — and was a prude and a bigot to boot — could never have accepted Blake's revolutionary, millenarian, romantic and libertine "solutions."

In agreement with Eliot, the one-time apostle of Modern Art in the 1920s, Roger Fry, criticized Blake's technical facility as an artist as well, especially his drawing, and in words that seem to reecho the hollow voice of Sir Joshua Reynolds *d'outre tombe*. Fry describes the figures so often depicted by Blake, with their space-flight or dream-space weightlessness, as having "the wavy unresistance of seaweed," in which "his lines wave about in those meandering nerveless curves which were so beloved by the Celtic craftsmen long before. He shows in this," Fry continues darkly, "a strange atavism which may not be unconnected with his mental malady." Fry, in fact, would have preferred to categorize all of Blake's work as "surrealism," as if that was that, but it bulked too huge and proved too anomalous even for the compendious grab bag.

How to define and where to assign Blake, in what genre or tradition, still perplexes critics. He somehow remains outside any circle of reference we attempt to draw him into, existing in an epicycle apart and his own. As a painter, he seems to belong to the same totemic clan as those magic-working shaman artists of prehistory who drew their own giant forms on the cave walls of Lascaux and Altamira; and as a poet, to the conclave of anonymous scribes and rhapsodic bards who invented the creation myths of the ancient religions. Yet he is no less in the present, perhaps more so to us now than to his own contemporaries, and, at the same time, futuristic as well. For the prophetic books have turned out to be just that, a kind of metaphysical science-fiction in which, miraculouly or coincidentally, many of the formative ideas of the 20th century, Nietzsche's as well as Heisenberg's, Freud's as well as Reich's, were at least glimpsed momentarily in his vision. ("The Nature of Visionary Fancy, or Imagination," he wrote in his *Vision of the Last Judgment*, "is not well known.") We might even have to accept him on his own terms, see him as he saw himself.

And the way he saw himself (as we have seen) with his fourfold vision raised to its height, was as W. B.[4] incorporated into the divine body of the Fourfold God-Man Albion, alias Adam Kadmon:

> Then those in Great Eternity met in the Council of God
> As one Man, for contracting their Exalted Senses
> They behold Multitude, or Expanding they behold as one,
> As One Man all the Universal family; . . .

he so stated in *Vala*. It is of course an ancient concept, sacred to Christianity, and envisioned also by the prophet Isaiah centuries before then. But Blake, being Blake, deliberately banished Old Nobodaddy and all other transcendent deities from their spheres above us. "Man can have no idea of anything greater than Man," he wrote, "as a cup cannot contain more than its capaciousness."

Within fairly recent times, the emergent but still inchoate existence of a spiritual Anthropos, in whom we live and move and have our being, was posited by Teilhard de Chardin's quasi-mystical evolutionary theory of a universal noosphere; also, the "collective unconscious" of this Anthropos was explored and analyzed symbolically by C. G. Jung and others; and, of course, his biography (or autobiography) as H.C.E., or "Here Comes Everybody," was spoken in tongues by James Joyce in *Finnegans Wake*. ("With pale blake," said Joyce in tribute, "I write tintingface.") The

6,000-year-old dream of Albion asleep has its obvious counterpart in the endlessly flowing "stream of consciousness" of Finnegan awake, but there is a crucial difference between them: for where Joyce's labyrinthine opus has no exit, but begins again where it seems to end, cyclically, Blake's reaches its climax in the ultimate redemption and awakening of Albion.

And this in itself, with fewer than 25 annual heartbeats remaining before the millennial year 2000, may account for the almost noumenal power of Blake's vision nowadays. For while the real existence of all men in "One Man" still seems no more than metaphysical science-fiction, the possible annihilation of mankind as a whole, through nuclear warfare or some other disaster, has come to be universally accepted. If not in life then in death — "the all tremendous unfathomable Non Ens" — Albion has assumed a paradoxically "real non-existence." Blake's words, at the conclusion of *Jerusalem*, thus seem to have been written for us in black fire on white fire:

> "Do I sleep amidst danger to Friends? O my cities & Counties,
> Do you sleep? rouze up Eternal Death is abroad!"
> So Albion spoke & threw himself into the Furnaces of affliction.
> All was a Vision, all a Dream: the Furnaces became
> Fountains of Living Waters flowing from the Humanity Divine.

(1976)

Notes

1. "Oothoon," with four ecstatic o's, speaks for herself as the personification of sexual joy and freedom in Beulah land. In a similar fashion, reminiscent not only of cabbalist abracadabra but also of primitive name-magic, Blake's malevolent demiurge "Urizen" is contained and revealed in the letter z, the shape of the zigzag thunderbolt with which, as a storm god, he inscribes himself upon the sky.

The Abyss of the Undermind: Blake's Illustrations of *The Divine Comedy*

During his last years, from 1821 to midsummer of 1827, Blake lived in near poverty and obscurity with his wife Catherine at 3 Fountain Court, Strand, a house kept by her brother-in-law, where they rented two small and sparsely furnished rooms on the first floor. The main front room, its walls hung with Blake's own pictures, was described by his biographer Alexander Gilchrist as containing a bed in one corner, a fireplace for cooking and warmth in another, a side table for meals, a second worktable for engraving that stood at a window overlooking Fountain Court, and two chairs; while the smaller back room, apparently little used, provided a view of the Thames shining beyond, as Blake said, "like a bar of gold." A frequent visitor to the Blakes in those days, John Thomas Smith, author of *Nollekens and his Times*, states that "he always painted, drew, engraved, and studied, in the same room where they grilled, boiled, stewed, and slept." Which was sufficient for the corporeal Blake, but of course the real Blake, the visionary Blake, lived elsewhere, in what he referred to as the "Divine Imagination," and that was expansive enough for him to contain even Dante's Heaven and Hell.

To Fountain Court on October 9, 1824, the then nineteen-year-old Samuel Palmer, whose eyes as an artist had recently been opened by Blake's pictures, made his first pilgrimage to see the seer himself. Accompanying

From *Blake's Dante*, by Milton Klonsky. First published 1980 by Harmony Books, a Division of Crown Publishers, Inc. Reprinted by permission of Harmony Books, a Division of Crown Publishers, Inc.

him at the time was Blake's patron and Palmer's future father-in-law, the painter John Linnell. As Palmer relates:

> We found him lame in bed, of a scalded foot (or leg). There, not inactive, though sixty-seven years old, but hard-working on a bed covered by books sat he up like one of the Antique Patriarchs, or a dying Michael Angelo. Thus and there was he making in the leaves of a great book (folio) the sublimest designs from his (not superior) Dante. He said he began them with fear and trembling. I said, "O! I have enough of fear and trembling." "Then," said he, "you'll do." He designed them (100 I think) during a fortnight's illness in bed!

The memory of that day still glowed in his mind more than thirty years later when Palmer, in a letter to Gilchrist dated August 23, 1855, declared: "Moving apart, in a sphere above the attraction of worldly honours, he did not accept greatness, but confer it. He ennobled poverty, and, by his conversation and the influence of his genius, made two small rooms in Fountain Court more attractive than the threshold of princes."

Blake was then chiefly engaged in completing the engravings of his *Illustrations of the Book of Job*, which had been commissioned in 1823 by Linnell. Soon after the official publication of the book, on March 8, 1825, Linnell proposed that he do a similar series of engraved illustrations of the *Divine Comedy*, and offered to pay him in installments of two or three pounds a week for as long as the work lasted. Except for the occasional rare sale of a picture or one of his books of "illuminated printing" to friends and collectors, Blake was dependent on Linnell's patronage for his livelihood. Upon his acceptance of the offer, Linnell presented him in October of that year with a folio of fine Dutch watercolor paper, measuring 25⅝ by 14½ inches, which may or may not have been the "great book (folio)" mentioned by Palmer.[1]

Blake now set out to learn Italian ("tho' before," declares the sculptor Frederick Tatham in his memoir, "he never knew a word"), and within a few weeks is said to have made sufficient progress to be able to read Dante in the original. The text he used was an edition of the *Divine Comedy* published in Venice in 1564, with notes and commentaries by Cristoforo Landino and Alessandro ("Sessi") Vellutello. To a large extent, however, he relied on the Reverend Henry Cary's translation of Dante's *terza rima* into Miltonic blank verse, which appeared in 1814. During this period he also formed an acquaintance with Cary, and no doubt must have discussed the poem with him.[2]

298

As he proceeded with the illustrations, Blake began to complain increasingly in his letters to Linnell of fits of shivering, jaundice, and excruciating stomach pain ("Pain too much for thought," he called it), symptoms of the gallstones and inflamed gallbladder from which he suffered. That "fortnight's illness in bed" mentioned by Palmer was in reality a sickness unto death. Blake's intermittent attacks, each more severe, left him enfeebled for sometime afterward ("only bones & sinews," he wrote. "All strings & bobbins like a Weaver's Loom"), but he continued working nonetheless. "I can draw as well a-Bed as up, & perhaps better," he informed Linnell, "but I cannot Engrave. I am going on with Dante & please myself."

In the midst of these Job-like afflictions, the Swiss-born artist Henry Fuseli (Johann Heinrich Füssli), a friend who had sustained and encouraged Blake throughout his career, died at the age of eighty-four on April 17, 1825; and not too long after, on December 7, 1826, another close and lifelong friend, the sculptor John Flaxman, also died. Both of these artists had been inspired by Dante to do some of their best-known work, especially Flaxman, who had published a series of illustrations of the *Divine Comedy* in Rome as early as 1793. Coming so close together, and at such a time, their deaths must have seemed to Blake a portent of his own. On the day of Flaxman's death, the news was brought to him by the literary journalist Henry Crabb Robinson, who was fascinated yet baffled by Blake and, as he ghoulishly confesses, "curious to know how he would receive the intelligence." In his journal Robinson reports that "he said with a smile, 'I thought I shd. have gone first.' He then said, 'I cannot think of death as more than the going out of one room into another.' And Flaxman was no longer thought of." Not so, however, for Blake was still haunted by his death months later, writing on April 27, 1827, to his friend George Cumberland: "Flaxman is Gone, & we must All soon follow, every one to his Own Eternal House, Leaving the delusive Goddess Nature & her Laws, to get into Freedom from all Law of the Members, into The Mind, in which every one is King & Priest in his own House."

A sense of foreboding and of urgency now becomes apparent in Blake's letters whenever he refers to the Dante project. It is as though he were fully aware that this was to be a summing-up of his lifework, both as artist and thinker, and how little time remained. "I go on without daring to count on Futurity," he wrote to Linnell on April 25, "which I cannot do without doubt & Fear that ruins Activity, & are the greatest hurt of an artist such as I am. . . . I am too much attach'd to Dante to think much of anything else." And in another letter to Linnell, undated, he declares: "I am still far from recovered, & dare not get out in the cold air. Yet I lose nothing by it. Dante goes on the better, which is all I care about." Blake had occasionally been able to visit friends and even to make excursions to Linnell's farmhouse in Hampstead, but by the beginning of July he was already too weak and yellowed with jaundice to leave his rooms at Fountain Court. Almost up to the day, August 12, 1827, when he himself passed into what he called "the all tremendous unfathomable Non Ens / Of death" (*Jerusalem* 98: 33–34), he was still working on the illustrations, lying propped up in bed with his folio open before him.

Blake left 102 designs in various states of completion, ranging from quick pencil sketches to luminous watercolors signed with his monogram. His procedure was to first make a preliminary drawing in pencil, altering it and adding details as his conception matured; he then emphasized the outlines with india ink, using a pen or fine brush; then he applied the colors in broad light washes; and finally, he worked over the whole surface (almost in the manner of Cézanne) by superimposing small touches of color after the ones beneath had dried. The number of illustrations based on subjects from the *Inferno* (72), from the *Purgatorio* (20) and from the *Paradiso* (10) are roughly equivalent to the literary as well as popular esteem in which the three parts of the *Divine Comedy* were held in Blake's era. There are only seven engravings, the engraved surface of each measuring 9½ by 13 inches and the plate mark approximately 13½ by 21 inches — the largest ever attempted by Blake — and all are from designs for the *Inferno*. Yet even these seven, except for the marvelously detailed Plate 103, "The Circle of the Lustful: Francesca da Rimini," remained unfinished at his death.

What T. S. Eliot once called the "continuous phantasmagoria" of the *Inferno* aroused in Blake, as it had for so many other artists over the centuries, all of his creative and imaginative powers. At the same time, however, he found the ingenious system of tortures contrived by Dante to punish the sinners in Hell morally abhorrent and repugnant to his most deeply felt religious beliefs. "Where are those who worship Satan under the name of God! Where are they?" he asks in *Jerusalem* 52. "Listen! Every Religion that Preaches Vengeance for Sin is the Religion of the Enemy & Avenger; and not of the Forgiver of Sin, and their God is Satan, Named by the Divine Name." Throughout his series of illustrations Blake makes it plain that he regarded Dante as one of "those," and that the Hell envisioned by him was "originally Formed by the Devil Himself & So I understand it to have been."

The severity of Blake's criticism, in Dante's case, is only poetic justice. There is a kind of algebra of retribution in the *Inferno* — though the equations are not always exact — by which the various types and degrees of torment are meant to be symbolic of the sins themselves, but raised exponentially in power before being returned upon the sinners. Blasphemers, for example, must lie supine upon burning sand under a fiery rain face to face with the Heaven they have insulted. Carnal lovers and adulterers, swept away by a tempest (of passion) as they were in life, are condemned to imprisonment in each other's arms for eternity. Religious and political schismatics are themselves split limb from limb by an avenging demon wielding a sword. To doubt the justice of their punishment is to doubt the divinity of the Law. Thus, when Dante encounters the sorcerers, fortune-tellers and false prophets in the eighth circle and weeps at their distress, he is rebuked by Virgil: "Art thou, too, like the other fools? Here piety lives only when pity is quite dead. Who is more impious than he that laments at God's judgment?" (Canto XX: 27–30). The saintly Thomas Aquinas himself, whose theology underlies the *Divine Comedy*, believed that one of the principal divertissements of the elect in Heaven would be the sight of the torments of the damned in Hell.

Though Dante in Canto V had swooned with pity over the fate of Paolo and Francesca, and in Canto XVI had even wished to throw himself down among the (literally) flagrant homosexuals in order to share in their suffering, he now takes Virgil's admonition to heart. How much so may be gauged by the famous incident involving Dante and the "Jovial Friar" Alberigo, described in Canto XXXIII, that occurs near the bottom of Hell in the frozen third region of Cocytus. There traitors are congealed face up in the ice, their tears forming a crust that prevents them from ever weeping again and thus easing their pain. Meeting him in this plight, Dante tricks and betrays the traitor Alberigo by promising to clear his eyes if he reveals his identity. After Alberigo does so, Dante contemptuously breaks his word. "To be churlish to him was courtesy," he remarks, thereby echoing Virgil's paradoxical conundrum on "pity" and "piety." Just as the devils encountered by Virgil and Dante in Canto XXI try to ensnare the poets by giving them false directions, Dante enveigles Alberigo, as if, in the course of the long descent through Hell, their own devilish nature had infected his own.

Even the most devout admirers of the *Divine Comedy* have found it difficult to explain away Dante's behavior in this instance. The artist Henry Fuseli, for one, who may have been the first to introduce the poem to Blake, thought it "betrayed a failure in moral feeling"; and Blake himself may have had it in mind when, about 1810, he wrote in *A Vision of the Last Judgment* (p. 93):

> In Hell all is Self Righteousness; there is no such thing there
> as Forgiveness of Sin; he who does Forgive Sin is Crucified as

an Abetter of Criminals, & he who performs Works of mercy
in Any shape whatever is punished, if possible, destroy'd, not
thro' envy or Hatred or Malice, but thro' Self Righteousness
that thinks it does God service, which Gos is Satan.

The rigor with which Dante worked out his infernal equations of crime
and punishment would not permit him to exempt or pardon even his closest
friends, his benefactors, or his own kinfolk. God's Law was more binding
than any human ties. *Item*, Cavalcante dei Cavalcanti, father of his fellow
poet Guido Cavalcanti, is condemned to be roasted eternally in one of the
fiery tombs reserved for heretics in the sixth circle for having believed, as
an Epicurean, that the soul dies with the body. *Item*, in the seventh circle,
where sodomites are compelled to run ceaselessly in packs beneath a rain of
fire, Dante recognizes his once revered teacher and counselor, the statesman-
poet Brunetto Latini, and greets him with: "Are you here, Ser Brunetto?" . . . surely one of the most profoundly moving and yet disingenuous
lines in literature, since, after all, it was Dante himself who put him there.
Item, members of the Donati family, to which Dante's wife Gemma belonged, are allotted different and separate destinies: Corso, a political opponent of Dante's, in Hell; his brother Forese in Purgatory; and their sister
Piccarda in Heaven—thereby dividing them from one another for eternity.
It is Piccarda, incidentally, who utters the words in the *Paradiso* (Canto
III: 85) that sum up Dante's conception of divine justice and the relationship between God and man: "*E'n la sua volontade è nostra pace*" ("And
in His will is our peace").

But for Blake such a peace, brought about by slavish obedience to the
dictates of so jealous and vindictive a deity, could only be the peace of
spiritual death. Throughout the series this deity appears as a glum-faced,
white-bearded, decrepit old tyrant, as in Plate 3, "The Mission of Virgil,"
where he is shown slumped wearily upon his throne receiving homage, with
an inscription over his head that identifies him as "The Angry God of This
World." The Supreme Being worshiped by Dante, as Blake saw him, can
therefore be none other than Urizen, sometimes referred to as "Old Nobodaddy," the sinister demiurge who plays a central role in his own mythological system. "O Urizen! Creator of men! mistaken Demon of heaven,"
Blake taunts him in *Visions of the Daughters of Albion* (5: 3–4), "Thy joys
are tears! thy labour vain, to form men to thine image." At once the tempter
and tormenter of mankind, Urizen plants the Tree of Good and Evil—the
"Tree of Mystery," Blake called it—whose forbidden fruit is wormy with
the sins that "reptilize upon the Earth." And though aware that "no flesh

302

nor spirit could keep / His iron laws one moment" (*Urizen* 23: 4), he promulgates the "ten commands" whose violators and/or victims populate Dante's Hell. He is, moreover, a boastful and vainglorious deity, threatening to take vengeance on all who deny him absolute supremacy. In *Milton* (9: 28–33), after "drawing out his infernal scroll / Of Moral laws and cruel punishments," Urizen arrives disguised as Satan:

> With thunder of war & trumpet's sound, with armies of disease,
> Punishments & deaths muster'd & number'd, Saying: "I am God
>   alone:
> There is no other! let all obey my principles of moral individu-
>   ality. . . ."

This is of course a caricature of the God of Genesis, the Elohim, and as such closely resembles the evil archon, known as Ialdabaoth, conceived by the ancient heretical Christian sect of the Gnostics. The church father Irenaeus's *Against Heresy*, with which Blake must have been familiar, relates a similar scene from the creation myth of the Gnostic cult of the Ophites (30: 4–6): "He [Ialdabaoth] boasted of what was taking place at his feet and said, 'I am Father and God, and there is none above me,' to which his mother [Ennoia, corresponding to another of Blake's characters, 'Aged Mother' Eno], retorts, 'Do not lie, Ialdabaoth, there is above thee the Father of all, the First Man [Christ], and Man the Son of Man.'" Besides their reechoing names — Ialdabaoth-"Old Nobodaddy" and Eno-Ennoia — they have other traits in common: Urizen is often depicted in Blake's prophetic books as blind, and Ialdabaoth is also so described in the Gnostic myths; and just as Urizen's emblem is a lion, Ialdabaoth frequently manifests himself in the form of "an arrogant beast of lion shape."

Crabb Robinson again, during one of his sly sidewise cross-examinations of Blake — he was trained as a lawyer — once led him into a discussion of the Creator in Genesis, and, he reports, "was triumphantly told that this God was not Jehovah, but the Elohim; and the doctrine of the Gnostics repeated with sufficient consistency to silence one so unlearned as myself." Though Robinson does not further specify this "doctrine," Blake could hardly have been more outspoken in his conversation with him than he already had been in his writings. "Thinking as I do," he declares in *A Vision of the Last Judgment* (p. 94), "that the Creator of this World is a very Cruel Being & being a Worshipper of Christ, I cannot help saying, the Son, O how unlike the Father! First God Almighty comes with a Thump on the Head. Then Jesus Christ comes with a balm to heal it."

A "Cruel Being" could only have created in his image a cruel world.

The torments of Hell, removed by Dante to an afterlife, were perceived by Blake to exist to a greater or lesser degree in this very life—and the fear of eternal damnation for sinners was not the least of them. "What seems to Be, Is, To those to whom / It seems to Be," he wrote in *Jerusalem* (36: 50–54), "& is productive of the most dreadful / Consequences to those to whom it seems to Be, even of / Torments, Despair, Eternal Death." For while he scoffed at the physical reality of a Hell such as Dante's (in an annotation to one of Lavater's *Aphorisms on Man* (309), he wrote, "Mark that I do not believe there is such a thing [Hell] litterally [*sic*]"), he never doubted its psychological reality within the abyss of the undermind. As he wrote in *Jerusalem* (71: 17–19):

> . . . in your own Bosom you bear your Heaven
> And Earth, & all you behold; tho' it appears Without
>   it is Within
> In your Imagination of which this World of Mortality
>   is but a Shadow.

W. B. Yeats, in his essay on the Dante illustrations in *Ideas of Good and Evil*, once characterized Blake as "a too literal realist of the imagination as others are of nature." To which Blake might have responded with one of the proverbs from *The Marriage of Heaven and Hell*: "What is now proved was once only imagin'd." For to digress a moment—if it is a digression—Dante's "imagin'd" *Inferno* was surely "proved," and in some ways improved, by the eruption into reality of the hells of Belsen and Auschwitz, which contained "real" enough devils and "real" enough furnaces, not to mention the Malebolgian gulags still in existence somewhere out in the tundras of Siberia. Urizen in the guise of a Hitler or Stalin makes no distinction between moral reprobates and racial or political deviants.

The Hell thus reified by Dante, with its ever-tightening screwlike grooves of greater and greater pain, was imagined by Blake as a series of spiritual states through which Everyman must pass in the journey through life. To distinguish between these eternal states and mortal individuals was, he believed, "the only means to Forgiveness of Enemies" (*Jerusalem* 49: 75). As he wrote in *A Vision of the Last Judgment* (p. 80): "These States Exist now. Man Passes on, but States remain for Ever, he passes thro' them like a traveller who may as well suppose that the places he has passed thro' exist no more. Every thing is eternal." But in Dante's *Inferno* individuals are identified with the sinful states in which they may find themselves— this one with lechery, that one with avarice, the other one with treachery— damning them all for eternity without hope of pardon or redemption.

304

"What I was living, that am I dead" (Canto XIV: 51), asserts the blasphemer Capaneus, still defiant even on the burning sands of Hell, thus exemplifying in himself the grim maxim attributed to the Greek philosopher Heraclitus: "A man's character is his fate." Such was also the belief of the spiritualist and theologian Emanuel Swedenborg, from whom Blake derived his conception of "states," as well as other doctrines, and whom he regarded as a "divine teacher." Yet on this point he opposed him passionately.

In one of his annotations to Swedenborg's *Divine Providence*, published in London in 1790, where Swedenborg wrote that "he who is in Evil in the World, the same is in Evil after he goes out of *the world; wherefore if Evil be not removed in the World, it cannot be removed afterwards* [Blake's italics]; . . . for Death is a Continuance of life; with this Difference, that then Man cannot be reformed," Blake responds: "Cursed folly! Predestination after this Life is more Abominable than Calvin's & Swedenborg is Such a Spiritual Predestinarian. . . ." According to Crabb Robinson, Blake considered "the visions of Swedenborg and Dante as of the same kind," adding only that "Dante was the greater poet." He saw both as "talking of what is Good & Evil or of what is Right or Wrong & puzzling themselves in Satan's Labyrinth" (*A Vision of the Last Judgment*, p. 90); and his characterization of Swedenborg applies to Dante as well: "O Swedenborg! strongest of men, the Samson shorn by the Churches, / Shewing the Transgressors in Hell, the proud Warriors in Heaven, / Heaven as a Punisher, & Hell as One under Punishment" (*Milton* 22: 50–52). In *The Marriage of Heaven and Hell*, Blake proclaims the yin-yang reciprocity of good and evil, for better and for worse, and states that one volume of Jakob Böhme's or of Paracelsus' was worth "ten thousand" of Swedenborg's. Böhme's essentially Gnostic vision of an emergent and suffering deity striving with the evil within himself, and Paracelsus' alchemical conception of man as both microcosmos and microtheos illuminated by the Divine Imagination, became part of hiw own mystical philosophy. To be born into this world, he believed, was to know Heaven and Hell from the inside.

The sentence of doom inscribed over the portals of Dante's Hell: "Abandon all hope, yet that enter," thus takes on for Blake an ironic and even darker meaning. In Plate 4, "The Inscription Over Hell-Gate," Virgil and the misguided Dante are about to step through these portals, but beyond them the five continents of our planet are shown in flames, the flames of "Old Nobodaddy"-Urizen, his ill will being done here on earth as it is in the abyss.[3]

Having drawn this line between them, Blake engages in a "Mental Fight" with Dante ("Thought," as he thought, "is act") that challenges his most fundamental ideas. Dante's adoration of Beatrice, which is at the heart of the *Divine Comedy*, Blake sees as self-imposed bondage to the "Female Will" and a betrayal of the "Poetic Genius"; Dante's veneration of Homer and Virgil, who celebrated warfare and extolled military prowess and heroism above all other human virtues, as an offense against Christianity and the Prince of Peace; and Dante's invocation of the classical Greek muses, the repressive and backward-looking daughters of Memory, as a rejection of the prophetic and freedom-loving daughters of Inspiration, the muses of the Bible. These charges may be discussed briefly and in order.

Sexual love, a "window" through which even in the Fallen World mortals could occasionally catch a glimpse of eternity, Blake believed to have been smeared, smutted over, and darkened by religious shame and guilt. "As the caterpillar chooses the fairest leaves to lay her eggs on," he wrote in *The Marriage of Heaven and Hell,* "so the priest lays his curse on the fairest joys." The cult of female chastity, nowhere better personified than in Dante's Beatrice, was to him an abomination that set the sexes apart in "Mutual Hate . . . & mutual Deceit & mutual Fear" (*Jerusalem* 69: 36). Out of this division sprang what Blake terms the "Female Will," by which the feminine half seeks to dominate the masculine by granting or withholding sexual communion. In *Europe* (6: 5–9), for instance, Enitharmon, the rebellious feminine emanation of Los, summons her children and commands them:

> Go! tell the Human race that Woman's love is Sin;
> That an Eternal life awaits the worms of sixty winters
> In an allegorical abode where existence hath never come.
> Forbid all Joy, & from her childhood shall the little female
> Spread nets in every secret path.

And in *Jerusalem* (34: 31–35), Los in turn cries out to the god-man Albion:

> O Albion, why wilt thou create a Female Will?
> To hide the most evident God in a hidden covert, even
> In the shadows of a Woman & a secluded Holy Place,
> That we may pry after him as after a stolen treasure,
> Hidden among the Dead & mured up from the paths of life.

Sexual repression, as it blights the human spirit, breeds pestilence in society. "He who will not comingle in Love," Blake wrote in *Jerusalem* (66: 56), "must be adjoin'd by Hate." And once more from *Jerusalem* (68: 62–

306

63), in lines that anticipate the radical post-Freudianism of Wilhelm Reich and his followers, Blake's pinup-sickened "Warrior" cries out: "I am drunk with unsatiated love. / I must rush again to War, for the Virgin has frown'd & refus'd."

In the revolutionary apocalypse envisioned by Blake, when Albion rouses himself from his deathlike sleep of 6,000 years, the strife between the sexes, along with the "Female Will,"[4] must vanish as they blend into one being. "This will come to pass," he prophesies in *The Marriage of Heaven and Hell*, "by an improvement of sensual enjoyment." What sort of jujitsu of the genders this will be like he suggests in *Jerusalem* (69: 43–44): "Embraces are Cominglings from the Head even to the Feet, / And not a pompous High Priest entering by a Secret Place."

In Plate 102, "The Queen of Heaven in Glory," a primly voluptuous, naked Beatrice, surrounded by nymphs, is shown perched upon a petal of the mystical "white rose" just below the Virgin Mary. On either side of her, without authorization from the text, Blake has introduced two massive and sphinxlike male figures. Each has a large closed book on its lap marked "Bible" and "Chain'd Round." Open wide beneath them are two other books, the one on the left labeled "Homer" (whom Dante in Canto IV, line 88, of the *Inferno* calls "the sovereign poet") and that on the right "Aristotle" (whom he calls in line 131 "the master of them that know"). Homer and Aristotle, Blake thus indicates, rather than the authors of the Holy Bible, provided the intellectual seeds out of which flowered the *Divine Comedy*.

"The Classics!" he exclaims in his commentary *On Homer's Poetry*, "it is the Classics, & not Goths nor Monks, that Desolate Europe with Wars." The scant historical knowledge of antiquity in Blake's time, and the difficulty in dating, made it possible for him to assert that the Hebrew Bible not only preceded the writings of all other peoples but (as he wrote in *Milton* I) had been "Stolen & Perverted" by them. In his commentary *On Virgil*, etched together with the one on Homer in 1820, he enlarges on this idea:

> Sacred Truth has pronounced that Greece & Rome, as Babylon & Egypt, so far from being parents of Arts & Sciences as they pretend, were destroyers of all Art. Homer, Virgil & Ovid confirm this opinion & make us reverence The Word of God, the only light of antiquity that remains unperverted by War. . . . Grecian is Mathematic Form: Gothic is Living Form. Mathematic Form is Eternal in the Reasoning Memory: Living Form is Eternal Existence.

By choosing Virgil as his "Guide" and "Master," therefore, Dante was led only deeper astray.

The classical Greek muses are said to have been begotten by Zeus in the course of nine unforgettable nights with Mnemosyne (Memory), offspring of Air and Mother Earth. They are depicted in Plate 7, "Homer, Bearing the Sword, and His Companions," where six of them float in homage about the martial figure of the poet. Upon this drawing Blake has inscribed: "Every thing in Dante's Comedia shews That for Tyrannical Purposes he has made This World the Foundation of All & the Goddess Nature [Memory] & not the Holy Ghost [Imagination]." Blake despised what he considered Dante's worldliness, his lifelong attempt to reestablish a new and holier Roman Empire, and his partisan involvement in the disputes of the squabbling Guelphs and Ghibellines, referring to him derisively (in his annotations to Boyd's *Historical Notes*) as "an Emperor's, a Caesar's Man." To Crabb Robinson he declared that Dante was "a mere politician and atheist, busied about the world's affairs." When Robinson "endeavoured to obtain from him a qualification of the term atheist, so as not to include him in the ordinary reproach," he was put off with the assurance that Dante was "*then* with God." (Blake was in constant communication with the spirit world and must have obtained the news of his conversion from Dante personally.) Afterward, however, Robinson learned that what Blake meant by atheism was the worship of nature rather than the Word of God. "For Nature," he told him, "is the work of the Devil."

Against the classical Greek muses, as already stated, Blake opposed the biblical daughters of Inspiration, who abide in the mythological realm he called Beulah (meaning "married," in Hebrew), between the Fallen World and Eternity, "where the sexes wander in dreams of bliss among the Emanations" (*Jerusalem* 79: 73). John Milton, whom Blake revered as a poet much as Dante did Virgil, had written in *The Reason of Church Government* that sacred poetry cannot be obtained "by the invocation of dame memory and her siren daughters but by devout prayer to that eternal Spirit, who . . . sends out his seraphim, with the hallowed fire of his altar, to touch and purify the lips of whom he pleases." As Blake's Milton (in *Milton* 41:4) announces that he comes "To cast off the rotten rags of Memory by Inspiration," so Milton himself at the beginning of *Paradise Lost* invokes the "Heavenly muse" of prophecy to assist him in his flight "above the Aonian mount" of Helicon, seat of the classical muses, and so surpass the heathen poets of Greece and Rome.

For Blake, who humanized and personified all things, to be inspired meant, literally, to be "in-spirited," attended and directed by spirits. "I am not ashamed, afraid, or averse to tell you," he wrote in a letter to his friend and benefactor Thomas Butts (dated January 12, 1802), "what Ought to be Told: That I am under the direction of Messengers from Heaven, Daily & Nightly." In another letter to Butts (dated April 25, 1803), he tells of having "composed an immense number of verses on One Grand Theme [most likely *The Four Zoas*] . . . from immediate Dictation, twelve or thirty lines at time, without Premeditation & even against my Will." Whether these "Messengers" (or angels, from the Greek *angelos*, meaning messenger) were projected, during the frenzy of creation, as hypnagogic images from his subconscious mind, or, as Blake's tutelary spirits, they were apparitions perceived through his own "fourfold vision," remains open to conjecture, but there can be no doubt that they visited him all his life. As they seemed so they were. In *A Descriptive Catalogue* (4), Blake wrote:

> A Spirit and a Vision are not, as the modern philosophy supposes, a cloudy vapour, or a nothing: they are organized and minutely articulated beyond all that the mortal and perishing nature can produce. He who does not imagine in stronger and better lineaments, and in stronger and better light than his perishing and mortal eye can see, does not imagine at all.

And they must have been present in their battalions at the time he engaged in his "Mental Fight" with Dante.

Blake's illustrations, therefore, could be no mere imitation of the text, in the usual sense, for that would have meant submitting to the supervision of "the siren daughters of memory," Dante's own muses, which had deceived him into mistaking Urizen's laws for justice and his mirages for reality. He declares in *Auguries of Innocence:* "We are led to Believe a Lie / When we see not Thro' the Eye." What Blake attempted instead was a "re-vision" of the poem, and the result is as much Blake's as Dante's. Seen "Thro'" Blake's eye, and in the glow of his own inner light, Dante's imagery undergoes a sort of alchemical, or rather al-chimerical, transmutation, similar to the one described in Canto XXV: 61–63 of the *Inferno*, where thieves turn into snakes that in turn turn into thieves, and, "as if they had been of hot wax, they stuck together, mingling their colors, and now neither the one nor the other appeared what it was before."

Blake would have found a biblical precedent for this in the second chapter of the Book of Daniel. There, with the sublime supererogation granted only to prophets, Daniel trumps and confounds all the magicians of Babylon by not only recalling for Nebuchadnezzar his own world-troubled dream, which the king had forgotten, but also by interpreting it. (The idol of gold, silver, brass, iron, and clay dreamt of by Nebuchadnezzar, Dante's "Grand Old Man of Crete," is depicted in Plate 30, "The Symbolic Figure of the Course of Human History Described by Virgil.") Later on, in the Book of Daniel (3: 20–25) when the Hebrew children Shadrach, Meshach, and Abednego refuse to worship the king's golden image and are "cast . . . into the burning fiery furnace," a fourth figure appears in the flames, and, it is written, "the form of the fourth is like the Son of God." (As the daughters of Inspiration, they are shown exulting in the flames of the Imagination in Plate 88, "Dante at the Moment of Entering the Fire.") These three, who become four, symbolized for Blake the successively ascending stages of what he called "fourfold vision." In a letter to Thomas Butts (dated November 22, 1802), he wrote:

Now I a fourfold vision see,
And a fourfold vision is given to me;
'Tis fourfold in my supreme delight
And threefold in soft Beulah's night
And twofold Always. May God us keep
From Single vision & Newton's sleep!

The first vision is sense perception alone, what we see *not* "Thro'" the eye; the second is the moral, which sympathizes with and humanizes all things; the third is the creative, which fuses thought and feeling; and the fourth vision is the mystical ecstasy which transcends and transforms the rest. At the end of *A Vision of the Last Judgment*, in an often-cited passage, Blake wrote:

I assert for My Self that I do not behold the outward Creation & that to me it is hindrance & not Action; it is as the dirt upon my feet, No part of Me. "What," it will be Questioned, "When the Sun rises, do you not see a round disk of fire somewhat like a Guinea?" O no, no, I see an Innumerable company of the heavenly host crying, "Holy, Holy, Holy is the Lord God Almighty." I question not my Corporeal or Vegetative Eye any more than I would Question a Window concerning a Sight. I look thro' it & not with it.[5]

But Dante, too, distinguishes between a natural and a spiritual sun, referring in his *Convivio* (IV:12) to "the spiritual sun, which is God." And, in their use of symbolism, there are other significant points of agreement between them as well. The left/right placement of hands and feet, employed by Blake here and elsewhere in his pictures to symbolize moral right and wrong (left = wrong), was originally invented by Dante and occurs through-out the *Divine Comedy*. Upon first entering the region of Hell called Malebolge, for instance, Dante relates (Canto XVII: 31–33) how he and Virgil descended "on our right and went ten paces along the edge, so that we might stay away from the sand and flames"—that is, they avoided evil by choosing the path of righteousness and walking the "ten paces," or com-mandments, of the Decalogue. Also, many of the features of the infernal landscapes described by Dante were adapted by Blake in his own prophetic books, though of course for opposite purposes, and lay submerged in memory (the daughters of Inspiration, be it remembered, abide in Beulah, where "Contrarieties are equally true"), so that when they reemerged at the time he did these illustrations they were already familiar territory. And finally, Blake's "fourfold vision" itself closely approximates Dante's famous fourfold method of interpretation, expounded by him in the *Convivio* 2: 1 and in his letter to Can Grande, by which he intended the *Divine Comedy* to be read for its literal, moral, allegorical, and anagogical meanings. Blake so read it, but "Thro'" his own eyes.

Sometimes he imposes his own point of view upon a scene by adding a slight yet crucial detail, as in Plate 81, "Dante and Virgil Approaching the Angel Who Guards the Entrance of Purgatory," in which the eyelids of the guardian angel are drawn half-shut; or else, as in Plate 91, "Beatrice Addressing Dante from the Car," he might obtrude his own mythic per-sonae into the picture disguised as Dante's, thereby entirely reversing his intent; or else he might anneal his own poetic symbolism onto Dante's im-agery, as in Plate 63, "The Primeval Giants Sunk in the Soil," to give it a meaning never thought of by Dante; or even, if his indignation be really inflamed, as in Plate 15, "The Goddess of Fortune," where the goddess is shown standing inside a privy, he might grossly burlesque Dante's con-ception, then vent his disgust still further by scrawling his opinion like graf-fiti across the page. There is nothing quite like it in the history of art and/ or poetry. As he was both painter and poet, no less himself in either role, Blake's picture-poems exemplify the famous saying attributed to the Greek poet Simonides of Ceos: "Painting is mute poetry, poetry a speaking pic-ture." The illustrations to Dante must therefore be "read" for their sym-bolical and intellectual content—"seen," that is, with the mind's eye—for their ideas to be made visible and their images to speak for themselves.

Blake had previously exhibited his uniquely evangelical-satirical style as an illustrator in the designs he made for the poems of Milton and Gray, Young's *Night Thoughts*, and especially *The Book of Job*. But nowhere is this style bolder or subtler than in the illustrations for the *Divine Com-*

311

edy. W. B. Yeats, in his *A Vision*, placed Blake in Phase 16 of the "Great Wheel," along with Rabelais, Aretino, Paracelsus, and "some beautiful women," and then goes on to describe them as follows:

> At one moment they are full of hate — Blake writes of "Flemish and Venetian demons" and of some picture of his own destroyed "by some vile spell of Stoddart's" — and their hate is always close to madness; and at the next they produce the comedy of Aretino and of Rabelais or the mythology of Blake, and discover symbolism to express the overflowing and bursting of the mind. There is always an element of frenzy, and almost always a delight in certain glowing or shining images of concentrated force: in the smith's forge; in the heart; in the human form in its most vigorous development; in the solar disc; in some symbolical representation of the sexual organs; for the being must brag of its triumph over its own incoherence.

Dante is placed in the very next, Phase 17, that of the "Daimonic Man," where he is characterized as "having attained, as poet, to Unity of Being, as poet saw all things set in order, had an intellect that served the *Mask* [or role in life] alone, that compelled even those things that opposed it to serve, and was content to see both good and evil." For Yeats, then, the "Mental Fight" between them was full of cosmic reverberations.

In his early essay on the illustrations, he wrote: "As Blake sat bent over the great drawing-book, in which he made his designs to the *Divine Comedy*, he was very certain that he and Dante represented spiritual states which face one another in eternal enmity." Yet it was a struggle of opposing visions, of dialectical "Contraries" (in Blake's sense) and not of "Negations." "Opposition," as he wrote in *The Marriage of Heaven and Hell*, "is true friendship."

Yeats thought Blake "the one perfectly fit illustrator for the *Inferno* and the *Purgatorio*," though somewhat less suited for the *Paradiso*, and called the series as a whole "the crowning work of his life." Dante's "Negation," however, might be found in the once widely popular illustrations by Gustave Doré, which Yeats condemned as "noisy and demagogic." By the end of the nineteenth century, when they appeared, the religious heart of the *Divine Comedy* had almost stopped beating. What chiefly excited the public was the Grand Guignol horrors of Dante's infernal freak show, and these Doré exhibited with characteristic flamboyance, adding a few erotic *frissons* of his own. To Blake they would have served as an example of "single vision," looking *with*, not "Thro'," the eye.

John Flaxman's 110 designs, engraved for him by Tommaso Piroli and published in Rome in 1793, were reissued in England under the title *Compositions from the Divine Poem of Dante* in 1807, when they were accompanied by passages from the translation by the Reverend Henry Boyd. Blake indignantly claimed at the time that Flaxman had taken over many of his ideas without acknowledgment. "How much of his Homer & Dante he will allow to be mine," he wrote in the *Public Address* (p. 53), "I do not know, as he went far enough off to Publish them, even to Italy, but the Public will know & Posterity will know." Yet even now it is hard to detect Blake's hand in Flaxman's austerely neoclassical line drawings, which, while impressive in themselves, are too narrow stylistically to encompass the emotional range and depth of the *Divine Comedy*. Blake himself must have been strongly influenced by the paintings of his friend Henry Fuseli based on subjects from Dante. In 1774, while in Rome, Fuseli did a series of six wash drawings illustrating the *Inferno* and *Purgatorio*, and he also exhibited several oils, all on the *Inferno*, at the Royal Academy in 1786, 1806, and 1818. When Fuseli's painting of "Count Ugolino" was attacked by critics in 1806, Blake wrote an angry letter in his defense (published in the *Monthly Magazine* of July 1, 1806), describing the effect of the picture as "truly sublime" and declaring furthermore that anyone persuaded to believe otherwise had been "connoisseured out of his senses."

Fuseli, who was as testily independent in his opinions as Blake, once compared the various Italian illustrators of Dante, asserting that the torments described in the *Inferno* were "far beyond the culinary abominations of Sandro Botticelli" (*Life and Writings*, vol. 3, p. 184). Blake of course never saw them, but they provide an illuminating contrast in style to his own. The critic Kenneth Clark, in an introductory essay to these ninety-two silverpoint drawings by Botticelli (*Drawings by Sandro Botticelli for Dante's Divine Comedy*) done for Lorenzo di Pierfrancesco de Medici in 1492, refers to the concordance between his "controlled simplicity" and Dante's "purity of diction." What may be lacking, however, is Dante's intellectual burr and rasp. For in accompanying Dante on his journey through the *Inferno* and the *Purgatorio*, Botticelli's exquisitely modulated violinlike line, for all its beauty, seems somehow out of place, a Paganini in Belsen, calling attention to itself rather than to the scenes it depicts. It is only in the *Paradiso*, where Dante, like an ecstatic moth, flutters up into the immense concentric chandelier of the ten-tiered heavens, that style and content in Botticelli's drawings become one. The opposite may perhaps be true in Blake's case.

But then there's Michelangelo, who, during his lifetime, was acclaimed as "the Dante of art." The almost suprahuman grandeur of the figures sculpted by Michelangelo and painted on the dome of the Sistine Chapel have their counterparts in Dante's own characters—Ulysses, La Pia, Farinata, Capaneus—whose features, formed from within, are often revealed in a single image or gesture. Conversely ("*Ut pictura poesis*," as Horace wrote—"As is painting so is poetry"), the hundred cantos of the *Divine Comedy* seem not so much written as carved and shaped out of words, words so compact with meaning and charged with energy that they strain in tension against the triple-barred stanzas that contain them. The kinship between the artist and poet seemed so close that a kind of saint's legend, based on wish fulfillment rather than any real evidence, sprang up that the "Dante of art" himself had actually illustrated the *Divine Comedy* in the margins of his own copy. This volume, so the story goes, was lost forever when a ship carrying all his belongings, at the time he traveled from Livorno to Rome to do the Sistine frescoes, was sunk by a storm at sea. (Kenneth Clark, in the aforementioned introduction to Botticelli's drawings, has traced the history of this legend as it first emerged from the mists of rumor, became thickened by repetition, and was finally concretized as fact.) As a result, the personages of the *Divine Comedy* that Michelangelo never depicted have assumed a second and even more spectral existence.

During Flaxman's stay in Rome, from 1787 to 1794, he heard the tale of Michelangelo's lost Dante, and upon his return to England must have transmitted it to Blake. From his earliest years Blake had held Michelangelo in awe as "the supreme glory" of Italian art and had sought to model his own style on his. And, though unknown to Blake, there is temperamental affinity between them as well. The irascible cockney poet-painter who wrote of himself in verses addressed to Thomas Butts (in a letter dated August 16, 1803):

> O why was I born with a different face?
> Why was I not born like the rest of my race?
> When I look, each one starts! When I speak, I offend;
> Then I'm silent & passive & lose every Friend.

would surely have recognized his own psychological features in those of the saturnine Tuscan genius who confessed in a letter to Pietro Gondi in 1504:

> No one ever entered into relations with me—I speak of work-
> men—to whom I did not do good with all my heart. Afterwards,
> some trick of temper or some madness [*pazzia*], which they say

314

is in my nature, which hurts nobody except myself, gives them
an excuse for speaking evil of me and calumniating my character.

All Blake knew of Michelangelo's work was, of necessity, at second remove
and derived entirely from engravings, especially those by the sixteenth-century
Mantuan engraver Ghisi, and from drawings copied from the frescoes in
the Sistine Chapel. But a still greater handicap was the lack of formal training during his youth, especially in drawing from the nude, which led him
into making sometimes grotesque errors in proportion and muscular structure. The most frequent charge made against him by critics ("those narrow
blinking eyes that have too long governed art in a dark corner," he called
them in the Preface to *A Descriptive Catalogue*), then as now, was that his
execution was not equal to his conception. "This Absurd assertion," he
declares in his *Public Address* (p. 24), "has done me & may still do me the
greatest mischief. . . . I know my Execution is not like Any Body Else. I
do not intend it should be so."

To which one can only agree and be grateful. Dante's characters in the
Divine Comedy have been envisioned in their setting and depicted with such
noumenal power that they no longer seem bloodless phantoms but actual
presences. In the *Descriptive Catalogue* (4), Blake wrote: "The Prophets
descibe what they saw in Vision as real and existing men whom they saw
with their imaginative and immortal organs; the Apostles the same; the
clearer the organ the more distinct the object." No doubt he must have included himself in this illustrious company. Throughout Dante's journey from
the abyss to the empyrean he keeps pace beside him like another shadow,
meanwhile protesting, declaiming, scoffing, pleading, expostulating, singing along in mock falsetto with the elect in Heaven, and speaking up eloquently for the damned in Hell, to give them a voice at last.

(1980)

Notes

1. The discrepancy in these dates had led Mona Wilson (in her *Life of William Blake*,
p. 343) to conclude that Palmer must have been mistaken about the year of his
visit. After a lapse of three decades this is quite possible, but it seems more likely
that Blake had begun the Dante illustrations even before the financial arrange-
ment was made with Linnell.

2. Cary had previously published a translation of the *Inferno*, together with the Italian text, in 1805–1806, but it had only a limited circulation and there is no evidence that Blake ever read it. The first English translation of the whole of the *Divine Comedy*, by the Reverend Henry Boyd, was published in 1802. Like Cary's, it was preceded by the publication of a version of the *Inferno* alone in 1785, a copy of which Blake annotated. Boyd translated — or, rather, transmogrified — Dante's *terza rima* into jingling six-line stanzas, never hesitating to "embellish" the original with his own imagery or even to alter the sense for the sake of a rhyme, so that what emerged was more Boyd than Dante. Blake's benefactor William Hayley, in his "Essay on Epic Poetry" (1782), translated the first three cantos of the *Inferno*, which, says Paget Toynbee (in *Dante in English Literature*, p. 360), "was the first published English translation of the *Commedia*, beyond a mere episode, and the first attempt to translate Dante in the meter of the original." Blake resided for three years, from 1800 to 1803, close to Hayley at Felpham, in Sussex, and while there painted a portrait of Dante in tempera as one of a series of eighteen-heads of the poets to decorate Hayley's library.

3. Dante's Hell, Purgatory, and Paradise roughly correspond to the four regions described in Blake's prophetic works. These are: *Ulro*, the material world, a spectral place of "cruelties," "unreal forms," and "dread sleep," in which the cause-and-effect Circle of Destiny is spun out; *Generation*, the Fallen World of sexual strife and the clash of contraries, but which is also the "Image of regeneration," containing the possibility of transcendence and redemption; *Beulah*, the place of dreams and visions, poetic inspiration, and amorous delight, where "Contrarieties [*sic*] are equally true"; and *Eden*, the dwelling place and sanctuary of the spirit, where male and female are conjoined in peace, joy, and freedom. All four coexist within the Divine Imagination.

4. Blake's animadversions on the "Female Will" would undoubtedly leave him open nowadays to the pot-and-kettle countercharge of "male chauvinism," and with some justice. The severe penalty pronounced against Eve after the Fall, that "thy desire shall be to thy husband, and he shall rule over thee" (Genesis 3:16), was one decree by "Old Nobodaddy" that he never seems to have challenged. Female characters in his prophetic books are always "emanations" of the male, moons to their suns. And yet, Blake was a friend and ally of the feminist Mary Wollstonecraft, author of *A Vindication of the Rights of Women*. His own *Visions of the Daughters of Albion*, published a year later, in 1793, was in great measure inspired by her book.

5. Blake may have been alluding here to an anecdote concerning the astronomer Sir William Herschel and the chemist Henry Cavendish. As told in the *Dictionary of National Biography*:

> When he, Herschel, began to observe, it was almost unheard of that a star should be seen without "rays" or "tails." Henry Cavendish, happening to sit next Herschel at dinner, slowly addressed him with, "Is

it true, Dr. Herschel, that you see the stars round?" "Round as a button," exclaimed the doctor, when the conversation dropped, till at the close of the dinner, Cavendish repeated interrogatively, "Round as a button?" "Round as a button," briskly rejoined the doctor and no more was said.

The planet Uranus was discovered by Herschel in 1781 and first named *Georgium Sidus* ("The Star of George") in honor of George III. Urizen, generally translated as "Your Reason," may thus be a doubly scatological and subversive pun on Uranus and Your Highness. Herschel was an occasional member of the intellectual circle that gathered at the home of the Reverend Anthony Mathew and his wife, sponsors of Blake's first book of poems, *Poetical Sketches*, in 1783, and Blake may have encountered him there in his youth.

Speaking Pictures:
An Introduction

Painting is mute poetry, poetry a speaking picture.

—Simonides of Céos, sixth century B.C.

Property was thus appall'd
That the self was not the same;
Single nature's double name
Neither two nor one was called.

—Wm. Shakespeare,
The Phoenix and The Turtle

Speaking Pictures: A Gallery of Pictorial Poetry brings together for the first time many of the chief works in a five-hundred-year-old yet still obscure tradition that, from the start, has been cast inevitably under the spell of Hermes. Throughout one can trace the presence of this elusive twilight god, famous for his benevolent duplicity, who loved to pose riddles and play practical jokes. For, as we have come to recognize—but only after one of the most baffling double-takes in literature—the genre of the picture-poem and/or poem-picture, with its reciprocal *presto-chango* of form, originated in Italy during the early Renaissance mainly as the result of what later proved to be a misconception of Egyptian hieroglyphs; then spread from Italy to all the centers of European culture, reaching its height in critical esteem and popularity by the mid-seventeenth century; after which, following a long period of decline, when picture-poetry as such seemed almost forgotten, it has only recently reemerged in our own time as the result of a strangely similar misconception of Chinese ideograms.

How all this came about is perhaps better shown than told, for Hermes's sleight-of-hand still has to be seen to be believed.

Around the year 1460, as it happened, within a decade of the fall of Constantinople to the Turks, there was smuggled out of Byzantium to the circle of humanist scholars at the court of the Medici in Florence a collection of rare and ancient Greek manuscripts. Among them were certain mystical dialogues, called the *Corpus Hermeticum*, in which an Egyptian hierophant (high priest) cast in the role of Hermes Trismegistus ("Thrice-Great Hermes") reveals the sacred mysteries to his disciple Asclepius. Historians nowadays have determined that these works, combining neoplatonist metaphysics, Persian mithraism, gnostic theosophy, magical incantations, and alchemical prescriptions, were composed in Alexandria sometime between 100-300 A.D., and probably served as the bible of an Egyptian religious cult; but at the time of their rediscovery in Florence they were hailed as a godsend out of remote antiquity, before the days of Moses, and to have been written by Hermes Trismegistus himself. "This huge historical error," asserts the Renaissance scholar Frances A. Yates, in her *Giordano Bruno and the Hermetic Tradition*, "was to have amazing results."

The legendary Hermes Trismegistus (or "Mercurius," as he is also called) had been described by Cicero in his *De Natura Deorum* as the culture hero who, during a sojourn in Egypt, assumed the identity of the god Thoth, inventor of hieroglyphs, and founded the holy city of Hermopolis. Following Cicero, St. Augustine as well as the Church Fathers Clement of Alexandria and Lactantius repeated this legend of Hermes Trismegistus, whom they regarded as the author of the so-called "hermetic" doctrines on black magic and idolatry that had sprung up about his name. So then, in turn, with the real existence of Hermes Trismegistus thus affirmed on such high authority, both pagan and Christian, the neoplatonist philosopher-poet Marsilio Ficino, who first translated the *Corpus Hermeticum*, assumed without question that Hermes Trismegistus had actually lived and taught in Egypt at one time. "In that age in which Moses was born," wrote Ficino, accepting the weird geneology devised by St. Augustine, "flourished Atlas the astrologer, brother of Prometheus the physicist and maternal uncle of the elder Mercury, whose nephew was Mercurius Trismegistus." But then Ficinio made a claim of his own just as astonishing: the Egyptian magus was declared to have been the pristine source of a sacred wisdom, a *prisca theologia*, no less, that had been passed on down the ages and through the sages in an unbroken succession from Orpheus to Pythagoras to Plato to Plotinus . . . up to, presumably, Ficino himself. For it was Ficino, along with his cospirit and disciple Pico della Mirandola, who became the apostles of that mystical Renaissance neoplatonism, with its newly discovered "hermetic" core of magic, which complemented but also in some ways rivaled the account of creation told in *Genesis*.

As envisioned in this cosmogony, the Mind of God, which contains all possible ideas as *logoi spermatikoi*, penetrates and impregnates the World Soul brooding over nature, thereby generating the forms infused into matter that are perceived by the senses. "Every particular thing," wrote Plotinus in the *Enneads*, "is the image within matter of the Intellectual Principle, which itself images the Divine Being; thus, each entity in the natural world is linked to that Divine Being in whose likeness it is made." The universe was conceived as a vast rebus, a cosmic riddle whose spiritual meaning lay hidden under the appearances of nature. In "imitating" nature, therefore, Renaissance artists under the spell of the hermetic philosophy mimicked the primal act of God himself, and their own creations stood to the larger Creation as microcosm to macrocosm. Such multilayered pictures as Botticelli's *Birth of Venus*, say, or Titian's *Sacred and Profane Love*, or Leonardo's *Leda and the Swan* were meant to be "read" hermeneutically for their symbolical and allegorical content — "seen," that is, with the mind's eye — for their poetic ideas to be made visible and their images to speak for themselves.

But all this is only part of the picture and/or story. For about the year 1419, long before the *Corpus Hermeticum* was discovered, there had arrived in Italy another apparent godsend of a manuscript out of Byzantium, the so-called *Hieroglyphika* of Horapollo (Horus Apollo). And here again this treatise, which claimed to have deciphered the *hieroglyphika grammata* ("sacred carved letters") of ancient Egypt, was also mistakenly believed to have been written in remote antiquity. As the *Corpus Hermeticum* had seemed to Ficino and his circle to contain a pure gnosis, unmediated by discursive reasoning, so also the *Hieroglyphika* might unriddle for them the secrets of a written language that reflected ideas directly, what (so to speak) the Sphinx would have spoken if it spoke in images rather than words. Horapollo, an Egyptian-born scribe who lived in Constantinople sometime in the fifth century A.D., assumed that hieroglyphs were simple pictographs — as in fact they had been around 3000 B.C. during the earliest stage of their evolution — so that his interpretations, though occasionally close to the mark, were no more than wild, if wildly ingenious, guesses. It was not of course until Champollion, as late as 1824, finally deciphered hieroglyphs with the aid of the Rosetta Stone that they were understood to be characters in a primitive syllabary, somewhat like our own alphabet, that signified not ideas as such but vocal sounds forming words.

Horapollo's *Hieroglyphika,* first published in Latin by the Venetian printer Aldus in 1505, appeared at a time when the invention of printing and the spread of literacy throughout Europe was in the process of transforming what had once been predominantly an aural into a visual culture. The book was subsequently translated into most European languages and published in numerous editions before the end of the century. Even the skeptical Erasmus, while dismissing as folly and superstition the notion that hieroglyphs were a "sacred language," believed they might serve as the model for a universal symbology of ideas that could be "seen through" as well as read — "a pure transparency," as Coleridge once expressed it, "that intercepts no light and adds no stain" — and thus constitute a sort of philosophical algebra for the family of mankind. The great French printer and neoplatonist mystic Geofroy Tory, whose *Champ Fleury* in 1529 was inspired by the *Hieroglyphika,* attempted to devise such an international iconic alphabet by recasting the shapes and proportions of letters. And his own typographical designs, though they never fulfilled the high purpose for which they were invented, led to other experiments by the master printers of the Renaissance.

For most artists and poets of that era, who regarded as self-evident Horace's gnomic remark, *Ut pictura poesis* ("As is poetry so is painting"), this very resemblance, so close that they seemed integral, also suggested that a disintegration must have occurred in the past. The belief was then widely held that in some lost arcadian foretime mankind had actually possessed a single sacred language in which idea and image were one. Thus, on the margin of a copy of the *Hieroglyphika,* Albrecht Dürer drew a number of sketches illustrating Horapollo's essentially poetic interpretations, which, had he done so for the rest, would have made it the earliest book of what came to be known as "Emblem poetry."

That, it turned out, was to be Andrea Alciati's *Emblematum Liber,* published in 1531, not only the most famous but the prototype of all that followed. The engravings by various artists and the accompanying poems by Alciati, mainly translations from the *Greek Anthology,* were conceived as indivisible, meant to reflect, and to reflect upon, one another in multiple facets of meaning. . . . [One] example is Alciati's *Emblema 132,* with the motto: "From the pursuit of literature one acquires immortality." . . .

An English version of the poem by George Boas (who was, incidentally, also the modern editor of the *Hieroglyphika*) reads as follows:

Neptune's trumpeter, whose body is a sea-beast and whose appearance shows that he is a sea-god, Triton, is enclosed in a circle made by a serpent which holds its tail in its mouth [Uro-

boros, symbol of immortality]. Fame follows men outstanding
in mental powers and glorious deeds, and demands that their
name be spread throughout the world.

Upon which Boas comments: "Literally, the picture is of a sea-beast blowing a trumpet as he rises from the waves. Allegorically, the beast is the
god Triton, blowing a conch. Tropologically, the trumpet is fame and the
serpent eternity. Anagogically, it conveys the message contained in the motto
heading the picture . . ." and so forth.

The intellectual effort required to "get the picture" was intended by Alciati as a necessary veil, or cloud-cover, to conceal the mysteries from the
profane. (Hermes, among his other magical functions, was both a gatherer
and disperser of mists and clouds.) Even more cryptic emblems called
imprese—whose meanings, for most people at that time, as for us, lay
buried within their crypts—became fashionable throughout Europe in the
following decades, pointing the way for the inwrought "metaphysical" style
in poetry represented by Gongora in Spain, Scève in France, Marino in
Italy, Donne in England.

Nature itself, as the Logos of God brought down to earth and made
manifest, was not exempt from such riddling obfuscation. One Italian enthusiast, the poet Emanuele Tesauro, visualized the sky in the image of
"a vast cerulean shield, or empty canvas, or blank page, on which skillful
Nature draws what she meditates: forming heroical devices, and mysterious
and witty symbols of her secrets"; and, as such, the thunderbolts of Jove-
Jehovah could be no less than cosmic wisecracks, "formidable witticisms
of God, having the bolt of lightning for their device and the thunder for
their motto." In sum, the Emblem of emblems. Shakespeare might have
had this sort of hieroglyphical frenzy in mind when he wrote the passage
in *Hamelt* (Act III, Scene 2) wherein the merry Dane taunts Polonius
by persuading him to interpret then reinterpret the mercurially shifting
rorschach-blot of a cloud:

> *Ham.:* Do you see younder cloud that's almost in shape of a
>   camel?
> *Pol.:* By the mass, and 'tis like a camel indeed.
> *Ham.:* Methinks it is like a weasel.
> *Pol.:* It is backed like a weasel.
> *Ham.:* Or like a whale?
> *Pol.:* Very like a whale.

The cult of Emblem poetry, and the hermetic philosophy which was its source, had been established in Europe for half a century before reaching Elizabethan England. But by 1583, when the most celebrated Magus of the age, Giordano Bruno (considered by some scholars to have been Shakespeare's model for the exiled wizard Prospero in *The Tempest*) took refuge from the Inquisition in England, where he sojourned for a year at Oxford, he found there many devoted as well as powerful adherents to his cause. Bruno received the patronage of the poet-courtier Sir Philip Sidney, in whose circle at the time was the young Edmund Spenser, who, as his work attests, must also have been initiated into the mysteries. Spenser had already published the emblematic pastorals of *The Shepherd's Calendar*, and was then engaged in weaving the elaborate and inwrought tapestry of that "dark conceit" (as he called it) which became *The Fairie Queene*. By its fusion of medieval allegory and Italian epic romance, classical mythology and Christian theology, in an indivisible compact, *The Fairie Queene* was conceived in the same spirit that had produced Emblem poetry.

In fact, the first such collection in English, Geoffrey Whitney's *Choice of Emblemes*, published in Leyden in 1586, reveals throughout the influence of Spenser's poetic vision and ideas. "Herein," declared Whitney in his Preface, "by the office of the eie, and the eare, the mind may reape dooble delighte through holsome precepts, shadowed with pleasant devises." In keeping with the magpie custom of the time, Whitney had filched the engravings and most of the accompanying poems (which he later translated) for his book from the many collections of Emblem poetry that had appeared on the continent; and, in turn, Elizabethan poets, designers and artists not only reaped "dooble delighte" from his *Choice of Emblemes* but distilled from it imagery to produce their own works. Queen Elizabeth herself, it is said, encouraged the vogue for emblems at the court by having a jacket bejewelled and embroidered with "pleasant devises" copied from Whitney. Emblems and *imprese* of all sorts now figured in heraldry, tournaments, carvings, tapestries, pageants, and, especially, in those communal theatrical extravaganzas of the nobility (once characterized by Ben Jonson as "court hieroglyphs") known as masques.

It was through masques, as Frances A. Yates has pointed out in her *Theatre of the World*, that "the connection in the Renaissance mind between magic and mechanics finds expression . . . and in them mechanics were being used, partially at least, to form a vast moving and changing talisman which should call down divine powers to the assistance of the monarch." Allegorical figures who personified Justice, Truth or Beauty in a masque by Ben Jonson, as produced and staged by Inigo Jones, were actually thought to contain within themselves some trace of the original ideas of Justice, Truth or Beauty within God's Mind. This "natural" magic, as Ficino called it—to distinguish it from the "black" magic of sorcerers in cahoots with Satan—was accomplished by a reverse upward movement along the great spiritual chain of neoplatonism, whereby "every entity is linked to that Divine Being in whose likeness it is made," just as the ancient Egyptian priests described in the *Corpus Hermeticum* once made the statues of the gods in their temples move and speak.

Likewise, the so-called "iconic," or shaped, poems of George Puttenham, George Herbert, Robert Herrick, et al.—among the earliest examples of a genre that appears throughout this *Gallery*—also assumed a magical reciprocity between printed words shaped into images and the ideas they both contained and reflected. The picture-poem so conceived might be considered an amulet, even a sort of primitive fetish. Though the makers of iconic poems could hardly have been aware of this at the time, by such typographical necromantics they were conjuring up the instinctive religious rites of a true pristine theology, or *prisca theologia,* far more ancient than ancient Egypt's, in use before the invention of writing, relics of which can be found in the magic-working pictures of totemic animals painted on walls of caves like those at Lascaux and Altamira millennia ago. A superstitious belief in the substantiality of names and images—and their consubstantiality—underlies all mythical thinking. As Ernst Cassirer points out: "The image or name does not represent the 'thing,' it *is* the thing; it does not merely stand for the object, but has the same actuality." And from this belief stems the principle of *pars pro toto,* the part standing for the whole as species to genus, microcosm to macrocosm—and thus "linked" as an idea to Ficino's own natural magic—which makes possible the hocus-pocus of spells and charms as well as the presto-chango of metaphor.[1]

Toward the end of Elizabeth's reign in England, the widespread diffusion, and hence vulgarization, of hermeticist literature down to the pious and upward striving middle classes, was regarded by its votaries as something of a sacrilege. But this process, swelled by the social and religious tendencies of the age, was to continue deep into the next century.

"The century which produced the greatest mystics," declares Mario Praz, "produced also the Emblem poets: they seem opposites, yet frequently these opposites are found united in the same person." That baroque passion for the joining of contraries into a higher unity, a *discordia concors*, which was shared by all these visionary poets, would be exemplified accordingly even in their own lives. At the time, however, they were dragooned and

324

impressed into the total religious civil war dividing Europe between the forces of the Protestant Reformation and Catholic Counter-Reformation. Such suspiciously heretical doctrines as the *prisca theologia* of Hermes Trismegistus, "natural" magic, cabalistical abracadabra, and so forth, were now muffled or suppressed on both sides; and Emblem poetry came to assume instead an almost entirely pietistic and evangelical character. The picture-poem itself was no longer conceived in a mystical sense as a higher unity, but rather separated hyphenetically as sermon (poem) to text (picture). Mysticism, as Cardinal Newman once cracked, wisely, "begins in mist and ends in schism."

What still endured, nonetheless, was a neoplatonist faith in the essential oneness of the Word and the Work — both having issued from the Mind of the Creator — so that Nature was often referred to as God's other "Book." The most famous of seventeenth-century English Emblem poets, Francis Quarles, declared: "Before the knowledge of letters, God was known by *Hieroglyphicks*; and, indeed, what are the Heaven, the Earth, nay every creature, but *Hieroglyphicks* and Emblems of His Glory?" And Quarles's contemporary, John Milton, whose *Paradise Lost* was intended to add to that Glory, asked almost the same rhetorical question:

> What if earth
> Be but the shadow of Heaven, and things therein
> Each to each other like, more than on earth is thought?

Quarles qua poet hardly deserves comparison nowadays with Milton, yet during their own lifetimes, as Horace Walpole observed: "Milton had to wait for his due until the world had finished admiring Quarles." His *Emblemes*, published in 1635, was the most widely read book of poetry of any sort in the seventeenth century, suiting the taste of the age for metaphysical fancy and moral self-flagellation. Though he declared himself "a true sonne of the Church of England," Quarles had no scruple in taking his emblems from Jesuit collections published in Europe; nor, for that matter, did his fellow Emblem poets, such as Christopher Harvey or Robert Farley or even the fanatically anti-Catholic George Wither, who used the emblems against themselves as texts on which to preach an opposing faith. Some occasional squibs and flashes of wit in these poems serve now and then to relieve an otherwise impenetrable miasma of Calvinist gloom. Still, their bathetic religiosity has in the course of time acquired a modern patina of "camp," which may yet save them entirely from oblivion.

The great English poet-mystics of the seventeenth century, who include Donne and Herbert, Vaughn and Crashaw, worked outside the tradition of Emblem poetry. Yet they were all nonetheless profoundly influenced in their style and sensibility. Of Crashaw, especially, the assertion has often been made by critics that his rhapsodic hymns lack only the accompanying emblems to have become the masterpieces of the genre. Crashaw's own spiritual agony, in which he was torn (as he wrote) "twixt in and out, twixt life and death," finally to be resolved by his self-exile and conversion to Catholicism in Rome, foreshadowed the conflicting religious and political passions that later erupted into civil war in England.

The midpoint of the century was also the zenith of Emblem poetry. With the Restoration of Charles II in 1660, after the long interregnum of the Puritan Commonwealth, the wits and wordlings of the court must have found Emblem poetry itself emblematic of the religious bigotry and obscurantism of a time best forgotten. But, most important, the neoplatonist cosmology which had provided its *raison d'être* was to be displaced in the following decades by the new scientific world order of Newton and Descartes. The rift between mind and matter, the Word and the Work, henceforth grew steadily wider; and man himself, from being the microcosm of the Creator, became a mere spectator, enclosed within his own sensorium, of a world indifferent to his existence — "a world," as the philosopher E. A. Burtt has put it, "hard, cold, colorless, silent and dead; a world of quantity; a world of mathematically computable motions in mechanical regularity" — which is to say, the sort of world we still make do with.

The last noteworthy collection of English Emblem poetry, John Bunyan's *Divine Emblems; or, Temporal Things Spiritualized*, with the subtitle, *Calculated for the Use of Young People*, appeared in 1686, exactly a hundred years after the publication of Geoffrey Whitney's *Choice of Emblemes*. What Bunyan's own homespun Baptist allegory, *The Pilgrim's Progress*, was to Spenser's *The Fairie Queene*, his pious book of Emblem poetry was to Whitney's. Thus, a tradition that had begun at the dawn of the Renaissance as an attempt to recover the "sacred language of the gods" now closed with a book of homilies for the humbler classes that endeavored, Polonial-fashion, to point a moral and adorn a platitude.

The revulsion against Emblem poetry, and all it stood for, inevitably grew deeper during the positivist and deist Age of Enlightenment. One of its chief luminaries, the Earl of Shaftesbury, in his *Second Characters, or The Language of Forms*, published in 1713, there buried it under a heap of stony epithets, such as "enigmatical, preposterous, disproportionate, gouty and lame, impotent, pretentious, Egyptian, magical, mystical, monkish, and" — most crushing of all at the time — "gothic." And yet, for all that, reprints of Quarles and Withers as well as translations of foreign Emblem poets, such as the Dutch Jacob Cats, appeared from time to time; and Cesare Ripa's great *Iconologia*, republished in various editions throughout the century, still served as a source of symbolic imagery for painters and engravers. But Hermes himself—at least in his manifestation as Hermes Trismegistus—had apparently gone into a disappearing act that would last forever.

Or so it seemed. Under the spell of the hermetic philosophy, still potent even in that skeptical age, the visionary poet Christopher Smart (whose fragmentary epic, *Rejoice in the Lamb*, was written while he was confined in a madhouse) sought to reconcile the breach between spiritual and material reality, the Word and the Work, brought about by Newtonian science. Robert Browning, who rediscovered Smart's poetry, wrote of him in homage that he had "pierced the screen / Twixt word and thing"; and Smart, in his *Rejoice in the Lamb*, said of himself: "For my talent is to give an impression upon words by punching, that when the reader casts his eye upon 'em, he takes up the image from the mold which I have made." The same "talent," in essence, was shared by Smart's kindred spirit and true successor, William Blake, who also sought to recover the "Holy Word"

> That might controll
> The starry pole,
> And fallen, fallen light renew!

Blake's *The Gates of Paradise*, the centerpiece in our *Gallery*, was first conceived by him in 1793, when he gave it the subtitle *For Children*; but in 1818, toward the end of this creative life, he made several minor improvements in the emblems and added the epirammatic poem that unites them all, at which time he changed the subtitle to *For the Sexes*. Not only does *The Gates of Paradise* sum up his own career as a picture-poet, but it consummates the genre of Emblem poetry as well. The lowly social and aesthetic status to which it had declined suited his alchemical genius for transmuting base into high forms of art, as he had already demonstrated in making the *Songs of Innocence and of Experience* out of the plain speech and tic-toc meters of London street ballads and church hymnals.

The mystical ideas imagined and inscribed on *The Gates of Paradise* were, as we know, the distillation of his lifelong study of occult literature, such as the Cabala and the *Corpus Hermeticum*, the works of Paracelsus, Cornelius Agrippa, Robert Fludd, Jacob Boehme, Swedenborg, and the rest. In the self-esteemed Age of Reason these were dangerous ideas: for though religious heretics and ecstatics, ranters and necromancers, were no longer burned at the stake, as was the sixteenth-century Magus Giordano Bruno, they still ran the risk of being clapped into Bedlam. ("If Blake had a crack," wrote his disciple Samuel Palmer, "it was a crack that let the light through.") Blake's mysticism, regarded by others as religious frenzy and/or poetic madness, was what he himself referred to as "vision," that druidic faculty of "into-it-iveness" possessed by the prophets and seers of ancient times. "I rest not from my great task," he declared, not without a certain Churchillian grandiloquence,

> To open the Eternal Worlds, to open the immortal Eyes
> Of Man inwards into the Worlds of Thought, into Eternity
> Ever expanding in the Bosom of God, the Human Imagination.

Toward the end of life, in the 1820s, the painters Samuel Palmer and Edward Calvert and other admirers in a group calling themselves the "Shoreham Ancients" formed a charmed circle around the poet; but for the rest of the century and almost up to our own time, his work, except for several of his early lyrics, remained largely unknown.

By his original subtitle to *The Gates of Paradise*, namely, *For Children*, Blake of course did not mean that it was intended solely for them, but rather for all who had to become as such, in order to pass through "The Gates." Ironically, this subtitle turned out to be prophetic in a way he could not have foreseen. For the two most important picture-poets to appear in the later nineteenth century, Edward Lear and Lewis Carroll, for whom the play of the imagination was as profoundly serious as even their most profound ideas were playful, did conceive their books expressly for them.

> The Child's Toys & the Old Man's Reasons
> Are the Fruits of the Two Seasons,

wrote Blake in his "Auguries of Innocence." The magical potential of names and images to conjure up what they represent — *"Rumpelstiltskin!"* — seems to children of whatever historical epoch or society as much in the nature of things as such names once did universally to primitive man. Lear's totemic fantasies and Carroll's metalogical trip through the looking-glass thus belong to the same once-upon-a-time mythopoeic Dream Time. No wonder, then, that the only other eminent Victorian author of children's books who deserves comparison with them, Robert Louis Stevenson, was also to take up the by now almost forgotten form of Emblem poetry, if merely and mischievously to parody it, with the type of humor that has since become known as "black." (Dr. Jekyll might have composed the sentimental lyrics of Stevenson's *A Child's Garden of Verses*, Mr. Hyde his *Moral Emblems*.) But even this flickering revival of the hermetic spirit indicated that the god was abroad once more.

In France about this time, where the modernist movement in art and poetry was already under way, there could be no doubt. Following Baudelaire, the Symbolist poets, who revered him as a kind of Magus, took as their own credo his metaphorical conception of reality as a "forest of correspondences"; which conception, of course, itself corresponded to the one conceived long ago by the neoplatonist and hermetic philosophers. But for Baudelaire both parts of his metaphor had equal weight: it was a *forest*, one in which mankind was lost, not a metaphysical highway (or *circuitus spiritualis*, as Ficino called it) paved with logic that led from *ergo* to *ergo* straight to the Mind of God. Rimbaud, who hoped by such correspondences to discover for himself *"l'alchimie poétique,"* acclaimed Baudelaire as "the first see-er," a poet able "to inspect the invisible and to hear the unheard"; but then he added that "his much-praised form is a poor thing. Inventions of unknownness demand new forms." However, it was not the "wild" Rimbaud *("un mystique à l'état sauvage,"* as Claudel once described him), but his temperamental opposite, the milquetoast mandarin Mallarmé, who was destined to invent these new forms. A correspondence of sorts exists, after all, between the petasus and caduceus of Hermes, the conical hat and hazel wand of a Renaissance Magus, and the tasseled nightcap and cigar of Mallarmé.

Mallarmé had based his own poetic faith, from which he never wavered, on another of Baudelaire's oracular pronouncements: "There is in the Word something sacred which prohibits us from making it into a game of chance." A poem therefore had to be no less than an ikon of the Absolute, with all the density, mystery, and inevitability of a "thing in itself." From his early "L'Après-Midi d'un Faune" to the baffling sonnets of his later years, the progressive obscurity of his style ensued from this lifelong effort to fix his vision of the Word into poetry that, no matter how self-referential and sealed from within, kept escaping into mere words.

In 1897, a year before his death, he published his most orphic and original poem, *Un Coup de Dés (A Throw of Dice)*. At the time it first appeared in the Paris revue *Cosmopolis*, the young André Gide, awe-struck, called it "the farthest point to which the human spirit has yet ventured"; and Mallarmé himself — who would refer to it, only half-humorously, as "The Book" — believed that he had created a new kind of visual poetry: "words led back to their origin, the twenty-four letters of the alphabet, so gifted with infinity that they will finally consecrate language."

If God, as Einstein once said, refused to "play dice with the universe," neither would Mallarmé do so with the Word. *Un Coup de Dés*, in point and in fact, was a literary *coud d'état* designed not merely to change the rules but to abolish the "game" itself, in which poetry, by definition, could be no more than a "miscellany of chance inspirations." This meant, first of all, that its basic unit, the line, had to be annulled. "Let us have an end," he wrote in an essay called "The Book: A Spiritual Instrument," published in 1895, "to those incessant, back-and-forth motions of our eyes, traveling from one line to the next and beginning all over again": furrow after furrow, that the poet, plodding behind an earth-bound blinkered Pegasus, foot by foot, had previously laboriously sown with his *logoi spermatikoi*. What he proposed instead, and realized in *Un Comp de Dés*, was that the whole page – or, rather, the double-page spread – become the unit of the poem. The various motifs, or idea-images, each represented by its own peculiar type-face and surrounded like star-clusters by a "white silence," would thus have the simultaneity of a picture and yet unfold from page to page in a musical sequence. In the by-now classic typographical version of *Un Coup de Dés*, published by *La Nouvelle Revue Française* in 1914, the dismembered sentences, phrases scattered throughout here and there, isolated words dangling in midpage, like exposed nerve ends that are related and joined to one another by synaptic cross-currents of meaning and metaphorical sidelights, seem to comprise an uncanny X-ray photo, in words, of Mallarmé's mind in the process of composing his poem.

Un Coup de Dés has remained a unique, and uniquely inscrutable, work, with many talmudic exegeses and commentaries over the years but no successors in poetry. The "game," as Mallarmé had termed it, went on as before. For Guillaume Apollinaire, the most innovative French poet of his era, *Un Coup de Dés* must have served as the baptismal font for his own typographical picture-poems published in *Calligrammes* in 1918. And, of course, James Joyce, who also attempted like Mallarmé ("My shemblable! My freer!") to write "The Book," begorra, in *Finnegans Wake*, recognized in his poem its only rival. ("But jig jog jug as Day the Dicebox Throws, whang, loyal six I lead.") Yet the great Pascalian wager made by Mallarmé on the formal structure of his picture-poem – or, rather, moving picture-moving poem, like the unwinding scroll of a Chinese landscape – that it would "consecrate language," has, as said before, found no takers among other poets.

What was already a strong oriental current in art at the time of Mallarmé, evident in the painting of Whistler, Manet, and others of the post-Impressionist school, now entered the mainstream of Western poetry as well. By the year 1912 the Imagist movement, led by Ezra Pound in London, had begun its reconstruction of English poetics according to principles derived from Pound's study of Chinese and Japanese forms, which he knew, however, only in translation. The *haiku*, especially, assumed a paradigmatic importance for Imagism

IN A STATION OF THE METRO
The apparition of these faces in the crowd;
Petals on a wet, black bough.

comparable to that of the epigram for Emblem poetry. "The point of Imagism," Pound wrote, "is that it does not use images as *ornaments*. The image is itself the speech." Furthermore, the "Image" — exalted by him this way and enshrined in quotes — not only "presents an intellectual and emotional complex in an instant of time," but also "is real because we know it directly." It had to be, then, the very dingdong *ding an sich* of poetry. The Imagist credo was reechoed in the United States some years later by Wallace Stevens: "The poem is the cry of its occasion, part of the *res* itself and not about it." And, expressed most succinctly, it became W. C. Williams's slogan: "No ideas but in things."

Pound, as T. S. Eliot said of him, is "the inventor of Chinese poetry for our time": not entirely out of whole cloth, though he was incapable of reading the poems of Li Po in the original, but by reworking the notes and glosses on them made around the turn of the century by the sinologoist Ernest Fenollosa — who was himself dependent for his interpretations on a Japanese tutor — into the "translations" published as *Cathay* in 1915. The confusion that inevitably resulted was further compounded by the fact that Chinese characters contain no indications of number, tense, and gender; that Fenollosa often misunderstood — or else his tutor misunderstood — their meaning; and that Pound, in turn, sometimes misread Fenollosa's notes or else arbitrarily supplied his own versions. He therefore, as the French say, "Robinsonized" (adopting Rimbaud's noun-verb derived from the famous castaway who remade a barren island into a bit of seventeenth-century England), by transforming the — to him — virgin territory of Chinese poetry into a *chinoiserie* that was a replica of his own Symbolist and Imagist poetics. But in the process (as Pound so stated some fifty years later) he "gathered from the air a live tradition" — Western, of course, not Chinese — and forged the complex pictorial style of the *Cantos*.

As Fenollosa's literary executor, Pound also inherited his notes and papers for a lecture on Chinese ideograms, which he then incorporated into an essay, first published in *The Little Review* in 1919, entitled "The Chinese Written Character as a Medium for Poetry." And this, too, was destined to have an unforeseen effect on the course of modern literature.

"A true noun," wrote Fenollosa, "an isolated thing, does not exist in

331

Nature. . . . Neither can a pure verb, an abstract motion, be possible in Nature. The eye sees noun and verb as one: things in motion, motion in things, and so the Chinese conception tends to represent them." He then cited several examples, e.g.: "The sun underlying the bursting forth of plants = spring"; or, "'Boat' plus 'water' = boat-water: a ripple"; and so forth. Ergo, he concluded, "Chinese notation is something more than arbitrary symbols: it is based upon a vivid shorthand picture of the operations of Nature. . . . In reading Chinese we do not seem to be juggling mental counters, but to be watching *things* work out their fate."

So there it is, once more, the primal uroboric serpent biting its own tail. Though Chinese characters, like Egyptian hieroglyphs, must have originated as simple pictograms, they, too, evolved in the course of time into far more sophisticated phonetic symbols. Only a very small percentage are still directly representational. But by focusing almost exclusively on the pictorial aspect of the ideogram, Fenollosa (and Pound, too, as a result) muted its equally significant aural component, "the cry of its occasion." With a visionary enthusiasm that recalls that of Ficino and the other Renaissance hermetists when they first discovered Horapollo's *Hieroglyphika*, he declared, "Such a pictorial method, whether the Chinese exemplified it or not, would be *the ideal language of the world.*" (Editor's italics.)[2]

Dr. J. Y. Liu, in his *The Art of Chinese Poetry*, asserts:

> There is a fallacy still common among Western readers . . . that *all* Chinese characters are pictograms or ideograms. Ernest Fenollosa stressed this misconception and admired . . . their alleged pictorial qualities. While one is flattered by his attribution of superior poetic qualities to one's mother tongue . . . his conclusions are often incorrect, largely due to his refusal to recognize the phonetic element of Chinese characters. . . . As an introduction to Chinese poetry, the Fenollosa approach is, to say the least, seriously misleading.

Still, by being misled down this fork in the garden path—no doubt with Hermes showing the way in the gloaming—the followers of Ezra Pound, who himself followed Fenollosa, arrived in turn at the conception of what has become known as Concrete poetry.

The name was adopted, in 1955, after a meeting between the Brazilian poet Decio Pignatari and the Swiss but Bolivian-born poet Eugen Gomringer at Ulm in south Germany—the sister city, by the way, of Augsburg, where Alciati's first book of Emblem poetry was published—at which time they also agreed on a common program for what was already an international movement. Pignatari, together with the poets Augusto and Haroldo de Campos, had founded a magazine in 1952 in São Paulo, Brazil, called *Noigandres*, a name derived from a Provençal word of obscure provenance used by Arnaut Daniel and mentioned in one of Pound's *Cantos* ("Noigandres, eh, *noi*gandres, / Now what the DEFFIL can that mean!"), whose baffling signification, they must have felt, suited a kind of poetry that had not yet defined its scope. Gomringer, setting his sights through Mallarmé's *Un Coup de Dés*, had originally called his own ideographic poems "constellations." But the new name Concrete, thus fixed, became part of the *res* itself.

As one of its best-known practitioners as well as its chief theoretician, Gomringer conceived of Concrete poetry as a "tension of thing-words in space-time" that presented a simultaneous image-idea. By grasping the identity of this image-idea ("Single nature's double name"), and thus sharing mentally in its re-creation, the reader-viewer would experience a momentary arrest, or doubletake, like the flash of insight followed by intellectual comprehension that occurs in solving a riddle. And a riddle, unriddled, is a metaphor whose terms, so to speak, have been "spelled" out. In that sense, therefore, the term Concrete poetry may be a misnomer, an instance of what the philosopher Whitehead once called the "fallacy of misplaced concreteness," for its source lies not in any Einsteinian "space-time" but in

> The Mind, that Ocean where each kind
> Does streight its own resemblance find,

as Andrew Marvell once wrote.

During the five hundred years that separate the picture-poems at either end of this *Gallery*, Emblem and Concrete, the idea of the visual symbol, which is the symbol itself as idea, has undergone a Circean metamorphosis. As perceived by modern depth psychology, the symbol not only has a rational side but a sensuous, figurative component as well that (according to Jung) is "inaccessible to reason, since it is composed . . . of the irrational data of pure inward and outward perception." So then, to bring this Introduction round as well, the *logoi spermatikoi* of neoplatonism have apparently made another descent, historically and psycholoically: from the spirit, as metaphysical essences, down to the human consciousness, as logical forms and categories, then down once more to the undermind, as primordial archetypes and ghostly eidolons. "The aim of the poet," wrote Giambattista Marino, "is the marvelous"—that is, to enlarge the imagination the way light expands the eye.

(1975)

Notes

1. An Egyptian myth tells how the goddess Isis once compelled the sun god Ra by sorcery to reveal his secret name, thereby obtaining dominion over him and all his power. In the name of Ra, incidentally, and its hieroglyph — which survives as our astonomic symbol for the sun — we can also find the Indo-European root of the words *rajah* and *rex*, perhaps pointing to a common derivation. A palimpsest-echo of the great picture-name itself, reaching us from the depths of the Pliocene (anything so far-out has to be far-fetched) may still be heard in one of the earliest cries of proto-human language: the wide-open-mouthed, sun-greeting *rrrrrrrahhhh-rrrrrrrahhhh* growled by lemurs at dawn along the Ganges and the Nile. Cheerleaders nowadays still rouse themselves into eurhythmic frenzies of propitiation with the same primordial *rrrrrrrahhhh*. "One thought," as Blake said, "fills eternity."

2. It should be mentioned that Fenollosa shared this belief with some illustrious company in the past. At the time when Europe was becoming aware, through the reports of Jesuit missionaries in China, that a living hieroglyphical language was in use by the Chinese, Francis Bacon (in the *Advancement of Learning*, VI, 1) expressed the hope that "real, not nominal, characters, to express, not . . . letters or words, but things and notions" might also be employed in Europe. And in the seventeenth century, the author of the *Pseudodoxia Epidemica,* Sir Thomas Browne, as well as the German philosopher and coinventor of the calculus, Wilhelm Leibniz, thought likewise.

Bibliography

"The End Pocket" (poem). *Chimera* 1:2 (Autumn 1942).

Review of *Blood for a Stranger* by Randall Jarrell. *Chimera* 1:3 (Winter 1943).

"The Trojans of Brighton Beach: Life on the Old Block." *Commentary* 3:5 (May 1947).

"The Poetry of Samuel Greenberg: 'Neither the Time nor the Poet Was Ripe.'" *Commentary* 6:4 (October 1948).

"Greenwich Village: Decline and Fall. Bohemia's Age of Lead." *Commentary* 6:5 (November 1948).

"Along the Midway of Mass Culture." *Partisan Review* 16:4 (April 1949).

"On the Margin in France: Life in a World of Uneasy Moneys." *Commentary* 8:5 (November 1949).

"A Guide through the Garden." *Sewanee Review* 58:1 (Winter 1950).

"The Importance of Being Milton: That Talent Which Is Death to Hide." *Commentary* 14:4 (October 1952).

"Jack the Giant Killer" (poem). *Hudson Review* 5:3 (Autumn 1952).

"Selected Spooks, Stars, Gods, and Celebrities." *Discovery* 3 (edited by Vance Bourjaily, published by Pocket Books, 1954).

"The Descent of the Muse" (poem). *Hudson Review* 7:4 (Winter 1955).

"The Old Magi at the Burlesque" (poem). *Hudson Review* 7:4 (Winter 1955).

"Annus Mirabilis: 1932. Boyhood Diary." *Commentary* 24:2 (August 1957).

"Squash & Stretch: Maxwell Bodenheim in the Village." *Esquire* (December 1963).

"Mc²Luhan's Message, or: Which Way Did the Second Coming Went?" *New American Review* No. 2 (January 1968).

"Down in the Village: A Discourse on Hip. Or, Watch Out for the Cynosure." *New American Review* No. 13 (1971).

Introduction to *Shake the Kaleidoscope: A New Anthology of Modern Poetry*, edited by Milton Klonsky. New York: Pocket Books, 1973.

335

"Art & Life: A Menippean Paean to the Flea; or, Did Dostoevsky Kill Trotsky?" *American Review* No. 20 (April 1974).

Introduction to *Speaking Pictures: A Gallery of Pictorial Poetry from the Sixteenth Century to the Present*, edited by Milton Klonsky. New York: Harmony Books, 1975.

"Two in the Bush," "Palimpsest," "Chinoiserie," and "The Bogie Man Cometh" (poems). In *Speaking Pictures: A Gallery of Pictorial Poetry from the Sixteenth Century to the Present.*

"W. B.[4]: or, The Seer Seen by His Own Vision." In *William Blake: The Seer and His Visions*, edited by Milton Klonsky. New York: Harmony Books, 1977. The essay also appeared in *American Review* No. 25 (October 1976).

Introduction to *Blake's Dante: The Complete Illustrations to the Divine Comedy*, edited by Milton Klonsky. New York: Harmony Books, 1980.

"A Writer's Education," *New York Times Book Review* (7 March 1982).

"Maxim Gorky in Coney Island" and "First Acquaintance with Poets." In *From Mt. San Angelo: Stories, Poems, & Essays*, edited by William Smart. Mt. San Angelo, Sweet Briar: Virginia Center for the Creative Arts, 1984.

Editions by Klonsky

Light on Dark Corners: A Complete Sex Science and Guide to Purity by B. G. Jefferis and J. L. Nichols. New York: Grove Press, 1967.

Shake the Kaleidoscope: A New Anthology of Modern Poetry. New York: Pocket Books, 1973.

The Fabulous Ego: Absolute Power in History. New York: Quadrangle Books, 1974.

Speaking Pictures: A Gallery of Pictorial Poetry from the Sixteenth Century to the Present. New York: Harmony Books, 1975.

William Blake: The Seer and His Visions. New York: Harmony Books, 1977.

Blake's Dante: The Complete Illustrations to the Divine Comedy. New York: Harmony Books, 1980.

Ted Solotaroff edited the *New American Review* (later the *American Review*) and is the author of two essay collections, *The Red-Hot Vaccuum* and *A Few Good Voices in My Head.*

Mark Shechner is professor of English at the State University of New York in Buffalo. He is the editor of *Preserving the Hunger: An Isaac Rosenfeld Reader* and the author of *Joyce in Nighttown: A Psychoanalytic Inquiry into Ulysses, After the Revolution: Studies in the Contemporary Jewish Imagination,* and the essay on Jewish writers in *The Harvard Guide to Contemporary American Writing.*

The manuscript was edited by Robin DuBlanc. The book was designed by Mary Primeau. The typeface for the text is Times Roman. The display face is Rob's Medium and Times Roman.

Manufactured in the United States of America.